THE ULTIMATE GUIDE TO
MARATHONS

BY DENNIS CRAYTHORN AND RICH HANNA

MP

MARATHON PUBLISHERS, INC.
SACRAMENTO, CALIFORNIA

An Important Note to Fellow Runners (a.k.a. Disclaimer)

Races change constantly. We have made every conceivable effort to ensure the information in this book is as up-to-date and accurate as possible. However, there will be changes after this book is printed. So, please, before making any plans or final decisions, contact the races themselves to get the latest information, *especially race dates*. Every year, many races change their dates for a variety of reasons. Once the book is printed, there is little or nothing we can do about it. It is therefore incumbent upon you to check with the race before you make any reservations, buy any tickets, or request any time off from work. We cannot be responsible for any inconvenience, loss, or other unhappiness you encounter. If you do have any suggestions, updates, or differing opinions, please let us know. Be as specific and constructive as you can; generic comments are of little use. Your comments will play a large role in improving the next edition of THE ULTIMATE GUIDE TO MARATHONS.

Direct all correspondence to:

THE ULTIMATE GUIDE TO MARATHONS, SECOND EDITION
c/o Marathon Publishers, Inc.
P.O. Box 19027
Sacramento, CA 95819

TABLE OF CONTENTS

TABLE OF CONTENTS

PREFACE

Three years ago, we embarked upon an adventure. No one had ever written a guidebook for the traveling runner, so we took it upon ourselves to write one. THE ULTIMATE GUIDE TO MARATHONS turned out to be a hit; it was so successful that we have since written two other books, THE ULTIMATE GUIDE TO INTERNATIONAL MARATHONS and THE ULTIMATE RUNNER'S JOURNAL. You could say that we've been busy.

Now it's time to update the original. This second edition of THE ULTIMATE GUIDE TO MARATHONS contains quite a few improvements over the first. Our section on the top 100 marathons has been expanded to include the top 110 races to give you more detailed information on 10 more events. Some new races have come. Some old races have gone. Many races that have stuck around have undergone changes, like debuting new courses, moving to a different time of year, or breaking in a tenderfoot race director. In short, much has changed, and in this second edition, we chronicle it all for you.

We have also added several features to improve the book's readability, like an expanded table of contents listing the top 110 races by month, indicating each race's ranking in the race data section, and cross-references in the appendix to make it easy to find each race.

If you know our previous book, we hope that you like the second edition as much or better than the first. If you are a new reader, welcome to the world of the traveling marathoner. There are many great races waiting for you to discover them. We hope the second edition of THE ULTIMATE GUIDE TO MARATHONS helps you find them.

Dennis Craythorn
Rich Hanna
October, 1998

ACKNOWLEDGMENTS

We find ourselves indebted to many of the same people for this second edition of THE ULTIMATE GUIDE TO MARATHONS as the first edition. We would like to single out a few individuals who made a particular contribution to this edition.

Several race directors again distinguished themselves providing us with the information we required for this book—and then some. Thanks to Bob Craver, Wally Kastner, Les Smith, Tom Bradley, Deanna Broglia, Hermine Higgins, Colin Atkinson, Carey Pinkowski, Mike Nishi, Connie Hessburg, Joan Riegle, Mike Doyle, Lynn Von Wald, Andrea Riha, Ski Pisarski, and Jay Glassman.

And now for the flip-side of the on-the-ball race director list. Some of you may be wondering why a particular race ended up in the Mid Pack section as opposed to the Lead Pack. In most cases, these decisions involve judgements on our part, but in a few cases it resulted from an utter lack of cooperation by the race directors. So, for the record, here is the list of races that we wanted to place into the top 110 marathons, but were unable to do so because of a refusal by the race organization to provide us with any information whatsoever: Atlantic City Marathon; Long Island Marathon; Duke City Marathon; and Trail's End Marathon.

There are several runners who, due to their sheer love of running or a particular race, provided us with invaluable information. Thanks Jonathan DeHart, Ben Jones, Cary Craig, Taylor Palomis, Bruce Cannon, Steve Bainbridge, Andre Tocco, Leonard Fisher, and Ruth Carter.

INTRODUCTION

HOW TO USE THIS BOOK

This book was written for runners who want to travel to a marathon, whether it be for a vacation or to try for a PR. It is divided into two main sections—The Top 110 Destination Marathons and 56 Local Marathons. Within each section, races are listed chronologically. The Appendix contains a number of useful rankings, and course profiles, arranged in alphabetical order, for about half of our Top 110 races.

HOW TO READ THE RATINGS

Beneath the title of each entry there is a series of ratings. The overall rating indicates our cumulative assessment of the race as a destination marathon, *i.e.*, a marathon that a runner may want to travel to and perhaps build a vacation around. The top-ranked marathon, the Big Sur Marathon, was assigned a score of 100, and every other race's score is a percentage of Big Sur's. The factors that make up the overall score are: course beauty, race organization, level of crowd support, and destination value of the location. The next five ratings (course beauty, course difficulty, appropriateness for first timers, race organization, and crowd support) are based on a 10-point scale and are modified by pluses and minuses, just like school grades. Therefore, a score of 9- exceeds an 8+. The following legend applies to our scores for course beauty, appropriateness for first timers, and race organization:

10	EXCEPTIONAL	For course difficulty:	
9	VERY GOOD	9-10	EXTREMELY DIFFICULT
8	GOOD	7-8	VERY DIFFICULT
7	FAIR	5-6	MODERATELY DIFFICULT,
<6	POOR		ROLLING WITH SOME
For crowd support:			GOOD GRADES
9-10	EXCEPTIONAL	4	AVERAGE DIFFICULTY,
7-8	VERY GOOD		MOSTLY ROLLING
5-6	MODERATE	3	SLIGHTLY ROLLING
3-4	LIGHT	2	MOSTLY FLAT
1-2	VERY LITTLE	1	PERFECTLY FLAT OR
0	JUST YOU AND THE WIND		SLIGHT DOWNGRADE,
			FEW TURNS

The **COURSE BEAUTY** rating scores just that. We tend to mark down courses that pass strip malls, urban blight, and industrial parks. We also tend to cast disfavor on monotonous scenery and never-ending brownness. So much for our biases. The **COURSE DIFFICULTY** rating considers the elevation changes along the route (*i.e.*, hills), number of turns, running surface, altitude, and average weather conditions. The higher the score, the more difficult the course. You may use this rating as our equivalent of the relative quickness of the course. Races with the notation **(SEE APPENDIX)** have an elevation profile in the Appendix. The **RACE ORGANIZATION** score consists of an overall evaluation of the race structure. It considers a wide range of factors, including professionalism of race personnel, amount and quality of race amenities (aid stations, pre/post-race activities, transportation, awards), volunteers, and general quality of the race. The **APPROPRIATENESS FOR FIRST TIMERS** is our attempt to help novice marathoners choose the right race for them. To us, the perfect first-timer marathon has a scenic course, excellent race organization, lots of aid stations, few hills, and huge crowds. We consider all of these factors in compiling this score. Finally, **CROWD SUPPORT** indicates the approximate number of spectators along the route. It also considers course-side entertainment.

WHAT'S IN AN ENTRY?

Following the ratings is a boxed section called **RACE DATA** with useful information about the race.

The first narrative section consists of race **HIGHLIGHTS**. Here we try to capture the essence of the race; what makes this marathon special or not so special. Some races have interesting or noteworthy **RACE HISTORIES**. These histories follow the highlights section. The **COURSE DESCRIPTION** contains a detailed account of the course from a runner's perspective. It tells you what you see along the way and the location of major hills and terrain changes. **CROWD/RUNNER SUPPORT** discusses the level of crowd support along the course and the locations of the greatest concentration of spectators. It also details the aid stations, medical assistance, and entertainment during the race. **RACE LOGISTICS** explains how to get to the race start and back. **ACTIVITIES** enumerates the pre- and post-race activities offered by the event, including where to get your race packet, the pasta dinner, expo, victory party, awards ceremony, and any other activities. **AWARDS** lets you know about T-shirts, medals, age-group awards, prize money, and other relevant goodies. Races that have programs for elite runners contain an **ELITE RUNNERS INFORMATION** section. We also list some **ACCOMMODATIONS** convenient to the race site, including the host hotel, hotels offering discounts to marathon entrants, and in some cases other lodging options. All prices are in the local currency unless otherwise noted. **RELATED RACES/EVENTS** lists other races that run in conjunction with the marathon, such as a marathon relay, half marathon, 10K, 5K, and kids races. Finally, the **AREA ACTIVITIES** section gives you a general idea of the sights and things-to-do in the area. Not an exhaustive list, this section is intended only to help you decide whether to attend that particular marathon.

APPENDIX:
RANKINGS AND COURSE PROFILES

Most of the rankings in this section are self evident, except perhaps for our **TOP 30 FASTEST MARATHONS** ranking. The fastest marathons ranking indicates what we believe to be the fastest races in the North America. Similar rankings in other publications have used such things as course records, percentage of PRs, and the like. We believe such criteria are misleading at best. Instead, we try to consider the factors that affect a runner's performance at a given race, so our ranking considers three broad factors in descending order of importance: course difficulty, race organization, and crowd support. The most important ingredient is the course. Is it flat, rolling, or hilly? Where are the biggest hills? Do the turns disrupt a runner's rhythm? What is the running surface? The second ingredient to producing a fast race is organization. The more support a runner has before, during and after a race the better his prospects for a fast time. The third ingredient is crowd support. Any runner can tell you that the extra lift provided by spectators can make the difference between pushing through the hurt and giving in to the struggle. The energy at Boston and New York contribute to faster times than would otherwise be run on those courses. We believe that the ranking of the fastest races based on our formula is the most accurate yet produced. There is always room for fine-tuning, however, and we welcome your comments.

THE LEAD PACK

TOP 110 DESTINATION MARATHONS

WALT DISNEY WORLD MARATHON

OVERALL: 89.5

COURSE BEAUTY: 9-

COURSE DIFFICULTY: 3-

APPROPRIATENESS FOR FIRST TIMERS: 10-

RACE ORGANIZATION: 9

CROWDS: 4

RACE DATA

Overall Ranking:	23
Quickness Ranking:	28
Contact:	Walt Disney World Marathon
	P.O. Box 10,000
	Lake Buena Vista, FL 32830-1000
	Tel. (407) 939-7810
Date:	January 10, 1999; January 9, 2000
Start Time:	6:00 a.m.
Time Course Closes:	1:00 p.m.
Number of Finishers:	6,527 in 1998
Course:	Near loop
Certification:	USATF
Course Records:	Male: (open) 2:11:50; (masters) 2:20:26
	Female: (open) 2:31:54; (masters) 2:49:44
Elite Athlete Programs:	No
Cost:	$55/65
Age groups/Divisions:	18-24, 25-29, 30-34, 35-39, 40-44, 45-49, 50-54,
	55-59, 60-64, 65+ (F), 65-69, 70+ (M)
Walkers:	Yes
Requirements:	None
Temperature:	45°- 75°
Aid/Splits:	20 / digital clocks every mile

HIGHLIGHTS Do you remember running through Walt Disney World as a child, rushing from the Pirates of the Caribbean to It's a Small World? Or maybe you never got a chance to visit the home of Mickey Mouse, Goofy, Tinkerbell, and all their friends. Well, here's your opportunity to run as fast as you like through the Magic Kingdom and not be told to slow down by pesky parents. The Walt Disney World Marathon is blooming into a compelling, runner-friendly event with Disney's one-of-a-kind flair. Runners complete a flat course, weaving through four theme parks including Disney's newest attraction, the Animal Kingdom. Though fun and entertaining through the theme parks, be aware that the course also runs unceremoniously along park service roads much of the way. As you would expect, Disney puts on quite a spectacle, including light shows, a torrent of fireworks, lasers, and music. The race offers a number of packages, including entry fee, two-nights accommodations, carbo-load party, and transportation. Walt Disney World is a particularly great race for families. This quality alone makes it a good destination marathon. Leon Roby Blue of

Searcy, Arkansas says, *"It is a good way to include the whole family in the marathon experience. Something for everyone."*

COURSE DESCRIPTION The Disney World Marathon begins just outside Epcot and passes under Epcot's Spaceship Earth at the 3-mile mark. Runners then proceed to the World Showcase before heading to the Magic Kingdom, passing Disney's Contemporary Resort. While in the Magic Kingdom, runners visit Main Street's Town Square, Tomorrowland, Fantasyland, Cinderella's Castle, Liberty Square, the Hall of Presidents and Splash Mountain. Returning to Floridian Way, the route passes several of Disney's 99 Holes of Golf, as well as a few resort hotels. While the half marathoners finish at the Magic Kingdom Pluto Parking area, full marathoners continue to Disney's newest attraction, the Animal Kingdom. The 16-mile mark greets runners as they enter a backstage area the giraffes and rhinos call home. Entering the Animal Kingdom in Asia, runners continue past the park's centerpiece, the Tree of Life, and then tour Dinoland before leaving the park at the entrance near the Rainforest Cafe. After a brief spin around Disney's Wide World of Sports Complex (mile 20), runners continue on to the MGM Studios. The course follows Sunset and Hollywood Boulevards before returning to Epcot via Disney's Boardwalk, the resort's entertainment district. Upon reaching Epcot, runners pass the eleven-country World Showcase before finishing just outside of Spaceship Earth. *(Note: The Disney Marathon course changes almost yearly in an effort to showcase new areas of the ever-growing property).*

CROWD/RUNNER SUPPORT Once known as one of the loneliest marathons because of thin crowds, the Walt Disney World Marathon has made significant strides in remedying this concern. Monorail takes spectators to several sites along the course, but most of the onlookers stay in Epcot and the other theme parks. In part to make up for smaller crowds, Disney packs in the entertainment along the course from Disney characters, to light presentations, to music. Steve Bainbridge of Fairbanks, Alaska calls the race, *"A sensory overload! Nonstop entertainment."*

RACE LOGISTICS Runners take the monorail system or shuttle buses from their Disney Resort hotels to the start. The same transportation can return runners back to their hotels following the race. If you are staying outside the Disney complex, you must provide your own transportation.

ACTIVITIES On Friday and Saturday visit the Health and Fitness Expo located at Disney's Wide World of Sports Complex. There, you have your choice of dozens of Disney Marathon souvenirs. On Saturday evening, devour mounds of pasta at the carbo-loading dinner. Following the race you can reload at the generous fruit and bagel tables. The day after the marathon, complete results and finishers' certificates are available at Disney's Wide World of Sports Complex from 9:00 a.m. to 6:00 p.m.

AWARDS Every entrant receives a long-sleeve T-shirt and an official race program. Marathoners who finish under six hours are awarded heavy Mickey Mouse Medallions and finishers' certificates. The top five finishers in each division earn additional awards. Disney no longer awards prize money or recruits elite athletes.

ACCOMMODATIONS For information on resort packages call your travel agent or (407-939-7810) and reference the 1999 or 2000 marathon weekend.

RELATED EVENTS/RACES Kids Foot Locker presents the FamilyFun Magazine's FamilyFun Run on Saturday morning beginning at 7:30 a.m. at Epcot. Open to the public, the 5K runs through Epcot with a finish at the marathon finish line. Participants receive long-sleeve T-shirts. There are also shorter events for youngsters. In addition, meet celebrity runners at the press conference following the FamilyFun Run.

AREA ATTRACTIONS The big attraction in the area is the Walt Disney World complex itself, with its four theme parks, nighttime entertainment complex, three water parks, a

zoological park, golf, tennis, and even an Indy Car track. After opening in May of 1997, Disney's Wide World of Sports Complex has hosted hundreds of sporting events. The 200-acre, state-of-the-art sports complex features a 9,000-seat baseball stadium used as the spring training home of the Atlanta Braves, an eleven-court tennis center home to the U.S. Men's Clay Court Championships, the Foot Locker Track and Field complex, the multi-purpose Fieldhouse, and the Official All-Star Cafe, a sports-themed family restaurant owned by several sports celebrities. In all, the facility accommodates over 32 different sports.

HOUSTON MARATHON

OVERALL: 90.6

COURSE BEAUTY: 7-

COURSE DIFFICULTY: 2

APPROPRIATENESS FOR FIRST TIMERS: 9

RACE ORGANIZATION: 10

CROWDS: 9-

RACE DATA

Overall Ranking: 19

Quickness Ranking: 5

Contact: Methodist Health Care Houston Marathon
720 North Post Oak Road, Ste. 335
Houston, TX 77024
Tel. (713) 957-3453
Fax (713) 957-3406
http://www.houstonmarathon.com

Date: January 17, 1999; 2000 date TBA but generally held on Martin Luther King holiday weekend

Start Time: 8:00 a.m.

Time Course Closes: 1:30 p.m.

Number of Finishers: 4,440 in 1998

Course: Loop

Certification: USATF

Course Records: Male: (open) 2:10:04
Female: (open) 2:27:51

Elite Athlete Programs: Yes

Cost: $45/60

Age groups/Divisions: ≤19, 20-24, 25-29, 30-34, 35-39, 40-44, 45-49, 50-54, 55-59, 60-64, 65+ (F), 65-69, 70-74, 75+ (M)

Walkers: No

Requirements: None

Temperature: 45˚ - 50˚

Aid/Splits: 24 / every mile from mile 2

HIGHLIGHTS Do you like hoopla, the noisy, uplifting, and often crazy entertainment along so many marathon routes today? Pioneering the hoopla phenomenon, the Houston Marathon does it better than most. With nearly every mile packed with some form of entertainment, the course loops through the city and its suburbs. A good place to try for a PR, the race offers excellent organization, superb runner support, usually ideal weather conditions, and substantial crowds.

RACE HISTORY A five-mile loop course marked by a parked station wagon debuted as the Houston Marathon in December 1972. Seventy-three runners endured that race and were treated to beef stew afterwards. Taking up sponsorship of the race in 1980, Tenneco Energy helped it blossom. In fact, in 1992, Houston was the site of the women's Olympic Marathon Trials. Tenneco ceased its support of the race in 1996, ending one of the longest standing marathon partnerships. The race has shown little impact, however, and in 1998 Houston hosted the U.S. Women's Marathon Championships. Over the years, Houston has witnessed some remarkable races, including perhaps the closest marathon finish in U.S. history: in 1984, a photo revealed that Charlie Spedding literally won by his foot.

COURSE DESCRIPTION The Houston Marathon's loop course starts and finishes downtown at the George R. Brown Convention Center. Passing through many of Houston's ethnically diverse neighborhoods, the race is completely closed to vehicular traffic. Houston sports a dual start, with men departing from LaBranch Street and women beginning on Crawford Street. After the cannon-blast start, runners head for the Elysian Viaduct. At mile 1, which is on the viaduct, the course reaches one of its highest points at 85 feet. One of Houston's oldest neighborhoods, a Hispanic barrio in the near north side, awaits runners on the down side of the viaduct, providing a fiesta atmosphere as runners pass mariachi bands and dancers. As the men and women merge at 2.5 miles, they head back into downtown, crossing the Main Street Bridge in front of the University of Houston's Downtown campus. After passing the 5-mile mark in the midst of downtown skyscrapers, runners continue south down Main Street toward its booming Asian office and retail centers. Mile 7 takes runners through a middle class neighborhood where residents bring the kids out to view the race. Mile 8 brings the Herman Park Rose Garden and the Mecom Fountain. Between 8 and 9, competitors enjoy the oak trees arching over Main Street as they run toward the beautiful Rice University campus. Around 10.5 miles, runners enter trendy, fashionable West University Place, featuring some of Houston's finer homes. Soak in the encouragement here to fortify yourself for the Westpark Hump at the halfway point, a 35-foot climb over a quarter mile, and the following commercial sections of the course. Houston's well-known Galleria shopping area provides good crowd support, while runners pass the Transco Tower, the tallest building in the country that is outside a downtown area, and its sculptured "Water Wall." It's a tough time for runners as they again turn away from downtown at mile 15. Between 15 and 20 miles you pass through the residential and commercial areas Riverway, Tangelwood, and Church. At mile 18 you head toward downtown, passing George Bush's church. Look for the former president as he's usually watching the runners as they continue downtown toward the finish. Miles 20 to 21.5 lead you through Memorial Park, the training ground for Houston's runners. Leaving the park, runners sense the finish, but must conquer the hills of Allen Parkway, actually two street underpasses that at 23.5 can be difficult for many marathoners. After making it through the Allen Parkway bumps, runners make one last pass through downtown. The last mile decorated with confetti streamers is a welcome sight, with the Convention Center finish within view.

CROWD / RUNNER SUPPORT The Houston Marathon provides unparalleled hoopla lining most of the marathon route. The entertainment consists of everything from belly dancers, bands, ballet, gymnastics, and bagpipers, to cheerleaders. Complementing the hoopla are approximately 250,000 spectators at various sections of the course. Add on to that water stations and split times every mile, and you have outstanding runner support. Together with the other 6,500 runners, you shouldn't be too lonely out there. The Houston Marathon also supports the Run for a Reason program, where marathoners help raise money for any number of area charities.

RACE LOGISTICS The GRB Convention Center offers excellent indoor facilities for runners before and after the race.

ACTIVITIES Houston hosts a large, two-day Health and Fitness Expo at the GRB Convention Center on Friday and Saturday. There you can attend numerous seminars on running and fitness topics, pick up your race packet, or register late. There is no race-day registration or packet pick-up. After the marathon, relax at the post-race party in the Convention Center.

AWARDS Each entrant receives a marathon T-shirt. Runners who finish under five and one-half hours also are awarded finisher medals, glass mugs, and certificates. Trophies are given to age-group winners, while top athletes compete for about $162,000 in prize money. The first local male and female finishers receive a trip to a top international marathon.

ELITE RUNNERS INFORMATION World-class runners could be offered lodging, travel, and expenses. Elite runners compete for the approximately $162,000 prize money. Open winners receive $25,000, with $16,000 for second, $10,000 for third, $6,200 for fourth, $4,200 for fifth, $2,200 for sixth, $1,700 for seventh, $1,200 for eighth, $750 for ninth, and $500 for tenth. Masters prize money goes five deep, with $3,000 for first and $200 for fifth.

ACCOMMODATIONS The DoubleTree Hotel at Allen Center, 400 Dallas Street (800-231-6310), serves as the headquarters hotel for the Houston Marathon. The DoubleTree offers runners special room rates. Also convenient are the Hyatt Regency, 1200 Louisiana (800-233-1234); the Four Seasons Hotel, 1300 Lamar Street (800-332-3442); and The Lancaster, 701 Texas Avenue (800-368-5966). A little further out, try the Allen Park Inn, 2121 Allen Parkway (800-231-6310); Harvey Hotel, 2712 Southwest Freeway (713-523-8448); and Ramada Hotel-Galleria, 7787 Katy Freeway (713-681-5000).

RELATED EVENTS / RACES Houston also hosts the Downtown 5000, starting just after the marathon at the GRB Convention Center. The 5K draws more than 1,500 runners and tours the downtown area. There is no race-day registration.

AREA ATTRACTIONS While in Houston, you may want to catch a Houston Rockets basketball game at The Compaq Center, 10 Greenway Plaza. Also tour Space Center Houston for hands-on exhibits and a behind-the-scenes peek at the Johnson Space Center. Bone up on Texas' battle for independence at the San Jacinto Battleground State Historical Park. Houston boasts numerous museums, including the Houston Museum of Natural Science, and its Cockrell Butterfly Center, the Museum of Fine Arts, the Contemporary Arts Museum, and the Menil Collection.

SAN DIEGO MARATHON

OVERALL: 83.2

COURSE BEAUTY: 8+

COURSE DIFFICULTY: 4 (SEE APPENDIX)

APPROPRIATENESS FOR FIRST TIMERS: 7+

RACE ORGANIZATION: 9+

CROWDS: 2

RACE DATA

Overall Ranking: 66
Quickness Ranking: 58
Contact: San Diego Marathon
511 S. Cedros Avenue, Suite B
Solana Beach, CA 92075
(619) 792-2900
http://www.sdmarathon.com

Date: January 17, 1999; January 1, 2000 (tentative)
Start Time: 7:30 a.m.
Time Course Closes: Noon
Number of Finishers: 2,700 in 1998
Course: Loop
Certification: USATF
Course Records: Male: (open) 2:23:08
Female: (open) 2:48:17
Elite Athlete Programs: Yes
Cost: $45/50/60
Age groups/Divisions: ≤17, 18-24, 25-29, 30-34, 35-39, 40-44, 45-49,
50-54, 55-59, 60-64, 65-69, 70-74, 75-79, 80+
Walkers: Yes (5:30 a.m. start)
Requirements: None
Temperature: 45° - 72°
Aid/Splits: 26 / 10 points on course

HIGHLIGHTS   The San Diego Marathon mixes all the ingredients that make Southern California famous—great weather, beaches, and beautiful scenery—into an appetizing race. The temperate January weather makes for excellent running conditions. The course takes in about 10 miles of the Pacific coastline and the Carlsbad flower fields. But you won't find one of the area's biggest headaches—traffic. The race course is completely closed to vehicles. Known more for its larger half marathon, San Diego hopes to grow the full race into the premiere event. The race also makes a strong effort to attract runners of all abilities by offering early start times.

COURSE DESCRIPTION   San Diego's rolling, loop course starts at Plaza Camino Real shopping complex and then heads directly to the coast, passing the Buena Vista Lagoon before reaching the Pacific Ocean near mile 1. Turning south along Carlsbad Blvd., runners pass through the village of Carlsbad while paralleling the water. Angling inland on Palomar Airport Road (PAL) at mile 5, the route loops a business park area before running through the Carlsbad flower fields, climbing over 120 feet from mile 11.5 to 13. Turning around in another business park complex, runners return on PAL through the flower fields and rejoin Carlsbad Blvd. near mile 15. The next three miles run south beside the ocean and include a 40-foot climb to the turnaround at La Costa Avenue. From mile 18 to the finish, runners head north on familiar Carlsbad Blvd. as they make their way back to Plaza Camino Real.

CROWD/RUNNER SUPPORT The race features entertainment—rock bands, bag pipers, Taiko drummers—at a number of locations on the route. Otherwise, crowd support is limited to a few areas. Organizers generously provide aid stations every mile of the course, with water, electrolyte replacement drink, petroleum jelly, and portable toilets generally available. Fruit provides a needed sugar boost at the final 6 stations.

RACE LOGISTICS Entrants staying at the official hotel can take advantage of shuttle service to the marathon start. Other runners need to provide their own transportation to the start. You may park at Plaza Camino Real or in adjacent areas, but arrive early since access roads may be closed by 6:00 a.m. Entrants who intend to walk the marathon should start at 5:30 a.m. Others who expect to take longer than 4:30 to complete the race should begin at 6:15 a.m. However, if you start at 6:15 a.m. and run faster than 4:30, you will unfortunately be disqualified.

ACTIVITIES Pick up your race packet or register during the All About Fitness Expo at Plaza Camino Real on Friday, 2:00 p.m. to 7:00 p.m., or Saturday, 8:00 a.m. to 6:00 p.m. On Saturday, the expo features a number of running-related clinics. The Carbo Pasta Party with entertainment takes place at the headquarters hotel on Saturday evening from 5:00 p.m. to 8:00 p.m. The post-race party features plenty of food, refreshments, live entertainment, and massages. The awards party at 2:00 p.m. at the official hotel features complimentary hors d'oeuvres.

AWARDS All entrants get T-shirts, and medals are awarded to all finishers. The top three in each age group also receive awards.

ACCOMMODATIONS The Holiday Inn in Carlsbad (619-792-5200), is the official hotel. The Carlsbad Visitors Bureau (800-227-5722) can assist you with other hotel reservations in Carlsbad.

RELATED EVENTS/RACES On Saturday, the day before the marathon, there are a 5K Run/Walk and a Kids Marathon Mile for children 12 and under. A five-member marathon relay runs with the marathon. The first four team members each run 5-mile legs, and the last runner completes a 10K. Shuttle buses transport team members to the relay exchange points. The half marathon is even better known than the marathon, attracting a national-class field.

AREA ATTRACTIONS The San Diego area has a lot to offer visitors. You must visit the awesome San Diego Zoo in beautiful Balboa Park. Kids may also enjoy a day at Sea World and Wild Animal Park. Old Town provides that western/Mexican flair. Warm weather brings out the hoards to Mission Beach and La Jolla. Great shopping can be had at Hortons Plaza.

MARDI GRAS MARATHON

OVERALL: 83.6

COURSE BEAUTY: 9-

COURSE DIFFICULTY: 2+

APPROPRIATENESS FOR FIRST TIMERS: 8-

RACE ORGANIZATION: 9-

CROWDS: 3-

RACE DATA

Overall Ranking:	62
Quickness Ranking:	20
Contact:	Chuck George
	Nokia-Sugar Bowl Mardi Gras Marathon
	New Orleans Track Club, Inc.
	P.O. Box 52003
	New Orleans, LA 70152-2003
	(504) 482-6682
	E-mail: NOTC@runNOTC.org
	http://www.runNOTC.org
Date:	January 30, 1999; January 29, 2000
Start Time:	8:00 a.m.
Time Course Closes:	2:30 p.m.
Number of Finishers:	1,000 in 1998
Course:	Out and back with a loop
Certification:	USATF
Course Records:	Male: (open) 2:23:57
	Female: (open) 2:55:03
Elite Athlete Programs:	No
Cost:	$45/55
Age groups/Divisions:	<19, 20-24, 25-29, 30-34, 35-39, 40-44, 45-49, 50-54, 55-59, 60-64 , 65-69, 70+
Walkers:	Yes
Requirements:	None
Temperature:	40° - 65°
Aid/Splits:	18 / every mile

HIGHLIGHTS New Orleans pops like a firecracker—always explosive, fiery, flashy, illicit, and just this side of dangerous. Hence the appeal. The city's cultural melange provides much of the powder and the spark for the brilliant show, most notoriously exemplified by that brazen February rite known as Mardi Gras. Taking its name from the crazy festival, the Mardi Gras Marathon passes through the site of the festival's madness—the French Quarter—and many other New Orleans attractions including Bayou St. John and Esplanade Avenue. Nearly doubling in size in the last two years, Mardi Gras is growing into one of the most popular marathons in the south.

COURSE DESCRIPTION Mardi Gras' closed, loop course covers many of its roads twice, giving it an out-and-back quality. The race starts in Tad Gormley Stadium, site of the 1992 Olympic Track Trials and situated in 1,500-acre City Park. Heading to Marconi Drive, the course borders the park until just past the 2-mile mark where it does an about face returning past the stadium and down Roosevelt Mall. After a right turn on Stadium, the route passes through City

Park alongside the Peristyle and Bandstand until hitting the Bayou St. John at mile 6. Lined with old historic houses and mansions, Bayou St. John may be the highlight of the course. Mile 7 runs out and back on Bell and Ursulines Avenues, a stretch that seems to go back in time 100 or more years. Turning onto Esplanade Avenue at mile 8.3, runners proceed towards the French Quarter, reaching it by mile 10. After cutting through the heart of the French Quarter and then downtown, the route reaches Prytania Street, home to the famous Crescent City Classic 10K, site of numerous world and American records. Running along Prytania at mile 12, the course passes through the scenic Garden District and Uptown before entering Audubon Park. A loop of Audubon Park between miles 16 and 17.6 offers a peaceful setting alongside Tulane University, Loyola University, and the famous St. Charles Avenue streetcar line. Leaving Audubon Park, the course retraces itself to Prytania, through the city center and as luck would have it, right back through the French Quarter. Beware as the renowned Hash House Harriers coordinate the water station in the French Quarter. Back on Esplanade at mile 23, runners return to City Park, loop the New Orleans Museum of Art, and then travel down Roosevelt Mall to the entrance of Tad Gormley Stadium and the finish line.

CROWD/RUNNER SUPPORT   Although more spectators come out along the new course, don't expect huge crowds along the way. Areas of greatest support include Moss Street, the French Quarter, and near the turnaround in Audubon Park. Numerous live musicians entertain runners in the French Quarter, and expect lots of mardi gras flavor around the aid stations as all eighteen of them compete for prize money in a costume/decoration contest. Portable toilets also sit at several points along the course.

RACE LOGISTICS   Race organizers provide bus transportation from the race headquarters hotel to Tad Gormley Stadium from 6:30 a.m. to 7:15 a.m. The race also gets you back to the hotel afterwards from 10:00 a.m. to 3:00 p.m. If you prefer to drive, park at the Stadium or on Victory Avenue, or Marconi Drive, but not on Roosevelt Mall.

ACTIVITIES   You can pick up your race packet or register at the expo held in the headquarters hotel on Thursday or Friday from 12:00 p.m. to 7:00 p.m. Refreshments, including Mardi Gras King Cakes and lots of beer, follow the marathon.

AWARDS   Every Mardi Gras runner takes home a long-sleeve T-shirt, and finishers receive a medal, certificate, and results booklet. Age-group awards go 2 or 3 deep, and commemorative awards are given to the top three overall and the top masters runners.

ACCOMMODATIONS   The Radisson Hotel, 1500 Canal Street (800-824-3359) serves as the official race hotel offering discount rates to Mardi Gras Marathon participants. Other possibilities include the Omni Royal Orleans, 621 St. Louis Street (504-529-5333); Monteleone, 214 Royal Street (504-523-3341); Windsor Court, 300 Gravier Street (504-523-6000); or Westin Canal Place, 100 Iberville Street (504-566-7006).

RELATED EVENTS/RACES   Race organizers also offer a half marathon (1,000 runners) and 5K (1,000 runners).

AREA ATTRACTIONS   Although best known for its spicy French Quarter, New Orleans does contain other points of interest. St. Charles Avenue boasts impeccable 19th-century homes, as does the Garden District. Get in your warm-up or warm-down run at Audubon Park, and return later to roam the excellent Audubon Zoo. The swamp curious should tour the Barataria Preserve along Lake Salvador.

CAROLINA MARATHON

OVERALL: 77.3

COURSE BEAUTY: 8

COURSE DIFFICULTY: 5 (SEE APPENDIX)

APPROPRIATENESS FOR FIRST TIMERS: 7-

RACE ORGANIZATION: 9

CROWDS: 1+

RACE DATA

Overall Ranking: **104**
Quickness Ranking: **76**
Contact: **Carolina Marathon Association**
P.O. Box 5092
Columbia, SC 29250
(803) 929-1996
http://www.carolinamarathon.org

Date: **February 6, 1999; February 26, 2000**
Start Time: **8:00 a.m.**
Time Course Closes: **1:00 p.m.**
Number of Finishers: **261 in 1998**
Course: **Loop**
Certification: **USATF**
Course Records: **Male: (open) 2:43:42; (masters) 3:04:19**
Female: (open) 2:29:54; (masters) 2:40:36
Elite Athlete Programs: **No**
Cost: **$30/40**
Age groups/Divisions: **<19, 20-24, 25-29, 30-34, 35-39, 40-44, 45-49,**
50-54, 55-59, 60-64, 65-69, 70+
Walkers: **No**
Requirements: **None**
Temperature: **46°**
Aid/Splits: **12 / none**

HIGHLIGHTS The 1996 U.S. Women's Olympic Trials served as a coming-out party for both its host and winner. Virtual unknown Jenny Spangler shocked the pundits by surging to a strong victory over the pre-race favorites. The Trials also pulled the Carolina Marathon out of southern obscurity. Historically a small race, Carolina runs on a difficult course through Columbia's downtown, suburbs, Fort Jackson Army Base, and University of South Carolina campus. South Carolina's capital city, Columbia provides a hospitable setting for the now recognizable race.

COURSE DESCRIPTION Starting on Main Street near the South Carolina State House, the course circles downtown passing the landmark Hampton Preston Mansion and Robert Mill House before returning to the State House near mile 2. Heading west, runners cross the Congaree River before mile 3 and pass through the residential communities of West Columbia and Cayce while dropping 150 feet to mile 6. Crossing back over the river near the 6-mile mark, the route contains two 100-foot hills between miles 5 and 8. After passing through the University of

South Carolina, runners head through the quiet, shady neighborhoods of Shandon and Heathwood. At mile 11, runners descend 150 feet through Lake Katherine's residential community. Near mile 12, the course enters Fort Jackson (miles 12 to 19), one of the country's largest Army training centers. Gaining 170 feet over 2 miles, the route also contains several long downhill sections to mile 20. Exiting the fort after mile 19, runners head back toward downtown through suburban areas climbing 120 feet from mile 21 to mile 23. From here, runners stride down Devine Street for a 1-mile straightaway on Main Street leading to the NationsBank Plaza finish.

CROWD/RUNNER SUPPORT Runners find the bulk of the crowd support downtown, at Five Points shopping center, and in Fort Jackson Army Base, where the soldiers come out in force to cheer. Some spectators also scatter in the many residential communities along the route. The aid stations, located every two miles, offer water and electrolyte replacement drink.

RACE LOGISTICS Runners staying at the race headquarters hotel can walk to the starting line. Several other downtown hotels are within walking distance of the start. If you're staying further out, you will need to drive and park in the vicinity.

ACTIVITIES Browse the expo and pick up your race packet from 12:00 p.m. to 9:30 p.m. on Friday at race headquarters (site undetermined at press time). You can also retrieve your packet from 6:30 a.m. to 8:00 a.m. on race day, but there is no race-day registration. On Friday evening, the race holds a pasta party starting at 5:30 p.m. After the marathon, partake in the traditional luncheon starting at 1:00 p.m.; the awards ceremony begins at 1:30 p.m.

AWARDS Every entrant receives a marathon T-shirt, and finishers take home a medal and certificate of completion. The top overall finishers receive small cash awards, while the top three division winners receive trophies.

ACCOMMODATIONS The official race hotel had not been determined at press time. The Adam's Mark, 1200 Hampton Street (803-771-7000) served as the race headquarters in the past. Other nearby hotels include: Comfort Inn Capital City, 2025 Main Street (803-252-6321); and Governor's House, 1301 Main Street (803-779-7790).

RELATED EVENTS/RACES Columbia's reputation for holding national-class running events continues over the next few years as it hosts the U.S. Women's National 8K Championship in 1999 and the U.S. Women's Olympic Marathon Trials in 2000. Both races are held in conjunction with the Carolina Marathon. Those of us non-elites can choose from a 10K run or walk beginning at 9:30 a.m., and kids (6-15 years old) can compete in the youth races held in nearby Finlay Park.

AREA ATTRACTIONS Columbia features one of the nation's best zoos, the Riverbanks Zoo and Garden. Visitors can also glimpse antebellum Columbia at the Robert Mills Historic House and the Hampton-Preston Mansion.

LAS VEGAS MARATHON

OVERALL: 79.3

COURSE BEAUTY: 7+

COURSE DIFFICULTY: 1+ (SEE APPENDIX)

APPROPRIATENESS FOR FIRST TIMERS: 8-

RACE ORGANIZATION: 8

CROWDS: 2

RACE DATA

Overall Ranking: **89**
Quickness Ranking: **3**
Contact: **Al Boka**
Las Vegas International Marathon
P.O. Box 81262
Las Vegas, NV 89180
(702) 876-3870
E-mail: lvmarathon@aol.com
http://www.lvmarathon.com

Date: **February 7, 1999; February 6, 2000**
Start Time: **7:30 a.m.**
Time Course Closes: **12:30 p.m.**
Number of Finishers: **2,100 in 1998**
Course: **Point to point**
Certification: **USATF & AIMS**
Course Records: **New course in 1999**
Elite Athlete Programs: **Yes**
Cost: **$45/55**
Age groups/Divisions: **18-24, 25-29, 30-34, 35-39, 40-44, 45-49, 50-54,**
55-59, 60-64, 65-69, 70+, Clydesdale
Walkers: **No**
Requirements: **None**
Temperature: **38° - 60°**
Aid/Splits: **15 / every five miles**

HIGHLIGHTS Known as the entertainment capital of the world, Las Vegas' fast-paced action occurs along "The Strip," a long stretch that contains the lavish theme hotels not to mention their accompanying casinos, showgirls, nightclubs, and entertainers that make Vegas famous. However, once a year, the spotlight shifts to a lesser known strip—26 miles of pavement just south of downtown—which features fast-paced action of a different variety. Nestled below the barren Las Vegas mountains, the rural point-to-point Las Vegas International Marathon (LVM) course lies in stark contrast to the neon-splashed 24-hour city located only a few miles from the finish. With a net downhill of 600 feet, Vegas offers excellent odds for a personal record. So, if you're looking for a fast winter marathon with a lot of glitz and glamour on the side, try your luck at Las Vegas.

RACE HISTORY The LVM was founded in 1967 by Hank Greenspun, publisher of the Las Vegas Sun newspaper. Heralded as the World Master's Marathon, the race drew 141 runners. Three years later, the newspaper dropped its sponsorship. The newly formed Las Vegas Track Club (LVTC) continued the race until 1982 when it, too, decided to end its involvement with the race. Up stepped LVTC member Al Boka who refused to let the race die and resolved to continue the race with the objective of transforming it into a much larger event. Today, the race draws over 2,000 marathoners and 3,500 half marathoners.

COURSE DESCRIPTION Las Vegas unveils a partially new, faster course in 1999. And no, despite the wishes of many participants, the race does not run down "The Strip." Rather, the race starts in Jean, NV, on State Road 604 (elevation approximately 2,875 feet). Race veterans should recognize the first 22 miles, as they are miles 3.5 through 26 of the former course. Paralleling I-15 for these first 22 miles, runners enjoy little in the way of visual stimulation— remember the course is designed for speed, not aesthetics. Mostly high desert, sage brush, and jack rabbits mark the course as it gradually climbs 150 feet to mile 7. Here, runners catch sight of the Las Vegas skyline in the distance as they begin the 'very fast but runable' 750-foot descent over the next 19 miles. And despite what you may think, the Vegas skyline is not just a desert illusion. You really are getting closer. At mile 22, the route heads east, winding through the Callaway Golf Center before emerging onto Sunset Road. After following the southern perimeter fence of McCarran International Airport, runners head south onto Eastern Avenue for last half mile to the finish.

CROWD/RUNNER SUPPORT Not surprisingly, few casino goers flee the slot machines and card tables to cheer the marathoners. In fact, as a rural, point-to-point course, the LVM is not particularly conducive to large crowds. Although the road is partially open and accessible to spectators after mile 12, most spectators assemble at the relay exchange points and at the finish where bleachers enhance the chance of spotting your favorite runner.

RACE LOGISTICS The race start in Jean, NV, is thirty minutes south of downtown. Free, mandatory bus transportation to the start is provided. Buses leave from the MGM Grand Hotel/Casino parking lot. Transportation back to the hotel is also provided. Specific details are provided in race packets.

ACTIVITIES The LVM features a three-day Health & Fitness Expo starting at noon on Thursday at the new MGM Grand Hotel and Casino Expo Center. Race packets are distributed here from 11:00 a.m. to 6:00 p.m. on Thursday and Friday, and Saturday from 10:00 a.m. to 6:00 p.m. Course bus tours ($12 pre-paid) are available on Saturday leaving at 1:00 p.m. from the MGM. A pasta party takes place at the Tropicana Hotel and Casino directly across the street from the MGM Grand. Food bags and beverages are available at the finish for runners along with an "International Food Festival" in the park. The awards presentation begins at 5:00 p.m. at the Tropicana.

AWARDS Each marathoner receives a race T-shirt at the packet pickup. Medallions are awarded to all finishers, and result booklets are mailed to all participants. With Las Vegas being, well, Las Vegas, it's only fitting that the prize money structure is about as unique as they come. Money is not limited to the very top finishers. Sure, the top open and masters runners are awarded prize money which varies from year to year depending on budget constraints. But, age groupers, usually excluded from the prize money fold, also compete for small purses for the top one or two places. Various time bonus money is also available. Plaques are awarded to tenth place in some divisions. Although the plaques are presented at the awards ceremony, prize money winners should not plan on racing to the casinos to parlay their earnings into a huge jackpot—the checks are mailed within thirty days of the event.

ELITE RUNNERS INFORMATION Complimentary entries and possible, limited shared accommodations, are given to sub 2:20 men and sub 2:45 women.

ACCOMMODATIONS Although there are more than 100,000 hotel rooms in Las Vegas, amazingly, they can fill, so book your reservation early. If you can stay on "The Strip" on Las Vegas Boulevard, do it! The various theme hotels are unparalleled, if you don't mind gaudy. You can choose between the co-hosts MGM Grand Hotel and Theme Park, the world's largest hotel with 5,009 rooms, $119/night (800-288-1000), and the exciting Tropicana Resort & Casino, $110/night (800-634-4000); or the other hotels offering room blocks for marathoners: San Remo, Luxor and Monte Carlo.

RELATED EVENTS/RACES The LVM features a half marathon run and race walk which take place on the lightning-fast second half of the marathon course, beginning at 6:45 a.m. On Saturday, a 5K "International Friendship Run" brings together runners from around the world for a pre-marathon tuneup. The race takes place on the famed "Strip" beginning at 6:30 a.m.

AREA ATTRACTIONS The hotels alone offer so much entertainment for adults and children that you can easily do without a car. In fact, you may experience greater fatigue from hotel/casino activities than from the marathon. If it's culture you want, the Las Vegas Art Museum is one of the finest in the country. If you're interested in sights outside Las Vegas, visit Hoover Dam (30 minutes to the southeast), Lake Mead, the largest man-made lake in America (45 minutes north), or Laughlin, with its slower paced casinos and impressive views of the Colorado River (60 minutes south).

AUSTIN MARATHON

OVERALL: 85.5

COURSE BEAUTY: 8

COURSE DIFFICULTY: 3- (SEE APPENDIX)

APPROPRIATENESS FOR FIRST TIMERS: 9+

RACE ORGANIZATION: 10

CROWDS: 5-

RACE DATA

Overall Ranking:	46
Quickness Ranking:	24
Contact:	Motorola Austin Marathon
	P.O. Box 684587
	Austin, TX 78768-4587
	Tel. (512) 505-8304
	Fax (512) 505-8312
	E-mail: momar1@email.sps.mot.com
	http://www.motorolamarathon.com
Date:	February 14, 1999; February 20, 2000
Start Time:	7:00 a.m.
Time Course Closes:	1:00 p.m. (runners must maintain 14 min. pace)
Number of Finishers:	1,700 in 1998
Course:	Out and back
Certification:	USATF
Course Records:	Male: (open) 2:15:19; (masters) 2:18:07
	Female: (open) 2:36:45; (masters) 2:41:01
Elite Athlete Programs:	Yes
Cost:	$40/50
Age groups/Divisions:	≤19, 20-24, 25-29, 30-34, 35-39, 40-44, 45-49,
	50-54, 55-59, 60+ (F), 60-64, 65-69, 70+ (M),
	Clydesdales & Fillies open & masters, and wheelchair
Walkers:	No
Requirements:	None
Temperature:	43° - 65°
Aid/Splits:	25 / every mile

HIGHLIGHTS "Six Sigma" is Motorola jargon for doing things with near-perfect quality. Well known for its superior products, Motorola hosts a "Six Sigma" marathon. The race organization's attention to detail is impressive, with aid stations, split and pace times, and portable toilets every mile; good transportation; a well-marked and patrolled course; an announcement of every runner's name as they cross the finish line; and excellent T-shirts. A fast course, the second half in particular becomes scenic as it runs through parkways near Town Lake. All of the amenities and the easy course make the race an excellent choice for first-time marathoners. The only wild-card is Texas weather. Race organizers moved the race from March to February to enhance the chances for cool weather, but there remains a real possibility for warm, humid conditions.

COURSE DESCRIPTION The course begins in northwest Austin and proceeds through a gently rolling loop, doubling back on itself at the 2.5-mile mark. Continuing slightly downhill through a light commercial/industrial area until mile 6, the course then winds downhill along the shaded boulevards of Shoal Creek and Lamar, losing approximately 250 feet in elevation. The Austin skyline appears just past the 14-mile mark. At mile 15, runners encounter a sharp U-turn on Sixth Street and return along Fifth Street. Mile 16 marks the beginning of the most scenic section of the route, the river front parkways lining Austin's Town Lake (actually part of the Colorado River). Mostly rolling between miles 17 and 22, the course then sharply descends on Riverside Boulevard before flattening on Barton Springs Road. The final 5K run flat through "Restaurant Row" before finishing in the heart of handsome Zilker Park.

CROWD/RUNNER SUPPORT Enthusiastic crowds at the relay exchanges and the finish area spur you along with the help of a few bands. Scattered crowds pop up in the neighborhoods and along the major thoroughfares. Competing against each other for offering the best support, over 2,200 volunteers operate aid stations and provide other necessary assistance.

RACE LOGISTICS Race organizers provide bus service from the finish line to the start, from the start to the various relay exchanges and ekiden exchange zones, and from exchange zones to the finish. Since buses are limited and service can take a little time, race officials urge runners to provide their own transportation if possible. The race also transports any clothes you may wish to have waiting for you at the finish. Though parking exists at both the start and finish areas, arrive early.

ACTIVITIES The marathon holds a two-day expo with about 30 exhibitors. On Saturday, a free fitness symposium addresses running-related topics. Pre-race activities culminate in the pasta dinner (about $9 in addition to the race entry fee). After the race, participants celebrate with a victory party featuring food, drinks, live music, kids' games, massage, and an awards ceremony.

AWARDS Every runner receives a great T-shirt and results booklet. All marathon finishers receive a medallion and finisher's T-shirt. There are distinctive age-group awards three to ten deep. About $40,000 in prize money is split among the top overall (ten deep), masters (ten deep), veterans (three deep), and wheelchair (three deep) athletes. Overall male and female winners receive airline tickets from American Airlines.

ELITE RUNNERS INFORMATION Participants interested in the elite runner program should contact John Conley (512-933-8739).

ACCOMMODATIONS Several hotels throughout the city of Austin offer special rates for Motorola Marathon participants. For information contact Tramex Travel (512-473-8585).

RELATED EVENTS/RACES If you're not ready for the full marathon, consider the two-person relay or the new, five-person ekiden. The ekiden is broken into two 10K legs, two 5K legs and a 12K leg. The race provides excellent transportation between the relay exchange points and the finish line.

BLUE ANGEL MARATHON

OVERALL: 79.3

COURSE BEAUTY: 8

COURSE DIFFICULTY: 3+

APPROPRIATENESS FOR FIRST TIMERS: 7+

RACE ORGANIZATION: 9+

CROWDS: 2

RACE DATA

Overall Ranking:	89
Quickness Ranking:	41
Contact:	Blue Angel Marathon
	190 Radford Blvd., Bldg. 632
	MWR Dept., NAS
	Pensacola, FL 32508-5217
	Tel. (850) 452-2843
	Fax. (850) 452-3133
	http://www.mwr-pcola.navy.mil
Date:	February 27, 1999; February 26, 2000
Start Time:	7:00 a.m.
Time Course Closes:	12:00 p.m.
Number of Finishers:	1,090 in 1998
Course:	Out and back with a few loops
Certification:	USATF
Course Records:	Male: (open) 2:20:50; (masters) 2:32:47
	Female: (open) 2:51:23; (masters) 3:07:21
Elite Athlete Programs:	No
Cost:	$28/35
Age groups/Divisions:	14-19, 20-24, 25-29, 30-34, 35-39, 40-44, 45-49,
	50-54, 55-59, 60-64, 65-69, 70-74, 75-79, 80+
Walkers:	No
Requirements:	None
Temperature:	55°
Aid/Splits:	13 / miles 1, 5, 10, 15 & 20, digital clock at halfway

HIGHLIGHTS Heralded as the "Official Navy Marathon," the Blue Angel Marathon takes its name from the pride of the U.S. Navy—the Blue Angel Flight Demonstration Squadron based at Pensacola Naval Air Station. Open to both military and civilian entrants, this out-and-back course features a mostly flat, and partially rolling journey through historic NAS and downtown Pensacola, along the waterfront of Pensacola Bay, and around two meticulously manicured golf courses. Shunning the traditional marathon start involving a speech and gun-firing by a local dignitary, BAM's send off includes a Blue Angel fly by and cannon blast. Barring an invasion or declaration of war, the Blue Angel will continue as one of the most prestigious races in the southeastern United States.

COURSE DESCRIPTION The Blue Angel Marathon begins aboard Naval Air Station Pensacola, the "Cradle of Naval Aviation." Starting on the NAS waterfront, the course heads westward, wrapping around the National Cemetery, going by the National Museum of Naval Aviation prior to making a quick loop in front of the historic Light House. The Light House, constructed in

1858, is still in operation today. Once again, the course crosses past the National Museum of Naval Aviation. At the 4-mile mark, the course overlooks the impressive frontage of Ft. Barrancas and Barrancas Beach. Continuing on, the course leads runners off-base at the 6-mile mark. Winding down through Old Warrington Town, the runners see magnificent homes surrounding Pensacola Country Club at the 11- and 12-mile marks. Runners are greeted by the historic City of Pensacola, along with fisheries, boats, parks, and businesses as they travel the route adjacent to the waterfront. At mile 14, the runners turn left and journey up Palafox Street, the center of downtown Pensacola, continuing on to the highest point of the course at the 15-mile mark located at the top of Palafox Hill in beautiful Lee Square. Marathoners travel around Lee Square and down the hill with a left turn at the 17-mile mark. Then, onto Seville Square Historical District filled with beautiful old buildings, parks, gardens, stately homes with gingerbread trim, and quaint shops. Runners head back to the waterfront at mile 18 past the Vietnam "Wall South" Monument and Park overlooking Pensacola Bay and the numerous fishing and pleasure boats. Around the 22-mile mark, the course circles back through Old Warrington Town. Runners enter the Naval Air Station at mile 24 with a run by A.C. Read Golf Course, completing the Blue Angel Marathon on the waterfront aboard NAS Pensacola.

C R O W D / R U N N E R   S U P P O R T   A smattering of spectators gather in front of their homes and businesses to applaud the athletes. Added motivation comes in the form of keyboard players, bands, and high school cheerleaders. Thirteen well-staffed aid stations keep you hydrated in the frequently humid race conditions.

R A C E   L O G I S T I C S   Since the start and finish are located in the same place, your only transportation worry on race day involves getting to the start. Fortunately, plenty of parking is available on the tarmac behind the gym.

A C T I V I T I E S   A three-day Sports Expo and packet pick-up kicks off on Thursday from 8:00 a.m. to 4:00 p.m. in Gym Bldg. 632 on NASP and continues Friday from 8:00 a.m. to 9:00 p.m. Don't miss the spaghetti feed at the Mustin Beach Officer's Club Friday night from 6:00 p.m. to 8:00 p.m. On top of the carbo-loading, the evening includes door prizes, entertainment, and a video and slide show of the race course. The Sports Expo continues on race day from 5:00 a.m. to 3:00 p.m. with late packet pick-up between 5:00 a.m. and 6:30 a.m. There is no race-day registration. After finishing the race, hasten your recovery with complimentary pasta, beverages, fruit, and cookies. Enjoy music as you wait for the awards ceremony in the finish area at 1:00 p.m. You must be present to receive an award.

A W A R D S   Every marathon entrant receives a commemorative long-sleeve T-shirt, race poster, Blue Angel Marathon mug, and other souvenirs. Complete race results and finisher certificates will be mailed to all who complete the event within the 5-hour time limit. Overall male and female winners typically earn air fare to the Boston Marathon, running shoes, and a framed race poster. Masters winners receive running shoes, and the top five in each age group are awarded medals/rosettes.

A C C O M M O D A T I O N S   Hotels in the vicinity include: Beachside Resort, 14 Via Deluna Pensacola Beach (800-232-2416); Hampton Inn, 2 Via Deluna Pensacola Beach (800-320-8108); Best Western—Perdido Key, 13585 Perdido Key Drive (800-528-1234); Clarion Suites, 20 Via Deluna Pensacola Beach (800-874-5303); and Pensacola Grand, 200 E. Gregory Street (800-348-3336).

R E L A T E D   E V E N T S / R A C E S   If your racing plans don't call for an early season marathon, consider the Blue Angel 5K. The race runs entirely on the naval base and starts an hour after the marathon.

A R E A   A T T R A C T I O N S   Located on Florida's Gulf Coast, Pensacola's year round temperate climate and white sand beaches beckon the winter vacationer. On NAS don't miss the free Museum of Naval Aviation, with an IMAX theater and a virtual reality flight (at a charge). Historic Old Town also provides nice breaks from the omnipresent water recreation.

COWTOWN MARATHON

OVERALL: 81.5

COURSE BEAUTY: 8

COURSE DIFFICULTY: 4+

APPROPRIATENESS FOR FIRST TIMERS: 7

RACE ORGANIZATION: 9-

CROWDS: 5-

RACE DATA

Overall Ranking:	**75**
Quickness Ranking:	**63**
Contact:	**Cowtown Marathon** **P.O. Box 9066** **3515 W. 7th Street** **Ft. Worth, TX 76147** **(817) 735-2033** **http://www.cowtownmarathon.org**
Date:	**February 27, 1999; February 26, 2000**
Start Time:	**8:30 a.m.**
Time Course Closes:	**3:00 p.m.**
Number of Finishers:	**869 in 1998**
Course:	**Loop**
Certification:	**USATF**
Course Records:	**Male: (open) 2:20:13** **Female: (open) 2:45:51**
Elite Athlete Programs:	**No**
Cost:	**$30/35**
Age groups/Divisions:	**18-21, 22-27, 28-33, 34-39, 40-44, 45-49, 50-54, 55-59, 60-69, 70-79, 80+, Big Person (200 lbs. and over): Open and Masters (40+)**
Walkers:	**Yes**
Requirements:	**None**
Temperature:	**46° - 56°**
Aid/Splits:	**12 / every mile**

HIGHLIGHTS Frank Shorter, when asked why he returns to Cowtown year after year, called it the biggest small race he knows, and while he specifically referred to the 10K race which routinely draws over 11,000 entrants, the description aptly fits the marathon as well. Appearing like a small, community event with possibly a few ragged edges, Cowtown offers a barrelful of country energy and charm. Starting and finishing in the historic Fort Worth Stockyards lends a decidedly Western flavor to the race. Appropriately, the Stockyard Coliseum's rodeo pit doubles as the race registration area! The large number of 10K and 5K runners only adds to the already festive and boisterous atmosphere. The course winds through residential areas, down the trail along the Trinity River, and finishes in the Stockyards. Faster runners will find a huge crowd waiting for them at the finish. Slower runners (over 4 hours) will have to be content with the race announcers reading their names.

COURSE DESCRIPTION Cowtown's marathon route literally winds through Fort Worth in a loop course that begins and ends in the Stockyards, a relic of Fort Worth's cattle town past. Not particularly fast, the course twists and turns, challenging runners to find and maintain a rhythm. From the start, runners head through a commercial area to mile 3. Filing into one lane of a wide street, runners approach a 200-yard downhill followed by a slight 100-yard incline just after mile 2. Once you hit the 3-mile mark, the course moves into a nice residential area where it becomes slightly rolling. After mile 6, runners pass Rivercrest golf course and head 100 yards downhill into more neighborhoods for most of the next 12 miles. A 70-yard upgrade to mile 10 leads to the Hulen bridge over the railroad yard and the Trinity River. After 18, the course follows the scenic Trinity Trail downward along the river. Miles 19 to 20 pass through grassy Trinity Park with its gnarled oak trees, then on to Fairington Field, followed by a commercial district (mile 20 to 21.5). Runners cross the busy Founders Bridge, traverse the Tandy parking lot, and head back down to the Trinity Trail from mile 23 to 25. Runners exit the trail after going under the North Side Drive overpass, and head for the Stockyards finish on Exchange Avenue. Entirely open to traffic except for the Trinity Trail, the course is monitored by police officers, and cones protect runners from the passing traffic.

CROWD/RUNNER SUPPORT Cowtown is the big community event in Fort Worth. The Fort Worth Star-Telegram carries a special Cowtown supplement the day after the races with stories and complete results. Big crowds await you at the marathon start and finish if you can run 4 hours or so. Scattered along the course, crowds accompany high school cheerleaders at several points on the route. Volunteers read split times every mile.

RACE LOGISTICS The race provides bus transportation from the downtown hotels to the start at the Stockyards. Though difficult to find, shuttle buses back to the hotels wait down Mule Alley (across from the Coliseum) near the communications van. You can check in clothing and personal items before the race in the Coliseum. Even though you can find quite a bit of parking near the Stockyards, arrive early to avoid aggravation. Relay runners must provide their own transportation to the exchange points.

ACTIVITIES Register or pick up your race packet the week prior to the marathon at the Cowtown Marathon office, 3515 W. 7th Avenue in Fort Worth (817-735-2033) or at Luke's in the Fort Worth and Dallas areas. The evening before the marathon, the race hosts the Cowtown Spaghetti Dinner ($5). Following the race, relax at the festive post-race party with food and drink in one of the scenic stockyards buildings. The Stockyards lend a real Western atmosphere to the entire event. Get your picture taken with a bull, eat lunch at nearby restaurants or food stalls, or watch your fellow toilers coast down to the finish.

AWARDS Every entrant receives a terrific, colorful T-shirt which is one of our personal favorites. All marathon finishers receive a finisher's award and personalized certificate. Trophies are awarded to the top three age-group winners. Overall winners earn trips to the next Boston or New York Marathon, in addition to trophies. Miller Lite offers a $1,000 cash bounty for new course records. Complete race results are published in the Sunday Fort Worth Star-Telegram. Race results are posted on the race web site the evening after the race.

ACCOMMODATIONS The official race hotel changes from year to year. Lodging options include: Radisson Plaza, 815 Main Street in downtown Fort Worth (817-870-2100); Ramada Downtown, 1701 Commerce (817-335-7000); The Worthington Hotel, 200 Main Street (817-870-1000); or The Remington Hotel, 600 Commerce Street (817-332-6900).

RELATED EVENTS/RACES Three-person teams can enter the marathon relay and run legs of 10, 8 and 8.2 miles. Teams may be same-sex or coed. Over 150 teams participated in the 1998 version. The biggest draw is the 10K race, one of the largest in the country, which offers a fairly fast, loop course. The 10K begins one-half hour after the marathon start. In 1998, a 5K was added to celebrate Cowtown's 20th anniversary.

MYRTLE BEACH MARATHON

OVERALL: 85.9

COURSE BEAUTY: 9

COURSE DIFFICULTY: 2

APPROPRIATENESS FOR FIRST-TIMERS: 8+

ORGANIZATION: 9

CROWDS: 3

RACE DATA

Overall Ranking:	45
Quickness Ranking:	10
Contact:	Shaun Walsh
	Official All Star Cafe Myrtle Beach Marathon
	P.O. Box 8780
	Myrtle Beach, SC 29578-8780
	Tel. (843) 293-RACE
	Fax (843) 349-2862
	E-mail: Mbmarathon@coastal.edu
	http://www.coastal.edu/mbmarathon
Date:	February 27, 1999; February 26, 2000
Start Time:	6:00 a.m. (walkers); 7:00 a.m. (runners)
Time Course Closes:	2:00 p.m.
Number of Finishers:	1,041 in 1998
Course:	Near loop
Certification:	USATF
Course Records:	Male: (open) 2:30:30; (masters) 2:46:39
	Female: (open) 3:01:59; (masters) 3:18:26
Elite Athlete Programs:	No
Cost:	$35/65
Age groups/Divisions:	≤19, 20-24, 25-29, 30-34, 35-39, 40-44, 45-49, 50-54, 55-59, 60-64, 65-69, 70+, wheelchair, crankchair
Walkers:	Yes
Requirements:	None
Temperature:	50°-60°
Aid/Splits:	15 / digital clocks every mile

HIGHLIGHTS   The inaugural Myrtle Beach Marathon in 1998 proved quite a success, with over 1,000 finishers in the marathon. Like its South Carolina cousin, the Kiawah Island Marathon, Myrtle Beach is very flat, but it lacks the twisting turns of Kiawah. This means it has the potential to be a very fast race. The first 10 miles are particularly scenic as you follow the coastline, before you reach the commercial-laden second half of the route. February in Myrtle Beach is quite mild, perfect for Northerners sick of the winter cold. With these characteristics, this race has great potential to become a major winter destination marathon.

COURSE DESCRIPTION   The marathon starts and finishes on the former Myrtle Beach Air Force Base. The course is not entirely closed to traffic; participants generally run in coned-off lanes. The near-loop course (about .8 mile separates the start and finish lines) starts at 16 feet and reaches a peak elevation of 33 feet. It also contains relatively few turns, which means it should be fast, assuming the wind doesn't get you. From the base, the race quickly reaches Ocean

Blvd. where you get to enjoy the beach, waterfront, the "strip" and finally hotel properties and residential areas for the first 10 miles. Runners then turn onto Kings Highway, a major thoroughfare, heading back toward the base. Mostly commercial here, the course detours up 79th Avenue N and down 76th Avenue N before returning to Kings Highway. After mile 15, the race heads up 29th Avenue N making its way to the All Star Cafe (mile 17), Planet Hollywood, and the Hard Rock Cafe. It then goes around Broadway at the Beach before veering back down to Kings Highway (after mile 19), which here features restaurants, bars, and miniature golf courses. Turning onto AVX Drive, runners pass the quiet of Whispering Pines Golf Course, which soon is shattered as you run under the flightline of the Myrtle Beach Airport (mile 25). You then head back onto the base for the stretch run to the finish line.

CROWD/RUNNER SUPPORT This young race attracts about 5,000 spectators to its course. The loudest cheers typically come at the relay exchange points, the All Star Cafe, Ocean Blvd., and the finish. Several bands also play during the race to keep your spirits up and your legs going. Aid stations come every 2 miles (every mile after mile 22). The volunteers will hand you water and sport drink, with food available at miles 16 and 22. Portable toilets are roughly located near every other aid station, and medical assistance is also available at several points.

RACE LOGISTICS Shuttle buses take runners from the host hotel and the other participating hotels to the race start, and from the race finish back to the hotels. The list of participating hotels changes every year so contact the race to see which hotels offer shuttle buses this year. If you have a car, plenty of parking exists in the area.

ACTIVITIES Pick up your race packet at the official headquarters hotel on Friday, 2:00 p.m. to 9:30 p.m. While there, stroll through the expo. On Friday evening the race hosts a pasta party for about $15. You receive a complimentary ticket to the post-race party in your race packet; additional tickets are available for $12. The post-race bash includes food, entertainment, and door prizes. On Sunday morning you can attend the post-race breakfast ($5 adults and free for ages 17 and under) to swap race stories and commiserate about your aches and pains.

AWARDS Every participant receives a long-sleeve T-shirt, and finishers also earn medals and certificates. Trophies go to the top three runners in each age group. The overall race winners get sent on an all-expenses-paid trip to an All Star Cafe Grand Opening.

ACCOMMODATIONS The Holiday Inn Oceanfront, 415 S. Ocean Blvd. (800-845-0313) serves as the host hotel. The hotel is located about 3 miles from the start and finish areas. Other nearby hotels include: Yachtsman Resort Hotel, 1400 N. Ocean Blvd. (800-868-8886); Fairfield Inn, 1350 Paradise Circle (800-217-1511); La Quinta Inn, 1561 21st Avenue North (800-687-6667); Days Inn, 601 S. Ocean Blvd. (803-448-1491); Hampton Inn, 48th Avenue N and Highway 17 (800-833-1360); Hampton Inn, 620 76th Avenue N (800-543-4286); and Hampton Inn, Broadway at the Beach, 1140 Celebrity Circle (888-916-2001).

RELATED EVENTS/RACES Myrtle Beach also holds a marathon relay, with five person teams. The first four members run legs of 5 miles, while the fifth member completes 6.2 miles. The relay divisions include: open male, open female, open coed, masters men, masters women, masters coed, Team in Training, corporations, teachers/educators, high school students, juniors (under 15), restaurant, hotel, health care, law enforcement, military, fire departments, and penguins.

AREA ATTRACTIONS Myrtle Beach is a popular resort with all of the usual coastal attractions. Although the water will be bit chilly in February, you can still enjoy the uncrowded beauty of the place.

SMOKY MOUNTAIN MARATHON

OVERALL: 82.9

COURSE BEAUTY: 9

COURSE DIFFICULTY: 5+

APPROPRIATENESS FOR FIRST TIMERS: 7

RACE ORGANIZATION: 9

CROWDS: 1

RACE DATA

Overall Ranking:	67
Quickness Ranking:	82
Contact:	Sherman Ames
	Smoky Mountain Marathon
	6401 Baum Drive
	Knoxville, TN 37919
	Tel. (423) 588-7465
	Fax (423) 588-2883
Date:	February 27, 1999; February 26, 2000
Start Time:	8:30 a.m.
Time Course Closes:	1:30 p.m.
Number of Finishers:	405 in 1998, normally limited to 300
Course:	Out and back
Certification:	USATF
Course Records:	Male: (open) 2:32:40
	Female: (open) 3:02:52
Elite Athlete Programs:	No
Cost:	$20/25
Age groups/Divisions:	≤19, 20-24, 25-29, 30-34, 35-39, 40-44, 45-49, 50+ (F), 50-54, 55-59, 60+ (M), Hercules, Athena
Walkers:	No
Requirements:	None
Temperature:	40° - 49°
Aid/Splits:	10 / miles 1, 5, 10, 13.5, 15 & 20

HIGHLIGHTS One of marathoning's best deals, the Smoky Mountain Marathon prides itself on offering down-home, East Tennessee hospitality to its capacity field of 300 runners. From the open house fireside gathering on Friday evening to the post-race soup gala, you should not need to step foot in your car, making for a hassle-free weekend. Smoky Mountain's moderately difficult course traces the Little River, providing an intimate glimpse of Southern Appalachia.

COURSE DESCRIPTION The marathon starts and finishes in the Townsend Village Center on the cusp of Great Smoky Mountains National Park. Most of the first 7.5 miles follow largely flat Highways 337 and 321. Crossing the Little River, the course rolls and winds through pine thickets and hardwood forests as it follows the river for the up and back from miles 8 to 17. Runners get a real taste of Appalachia here, with rustic mountain cabins, spectacular modern homes, small farm plots, and sheer rock facings which crop up to and sometimes over the road. Peeling away from the river after 17, the course challenges runners with hills between 18 and

22 on a patchy, gravel road. Weary runners receive a nice respite as the road improves and the terrain flattens from 23 to the finish.

CROWD/RUNNER SUPPORT A rural race, the Smoky Mountain Marathon attracts few crowds outside of family, friends, and race volunteers. To lift the spirits of tired runners, the race plans a special theme aid station near the 23-mile mark. Past themes, complete with costumes and props, have included Mardi Gras, Margaritaville, Graceland, and the O.K. Corral (you should have seen the sheriff!)

RACE LOGISTICS With virtually no logistics, all race activities, the start, and finish are within a stone's throw of the headquarters hotel.

ACTIVITIES On Friday evening from 6:00 p.m. to 8:00 p.m., gather around the fire at the Valley View Lodge for complimentary soft drinks, beer, munchies, and camaraderie. Wander between the social and the $10 pasta dinner (from 6:00 p.m. to 7:30 p.m.). After the race, warm up with hot soup and good conversation at the post-race gala. The awards ceremony kicks off at 1:00 p.m.

AWARDS Every marathoner receives a long-sleeve, 3-button T-shirt, and commemorative hat and gloves. Finishers also reel in a medallion, finisher's certificate, finish-line photo, and a results booklet. All of this combined with the race activities add up to an excellent bargain. The top three overall and Hercules and Athena, and the top masters and grandmasters receive plaques. In recent years, overall winners received original sculptures. Age-group winners have received different awards over the years, ranging from coffee mugs, cloisonne pins, and plaques. There is also a drawing for Smoky Mountain crafts.

ACCOMMODATIONS For convenience, make every effort to stay at the race headquarters, the Best Western Valley View Lodge in Townsend (615-448-2237). Book early because the hotel does fill. Second choice is the Hampton Inn, 7824 E. Lamar Alexander Parkway, Townsend (615-448-9000).

RELATED EVENTS/RACES Some folks may prefer the Smoky Mountain 8K which starts at the same time as the marathon and goes to the 4-mile mark before returning to the start.

AREA ATTRACTIONS Most visitors like to explore Great Smoky Mountains National Park. Stop by the visitor's center in Cades Cove on Little River Road, 7 miles southwest of Townsend, to get information on the park. Dolly Parton fans may want to head to Dollywood (800-365-5996), an imaginary village in Pigeon Forge teeming with crafts people, rides, and country music, for a hefty price.

NAPA VALLEY MARATHON

OVERALL: 88.3

COURSE BEAUTY: 9+

COURSE DIFFICULTY: 2+ (SEE APPENDIX)

APPROPRIATENESS FOR FIRST TIMERS: 9-

RACE ORGANIZATION: 9

CROWDS: 2

RACE DATA

Overall Ranking: 28
Quickness Ranking: 21
Contact: Sutter Home Napa Valley Marathon
P.O. Box 4307
Napa, CA 94558-0430
Tel. (707) 255-2609
E-mail: shnvm@napanet.net

Date: March 7, 1999; March 5, 2000
Start Time: 7:00 a.m.
Time Course Closes: 12:30 p.m.
Number of Finishers: 1,532 in 1998
Course: Point to point
Certification: USATF
Course Records: Male: (open) 2:16:20; (masters) 2:26:04
Female: (open) 2:39:42; (masters) 2:54:46
Elite Athlete Programs: Yes
Cost: $45/50/60
Age groups/Divisions: ≤19, 20-24, 25-29, 30-34, 35-39, 40-44, 45-49,
50-54, 55-59, 60-64, 65-69, 70+
Walkers: No
Requirements: None
Temperature: 40° - 70°
Aid/Splits: 12 / miles 1, 5, 10, halfway & 20

HIGHLIGHTS Low key, rural, the Napa Valley Marathon ("NVM") runs along the famed Silverado Trail through vineyards swept with pruned grape vines, emerald grasses, and golden mustard. Stir this incredible setting into Napa's world-class attractions, add a competent, runner-friendly race organization, and you've corked one of the top destination marathons in North America. A particularly fine choice for runners who appreciate serenity but don't like to be out there alone, NVM also seems to be blessed with near-perfect weather, raining only once in 20 years.

RACE HISTORY Designed as an intimate, rural marathon, the Napa Valley Marathon began in 1979 by the Silverado Striders, a Napa-based running club. The fact that the distance between Calistoga, at the northern end of the valley, and Napa, at the southern end, happened to be 26 miles seemed too coincidental to overlook.

A number of local companies with national reputations have acted as the race's primary sponsors. For the first dozen years, the Calistoga Mineral Water Company sponsored the race—NVM's

start line is just 50 yards from the Calistoga plant. Sutter Home Winery took up sponsorship in 1993, and has installed a permanent trophy (a 7-liter bottle of Zinfandel) in its tasting room along Highway 29 south of Helena. Each year the male and female winners' names and times are etched into the bottle.

Throughout its first 10 years, the marathon remained a local secret, with 800 to 1,000 participants. However, in 1987 the race won notoriety when Dick Beardsley, the then second-fastest marathoner in America, used the course to make his comeback after a near career-ending leg injury. Intending to qualify for the 1988 U.S. Olympic Marathon Trials, he cruised to a course record of 2:16:20. The 1996 race was the first-ever RRCA California State Marathon Championship, the 1997 race was the RRCA Western Regional Marathon Championship, and the 1999 version is the RRCA National Marathon Championship.

COURSE DESCRIPTION NVM's paved, gently rolling, point-to-point course, framed by wooded hills and picturesque vineyards, follows the Silverado Trail, a two-lane country road, for approximately 23 miles before turning into Napa's side streets on its way to the Vintage High School finish. The first 13 miles and the final 3 are completely closed to traffic, while cones protect the runners on the shoulder the middle ten miles. At times the road's camber makes finding a comfortable place to run difficult, particularly from 13 to 23.

The race starts just outside downtown Calistoga. About mile 1.25, runners hit a good, winding upgrade to 1.6, followed by a nice downhill to the 2-mile mark. The course then flattens briefly, going gently up from 2.2 to 2.75. This second hill is again followed by a good downhill. The final significant hill, the largest and steepest of the race, lies at 5.25 miles. As the course descends following the rise, a particularly nice panorama of forested hills greets the runners. From there to the 21-mile mark, the course gently rolls, with some longer, gradual inclines and declines, but no major surprises. Runners pass some excellent wineries during this stretch, including Villa Mt. Eden at 12.7, Mumm at 13.5, Z-D Wines at 13.9, hilltop Silverado Vineyards just after 19, the low, stone buildings of Stag's Leap Wine Cellars at 21.5, followed closely by the ivy-covered Clos du Val. From 21 miles the course flattens. Runners reach the 23-mile mark on a small bridge on Oak Knoll Avenue, just after the turnoff from the Silverado Trail, and pass Monticello Cellars at 24 miles. After the right turn on El Centro, the route becomes residential until the Vintage High School finish.

CROWD/RUNNER SUPPORT As you might expect, small numbers of spectators come out to cheer the runners, mostly family and friends who congregate at several major intersections on the Silverado Trail. NVM supports the runners well with 12 aid stations offering water, electrolyte replacement drink, sponges, medical supplies, and portable toilets. On the last half of the course, fruit is also available. The race will also put out your own special drinks at the aid stations you designate. The relatively short aid stations mean you will probably have to slow down to find and retrieve your bottle, but having your special brew may more than make up for the delay. The mile markers, located at ground level, may be a bit hard to spot if you're in a group.

RACE LOGISTICS The race provides free bus transportation to the start. Monitors will direct you to the parking area at Vintage High School, with buses leaving between 5:15 a.m. and 5:45 a.m. sharp. With limited parking in Calistoga, it's best to use the bus. In addition, runners who park in Calistoga will have to find their own way back to the start, unless their handlers can meet them at the finish.

ACTIVITIES On Saturday, pick up your race packet at the Sports and Fitness Expo, held in the Napa Valley Marriott. The crowded expo also features guest speakers and panels, and NVM veterans discuss course strategy. Buy a raffle ticket for a chance to win some great Napa Valley prizes on Saturday with the proceeds benefitting local charities. Later that evening, hit the pasta feed (about $15 in Napa, $12 in Calistoga). After the race, enjoy some delicious hot soup, bread, fruit, and drink. All registered runners are eligible for random draw prizes, including wine. The drawing is held just prior to the awards ceremony.

AWARDS Every entrant receives a T-shirt, and finishers earn a medal and a pat on the back for a job well done. Plaques are awarded three deep in most age divisions. The top three overall winners receive prizes, including tasty Sutter Home wine. The top local finisher is also recognized.

ELITE RUNNERS INFORMATION Lack of prize money means most big-name runners stay away from NVM, but fast runners may be offered complimentary entry and possibly free lodging. Top prizes include a 6-liter etched bottle of Sutter Home Zinfandel and a set of luggage.

ACCOMMODATIONS The Napa Valley Marriott Hotel, 3425 Solano Avenue, Napa (707-253-7433), serves as the official race hotel, offering discounted rates to runners. Other possibilities in Napa include: Inn at Napa Valley, 1075 California Blvd. (707-253-9540); Best Western Inn, 100 Soscol Avenue (707-257-1930); John Muir Inn, 1998 Trower Avenue (707-257-7220); or Chablis Lodge, 3360 Solano Avenue (707-257-1944).

RELATED EVENTS/RACES NVM also sponsors the Three R's 5K Run, beginning and ending at the marathon finish line, and staged by the Vintage High School English Department. Run proceeds help upgrade the school's computer lab.

AREA ATTRACTIONS The Napa Valley Mustard Festival, with food, drink, and tasting of hundreds of mustards, coincides with NVM. Of course you must tour some of Napa's or nearby Sonoma's fabled wineries. Talk to locals to get tips on finding some lesser-known gems, or wander at will to make your own discoveries. After the marathon, pamper yourself with a spa and mud bath treatment in Calistoga. If the marathon didn't provide enough excitement, try a hot air balloon ride. Those who prefer more conventional locomotion can ride the Wine Train. Napa and Sonoma boast great restaurants and quaint shops. And if by some freak of nature you get bored, San Francisco lies nearby.

LA Marathon XIV
March 14, 1999

THE CITY OF
LOS ANGELES
MARATHON

Presented by
HONDA

for information call 310.444.5544

A\A
American Airlines

The Gas Company®

CEDARS-SINAI

SAUCONY

SecureHorizons®
Offered by PacifiCare

TYLENOL
acetaminophen

eb site: www.LAMarathon.com   e-mail: raceinfo@lamarathon.com

LOS ANGELES MARATHON

OVERALL: 92.8

COURSE BEAUTY: 7

COURSE DIFFICULTY: 4+ (SEE APPENDIX)

APPROPRIATENESS FOR FIRST TIMERS: 10+

RACE ORGANIZATION: 9+

CROWDS: 10

RACE DATA

Overall Ranking: 12

Quickness Ranking: 54

Contact: Los Angeles Marathon Office
11110 W. Ohio Avenue, Suite 100
Los Angeles, CA 90025
Tel. (310) 444-5544
Fax (310) 473-8105
E-mail: raceinfo@lamarathon.com
http:\\www.lamarathon.com

Date: March 14, 1999; 2000 date TBA

Start Time: 8:45 a.m.

Time Course Closes: 2:45 p.m. (must move to sidewalks after 13:00 pace)

Number of Finishers: 15,535 in 1998

Course: Loop

Certification: USATF

Course Records: Male: (open) 2:10:19
Female: (open) 2:26:23

Elite Athlete Programs: Yes

Cost: $40/50/55

Age groups/Divisions: ≤17, 18-24, 25-29, 30-34, 35-39, 40-44, 45-49, 50-54, 55-59, 60-64, 65-69, 70-74, 75-79, 80+, wheelchair

Walkers: Yes (including race walkers)

Requirements: None

Temperature: 59°

Aid/Splits: 25 / digital clocks every mile

HIGHLIGHTS If you like carnivals, and the entertainment capital of the world attracts you, you'll love the LA Marathon. This race has more characters than a Star Trek convention. The third-largest marathon in the United States, LA enjoys tremendous community support, with over one million residents making noise on your behalf. In addition to the crowds of fellow runners and spectators, highlights of the race include excellent aid stations, a superbly-monitored closed course, and entertainment every mile. We hope you're not hungry though because this course may pass more fast food joints than any other marathon in the world!

COURSE DESCRIPTION The LA Marathon offers an urban route, and like many urban courses, it is not particularly scenic, traveling through the major cultural centers of Los Angeles. While PRs are possible here, the course is not especially fast. The race starts on Figueroa in downtown LA. A nice, newly paved, wide street, Figueroa can accommodate the large number of runners. The course continues down Figueroa for about 3.1 miles, passing the LA Convention Center and the

University of Southern California (USC) turning right on Martin Luther King Blvd. The course skirts the LA Sports Arena and Memorial Coliseum before going right on Vermont. The route then heads down Exposition, going through lower-income residential neighborhoods for a couple miles. Runners encounter the first hill, a freeway overpass, near mile 7, then proceed gradually uphill for the next mile. Miles 8 and 9 gently roll with hills. Runners turn right on Olympic Blvd. (9.1 miles) on their way through Koreatown (9-11), where they encounter a series of short (50 yards) uphills and downhills, followed by two slightly longer upgrades to Wilshire Blvd. After the turn onto Wilshire (11.4 miles), a 200-yard descent precedes a quick uphill, followed by a long, gradual decline. This section is mostly commercial. Near mile 13, the course moves into wealthy residential neighborhoods, which includes a couple of short but good uphills. After mile 14.5, runners traverse N. Highland Avenue which features a palm-tree-lined median and Spanish-style homes. The course becomes more commercial a mile later as it reaches Melrose. As runners turn left on Vine Street, they face a long, gradual uphill until the left on W. Sunset Blvd. around mile 17. The course strolls down Hollywood Blvd. for nearly three miles, past tacky shops on rolling terrain into Sunset Blvd. Sunset contains a couple of long, tough hills at a tough time in the race—after 21 miles. Between miles 22 and 24, the course runs along Santa Monica Blvd. and Virgil Avenue before returning to Wilshire. Here runners stream into downtown, passing McArthur Park near mile 25. A left turn on Flower leads to the finish near the Public Library.

Los Angeles Marathon

As one would expect from a race of this caliber, the course is completely closed to traffic and is well monitored. Streets are in very good condition for the majority of the race. Quite visible, large mile markers stretch across the street. But beware—the banners don't necessarily mark the precise mile points. Look for the digital clocks.

CROWD/RUNNER SUPPORT The LA community strongly supports the marathon, with more than one million spectators cheering your every step. Over 100 live bands and performers provide entertainment along the course, with eleven designated entertainment centers meant to be representative of LA's diversity—including rock, rap, and Latin music. Lining both sides of the marathon route, 3,700 community volunteers effectively staff the 25 aid stations. The community also gets involved by training local residents for the marathon through the Los Angeles Roadrunners Training Program and Students Run LA. Created in 1987 by teacher Harry Shabazian, Students Run LA is designed to train nearly 1,700 "at-risk" Angeleno students who wish to run the LA Marathon.

RACE LOGISTICS The start/finish area lies near the downtown hotels, so transportation is not a concern. Shuttle vans roam between miles 7 and 24 to return runners to the finish area should they not be able to complete the race. In addition, the LA Metro Rail system offers free rides on the Green, Red, and Blue Lines the day of the race, delivering runners and spectators to within 100 yards of the start/finish lines.

ACTIVITIES The LA Marathon features a huge, three-day Quality of Life Expo with over 400 exhibitors, seminars, demonstrations, and games. Runners pick up their race packets here. Held at the LA Convention Center, the expo regularly attracts 100,000 people. The race hosts a carbo-load dinner (about $10) the night before the marathon. The dinner, which draws 4,000 runners, family, and friends, features music and live entertainment and sells out each year. After runners pass through the finish chute, they are provided with water, electrolyte replacement drink, and lots of food. The race hosts the Family Reunion Festival, a day-long party offering arts and crafts booths, entertainment, massage, medical tent, food, and restaurant kiosks; the festival serves as the meeting place for runners, their family, and friends.

AWARDS Every entrant receives a marathon T-shirt, poster, and stuffed goodie bag, all of which are obtained at the Quality of Life Expo. In addition, finishers earn an original medallion. Age-group winners earn plaques and other prizes.

ELITE RUNNERS INFORMATION LA actively recruits between 50 to 100 elite runners. The race offers prize money, incentives for breaking course records, accommodations, transportation, expenses, and new Honda automobiles for overall winners. The amount of cash and prizes varies yearly. In 1998, the prize purse totaled $150,000, with $30,000 (plus a Honda Accord EX V-6 Sedan) for first, $20,000 for second, $15,000 for third, $5,000 for fourth, $3,000 for fifth, and $2,000 for sixth. Contact race officials for the current prize structure.

ACCOMMODATIONS The Regal Biltmore Hotel serves as the official race headquarters (800-245-8673 or 213-612-1575). Perhaps even more convenient is the Omni Los Angeles Hotel (800-THE-OMNI). Adjacent to the race starting line, the Omni usually offers reduced rates for marathon entrants, about $110. For cheaper accommodations, try the Hotel Figueroa (800-421-9092), situated about one mile from the start/finish areas and within blocks of the LA Convention Center. Rates are about $50 to $60 per night. Many other hotels are convenient to the start/finish lines. Contact the marathon office for a complete listing of hotels.

RELATED EVENTS/RACES Marathon organizers also host two other events, The Los Angeles Marathon 5K and the Los Angeles Marathon Bike Tour. The 5K is held immediately following the marathon start and has its own pre-race and post-race activities and entertainment at the Convention Center. Celebrities, politicians and other VIPs often join in the 5K. LA is unique (some say for a reason) in offering a Marathon Bike Tour, a 21-mile ride that draws over 15,000 cyclists. Held before the marathon at 6:00 a.m., the tour features T-shirts, finisher medals, and a finish line festival.

CATALINA ISLAND MARATHON

OVERALL: 90.3

COURSE BEAUTY: 10

COURSE DIFFICULTY: 7+ (SEE APPENDIX)

APPROPRIATENESS FOR FIRST TIMERS: 4

RACE ORGANIZATION: 9+

CROWDS: 1+

RACE DATA

Overall Ranking: 21
Quickness Ranking: 100
Contact: Catalina Island Marathon
Pacific Sports
1500 S. Sunkist Street, Suite E
Anaheim, CA 92806
Tel. (714) 978-1528
Fax (714) 978-1505
Date: March 20, 1999; 2000 date TBA
Start Time: 7:00 a.m. (6:30 a.m. for walkers)
Time Course Closes: NA
Number of Finishers: 600 runner limit
Course: Point to point
Certification: None
Course Records: Male: (open) 2:39:58
Female: (open) 3:15:20
Elite Athlete Programs: No
Cost: $75
Age groups/Divisions: 15-18, 19-24, 25-29, 30-34, 35-39, 40-44, 45-49,
50-54, 55-59, 60-64, 65-69, 70-74, 75+, Buffalo
Division (open and masters): men over 200 lbs., and
women over 150 lbs., Island Residents
Walkers: Yes
Requirements: 15 years old
Temperature: 50° - 65°
Aid/Splits: 12 / none

HIGHLIGHTS   Celebrating its 22nd anniversary in 1999, the Catalina Island Marathon promises one of the most challenging and scenic runs of your life. A peaceful paradise 22 miles off the Los Angeles coast, Catalina Island features rugged mountain wilderness (complete with several hundred bison) encircled by 54 miles of pristine shoreline. Its breathtaking vistas soften the edges of a challenging, mostly dirt course that includes 3,700 feet of total climbing from the start in Two Harbors to the finish in Avalon. One of the top trail marathon destinations, Catalina's temperate weather and unspoiled beauty make for a perfect race-weekend getaway.

COURSE DESCRIPTION   Catalina's point-to-point course starts at sea level in Two Harbors on the west side of the island and ends at sea level in Avalon on the island's east side. In between, spectacular scenery and 3,700 feet of total climbing await you. Most runners finish about 20-25 minutes slower than their best road marathon time. From Two Harbors, the course starts flat but abruptly climbs 825 feet to the west summit around the 2.5-mile mark. Dropping and

rolling until you veer left onto Empire Landing Road, the course reaches an elevation of 920 feet at Big Springs Reservoir 4 miles into the race. Although pretty rough, the road flows mostly downhill from there to the junction of Big Springs Road. After a right turn on Big Springs, you continue downhill to Little Harbor Road, hitting sea level at Little Harbor (8.5 miles). You then begin two climbs with a peak of 350 feet at 10.8 miles. At this point you turn left onto Old Eagles Nest Trail—a now permanent detour made necessary by horrendous storms in 1995. Beginning downhill to an elevation of 260 feet, the trail has a series of three climbs with a peak of 700 feet. From that point it drops down toward Eagles Nest Lodge where you turn left onto Middle Ranch Road at 500 feet. From Eagles Nest, you begin a long steady and gradual uphill through Middle Ranch—often the hottest section of the course. Middle Ranch stretches for about 5 miles rising from 500 feet to 1,000 feet. Here, the infamous "Pumphouse Hill" awaits with a 360-foot rise in less than a mile; you finally reach the top at about 19 miles. Continuing to climb up a picturesque ridge featuring spectacular views of Avalon and the harbor below, you finally veer right past the Wrigley Reservoir back onto a dirt road and again head uphill along Divide Road. This section of the course is a series of rolling hills with a peak at 1,560 feet. At 23 miles, you begin to drop (almost literally) into Avalon, going from 1,500 feet to 270 feet in 2 miles. You enter the final stretch at 25 miles, heading downhill on paved Avalon Canyon Road on your way to the finish near Front Street.

CROWD/RUNNER SUPPORT With no rental cars allowed on the island, spectators stay in the start and finish areas. Encouragement is limited to aid station volunteers and Catalina's considerable wildlife population—most notably over 300 bison (descendants of 14 buffalo brought to the island in 1924 for a silent movie called "The Vanishing American"). The race provides portable toilets at five locations on the course.

RACE LOGISTICS Because the race is limited to 600 runners, your first consideration involves sending your registration early as the race generally fills by March 1. Next, participants must be on the island Friday night. Catalina-bound ferries leave regularly from the Los Angeles-area ports of Long Beach, San Pedro and Newport Beach, costing between $25 and $40 for the 60-70 minute ride. For reservations, call Catalina Cruises, Long Beach (800-228-2546), Catalina Passenger Service, Newport Beach (714-673-5245), or Catalina Express, Long Beach and San Pedro (310-519-1212). If you stay in Avalon Friday night, you need to reserve a seat on the Avalon-to-Two Harbors Marathon Boat leaving at 5:00 a.m. race morning (request a reservation on your entry form). The race provides a truck to transport your personal gear back to Avalon. Additionally, if your family or friends would like to be with you in Two Harbors on Friday night, the race provides a bus leaving from the start at 7:30 a.m., arriving in Avalon by 9:00 a.m. in plenty of time to catch the finish. Catalina welcomes marathon walkers and allows them and slower runners to start at 6:30 a.m.

A C T I V I T I E S   Packet pick-up occurs Friday night in Avalon at the Landing Bar and Grill from 4:00 p.m. to 9:00 p.m. and in Two Harbors from 4:00 p.m. to 9:00 p.m. After finishing the race, enjoy food and beverages while you await the awards ceremony starting at 2:00 p.m.

A W A R D S   Each marathon finisher receives a long-sleeve T-shirt, medal, pin, and special memorabilia. The top three overall and the Buffalo division winners receive plaques and merchandise awards. The top three finishers in each age group also receive awards, as do the first male and female Catalina residents and the second and third men and women in the Buffalo division.

A C C O M M O D A T I O N S   The marathon runs before the prime tourist season so accommodations are generally not hard to find. Marathon participants stay in either Avalon or Two Harbors. Avalon offers the Hermit Gulch Campground located just off Avalon Canyon Road one mile from Avalon (310-510-8368). Avalon hotels include: Pavilion Lodge, 513 Crescent Avenue (310-510-7788); Seaport Village Inn (800-2-Catalina); Hotel Atwater (310-510-2000); Catalina Canyon Hotel, 888 Country Club Drive (310-510-0325); Hotel Vista Del Mar, 417 Crescent Avenue (310-510-1452); and Hotel St. Lauren, Metropolis and Beacon (310-510-2299). If you'd rather awake in tiny Two Harbors on race morning, camp at the Little Fisherman Cove Campground, or on marathon weekend only, at the unimproved Buffalo Park behind the restaurant. The Banning Lodge (310-510-0303), a turn-of-the-century hunting lodge, is available for those who care to stay indoors.

R E L A T E D   E V E N T S / R A C E S   Catalina offers non-marathoners the opportunity to race on beautiful shorter courses in Avalon. At 8:00 a.m., a challenging 10K treats runners to stunning views of Avalon and its bay. A flat 5K gets going at 8:10 a.m. and takes runners along the water's edge and through the town of Avalon. Leaving no runner out, Catalina holds a half-mile Kid's Run for those under age 7, and a 1-mile run for those aged 7-12, starting at 9:00 a.m.

A R E A   A T T R A C T I O N S   Catalina offers visitors more than just her beauty. Some of the best scuba diving anywhere exists at Avalon's Underwater Park off Casino Point. If you'd rather see marine life from a further distance, hop on a glass bottom boat tour of a nearby cove. Touring the elegant estates of the Wrigley family and Zane Grey, the western novelist, are other options.

SHAMROCK SPORTSFEST MARATHON

OVERALL: 84.4

COURSE BEAUTY: 9-

COURSE DIFFICULTY: 2-

APPROPRIATENESS FOR FIRST TIMERS: 8+

RACE ORGANIZATION: 9+

CROWDS: 2

RACE DATA

Overall Ranking:	55
Quickness Ranking:	6
Contact:	Jerry Bocrie
	Shamrock Sportsfest, Inc.
	2308 Maple Street
	Virginia Beach, VA 23451
	Tel. (757) 481-5090
	Fax (757) 481-2942
	E-mail: sportsfest@juno.com
	http://www.shamrock.sportsfest.com
Date:	March 20, 1999; March 18, 2000
Start Time:	9:00 a.m.
Time Course Closes:	3:00 p.m.
Number of Finishers:	1,800 in 1998
Course:	Out and back
Certification:	USATF
Course Records:	Male: (open) 2:15:26
	Female: (open) 2:38:47
Elite Athlete Programs:	Yes
Cost:	$25/35
Age groups/Divisions:	≤24, 25-29, 30-34, 35-39, 40-44, 45-49, 50-54, 55-59, (F) 60+, (M) 60-64, 65-69, 70+
Walkers:	No
Requirements:	None
Temperature:	52°
Aid/Splits:	12 / mile 1 and every 5 miles

HIGHLIGHTS Providing intense excitement for runners crossing the finish line, the Shamrock Sportsfest Marathon—celebrating its 27th Anniversary in 1999—uses one of the few indoor finishes in North America. Held in Virginia Beach, VA, Shamrock boasts an extremely flat course through this resort area, turning around in Fort Story. Marathon weekend includes a world-class 8K, a terrific expo, a rocking beach party Saturday night, and enough free beer to intoxicate the Irish army.

COURSE DESCRIPTION Starting in front of the Virginia Beach Pavilion Convention Center on 19th Street, the Shamrock Sportsfest Marathon's out-and-back course heads straight toward the oceanfront. Just before reaching the beach (mile .75), the course turns right on Atlantic Avenue for 1 mile. Turning north, the route proceeds on the Rudee Loop with views of the Rudee Inlet and the beach's bungee jump. Miles 3 and 4 travel along the Virginia Beach Boardwalk past cafes and, in nice weather, springtime beach goers. Before the end of the boardwalk, the course takes you back to Atlantic Avenue for 6 miles, providing great views of beautiful beach homes and bungalows, and then turns toward False Cape State Park. As you run through Fort Story army base (miles 10 to 18), look for the country's oldest lighthouse and its contemporary replacement. Exiting the base, runners retrace their steps to the Convention Center getting an opportunity to eyeball their competition.

CROWD / RUNNER SUPPORT Without a doubt, the finish before thousands of spectators inside the Convention Center provides the race's greatest excitement. The 12 aid stations along the course carry water and electrolyte replacement, and medical assistance is available near miles 13 and 16. A trolley collects the tired and injured.

RACE LOGISTICS Most area hotels lie within 10 blocks of the Convention Center, a perfect warm-up on race morning. If you insist on driving to the start, some free parking exists at the Convention Center. The Virginia Beach YMCA offers sitter service (at the convention center) on race day from 7:00 a.m. to 1:00 p.m. with plenty of activities to keep kids out of trouble while you run the marathon.

ACTIVITIES A busy, compact race weekend in the Convention Center (on 19th Street) begins with the excellent Sports and Fitness Expo (where you also pick up your packet or register) on Friday from 2:00 p.m. to 10:00 p.m. Approximately 20,000 people plow through the expo making it one of the East Coast's largest. On Friday evening from 5:30 p.m. to 7:30 p.m., attend the all-you-can-eat Pasta Party, featuring plenty of free beer to assist in your carbo-loading efforts (about $15). If you didn't get enough to eat at the pasta dinner (or were too cheap to pay for it), crash the Hospitality Room for free fruit and more free beer, 5:00 p.m. to 10:00 p.m. The race typically sponsors a running clinic on Friday evening, too. You may pick up your race packet or register on race morning if you haven't already done so. After the race (which you may or may not have finished after all that free beer), treat yourself to a free massage, post-race goodies, and refreshments. You will need them to recuperate in time for the Post-Race Beach Music Party on Saturday night. The party offers food, entertainment, and plenty of beer.

AWARDS All runners receive race T-shirts; finishers are entitled to medals and parchment certificates. The top five runners in most age groups receive a custom cultured marble award, while the top five overall finishers earn tasteful etched marble awards. The top five overall runners also take home prize money of $1,000, $600, $400, $300, and $200. The top three masters runners take home $300, $200, and $100. Prize money recipients must be USATF members.

ELITE RUNNERS INFORMATION Elite runners may be offered travel expenses, free lodging, and complimentary entry. Interested runners should send their running resumes to Jerry Bocrie by February 14.

ACCOMMODATIONS The Shamrock Housing Bureau offers a lodging clearinghouse for Sportsfest participants complete with special rates. Simply indicate your top choices on your race application and the Bureau will take care of the rest. Closest to the Convention Center are the DoubleTree and the Quality Inn on 21st Street. Many of the other hotels sit near the beach.

RELATED EVENTS / RACES Parts of the Shamrock Sportsfest activities are the world-class 8K and Masters 8K (both with prize money), the 5K Walk, and the Children's Marathon (26.2 yards). Corporate teams also compete in the open 8K event. Several world records have been set on the 8K course in both the open and masters races.

AREA ATTRACTIONS The main attraction in Virginia Beach is, of course, the beach. Naval buffs may also want to explore the Virginia Marine Science Museum, and nearby Norfolk, the East Coast's largest U.S. Navy port. Learn about Colonial history at Williamsburg, about an hour drive north of Virginia Beach.

MAUI MARATHON

OVERALL: 93.4

COURSE BEAUTY: 10-

COURSE DIFFICULTY: 4-

APPROPRIATENESS FOR FIRST TIMERS: 7+

RACE ORGANIZATION: 9+

CROWDS: 3+

RACE DATA

Overall Ranking:	9
Quickness Ranking:	48
Contact:	Bob Craver
	Valley Isle Road Runners Association
	P.O. Box 330099
	Kahului, Maui HI 96733
	Tel. (808) 871-6441
	E-mail: bark@maui.net
	http://www.mauimarathon.com
Date:	March 21, 1999; March 19, 2000
Start Time:	5:30 a.m.
Time Course Closes:	1:30 p.m.
Number of Finishers:	1,314 in 1998
Course:	Point to point
Certification:	AIMS / USATF
Course Records:	Male: (open) 2:25:50
	Female: (open) 2:40:37
Elite Athlete Programs:	Yes
Cost:	US $50/60/75; Non-US $60/75/100
Age groups/Divisions:	18-24, 25-29, 30-34, 35-39, 40-44, 45-49, 50-54,
	55-59, 60-64, 65-69, 70+
Walkers:	Yes
Requirements:	18 years old
Temperature:	68° - 82°
Aid/Splits:	19 / yes

HIGHLIGHTS If your idea of a great marathon includes incredible scenery, excellent organization, small-race charm, and an unsurpassed vacation destination, then the Maui Marathon may be just your race! A well-kept secret for 27 years, the Maui Marathon word is starting to get out. The race grew from 574 runners in 1995 to 1,314 in 1998. For 1999, there is a 1,800 runner limit. Why the tremendous growth? In addition to the above, we know of no other race where you can watch humpback whales frolic offshore while you run, making the marathon's slogan, Run With The Whales, well suited. The race also hosts perhaps the best carbo-load party in the world, held at sunset on Kaanapali Beach with views of palm trees, the Pacific Ocean, and neighboring Lanai. The event boasts live Hawaiian music, hula dancers, entertainers, microbrewed beer, and a generous banquet spread. A great alternative to the Honolulu Marathon, Maui offers a lower-key event. One of the main sponsors of the race is Ryutaro Kamioka, the "Johnny Carson of Japan." He plugs the Maui Marathon regularly on his television show and radio programs in Osaka, which contributes to a large Japanese showing.

COURSE DESCRIPTION   The point-to-point course starts in Kahului at Kaahumanu Center (near the airport) and finishes in Kaanapali Resort at Whalers Village. The first 2 miles run in the dark on residential streets. The race then proceeds onto the shoulders of Highways 380 and 30 for the next 6 miles, covering the flat Central Valley sugar cane fields to Maalea fishing village. As you make the turn onto Honoapiilani Highway 30 after the 6-mile mark, there's a good chance you'll be pushed by a nice tailwind as you approach the rolling hills between miles 9 and 12.5. Sunrise over 10,023-foot dormant volcano Haleakala on your left and the rugged West Maui mountains on the right set the stage for inspired running. The next 4 miles hug the Pali (ocean cliffs) where humpback whales can be often seen playing in the waters below. The most difficult part of the course, this section includes moderate rolling hills between miles 9 and 12.5. Lacking large inclines, the hills come early enough so you should still be relatively fresh. If you are not concerned with time, whale searching can take your mind off the hills and the long road ahead. At mile 12.5, a welcomed, albeit short, break from the sun greets you in the form of a 100-meter tunnel. The tunnel signals the end of the hills and the beginning of a .25-mile downhill stretch prefacing the second half of the race. From this point to the finish, the course is flat and stays within 50 feet of sandy beaches and the Pacific Ocean, offering spectacular views of neighboring islands. At about mile 22, the course turns down Front Street into downtown Lahaina, a historic whaling town with many outstanding restaurants and shops. The final two miles are back onto the shoulder of Highway 30 and into Kaanapali Resort to the finish in Whalers Village. Well-marked, the course consists of asphalt in excellent condition as well as a not-too-steep camber of the shoulder. The one disadvantage with the course is that it cannot be closed to vehicle traffic (except for Front Street) since the highways are the only route to the airport and other destinations. The occasional passing tour bus can cause quite a gust in your face, but most traffic travels fairly slowly.

CROWD/RUNNER SUPPORT   Excellent for supporters to follow the race, the course highways are open to traffic and provide sufficient space on the side of the road to pull over and root for your favorite runner. Providing plenty of support, the aid station volunteers do a great job dispensing fluids and aid. Manned by various community groups, the aid stations compete for the "best aid station award" as chosen by the runners. Crowds along the course are sparse except for the start, Front Street in Lahaina, and the finish area. Announcers read the names of finishers as they come down home stretch. If you're lucky, your name will also be read in Japanese!

RACE LOGISTICS   Race organizers provide bus service from the Kaanapali Resort area to the start, with departures beginning around 3:30 a.m. (ouch!). Buses are limited and service can take a little time, so race officials urge runners to provide their own transportation if possible. Since most visitors to Maui rent a car anyway, this is not a big deal. Also, if your friends and family want to watch your progress, a car is the only way to go. If you do take the bus, the race will transport any clothes you may wish to have waiting for you at the finish. Though there is a good deal of parking at both the start and finish areas, arrive early. Additionally, shuttle buses are provided to return runners to Kaahumanu Center after the race.

ACTIVITIES   The Maui Marathon holds a Sports and Fitness Expo where you also can pick up your race packet, get a course briefing, and have your body kneaded. With an incredible view, party atmosphere, and great food, Maui's carbo-load party may be the best in the world. Held at the Maui Marriott, oceanfront at the Makai Garden, the party includes live music, Hawaiian entertainment, and an all-you-can-eat buffet with a wide variety of food. Refreshingly, there is not the usual parade of celebrity runners to bore you. Instead, the festive atmosphere abounds partly because it is held two nights before the race so runners feel free to partake in the all-you-can-drink beer. Tickets are $25 in advance and $30 at the door. Note that the party is limited to 900 guests and is practically guaranteed to sell out early. On Saturday morning there is a short (2.6 miles) charity fun run around Kaanapali Resort. Completely non-competitive, the run could serve as a nice day-before warm-up if you like to get up early. Otherwise, sleep in. All marathon finishers are treated to a post-race massage and refreshments.

AWARDS   Every finisher receives a nice Maui Marathon T-shirt, medallion, finisher's

certificate, and results booklet (both of which are available for pick-up on Monday at Whalers Village). There are age-group awards three deep in all categories. An awesome finisher's party with awards ceremony is held around 4:30 p.m., oceanfront at the Maui Marriott Makai Gardens (site of the pasta party). The party includes free beer, soda, and snacks while they last, so don't miss it!

ELITE RUNNERS INFORMATION Runners with PRs under the current course records will be considered for assistance with accommodations and inter-island airfare on an individual basis. In addition, the race offers about $10,000 in prize money to the top finishers. Contact the race director for more information.

ACCOMMODATIONS By far the most convenient area to stay is in Kaanapali Resort which boasts six beachfront hotels and four resort condominiums. The race headquarters hotel is the Maui Marriott (800-763-1333 or 808-667-1200). A discount for Maui Marathon participants makes it a good deal, but book early. Other Kaanapali possibilities are the Hyatt Regency (808-661-1234); and Westin Maui (808-667-2525). For less luxurious digs, try the Aston Maui Park (808-669-6622) located further down the highway and off the beach, or Lahaina.

RELATED EVENTS / RACES Held to coincide with the marathon, the 5K is a good way for family and friends to participate in race-day activities as the course finishes at about mile 23 of the marathon, allowing 5K runners to cheer on the marathoners as they run through Lahaina. In addition, a week-long celebration recognizing the humpback whale leads up to the marathon with many family-oriented activities. Marathoners can also get special sight-seeing tours, including cruises, whale-watching expeditions, helicopter tours, and snorkeling trips through the Do Maui Club (808-877-5303).

Maui MARATHON
Run With The Whales
A KAMIOKA CHARITY

SUNDAY, MARCH 21ST, 1999
SUNDAY, MARCH 19TH, 2000
2000 SUBJECT TO CHANGE

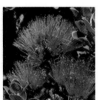

"One of the ten most scenic
marathons in America"
- Runners' World, February 1996

Because the field is limited, we recommend that you
register well in advance. For information call
Valley Isle Road Runners at (808) 871-6441
or visit our website at www.mauimarathon.com

VISIT MAUI...
*Condé Nast readers have repeatedly voted
Maui as the #1 island in the world!*

WIN A MARATHON TRIP!
*Enter the Ultimate Guide's Maui Marathon Sweepstakes
- see information in this edition!*

The Maui Marriott
Resort on Kaanapali
Beach is our Official
Headquarters Hotel and
the location of all race
week events.

MAUI **Marriott**
RESORT®
1-800-763-1333

TRAIL BREAKER MARATHON

OVERALL: 73.4

COURSE BEAUTY: 8

COURSE DIFFICULTY: 5-

APPROPRIATENESS FOR FIRST TIMERS: 6

RACE ORGANIZATION: 8

CROWDS: 1-

RACE DATA

Overall Ranking:	109
Quickness Ranking:	74
Contact:	MDA/Trail Breaker Marathon
	2949 N. Mayfair Road, Suite 106
	Wauwatosa, WI 53222
	Tel. (414) 453-7600
	Fax (414) 453-0706
Date:	March 27, 1999; March 25, 2000
Start Time:	8:00 a.m.
Time Course Closes:	1:30 p.m.
Number of Finishers:	NA
Course:	Out and back
Certification:	None
Course Records:	Male: (open) 2:44:21
	Female: (open) 3:12:00
Elite Athlete Programs:	No
Cost:	$26
Age groups/Divisions:	20-29, 30-34, 35-39, 40-44, 45-49, 50-54, 55-59,
	60-64, 65-69, 70-74, 75+
Walkers:	No
Requirements:	None
Temperature:	40°
Aid/Splits:	7 / none

HIGHLIGHTS   Held about 30 minutes outside Milwaukee, the Trail Breaker Marathon follows a converted railroad bed for 17 miles while the middle seven miles cut through southeastern Wisconsin's glaciated hills on the famous Ice Age Trail. The one-of-a-kind turnaround point lies at the top of the 70-step observation tower on Lapham Peak. Snow often appears at this race, once forcing organizers to change the course when the tower became encrusted with ice. Many of the area's sizeable ultramarathon community run Trail Breaker as a training run while raising money for the race's beneficiary, the Muscular Dystrophy Association.

COURSE DESCRIPTION   Trail Breaker's out-and-back course starts in Waukesha's Frame Park along the Fox River. After a brief stretch on cobblestones and city streets, the race goes on an asphalt path bordering the river to the Glacial Drumlin Trail. Runners follow the trail—a converted railroad bed of crushed limestone—for the next 6.5 miles, passing through hardwoods and under bridges. At mile 9.5, the course reaches the town of Wales, and by mile 10.3

runners hit the Ice Age Trail. The Ice Age Trail marks the edge of the glacier that covered much of Wisconsin 15,000 years ago. This rough trail leads to 1,233-foot Lapham Peak and its 60-foot observation tower at the halfway point. Formerly called Government Hill, the peak saw duty as a surveying vantage point, as a meteorological relay station between Pikes Peak and Chicago, and as a tuberculosis sanitarium. The hill provides great views of the Kettle Moraine Forest. After scaling the tower's 70 steps and trudging back down, runners head back the same route to Waukesha.

CROWD/RUNNER SUPPORT Trail Breaker doesn't attract large crowds, mostly runners' friends and family who tend to congregate near the start/finish and the halfway point. Handlers of runners can access the course at the aid stations and at Lapham Peak Tower (there is a $4 fee to enter the area).

RACE LOGISTICS Parking is available at the Schuetze Building and along the street. The heated indoor staging area provides showers for grimy runners.

ACTIVITIES After the marathon, enjoy hot food, beverages, and the cool sounds of a reggae band.

AWARDS Each marathon finisher who is early-registered receives a long-sleeve T-shirt that is customized with towers on the sleeve representing the number of Trail Breakers he or she has completed. Top open, master, and senior master runners, and the top three in each age group receive certificates.

ACCOMMODATIONS In Waukesha, try the: Country Inn, 2810 Golf Road (414-547-0201); Comfort Inn, 2111 E. Moreland Blvd. (414-547-7770); Fairfield Inn, 20150 W. Bluemound Road (414-785-0500); Motel 6, 20300 W. Bluemound Road (414-786-7337); Budgetel Inn, 20391 W. Bluemound Road (414-782-9100); Holiday Inn, 2417 W. Bluemound Road (414-786-0460); Super 8 Motel, 2501 Plaza Court (414-785-1590); Select Inn, 2510 Plaza Court (414-786-6015); or Hampton Inn, 575 Barney Street (414-796-1500).

RELATED EVENTS/RACES Trail Breaker makes everyone happy by having a few options. If you're not ready to tackle the Ice Age Trail and the Lapham Peak Tower, try the half marathon which starts at 9:30 a.m. The Fox River 5K Run/Walk goes along the Fox River and starts at 10:30 a.m. Finally, competitive race walkers can enter the judged, 5K race walk.

AREA ATTRACTIONS You must tour one of the many beer factories—Miller Brewery is located at 4251 W. State Street, and Pabst Brewing Company is at 915 W. Juneau Avenue. Friday nights in Milwaukee mean fish fry. Go to just about any restaurant to join in the tradition. Top it off with some frozen custard. Sneak a peek in the Pettit National Ice Center, 500 S. 84th Street, where some local runners do their winter training.

MULE MOUNTAIN MARATHON

OVERALL: 84.7

COURSE BEAUTY: 9+

COURSE DIFFICULTY: 5 (SEE APPENDIX)

APPROPRIATENESS FOR FIRST-TIMERS: 7

ORGANIZATION: 9

CROWDS: 1

RACE DATA

Overall Ranking:	53
Quickness Ranking:	78
Contact:	Leslie Woods
	Mule Mountain Marathon
	Department of the Army
	P.O. Box 12100
	Ft. Huachuca, AZ 85613
	Tel. 520-533-1065; Fax 520-538-2010
	E-mail: army-marathon@huachuca-emh1.army.mil
	http:\\huachuca-usaic.army.mil:80\Garrison\MMM\marathon.htm
Date:	April 10, 1999; April 8, 2000 (tentative)
Start Time:	5:00 a.m.
Time Course Closes:	11:00 a.m.
Number of Finishers:	234 in 1998
Course:	Point to point
Certification:	USATF
Course Records:	Male: (open) 2:29
	Female: (open) 2:48
Elite Athlete Programs:	No
Cost:	$25/45/55
Age groups/Divisions:	≤14, 15-19, 20-24, 25-29, 30-34, 35-39, 40-44, 45-49, 50-54, 55-59, 60-64, 65-69, 70+
Walkers:	No
Requirements:	None
Temperature:	45°-65°
Aid/Splits:	12 / none

HIGHLIGHTS Arguably the most scenic marathon in the Southwest, the Mule Mountain Marathon takes you through a See's Candy-assortment of scenery. Starting in the strikingly set historic town of Bisbee in the far southeastern corner of Arizona, the marathon climbs through picturesque mountains, drops past red rock formations, looks over valley vistas, and runs in Sonoran desert. Runners get to enjoy the beauty without having to worry about dodging cars on the completely closed course. This old mule is challenging, particularly in the first three miles and the final seven miles. Even a good part of the downhill portion is tough, with painfully sharp grades. This Army-run race (in fact it is nicknamed "The Army Marathon") offers participants solid organization with lots of military participants, especially in the relay event. And if you're fast, you might even win a new car in addition to the complimentary eye candy.

COURSE DESCRIPTION The Mule Mountain Marathon starts at the Convention Center in the old mining town of Bisbee (elevation 5,200 feet), one of Arizona's most charming locales. Quickly winding through the town, the Mule wastes little time in giving you a swift kick. You climb steadily up Tombstone Canyon before merging onto Highway 80 near mile 1.7. The course heads through Mule Pass Tunnel at 2.1 miles as it continues to climb up the Mule Mountains. After emerging from the tunnel, runners have beautiful views of the mountains and surrounding red rock hills, reaching the race pinnacle of just under 6,000 feet before mile 3. As you head down the sharp grade on the other side of the mountain range, the view opens up to a scenic canyon with pretty brushed hills. The descent becomes slightly less abrupt near 4.3 miles as more red rock crops up to your right. Runners face a few little bumps in the near elevator-steep downhill at miles 6.3, 7.2, and 8.1, while enjoying several gorgeous stretches of landscape. That last hill leads to the left turn onto Highway 90 (mile 8.6). On Highway 90, the descent becomes less severe as the San Pedro Valley unfolds beneath you. As you reach the valley floor, Sierra Vista appears ahead, still 14 miles away. Runners cross the San Pedro River bed at mile 16.3, your warning that the downhill is about to end. Mile 16.6 (just above 4,000 feet) marks the end of the downhill, and the beginning of the 500-foot climb out of the San Pedro Valley until the finish. It is not uphill the entire way, however, as several flat or downhill portions pop up during these final miles. The course enters the city limits of Sierra Vista at 20.5 miles. Runners turn right at Giullo Cesar Avenue at mile 22.5, and one-half mile later turn left onto Charleston Road which leads to Veterans Park. After completing a circuit in the park, runners finish amidst the Festival of the Southwest.

CROWD/RUNNER SUPPORT As you might expect from the closed course through the mountains and upper Sonoran desert, crowd support is sparse except for the finish area. Aid along the way comes every 2.5 miles, with water and food available. Portable toilets sit every 5 miles or so.

RACE LOGISTICS The race provides transportation from the official race hotel (Windemere Hotel) to the start and back to the hotel from the finish area.

ACTIVITIES The Windemere Hotel hosts a free pre-race pasta buffet for all runners on Friday evening. After the race, wander through the Festival of the Southwest, featuring food, entertainment, vendors, and art.

AWARDS Every entrant receives a T-shirt. The top three male and female marathoners receive $150, $75, and $50 in prize money, respectively. The first man to finish the marathon under 2:21 and the first woman under 2:50 receive a new Dodge Neon car. Note that if you are listed as one of the top 100 male or female international runners in USATF's Track and Field News, you are ineligible to win the cars. The top male and female master's runners receive $50 in prize money.

ACCOMMODATIONS The Windemere Hotel, 2047 S. State Highway 92 in Sierra Vista (800-825-4656) serves as the race headquarters hotel. Other possibilities in Sierra Vista include: Sun Canyon Inn, 260 N. Garden Avenue (520-459-0610); Motel 6, 1551 E. Fry Blvd. (520-459-5035); and Super 8 Motel, 100 Fab Avenue (520-459-5380). Lodging in charming Bisbee can be found at: Bisbee Grand Hotel, 61 Main Street (520-432-5900); Copper Queen Hotel, 11 Howell Avenue (520-432-2216); School House Inn Bed and Breakfast, 818 Tombstone Canyon (520-432-2996); and Inn at Castle Rock, 112 Tombstone Canyon (520-432-4449).

RELATED EVENTS/RACES Runners who are too stubborn to run the full Mule can participate in the marathon relay, half marathon, or 5K fun run. The marathon relay consists of six member teams, with five legs of 5 miles and one leg of 1.2 miles. Teams may be male, female, coed, or military. The half marathon runs along the final half of the full marathon course. All of the races together attract about 1,200 runners. The venerable Dual Mule Marathon (the 52.4-mile race starting at midnight) has been canceled.

AREA ATTRACTIONS Located only 12 miles from infamous Tombstone and Mexico, the region offers a plethora of activities including the mile-high bird sanctuary, San Pedro River Riparian Area, and Fort Huachuca (home of the Buffalo Soldier). Also make sure you spend a day in wonderful Bisbee.

CHARLOTTE MARATHON

OVERALL: 82.4

COURSE BEAUTY: 8

COURSE DIFFICULTY: 6+ (SEE APPENDIX)

APPROPRIATENESS FOR FIRST TIMERS: 8-

RACE ORGANIZATION: 9

CROWDS: 3-

RACE DATA

Overall Ranking:	68
Quickness Ranking:	90
Contact:	Marathon Administrator
	Charlotte Observer Marathon
	P.O. Box 30294
	Charlotte, NC 28230
	(704) 358-5425
	E-mail: promo@charlotte.infi.net
	http://www.charlotte.com
Date:	April 10, 1999; April 15, 2000
Start Time:	8:00 a.m. (tentative)
Time Course Closes:	2:00 p.m.
Number of Finishers:	1,094 in 1998
Course:	Loop
Certification:	USATF
Course Records:	Male: (open) 2:28:18
	Female: (open) 3:20:03
Elite Athlete Programs:	No
Cost:	$21
Age groups/Divisions:	≤14, 15-19, 20-24, 25-29, 30-34, 35-39, 40-44,
	45-49, 50-54, 55-59, 60-64, 65-69, 70-74, 75+
Walkers:	No
Requirements:	None
Temperature:	60°
Aid/Splits:	25 / every five miles

HIGHLIGHTS If you're the type of runner who has to run a PR each time out, then the Charlotte Observer Marathon, with its ever-present hills, probably isn't the race for you. If, however, you can pull yourself away from the PR chase, the Charlotte course offers a wonderful tour of some of the Queen City's most exclusive neighborhoods. Running under Charlotte's signature towering oak trees, the course takes you past the beautiful estate of golfer Arnold Palmer. You also run much of the same course used for the 1996 Olympic Marathon Trials, including the Providence Road pavement, between miles 23 and 24, where Trials winner Bob Kempainen made history by vomiting six times during a sub-five-minute mile.

COURSE DESCRIPTION The Charlotte Observer Marathon's hilly course runs on very smooth pavement through mostly residential and commercial areas of town. It's a challenging race. Although the first 10 miles produce a net drop of 150 feet, significant uphills keep you honest. The last 16 miles include more ups and downs than the stock market. Starting at Tryon and Stonewall Streets (the highest point on the course at 760 feet) in the heart of downtown, the course rises gently before turning left onto Morehead around the half-mile mark. After 1.5 miles, runners head through Myers Park, one of Charlotte's most exclusive neighborhoods and usually teeming with spectators. The first significant incline occurs at mile 2.8 on Queens Road West. At mile 3.2, the course turns right onto Selwyn Road, continues mostly downhill, and then goes sharply downhill from mile 4.8 to the turn onto Park Road at mile 4.9. With an already tough uphill from 4.9 to 5.5 miles, wind can also hinder you at this point as it is the barest part of the route. Another good uphill arises between miles 7.2 and 7.4 with a gradual descent from mile 7.6 to the turnaround at the 9.5-mile mark, possibly the race's fastest section. Tough and desolate, miles 10 to 11.9 roll with a net elevation rise of 40 feet. A nice downhill at 13.2 miles prefaces perhaps the most grueling climb on the course, 80 feet from mile 13.4 to 14.2. At 14.4 miles, the route begins to level off and is flat between miles 15 and 17 through high-traffic SouthPark (known for its shopping and upscale modern homes), providing a chance to recover from the preceding hills. Following a 30-foot drop from 18 to 18.3 miles, the road climbs 60 feet from 19.3 to 19.8 miles, turning left onto Randolph. Here, a brief downhill precedes a 3-mile incline before leveling off at the 21-mile mark. Relatively flat to mile 22.3, the race drops 50 feet between miles 22.8 and 23, followed by an easy rise to mile 23.5. Leveling off in Myers Park, the route climbs from mile 24.1 to 24.4 as it approaches downtown. Then mostly rolling, the race climaxes with a .25-mile gradual uphill on 2nd Street to the finish.

CROWD/RUNNER SUPPORT   Although Charlotte is better known for its beloved stock car racing, crowd support for the marathon increases every year. Scattered along the course, spectators mainly target Myers Park West (2 to 3 miles), SouthPark (15 to 16 miles), Myers Park East (23 to 24 miles), and the finish on 2nd Street. While open to traffic with one lane dedicated to runners, the roads allow supporters to maneuver easily around the route to cheer their favorite runners.

RACE LOGISTICS   The start and finish areas lie near the downtown hotels, so transportation is not a concern. There is transportation to the finish for dropouts. Baggage deposit is available at the start line, with pick-up at the finish.

ACTIVITIES   The Charlotte Observer Marathon features a two-day Health, Fun & Fitness Expo Thursday from 3:00 p.m. to 9:00 p.m. and Friday 11:00 a.m. to 9:00 p.m. at the Charlotte Convention Center, 501 South College. Packet pick-up, late registration, running clinics and the Carb-Up Party (5:30 p.m.) take place here. Unofficial finish times are printed in the Sunday edition of the Charlotte Observer newspaper. Official results are mailed with the Race Report a month after the race.

AWARDS   Every runner receives a T-shirt. Each finisher is presented with a custom-designed medallion. Additionally, handsome finisher certificates are available for $1. The first three finishers in each age group receive recognition awards.

ACCOMMODATIONS   The Hilton Hotel, 222 East Third Street downtown (704-377-1500), serves as the race headquarters. Other hotels near the start/finish area include the Radisson Plaza Hotel, 101 South Tryon Street (704-377-0400); Charlotte Marriott City Center, 100 West Trade Street (704-333-9000); Holiday Inn—City Center, 230 North College Street (704-335-5400); and Adam's Mark Hotel, 555 South McDowell Street (704-372-4100).

RELATED EVENTS/RACES   Race day features several other events for runners of all abilities. The Family Fun Run 1.2 Mile kicks off before the marathon. After the marathon start, in one of the largest 10K runs on the East Coast, 5,500 runners attack an out-and-back course over the first 3 miles of the marathon route. The 1999 edition of the marathon marks the debut of non-competitive bicycling and skating events.

AREA ATTRACTIONS   If you're planning to stay awhile in the Charlotte area consider cruising on Lake Norman, touring one of Charlotte's beautiful Victorian neighborhoods, or panning for gold at Reed Gold Mine where America's first big gold lode was discovered.

BOSTON MARATHON

OVERALL: 99

COURSE BEAUTY: 8

COURSE DIFFICULTY: 4- (SEE APPENDIX)

APPROPRIATENESS FOR FIRST TIMERS: NA

RACE ORGANIZATION: 10

CROWDS: 10+

RACE DATA

Overall Ranking:	5
Quickness Ranking:	37
Contact:	Guy Morse
	Boston Athletic Assn.
	131 Clarendon Street
	Boston, MA 02116
	Tel. (617) 236-1652
	Fax (617) 236-4505
Date:	April 19, 1999; April 17, 2000
Start Time:	Noon
Time Course Closes:	6:00 p.m.
Number of Finishers:	11,274 in 1999
Course:	USATF
Certification:	Point to point
Course Records:	Male: (open) 2:07:15
	Female: (open) 2:21:45
Elite Athlete Programs:	Yes
Cost:	$75
Age groups/Divisions:	18-34, 35-39, 40-44, 45-49, 50-54, 55-59, 60-64, 65-69, 70+, wheelchair
Walkers:	No
Requirements:	Qualifying time (see table on page 60), 18 years old
Temperature:	50° - 55°
Aid/Splits:	24 / every mile

HIGHLIGHTS The Mother of all Marathons, running's best friend, running's Mecca. Call it what you like, the 102-year-old Boston Marathon stands as the benchmark by which all other marathons are measured. Virtually all certified marathons in North America attest to Boston's pre-eminence in the sport by noting on their entry blank, "This is a Boston Qualifier." In addition to its age, part of the Boston mystique stems from the rigid qualification standards used to limit its field. If you're talented enough to qualify, expect to have an incredible running experience. One and a half million spectators frame the most famous course in the world; Hopkinton, Wellesley College, Heartbreak Hill, the Citgo sign, and Copley Square are all familiar landmarks of this landmark race.

RACE HISTORY Unchallenged as the world's oldest and most prestigious annual marathon, the Boston Marathon started on April 19, 1897 after Boston Athletic Association member and U.S. Olympic Team manager John Graham, so impressed with the spirit of the Olympic marathon, decided to stage one in the Boston area. Fifteen men participated in that first race, the second

marathon ever held in the United States (New York held a marathon the previous year). Held on Patriot's Day, commemorating Paul Revere's famous ride marking the American Revolution, Boston remains a race of tradition and distinction for its participants, volunteers, and spectators. Starting with John J. McDermott's inaugural win, Boston lore includes Clarence DeMar's record seven victories, John Kelley's two victories and 58 finishes, Roberta Gibb and Kathy Switzers' barrier breaking efforts for women runners, Bill Rodger's record performances, and current stars Cosmas Ndeti and Uta Pippig. While the world's elite marathoners dream of winning Boston, qualifying to run remains an aspiration of most other marathoners worldwide. After instituting qualifying times in the early 1970s, Boston has spurred many marathoners to times they never imagined possible. Whether an elite athlete, qualifier, spectator or volunteer, Boston represents the pinnacle of marathoning.

COURSE DESCRIPTION   Starting on Main Street in the rural hamlet of Hopkinton, Boston's point-to-point course features a 450-foot elevation loss as it winds through seven towns before finishing near Copley Square in Boston's Back Bay. Following Route 135, the race heads downhill through Ashland past the impressive Ashland clock tower and the stirring waters of the Sudbury River between miles 4 and 5. Here, runners enter Framingham, passing the historic Framingham Train Depot at the 10K mark. Continuing mostly downhill, the route skirts tranquil Lake Cochituate at 9 miles and the Natick Town Green at 10.5 miles. The male runners always seem to quicken their step as they near the halfway point to the screaming sirens of Wellesley College. Once there, however, many don't seem to be in any hurry. Now on Route 16, runners climb 50 feet between miles 15 and 16 before crossing the Charles River into Newton Lower Falls. After turning right at the fire station onto Commonwealth Avenue, the route traverses the Newton Hills (the infamous Heartbreak Hill) rising 175 feet between miles 17 and 22, paying homage to the John Kelley Statue at 19.5 miles. The course then descends 200 feet over the last 4 miles to the finish. Bearing right at the Chestnut Hill Reservoir, the route makes its way onto Beacon Street continuing mostly downhill past the landmark Citgo sign at the 25-mile mark in Kenmore Square. Here, the course rejoins Commonwealth Avenue turning right onto Hereford Street, then left onto Boylston Street to the finish line.

CROWD/RUNNER SUPPORT The largest single-day sporting event in New England, the Boston Marathon's crowd support is unparalleled, attracting more than 1.5 million spectators. Held on a holiday, the race draws onlookers over 10 deep at several points. Generations of families come out to cheer the runners, with kids holding out orange slices or water, dreaming of the day when they will take part in the spectacle. Several thousand volunteers help coordinate the start, finish and course logistics. If you miss one of the 24 aid stations, don't worry; unofficial neighborhood aid stations saturate the entire course. Additionally, American Red Cross aid stations occur every mile to assist anyone requiring medical attention. If it's media not medical attention you want, you have a very good chance of being captured in print or television by the approximately 1,100 media personnel representing more than 300 media outlets from around the world who cover the Boston Marathon each year.

RACE LOGISTICS Part of Boston's attraction comes from its unique qualification standards. The following qualifying times must be run within the 17 month window of October 1 of the previous year and March 1 of the year you would like to run Boston:

AGE GROUP	18-34	35-39	40-44	45-49	50-54	55-59	60-64	65-69	70+
MEN	3:10	3:15	3:20	3:25	3:30	3:35	3:40	3:45	3:50
WOMEN	3:40	3:45	3:50	3:55	4:00	4:05	4:10	4:15	4:20

There is a 20,000 runner limit for the race. If the limit is reached prior to March 1, you are out of luck. Elite foreign athletes must be registered with their country's federation. On race morning, shuttle bus transportation to the start is provided to runners from South Street and State Park.

ACTIVITIES Race packets may be picked up at the race headquarters hotel during the extraordinary, 2-day Sports and Fitness Expo all day on Saturday and Sunday. You may do more gawking than eating at the celebrity-laden Boston Marathon Pasta Party on Sunday night. After the race, enjoy the awards ceremony and the Post-Race Dance Party, including dinner, live music and entertainment.

AWARDS Each entrant receives a long-sleeve T-shirt and an official full-color Race Program. Runners finishing under 6 hours receive pewter medallions and certificates of completion. An official Results Booklet which chronicles the race and lists all official finishers is mailed after the event. Elite athletes compete for a portion of the $600,000 prize purse—largest in the sport. Division winners also receive special awards.

ELITE RUNNERS INFORMATION The B.A.A. recruits elite runners from every part of the globe, specifically men with sub-2:15 credentials and women under 2:35, though elite status may not always be this straightforward. The race covers travel, lodging and food expenses for elites. Prize money for open men and women extends 15 places with the winner receiving $100,000 and 15th place netting $1,500. Masters men and women compete for prize money extending 5 places with $12,000 earmarked for the winner and $1,000 for 5th place. In addition, bonuses are awarded for course records and world best performances.

ACCOMMODATIONS Hotels abound in the Boston Metropolitan area. In addition to the race headquarters hotel, the Copley Plaza Hotel (617-267-5300), your lodging options include: Four Seasons Hotel, 200 Boylston Street (617-338-4400); Ritz Carlton Hotel, 15 Arlington Street (617-536-5700); Sheraton Boston, 39 Dalton Street (617-236-2000); Westin, 10 Huntington Avenue (617-262-9600); and Marriott Copley, 110 Huntington Avenue (617-236-5800).

AREA ATTRACTIONS Not only the site of marathoning's most historic race, Boston rates as one of the country's best walking cities. You can visit some of the city's historic landmarks along the two-and-a-half mile red-painted line of the Freedom Trail through downtown Boston. Explore the Boston Massacre site, Paul Revere's House, and Bunker Hill Monument. Before catching a Boston Red Sox game at Fenway Park, the oldest major league ballpark, spend some time milling about the book stores and cafes of Harvard Square in nearby Cambridge. Shop on trendy Newbury Street near the marathon finish.

BIG SUR INTERNATIONAL MARATHON

OVERALL: 100

COURSE BEAUTY: 10+

COURSE DIFFICULTY: 6+ (SEE APPENDIX)

APPROPRIATENESS FOR FIRST TIMERS: 7-

RACE ORGANIZATION: 10

CROWDS: 5

RACE DATA

Overall Ranking:	1
Quickness Ranking:	87
Contact:	Big Sur International Marathon
	P.O. Box 222620
	Carmel, CA 93922-26200
	Tel. (831) 625-6226; Fax (831) 625-2119
	E-mail: info@bsim.org
	http://www.bsim.org/
Date:	April 25, 1999; April 30, 2000
Start Time:	7:00 a.m.
Time Course Closes:	12:30 p.m.
Number of Finishers:	2,437 in 1998 (limited to 3,000 entrants)
Course:	Point to point
Certification:	USATF
Course Records:	Male: (open) 2:16:39
	Female: (open) 2:41:34
Elite Athlete Programs:	Yes
Cost:	$65/70/75
Age groups/Divisions:	16-19, 20-24, 25-29, 30-34, 35-39, 40-44, 45-49, 50-54, 55-59, 60-64, 65-69, 70-74, 75-79, 80+, Active Military, Monterey County, Clydesdales (males over 195 lbs., females over 150 lbs.), Mozarctic
Walkers:	Yes
Requirements:	16 years old
Temperature:	50° - 60°
Aid/Splits:	12 / every mile, including pace & projected finish time

HIGHLIGHTS Unflappable and spectacular, the Big Sur International Marathon runs like Boots Randolph plays the saxophone, chipmunk cheeks making magical music. Not even the incredible storms of 1998, which washed away huge sections of Highway 1, could affect the quality of Big Sur's harmony. This race soars like the last note of *The Magic Flute*. Stunning. Breathless. Triumphant. It makes most other races seem a bit off-key. What makes this symphony of marathons so great? Big Sur has it all— a gorgeous course, quality race organization, outstanding entertainment, and an unbeatable location for a getaway vacation. Runners should savor this race; the difficult course and the spectacular scenery make PRs unimportant. And make no mistake, Big Sur is a very challenging race. Instead, take it all in: the Robert Louis Stevenson Orchestra, Jonathan Lee on the piano, the Bixby Bridge, the rocky coastline, the beautiful headlands and especially running down famous Pacific Coast Highway 1. Like any coastal race, the biggest drawback can be the weather; runners often face a stiff headwind. Despite the difficulty and the wind, Big Sur remains our number 1 marathon in North America because it always leaves us singing.

RACE HISTORY We do our best thinking on a run. Evidently, despite being a runner, Bill Burleigh does his best thinking in a car. While driving on Highway 1 from Carmel to his home in Big Sur, Bill noticed a road sign: "26 miles to Big Sur." Bill put twenty-six and point two (.2) together and founded one of the world's great marathons.

Debuting in 1986, Big Sur has become extremely popular lately. The race now quickly fills to its 3,000 runner capacity. Despite (possibly because of) the majesty of the surroundings, Big Sur organizers encourage humor and whimsy. One popular BSIM tradition, the naming contest started in 1988, asks runners to name everything from the 520-foot hill at mile 10 (Hurricane Point), the last hill at mile 25.5 (D minor Hill at D major Time), the 700-pound heifer mascot who gave birth near the course in 1989 (Tchaicowsky), a skeleton dressed in running clothes at mile 25.5 (DeComposer), and the slow-footed race founder (Bachward Burleigh). You may notice the classical music thread here, and for good reason; race organizers give extra points to classical connections.

COURSE DESCRIPTION The Big Sur International Marathon runs along U.S. Highway 1 from Big Sur to Carmel, passing spectacular redwoods, incomparable coastline, and seaside ranches. Runners have the whole road to themselves. Although downhill (the race starts at 300 feet and ends at 25 feet), the course contains plenty of uphills, providing a serious challenge for all runners.

BSIM starts on fairly narrow Highway 1 just south of Pfeiffer State Park at the State Park Maintenance Area. Redwoods dominate the early going, which lies away from the ocean. While BSIM loses 300 feet during the first 5 miles, it contains some strong undulations. The race goes mostly on a nice downgrade from the start until mile 1, where it climbs slightly to about 1.3 miles at the Fernwood Motel. Undulating downward, the course continues to wander under redwoods, in the shadow of the surrounding hills, to the Big Sur Village at mile 2.5. Soon out of the redwoods' embrace, runners face a good bump at 3.7 and another small hill at 4.5. After the downside of the hill, the race passes Andrew Molera State Park at the 5-mile mark. Quickly up another hill, runners view the Pacific Ocean for the first time at 5.4 miles. Flattening around 5.5 miles, the grassy Big Sur headlands appear, with textured hills and seaside ranches full of cows. The course rises from miles 6.4 to 6.7, 7.3 to 7.5, and 7.8 to 8.1. A mound of rock rises to the left, and by mile 8.8 runners descend the curvy highway to Point Sur at the 9-mile mark. Here you can make out the climb up Hurricane Point ahead of you. While you still have your breath, enjoy the incredible views of the Big Sur headlands and the crashing blue surf. Still gently down, the course ducks in a cove at 9.8 miles, crossing the Little Sur River Bridge; now the steady, 2-mile climb up 520 feet to Hurricane Point begins. Winds often intensify the challenge of the ascent. Once you top Hurricane Point, the route falls quickly downhill with more great views of the headlands, hills, and rugged, Big Sur rocks pounded by the ocean. At the halfway point, runners cross the famous Bixby Creek Bridge, preceding another winding downhill with incredible scenery. After another incline, the race heads back down past Palo Colorado Canyon. At mile 15.3, the road climbs about 80 feet to Rocky Point at 15.6 miles. Coming down Rocky Point, runners have a nice downgrade to the Garrapata Bridge at mile 16.8. Strongly rolling, with stretches of downgrade, the course forges the Granite Canyon Bridge at 18.2, where it continues to roll past Soberanes Point (mile 19). More stunning views appear after rounding the point. Still up and down, the course reaches the Carmel Highlands at mile 21.8 and a 90-foot hill to Yankee Point at 22 miles. The route here turns ever so slightly more residential as it pulls gently away from the water. You now enter the race's final stages, with another rise from mile 22.3 to 22.5. With a nice downgrade, you run over the Wildcat Creek Bridge at 22.9. With several discernible hills and rolls, you reach Point Lobos around 24 miles and can make out the town ahead. At 24.8 you head down to the Carmel River State Beach, where the course flattens before heading up "D minor Hill at D major Time" at mile 25.3. This tough little 80-foot hill, which should sap your legs of any remaining strength, leaves you more than ready for the finish line. You finish on a well-deserved downgrade into the Crossroads Shopping Center in Carmel. Congratulations. You are now a proud member of the Hurricane Point Survivors Association.

CROWD/RUNNER SUPPORT The Big Sur course naturally limits spectators' access to the race. As a result, the vast majority of crowds lie toward the finish. However,

musical inspiration awaits each runner along various parts of the route: a surprise group at the Little Sur River Bridge (mile 9.8); the 26-piece Robert Louis Stevenson Orchestra performs at Hurricane Point; Jonathan Lee plays a concert piano at Bixby Bridge; the Wild Coast Brass Quintet entertains at Rocky Point (mile 15); and Youth Music Monterey inspires at mile 17. At Point Lobos, brace yourself for the 60-member choral group, I Cantori. Bagpipes, radio stations, and a few other surprises support you on the majestic course. Aid stations stock water, electrolyte replacement drink, sponges, and fruit. Medical aid and toilet facilities are also available.

RACE LOGISTICS Race organizers provide shuttle bus service from Monterey to the start, and from the finish area to the start. Since the morning bus ride to the start travels the course in reverse, runners receive an excellent opportunity to check out the route. There is also transportation for your clothing and personal items to the finish.

ACTIVITIES The two-day Expo is held at race headquarters, the Monterey Conference Center. The good-sized expo contains all the usual goodies. On Saturday afternoon, race organizers offer a clinic on "How to Run the Big Sur Course." The clinic is presented by runners of all levels who have completed past races. On Saturday night, attend the group carbo meal for a pasta buffet, locally-grown artichokes, and live jazz (about $14). Reserve early since it sells out well ahead of time. After the race, relax to a classical music concert while receiving a well-deserved complimentary massage. You can shower up then celebrate at the post-race party with beer, fresh fruit juice, and a variety of foods and snacks. Awards ceremony follows.

AWARDS The entry fee for BSIM is one of the highest around and worth every penny. Each entrant receives a dri-release microblend, long-sleeve T-shirt, official results book, and race-day program. Finishers earn hand-crafted ceramic medals created by a local sculptor. Finishers also become members of the Hurricane Point Survivors Association, which entitles them to discounts on future BSIM entry fees. Unique awards, including merchandise prizes, go to the top five in each age division. Other random awards are doled out on race day. There is also approximately $20,000 in prize money.

ELITE RUNNERS INFORMATION The top three finishers get reimbursed for transportation and lodging, and the top five receive prize money ($2,500 for first, $1,000 for second, $500 for third, $250 for fourth, and $175 for fifth). Overall winners also receive round-trip airline tickets. If you do well, you can return as an invited elite runner and receive complimentary accommodations. Male runners who have run a recent 2:30, and females with a recent 2:40 could qualify as an elite athlete at BSIM. Non-invited elites receive free entry. A $2,000 bounty goes to the runner who sets a new course record.

ACCOMMODATIONS If you like to sleep in, try to stay in Big Sur with its 242 rooms and cabins and 431 campsites. For cabins call (800-424-4787). For more luxurious surroundings, try the award-winning Ventana Inn, starting at $195 (831-667-2331); or the Post Ranch Inn Resort, with rates beginning at $285 and a two-night minimum (from California 800-527-2200; others 831-667-2200). Monterey boasts a wider range of lodging but requires transportation to the bus-loading area. Call Monterey Travel (831-649-4292), and let them find you Monterey accommodations in your price range.

RELATED EVENTS/RACES For those of you who don't want to run the marathon, but would like to experience Big Sur, BSIM also offers a 10.6-mile walk that starts at Rocky Point (mile 15.6), a 21-mile Power Walk that begins at Molera State Park, a marathon relay for 5-member teams, and a 5K that starts and ends at the marathon finish area. Be aware that relay members may get stuck on the course awhile (because the race must convoy buses and other vehicles down the course at infrequent intervals), so be sure to bring plenty of warm clothing to wear while you wait. Most of the 5K race runs along the Pacific Ocean, and it serves as the USATF Pacific Association 5K Championship.

AREA ATTRACTIONS Big Sur has all the ingredients for a wonderful vacation. First and foremost is the coastline. You can also visit the Monterey Bay Aquarium, Cannery Row, Laguna Seca race track, shop in Carmel, golf at Pebble Beach or Spyglass, or just linger along 17-mile drive.

LAKE COUNTY MARATHON

OVERALL: 81.2

COURSE BEAUTY: 7+

COURSE DIFFICULTY: 3

APPROPRIATENESS FOR FIRST TIMERS: 8-

RACE ORGANIZATION: 9

CROWDS: 3-

RACE DATA

Overall Ranking:	77
Quickness Ranking:	35
Contact:	Lake County Races
	3100 Skokie Valley Road, 2N
	Highland Park, IL 60035
	Tel. (888) RUN-RUN1
	Fax (847) 266-7225
	E-mail: runlakeco@aol.com
	http://www.doitsports.com/lakecountyraces
Date:	April 25, 1999; April 23, 2000
Start Time:	8:15 a.m.
Time Course Closes:	1:45 p.m.
Number of Finishers:	NA
Course:	Point to point
Certification:	USATF
Course Records:	Male: (open) 2:16:55
	Female: (open) 2:50:36
Elite Athlete Programs:	NA
Cost:	$30
Age groups/Divisions:	≤14, 15-19, 20-24, 25-29, 30-34, 35-39, 40-44,
	45-49, 50-54, 55-59, 60-64, 65-69, 70-74, 75+
Walkers:	No
Requirements:	None
Temperature:	NA
Aid/Splits:	10 / miles 1, 3, 5, 10, 13.1, 20 & 22

HIGHLIGHTS From scary North Chicago to moneyed Highland Park, the Lake County Marathon shows a face of stark contrasts as it threads Lake Michigan's shore south from the Wisconsin/Illinois border toward Chicago. Offering a more exhaustive menu of races than the latest chain restaurant, Lake County attracts runners with its reasonably fast, point-to-point course and its something-for-everyone mentality.

COURSE DESCRIPTION Starting on Sheridan Road, a wide, unattractive stretch of asphalt, the Lake County Marathon cuts through strip malls, commercial districts, a warehouse area, and some low-income neighborhoods for most of the first 8 miles of the race. Cambered in some spots, the road contains some very gentle grades, but is mostly flat or downhill. Near mile 9, runners happily enter wooded Foss Park, marking a major change in the course's complexion. Miles 9 through 12 tour the Great Lakes Naval Base. Runners encounter Sousa Hill, the marathon's largest, at mile 10 on the base. Exiting the base is like bursting out of a 12-mile tunnel into the brilliant sunshine; it may take you a while to adjust. Now more rolling and winding, the course shows off Lake County's high society, passing estate after estate, mansion after mansion through the communities of Lake Bluff, Lake Forest, Highwood, and Highland Park to the finish. The merely large homes seem pedestrian, and thoughts of rundown North Chicago are a lifetime (and 4 miles) away.

CROWD / RUNNER SUPPORT You find most spectators scattered in the neighborhoods after exiting the Great Lakes Naval Base. Aid stations with water and electrolyte replacement and medical aid stations are located every 2.5 miles. Portable toilets sit at miles 3.5, 5, 6.2, 10, 13.1, 15, 20, and 23.5. Digital clocks show your progress at miles 1, 3, 5, 10, 13.1, 20, and 22.

RACE LOGISTICS We suggest you drive to Ravinia Park in Highland Park and take the free train to the start in Zion. The train departs Ravinia Park at 6:40 a.m. If you prefer, you can pick up the train at Clybourn Station in Chicago at 6:00 a.m. The train arrives in Zion at 7:15 a.m. If you must drive to the start, there is only one bus to take you back to Zion after the race. The bus leaves at 1:00 p.m. from the Western Gate of Ravinia Park in the parking lot. If you miss that bus, your only other alternative is to take the regularly scheduled (not free) METRA train at 3:21 p.m. from Ravinia Station. You may check your gear at the start for pickup after the race.

ACTIVITIES Race packet pickup and a Sports Expo are held on Friday from 3:00 p.m. to 8:00 p.m. and Saturday from 10:00 a.m. to 6:00 p.m. at the Sheraton North Shore. There is no race-day packet pickup or registration, but you may have your packet mailed to you for an extra charge. Hit the refreshments and snacks after the marathon.

AWARDS Every runner receives a Lake County Marathon T-shirt, and each finisher receives a memento. The top three runners in each age group and the top 10 overall are awarded prizes.

ACCOMMODATIONS The Sheraton North Shore Inn, 933 Skokie Blvd., Northbrook (800-535-9131), serves as the host hotel. Other hotels reasonably close to the marathon finish are: Hotel Moraine, 700 N. Sheridan, Highwood (847-433-5566); Residence Inn Deerfield, 530 Lake Cook Road, Deerfield (800-331-3131); Red Roof Inn Northbrook, 340 Waukegan Road (847-205-1755); Courtyard by Marriott, 1505 Lake Cook Road, Highland Park (800-321-2211); Hyatt Deerfield, 1750 Lake Cook Road (847-945-3400); and Embassy Suites Hotel, 1455 Lake Cook Road, Deerfield (847-945-4500).

RELATED EVENTS / RACES The Lake County Races offer six different races, including the marathon. The marathon, half marathon, 10K, and 5-person marathon relay share the same start time and location. The 3.5-mile Fun Run & Walk starts and finishes at Ravinia Park, while the Special Olympics Relay begins at the marathon's halfway point in Lake Bluff and finishes at Ravinia Park.

AREA ATTRACTIONS See the Chicago Marathon for area attractions.

MICHIGAN TRAIL MARATHON

OVERALL: 76.4

COURSE BEAUTY: 9-

COURSE DIFFICULTY: 8

APPROPRIATENESS FOR FIRST TIMERS: 3+

RACE ORGANIZATION: 8+

CROWDS: 1-

RACE DATA

Overall Ranking:	105
Quickness Ranking:	102
Contact:	**Randy Step**
	Running Fit
	123 E. Liberty
	Ann Arbor, MI 48104
	(734) 769-5016
Date:	**April 25, 1999; April 23, 2000**
Start Time:	**8:00 a.m.**
Time Course Closes:	**2:00 p.m.**
Number of Finishers:	**160 in 1998**
Course:	**Loop**
Certification:	**None**
Course Records:	**Male: (open) 2:58:45; (masters) 3:03:21**
	Female: (open) 3:40:30; (masters) 3:51:00
Elite Athlete Programs:	**No**
Cost:	**$15/20**
Age groups/Divisions:	**≤19, 20-24, 25-29, 30-34, 35-39, 40-44, 45-49,**
	50-54, 55-59, 60-64, 65-69, 70+
Walkers:	**No**
Requirements:	**None**
Temperature:	**50° - 60°**
Aid/Splits:	**10 / none**

HIGHLIGHTS   Up in Michigan there is a trail marathon run among the thin, bare trees, through swamps, and over rocky trails. Affectionately called The Beast, the Potawatomi Trail has claimed more than a few runners. The race director's motto is "No Wimps" because he doesn't want to hear any whining about skinned knees, bruised shins, and muddy countenances. Expect them. Despite the seemingly harsh attitude (meant in jest), the warm campfires at the aid stations and the camaraderie among the runners mark the true spirit of the race.

COURSE DESCRIPTION   Characterized by constant hills, muddy trails, and elevations ranging from 300 feet to 1,200 feet, Michigan Trail's double loop course begins along Silver Lake in the Pinckney Recreation Area just 20 miles north of Ann Arbor, Michigan. Quickly funneling onto the narrow, rocky and hilly Potawatomi Trail, runners huff and puff past dense woods, through occasional swamplands, and over several bridges. Sixteen lakes, fields of wildflowers, and budding trees help runners cope with the unrelenting hills. Race organizers ring a bell signaling the last lap—if you're doing the full marathon, the bell tolls for you.

CROWD/RUNNER SUPPORT Five aid stations dot the loop providing almost everything you may require: water, electrolyte replacement drink, GU, bananas, cookies, petroleum jelly, first aid (always a few falls) and cozy campfires. Usually in full party mode, aid station volunteers provide the bulk of your external encouragement along the course. At the halfway point and the finish, runners' families are often on hand picnicking along Silver Lake.

RACE LOGISTICS In keeping with the spirit of the race, you must find your own way to the start. Runners considering the race are clearly resourceful enough to handle this detail. The roving time limit requires you to maintain at least a 6-hour pace at each of the aid stations, or you will be forced to withdraw from the race.

ACTIVITIES Register or pick up your packet at Running Fit, 123 E. Liberty, Ann Arbor, on Saturday from 10:00 a.m. to 4:00 p.m. You may also take care of this on race morning near the start from 7:00 a.m. to 7:50 a.m. One of the race highlights is the legendary Saturday evening race meeting and campfire held at 7:30 p.m. at Crooked Lake Campsite on Silver Hill Road. Hear lies and stories about the race at this irreverent gathering, which also features storytelling and trivia contests. The raging bonfire should encourage you to new heights of exaggeration. Campers at Crooked Lake can enjoy the pizza loading party delivered to your campsite. Perhaps the most popular post-race activity involves a visit to the chiropractor.

AWARDS The entry fee does not include a T-shirt. If you would like a shirt, you must pay an extra $8 to $25 depending on the type of shirt desired. Marathon finishers receive commemorative awards, as do the top five runners in each age group. Men under 3:00 and women under 3:30 receive a $100 gift certificate.

ACCOMMODATIONS The official accommodation is the Crooked Lake Campground in the Pinckney Recreation Area. If you prefer a roof, try the Ramada Inn in Howell (517-546-6800).

RELATED EVENTS/RACES Runners who prefer a single scoop of mud can enter the half marathon, which is one loop of the course. Race weekend begins Saturday with a 5-Mile Trail Run that includes a patch near the start worse than any terrain on the marathon route.

AREA ATTRACTIONS Many of the participants enjoy a weekend of camping built around the marathon. If that seems just a bit too rustic for your tastes, head to Ann Arbor, the Berkeley of the Midwest. Home to the huge University of Michigan, Ann Arbor is an eclectic college town filled with restaurants, bars, and crunchy people.

SHIPROCK MARATHON

OVERALL: 78.5

COURSE BEAUTY: 8+

COURSE DIFFICULTY: 6+

APPROPRIATENESS FOR FIRST-TIMERS: 6

ORGANIZATION: 8+

CROWDS: 2+

RACE DATA

Overall Ranking: 93
Quickness Ranking: 94
Contact: Charlene Sanders/Santiago Zieu
Shiprock Marathon
P.O. Box 1676
Farmington, NM 87499-1676
Tel. (505) 326-6634
Fax (505) 598-8237
E-mail: casa04@Sprynet.com

Date: May 1, 1999; May 6, 2000
Start Time: 7:30 a.m.
Time Course Closes: No time limit
Number of Finishers: 131 in 1998
Course: Point to point
Certification: USATF
Course Records: Male: (open) 2:20:50
Female: (open) 2:52:58
Elite Athlete Programs: No
Cost: $25/30
Age groups/Divisions: 15-29, 30-39, 40-49, 50+ (W), 50-59, 60+ (M)
Walkers: No
Requirements: None
Temperature: 42°-75°
Aid/Splits: 13 / none

HIGHLIGHTS The Shiprock Marathon has a strong Native American feel to it, and for good reason since the race runs through a Navajo Reservation. Tse Bit Ai (the rock with wings) towers 1,700 feet above the surrounding desert plain and is visible during most of the race. This huge volcanic rock was formed in Pliocene times (over 3 million years ago), and is sacred to the Navajo who believe that it is the great bird that brought them from the north to the desert (hence the name "Shiprock"). The Navajo influence runs from the native drumming at the race start and continues in the Native American race awards. In between the start and collecting any potential prizes, runners complete a challenging course with very few flat sections. Although the route drops 1,000 feet from start to finish, there are plenty of hills to test your legs. Hopefully your training carries you through since it looks like the transportation days of the Shiprock are over.

COURSE DESCRIPTION The Shiprock Marathon starts about 2 miles east of Red Rock Trading Post on Red Rock Highway (approximate elevation of 6,000 feet). The very scenic start venue includes views of red rock hills, tableaus, and high desert. From the start, runners face a slight upgrade, with a steeper pitch as they approach the turnaround at mile 1. They then proceed back to the start where they do a second about face and retrace their steps (essentially completing mile 1 three times). At mile 3, the route heads along a curving downhill—fairly steep for .75 mile—with beautiful rock formations to the left. By 4.8 miles, runners climb a good, quarter-mile hill through the desert of the Navajo reservation. With the town of Shiprock and snow-covered mountains to the left, runners continue a slight climb to mile 6, going gently down between miles 6 and 6.5. As you check out the spine of rocks formation leading to the head of the Shiprock, enjoy just about the only flat section of the race (mile 6.5 to 7.3). A slight incline (mile 7.3 to 7.6) precedes a gradual descent from mile 7.6 to mile 9.5. The route then rises for 2 miles before falling for 1 mile as it passes the spine of rocks at mile 12.5. A tough 1-mile climb—marked by several plateaus to the right—is followed by a nice 1.5-mile downhill. At mile 15, runners must climb for a half mile before going back down again until mile 17 where another tough rise awaits (miles 17 to 18.3). An easy downhill deposits you at Highway 666 (mile 20), where you now begin the journey to Shiprock. While mostly downhill, Highway 666 does contain some rolling hills between miles 23.5 and 24.5. The race finishes at the City Market shopping center.

CROWD/RUNNER SUPPORT The race kicks off to the beat of Navajo drummers. From there, most of the crowd support comes from friends and family of the runners. The aid stations—with water, sport drink, and sponges—occur every 2.0 miles, and then every mile after mile 20.

RACE LOGISTICS You need to drive to the finish area at City Market shopping center in Shiprock, about a forty minute drive from Farmington. From there, buses transport you to the start line.

ACTIVITIES Early race packet pickup takes place at the host hotel on Friday evening or you can pick up your race number at the starting line from 6:15 a.m. to 6:45 a.m. After the challenging marathon, browse the Native American Arts and Crafts Fair in the finish area.

AWARDS All entrants receive a T-shirt designed by a local Navajo artist; finishers receive medals. The top 3 in each age group and the overall winners receive Native American pottery. All runners receive race results in the mail.

ACCOMMODATIONS The race has not determined the host hotel for future races. Hotels in the Farmington area include: Best Western, 700 Scott Avenue (tel. 505-327-5221; fax 505-327-1565); Holiday Inn, 600 E. Broadway (tel. 505-327-9811; fax 505-325-2288); La Quinta, 675 Scott Avenue (tel. 505-327-4706; fax 505-325-6583); and Ramada Inn, 601 W. Broadway (tel. 505 325-1191; fax 505-325-1223).

RELATED EVENTS/RACES A five-person marathon relay runs in conjunction with the marathon, with one leg of 6.2 miles and 4 legs of 5 miles. All teams must have at least one female. Walkers can participate in the half marathon race walk or fun walk.

AREA ATTRACTIONS The Shiprock area is a good place to delve into Native American culture. Visit the sites of the Navajo Reservation, including Canyon de Chelly and Monument Valley, and trading posts for a taste of native culture. You may also want to consider Mesa Verde National Park and Chaco Canyon National Park. Golfers could hit some shots at the Piñon Hills Golf Course in Farmington, one of the country's top-rated public courses.

WHISKEY ROW MARATHON

OVERALL: 81.2

COURSE BEAUTY: 9+

COURSE DIFFICULTY: 9 (SEE APPENDIX)

APPROPRIATENESS FOR FIRST-TIMERS: 2

ORGANIZATION: 8+

CROWDS: 1-

RACE DATA

Overall Ranking:	77
Quickness Ranking:	106
Contact:	Jen Klement
	Prescott YMCA
	750 Whipple Street
	Prescott, AZ 86301
	Tel. (520) 445-7221
	Fax (520) 445-5135
Date:	May 1, 1999; May 6, 2000
Start Time:	6:00 a.m. (5:00 a.m. early start)
Time Course Closes:	Noon
Number of Finishers:	183 in 1998
Course:	Out and back
Certification:	None
Course Records:	Unknown
Elite Athlete Programs:	No
Cost:	$17/20
Age groups/Divisions:	≤19, 20-24, 25-29, 30-34, 35-39, 40-44, 45-49, 50-54, 55-59, 60-64, 65-69, 70+
Walkers:	No
Requirements:	None
Temperature:	60°-80°
Aid/Splits:	15 / none

HIGHLIGHTS   In the late 1800s, booze poured freely down Prescott, Arizona's Montezuma Street, which came to be known as Whiskey Row. Now in the late 1900s, Montezuma Street hosts a slightly more healthy activity, the Whiskey Row Marathon and its associated half marathon, 10K, and 2 Mile Fun Run/Walk. At the end of the longer races, however, you'll yearn for the good ol' days when you could drown your pain with a rocks glass of stiff whiskey in the neighboring saloons. And you will be hurting after running up and down 3,000 or so feet in the thin mile-high air, which gets even thinner as you climb to about 6,900 feet in the first seven miles. The first and last four miles run along open, paved roads, while the remainder of the race cuts through the Ponderosa pine-covered Prescott National Forest on dirt roads. While shady and beautiful, the course can lose its rustic appeal when a caravan of tourist buses clank past you in a cloud of dust. Makes you again wish for the old days when Whiskey Row was indeed whiskey row.

COURSE DESCRIPTION   The entire Whiskey Row Marathon course from downtown Prescott to the base of Thumb Butte and back is open to traffic. Runners stay on the shoulder during the paved first and last four miles of the race. While light in the morning, the traffic picks up dramatically by the time you return for the final four miles. Runners must continue to watch out for cars, trucks and buses on the dirt Forest Service roads (miles 4 to 22). The first 8 miles are essentially uphill (about 1,600 feet net climb), while miles 8 to the turnaround at 13 go steadily downhill (net loss of about 1,300 feet). Then, of course, miles 13 to 18 head up, while the final 8 miles run largely down.

The out-and-back course begins at an elevation of 5,280 feet next to Courthouse Plaza on Montezuma Street. After a couple of blocks, runners leave the historic downtown and climb the first of many hills. The course heads right onto Copper Basin Road at mile 1, where a gentle downgrade past a mobile home park takes runners to a gradual climb through a residential area by mile 1.3. Following a brief stretch of level road at mile 1.9, the race continues its climbing ways, becoming fairly steep between miles 2.2 and 2.5 and miles 3.5 to 4.2. At mile 4, the course surface changes from asphalt to dirt Forest Service roads through the lengthy shade of the Ponderosa pines. Runners enjoy a short downgrade from mile 4.2 to 4.4, then it's back to reality as the road climbs steeply to mile 5. After rolling generally uphill, the course contains another challenging climb from mile 5.6 to the half-marathon turnaround at mile 6.5. Another tough hill occurs right after mile 6.5, preceding the right turn at 7 miles. Rolling for a half mile, the course goes back up near 7.5 miles leading to the race's most beautiful spot, a stunning vista overlooking the valley at 7.9 miles (about 6,900 feet). Now out of the thick trees, runners can take in the view for the next half mile as they begin the steady descent of the mountain. Short pines pop up near mile 8.5, soon becoming taller and more shady. A short upgrade meets you at mile 9.2, quickly giving way to more nice downhill (with short breaks at miles 10, 11.4, 12.1, 12.3, and 12.7). The course turns right at the intersection near 11.5, where the road improves until the turnaround near mile 13 (about 5,600 feet).

CROWD/RUNNER SUPPORT   A small legion of folks gathers at Courthouse Plaza for the start and finish, otherwise it's just you, your fellow runners, and some cars and tourist buses. The small aid stations hand out water and sports drink about every 2 miles.

RACE LOGISTICS   If you stay in downtown Prescott, you can easily walk to the start. Otherwise, it is easy to find parking within a few blocks of Courthouse Plaza. While the race will store your warmups while you run, they prefer that you take care of them yourself.

ACTIVITIES   Pick up your race number or register at the race headquarters, the historic Hotel St. Michael, on Friday 3:00 p.m. to 8:00 p.m., or on race morning from 5:00 a.m. to 7:15 a.m. (for the later races). The hotel is located adjacent to Courthouse Plaza on the corner of Gurley and Montezuma Streets. On Friday evening, the hotel hosts an all-you-can-eat pasta bar ($10) from 5:30 p.m. to 8:00 p.m. The cost is about $10. The awards ceremony takes place near the Courthouse steps adjacent to the finish line (or in the Hotel St. Michael if bad weather). Rejuvenate your thrashed legs with a post-race massage in Courthouse Plaza.

AWARDS   Each entrant receives a T-shirt and access to the YMCA facilities during race weekend. Each marathon finisher receives a small medal, as do the top three runners in each age group.

ACCOMMODATIONS   For convenience and charm, it's hard to beat the race headquarters, Hotel St. Michael, 205 West Gurley Street (800-678-3757). Another great choice is the historic Hassayampa Inn two blocks away (800-322-1927). The Best Western Prescottonian also usually offers discount rates to runners (520-445-3096), although you must book at least 30 days in advance for the best rates.

RELATED EVENTS/RACES   Runners can test their fitness in the very grueling half marathon, which completes the first and last 6.5 miles of the full marathon course. The half marathon climbs about 1,700 feet, including some very steep sections. The 10K turns around after 3 miles, missing the most difficult climbs. Finally, the fitness-minded can participate in the 2 Mile Fun Run/Walk.

AREA ATTRACTIONS   After exploring Prescott's historic downtown, head to the red rocks of Sedona a short drive away. There is great hiking all around the area, including near hip Flagstaff. And, of course, the Grand Canyon gapes within a two-and-a-half hour drive from Prescott.

AVENUE OF THE GIANTS MARATHON

OVERALL: 87.6

COURSE BEAUTY: 10

COURSE DIFFICULTY: 2 (SEE APPENDIX)

APPROPRIATENESS FOR FIRST TIMERS: 8+

RACE ORGANIZATION: 9-

CROWDS: 1-

RACE DATA

Overall Ranking: 32

Quickness Ranking: 12

Contact: Avenue of the Giants Marathon
281 Hidden Valley Road
Bayside, CA 95524
(707) 443-1226
E-mail: avenue@humboldt1.com
http://www.humboldt1.com/~avenue

Date: May 2, 1999; May 7, 2000

Start Time: 9:00 a.m.

Time Course Closes: No time limit

Number of Finishers: 500 in 1998

Course: Two separate out and backs

Certification: USATF

Course Records: Male: (open) 2:17:43
Female: (open) 2:45:40

Elite Athlete Programs: No

Cost: $55/60/65

Age groups/Divisions: ≤14, 15-19, 20-24, 25-29, 30-34, 35-39, 40-44, 45-49, 50-54, 55-59, 60-64, 65-69, 70-74, 75-79, 80+

Walkers: Yes

Requirements: None

Temperature: 45° - 70°

Aid/Splits: 9 / miles 1, 5, 15 & 20

HIGHLIGHTS Few marathons match the natural beauty contained in northwestern California's Avenue of the Giants Marathon. Staged in Humboldt Redwoods State Park, Avenue's gently undulating route weaves along the South Eel River Valley through a canopy of prehistoric Giant Redwoods that in some places barely allows enough sunlight to nourish the luscious ferns and wild iris growing below. In its heyday 20 years ago, Avenue reigned as one of California's most popular marathons filling its 2,000 runner limit in days. While participation has waned recently due to other excellent races coming along, Avenue remains a quality event through one of earth's most remarkable environments.

COURSE DESCRIPTION Avenue of the Giants runs on the same V-shaped course as autumn's Humboldt Redwoods Marathon, except Avenue completes the Bull Creek leg first and the Avenue of the Giants leg second, while Humboldt does the reverse. See Humboldt Redwoods Marathon on page 220 for more detail.

CROWD/RUNNER SUPPORT If your performance hinges on the support of boisterous spectators, the almost eerie quiet of Avenue may not be for you. Your greatest support, in addition to the aid station volunteers every 2.5 to 3 miles, comes from the "ambassadors from another time," as John Steinbeck referred to the mammoth redwoods. These goodwill ambassadors provide a protective canopy for most of the route, effectively insulating you from wind and direct sunlight.

RACE LOGISTICS Unless camping nearby, you'll probably need to drive to the start since lodging is scarce in the immediate vicinity. If you are traveling north on Hwy. 101, take the Weott or Honeydew exit, while southbound travelers should take the second Redcrest exit. The race's staging area lies on the north side of the Dyerville Bridge and overlooks the convergence of the south and main forks of the Eel River. Parking is located on the Eel River flats adjacent to the staging area. You can avoid the congestion by arriving early.

ACTIVITIES Containing none of the pomp and circumstance that you find at many other marathons, Avenue's principal attraction is its spectacular course. The race staging site, north of the Dyerville Bridge, serves as the race registration location on Saturday from 2:00 p.m. to 5:00 p.m. Local George Crandell presents an informative slide show/talk about the area starting at 4:30 p.m. at Humboldt Redwoods State Park. Avenue allows race-day registration from 7:30 a.m. to 9:00 a.m. An all-you-can-eat pasta dinner gets going at 5:00 p.m. at Weott Veterans Hall. After the race, enjoy refreshments while waiting for the awards ceremony at 1:00 p.m.

AWARDS All participants receive race T-shirts, and finishers receive medals and certificates. Overall and age-group winners receive framed renditions of the T-shirt graphic—usually an animal depicted in its forest habitat. A results booklet is mailed to each participant a few months following the event.

ACCOMMODATIONS Avenue does not have an official race hotel, but several hotels exist in nearby small towns. In Weott (about 2 miles away), try the Sequoia Motel, 151 Weott Heights Road (707-946-2276). Possibilities in Myers Flat (8 miles away) include: Log Chapel Inn, Avenue of the Giants (707-943-3315); and Myers Flat Country Inn, Avenue of the Giants (707-943-3259). Redcrest (4 miles away) houses the Redcrest Motor Inn on the Avenue of the Giants (707-943-4208); and Garberville (25 miles away) offers the Benbow Inn, 445 Lake Benbow Drive (707-923-2124); and Motel Garberville, 948 Redwood Drive (707-923-2422). Campgrounds dot the area; campsite assignments are made at Burlington Campground near Humboldt Redwoods State Park Headquarters, 1.5 miles south of Weott on the Avenue of the Giants. For other accommodations, see the entry for Humboldt Redwoods Marathon on page 221.

RELATED EVENTS/RACES You don't have to be a marathoner to enjoy a gorgeous run through the redwoods. Avenue offers a related 10K which starts at 9:10 a.m. heading south on an out-and-back course along the redwood-lined Avenue of the Giants.

AREA ATTRACTIONS Although your kids will go nuts over some of the touristy attractions like the Drive-thru Tree near Leggett, the best way to appreciate the majestic redwoods involves escaping to the less crowded trails. Rockefeller Forest (which you pass in the first half of the marathon) contains a grove with the largest redwoods in the world. If you have some time, obtain a hiking guide and explore the dramatic sea cliffs and rugged wilderness along the nearby Lost Coast, so named because no coastal highway exists along its 31 miles. (For other options, see Humboldt Redwoods Marathon.)

CLEVELAND MARATHON

OVERALL: 83.9

COURSE BEAUTY: 8-

COURSE DIFFICULTY: 2+

APPROPRIATENESS FOR FIRST TIMERS: 9-

RACE ORGANIZATION: 9+

CROWDS: 5+

RACE DATA

Overall Ranking: 60
Quickness Ranking: 14
Contact: CVS-Cleveland Marathon
29525 Chagrin Blvd., Suite 316
Pepper Pike, OH 44122
Tel. (216) 378-0141
Fax (216) 378-0143
E-mail: jackstaph@sprintmail.com

Date: May 2, 1999; May 7, 2000
Start Time: 8:00 a.m.
Time Course Closes: 1:30 p.m.
Number of Finishers: 1,360 in 1997
Course: Out and back
Certification: USATF
Course Records: Male: (open) 2:11:30; (masters) 2:19:21
Female: (open) 2:30:15; (masters) 2:49:23
Elite Athlete Programs: Yes
Cost: $25/30
Age groups/Divisions: ≤14, 15-19, 20-24, 25-29, 30-34, 35-39, 40-44, 45-49, 50-54, 55-59, 60-64, 65-69, 70+
Walkers: No
Requirements: None
Temperature: 50° - 73°
Aid/Splits: 15 / every mile

HIGHLIGHTS When the Cuyahoga River caught fire in the 1970s, Cleveland residents realized something had to be done to clean up their city. An all-out revitalization effort ensued that has transformed Cleveland from the butt of all jokes to a pleasant place to live and a vibrant tourist destination. The Cleveland Marathon takes runners past many of the city's new showpieces such as Jacobs Field and The Flats, all the while surrounding runners with expert race organization. Cleveland offers 15 aid stations, pre- and post-race massages, and one of the richest prize purses in North America. It also offers a flat course, which means Cleveland should appeal to those runners seeking good times.

COURSE DESCRIPTION The Cleveland Marathon's out-and-back course begins at the Cleveland State University campus at E. 18th and Euclid Avenue, first making a loop to the northeast, returning downtown, and then heading west paralleling the shore of Lake Erie. About six blocks into the race, on Euclid Avenue, runners pass Playhouse Square, the second largest theater district in the United States. After rounding the corner toward Superior Avenue, runners pass Public Square (mile .75), site of the modern BP America Building, Soldiers & Sailors Monument, and the U.S. Courthouse. Just beyond lie the Cleveland Public Library and the Federal Reserve Bank. Runners turn left on E. 45th and then left on St. Claire Avenue (mile 3) to begin the trek back to the heart of downtown. At mile 4.75 near the Galleria, crane your neck to the north up E. 9th Street to catch a glimpse of The Rock 'n' Roll Hall of Fame and the Great Lakes Science Museum. You hit the other side of Public Square near mile 5, going left on Ontario with the distinctive spires of the Terminal Tower (mile 5.25) and the Landmark Tower (mile 5.4) coming into view. At mile 5.5, the course goes by Jacobs Field, home of the Cleveland Indians, and the Cavaliers' Gund Arena. Runners cross the Hope Memorial Bridge, an early 1900s span overlooking the Cuyahoga River and the industrial flats, at mile 6 and enter the West Side Market (mile 6.9), a beautiful farmers market with Old World charm. By mile 8 on Detroit Avenue, the course turns residential with some views of Lake Erie. Lakewood, an eclectic middle-class neighborhood, lies near mile 10, and gracious Rocky River near 14. Runners turn around at mile 15.5, retracing their steps on Lake and Detroit Avenues (miles 15.5 to 24). As you return downtown via the Veterans Memorial Bridge, look down at The Flats entertainment area (mile 24.25) bordering the Cuyahoga River. Once over the bridge's hump, you have practically a straight shot for the final 1.2 miles through the city to the finish at Cleveland State University.

CROWD/RUNNER SUPPORT The largest crowds gather downtown and in the westside neighborhoods of Lakewood and Rocky River. One happy consequence of Cleveland's former status as a constant punch line is that its residents go out of their way to project a positive image of their city to guests. Many residents hold marathon parties, where friends and neighbors congregate to spur on the runners and celebrate their own good judgment for not entering the race. While many a church delegation has forced a marathon to change its starting time to accommodate its flock, one Cleveland church actually changed its hours so that members could participate as volunteers! Including the church delegation, Cleveland's plentiful volunteers man the 15 aid stations well stocked with water, electrolyte replacement drink, sponges, petroleum jelly, and bandages.

RACE LOGISTICS Several downtown hotels are within walking distance of the start. Runners staying at other hotels will have to drive; parking is available near the start and in CSU lots. The race maintains a secured area for your sweats in the gymnasium at the CSU Physical Education Building, 2451 Euclid Avenue.

ACTIVITIES Stop by the CSU Physical Education Building for race packet pick-up, late registration, and the runners expo. Hours are Friday, noon to 8:00 p.m., Saturday 10:00 a.m. to 6:00 p.m., and race day at 6:30 a.m. to 8:00 a.m. Work out your pre-race jitters with a free massage. To supply your carbo-load needs, the race coordinates Restaurants for Runners, where a number of area restaurants offer special deals to marathon participants. After the race, shower in the CSU gym, and then replenish those glycogen stores with the post-race food and beverages.

AWARDS Every marathon entrant bags a T-shirt and results booklet. If you make it through the 26.2 miles under the cut-off, you also receive a custom medallion, personalized certificate, and results postcard (within two days). The top three finishers in each age group receive awards, and the fastest overall and masters runners compete for approximately $115,000 in prize money.

ELITE RUNNERS INFORMATION Cleveland does recruit elite runners, men under 2:13 (sometimes under 2:15) and women under 2:40. Depending on your resume, you could be offered travel, lodging, expenses, and entry. Regardless, you will have a shot at the $115,000 prize purse. The top seven overall rake in $15,000, $10,000, $7,500, $5,000, $3,000, $2,000, and $1,000, respectively (plus $10,000 for a course record). The first Ohioan receives $1,000. The first three masters runners earn $1,000, $750, and $500, respectively, and the top Ohioan masters runner receives $250. Note that you may not win two awards; simply take the highest amount.

ACCOMMODATIONS Remember to book your hotel early to get the special rates because many out-of-towners come for the large CVS Cleveland 10K race. The Wyndham Cleveland Hotel at Playhouse Square, 1260 Euclid Avenue, 2 blocks from the start (800-WYND-HAM), serves as the official host hotel. Other downtown hotels with special deals for Cleveland runners include: Comfort Inn Downtown, 1800 Euclid Avenue, 1 block from the start (800-221-2222); Holiday Inn Lakeside City Center, 1111 Lakeside Avenue, 1 mile from the start (216-241-5100); Omni International Hotel, 2065 E. 96th Street, 3 miles from the start (800-THE OMNI); Radisson Plaza Suite Hotel Cleveland, 1701 E. 12th Street, .4 miles from the start (800-333-3333); Ritz-Carlton Hotel Cleveland, 1515 W. Third Street, .75 miles from the start (800-241-3333); Sheraton Cleveland City Centre Hotel, 777 St. Clair Avenue, 2 miles from the start (800-321-1090); and the Marriott Society Center, about .75 miles from the race start, 127 Public Square (800-228-9290).

RELATED EVENTS/RACES Gobs of runners enter the fast CVS Cleveland 10K. Run mostly in downtown Cleveland, the 10K attracts top runners from around the world, and about 5,700 others. In the 1996 race, Joseph Kimani of Kenya set a road 10K World Record (27:20), which fell soon thereafter.

AREA ATTRACTIONS Music fans should take note of the Rock 'n' Roll Hall of Fame, 1 T Plaza. The respected Cleveland Museum of Art, 11150 East Blvd., also may catch your interest. If not, watch the Indians play in awesome Jacobs Field, or catch the Cavaliers at Gund Arena. For nighttime entertainment, head to The Flats, the restored warehouse district on the banks of the Cuyahoga River now bursting with nightclubs, bars, restaurants, and shops.

LINCOLN MARATHON

OVERALL: 80.3

COURSE BEAUTY: 7+

COURSE DIFFICULTY: 4 (SEE APPENDIX)

APPROPRIATENESS FOR FIRST TIMERS: 7

RACE ORGANIZATION: 10-

CROWDS: 3+

RACE DATA

Overall Ranking: **85**

Quickness Ranking: **53**

Contact: **Nancy Sutton**
Lincoln/All Sport Marathon
882 N. Lakeshore Drive
Lincoln, NE 68528
(402) 435-3504
http://www.lincolnrun.org

Date: **May 2, 1999; May 7, 2000**

Start Time: **7:00 a.m.**

Time Course Closes: **12:00 p.m.**

Number of Finishers: **988 in 1998**

Course: **Out and back with a loop**

Certification: **USATF**

Course Records: **Male: (open) 2:20:09; (masters) 2:29:11**
Female: (open) 2:42:45; (masters) 2:56:58

Elite Athlete Programs: **No**

Cost: **$25/30/40**

Age groups/Divisions: **12-19, 20-24, 25-29, 30-34, 35-39, 40-44, 45-49,**
50-54, 55-59, 60-64, 65-69, 70-74, 75-79, 80+

Walkers: **No**

Requirements: **None**

Temperature: **45° - 60°**

Aid/Splits: **12 / every mile, 10K & halfway**

HIGHLIGHTS Although possessing the classic runner build, President Abraham Lincoln probably wasn't the slave to mileage like President Clinton. Nonetheless, his memory enjoys an interesting connection with the world of marathons. The Marine Corps Marathon runs past the Lincoln Memorial. Maryland's Northern Central Trail Marathon travels along a former railroad bed traced by the train that carried "Honest Abe's" body back to Illinois after his assassination. And, Nebraska's Lincoln Marathon is held in the city bearing his name. One score and zero years ago, the Lincoln Marathon offered runners a not-so-glorious tour of area cornfields. Since the recent renovation of the city's downtown, the race offers runners more than a run through "amber waves of grain." Instead, the route takes runners on a citywide tour passing many area landmarks including the breathtaking Capitol Building—the "Tower of the Plains." As a testament to Lincoln's stellar race organization, the Army National Guard has chosen Lincoln, fourteen straight years, as its marathon trials to decide its World Military Games marathon team.

COURSE DESCRIPTION Runners assemble in front of Memorial Stadium, home of the National Champion Cornhusker football team, on the University of Nebraska campus. The National Guard Band plays marching music to rouse the runners for a peak performance. After two blocks, the race turns south on 16th Street for 2 miles. At the 1-mile mark, runners see the Nebraska State Capitol Building, a jewel among state capitols. Turning left on South Street, runners follow historic Lincoln Sheridan Blvd. for 2 miles past many of the finest old homes in the city, climbing about 100 feet between miles 2 and 3. At the 5-mile mark, runners turn at 48th and Calvert, the highest point on the course. Traveling through College View, a community of small shops and student hangouts, runners are greeted by the students of Union College. After a gradual downhill to 10K, runners veer onto a paved bike path, following it for 2.5 miles. At 20th Street, runners exit the trail making their way north to the Country Club of Lincoln. This uphill stretch past the Country Club may be one of the toughest in the first half of the race. Coming down the other side of the hill, runners enter Van Dorn Park, a pleasant neighborhood of tree-lined streets. Proceeding down 10th Street, the City of Lincoln approaches as runners pass the County-City Building and the "Big Red N" over the football stadium looms ahead. Half marathoners peel away, finishing on Ed Weir Track, while marathoners circle the baseball stadium, cruise through the University campus, and return to 16th Street heading toward the Capitol building. At the Capitol, runners turn onto flat Capitol Parkway (which becomes Normal Blvd.) as they head toward Holmes Lake Park. The beautiful lily pads of the Sunken Gardens lie at 27th and Capitol Parkway. Winding its way past the Children's Zoo, the course then proceeds along the Ager Memorial Jr. Golf Course and Antelope Park. At about 17.5 miles, runners return to a bike path for a half mile and begin a 100-foot climb into Holmes Lake Park, the city's most beautiful park. Ducks and geese fill the water, and bands and giant balloons encourage runners. The climb up the dam to the park and the climb up 70th from Holmes Park to Van Dorn may be the two toughest stretches in the race. Looping around Holmes Park (19-20), the course returns down Normal Blvd./Capitol Parkway on a gradual downgrade, giving runners a chance to view their compatriots going in the opposite direction. The marathon finishes on Ed Weir Track on the UN-L campus.

CROWD/RUNNER SUPPORT Although nothing like a Nebraska Cornhusker football game, Lincoln attracts several thousand spectators along its citywide route. Most of the onlookers collect around the start/finish, where they can see the half marathon finish and cheer the marathoners embarking on the second half of the race, and in the residential areas. Twelve aid stations throughout the course carry ice, water and electrolyte replacement in cups with lids and straws, and orange slices after halfway. Particularly noteworthy, Lincoln General Hospital operates an imaginative and uplifting aid station near mile 9. Shag wagons roam the course to scoop up pooped-out runners.

RACE LOGISTICS If you're staying at the Ramada or at a neighboring hotel, you'll experience few hassles on race day as the start/finish is a short walk away. If you cannot complete the marathon in 5 hours or less, the race offers the option of starting at 5:30 a.m.

ACTIVITIES The Runner's Expo and Packet Pickup take place on Saturday from 10:00 a.m. to 7:00 p.m. at the race headquarters in the Ramada Hotel & Convention Center, 141 N. 9th Street. All participants over 50 years old are invited to attend the Harry Crockett over-50 Club's annual luncheon held at 11:30 a.m. at Spaghetti Works, 228 N. 12th Street. Runners, their families and volunteers are invited to enjoy a free spaghetti dinner at the Pastathon from 4:00 p.m. to 7:00 p.m. at the UN-L Fieldhouse. After your marathon, relax with a massage, enjoy food and beverages, and call your friends long distance for free to brag about your accomplishment. A post-race party kicks off at 12:00 p.m. followed by the awards ceremony and door prizes at 1:30 p.m.

AWARDS Whether it's effective budget management, excellent sponsorship, or both, you get more than what you pay for at Lincoln. Each participant receives a race T-shirt, finisher's medal, free night-before pasta party, pre- and post-race booklet, and finisher's photograph. Every woman finisher receives a rose. Faster runners compete for modest prize money with the following breakdown: $500-first, $250-second, $125-third, $100-fourth, $75-fifth, and $50-sixth through tenth. Masters prize money extends two deep, $125 and $75, respectively. Course record bonuses, $500 for open and $125 for masters, are also offered. Plaques are presented to the first three to eight men and women in each age division, depending on the number of runners. Runners breaking certain age-graded time standards receive an athletic bag.

ACCOMMODATIONS The Ramada Hotel, 141 N. 9th Street (402-475-4011), serves as the race headquarters offering special marathon rates. Other hotels featuring special marathon rates include: Cornhusker Hotel, 333 S. 13th Street (800-793-7474); Days Inn, 2920 NW 12th Street (402-475-3616); Motel 6, 3001 NW 12th Street (402-475-3211); and Town House Mini-Suite, 18th Street (402-475-3000).

RELATED EVENTS/RACES Race weekend gets going with the KFRX Mayor's Children Run on Saturday at 8:30 a.m. Kids in eighth grade or younger participate in a one-mile run around the Nebraska State Capitol. Additionally, Lincoln offers a half marathon which runs on the first half of the marathon course and starts along with the longer race.

AREA ATTRACTIONS After running by the architectural wonder in the marathon, you'll likely want to see the interior of Lincoln's impressive State Capitol Building. Free tours are available every hour. Afterward, roam the botanical gardens in Antelope Park or visit the Sunken Gardens at 27th and D Streets.

PITTSBURGH MARATHON

OVERALL: 88.6

COURSE BEAUTY: 8-

COURSE DIFFICULTY: 3 (SEE APPENDIX)

APPROPRIATENESS FOR FIRST TIMERS: 9

RACE ORGANIZATION: 10-

CROWDS: 8

RACE DATA

Overall Ranking:	27
Quickness Ranking:	29
Contact:	Larry Grollman
	City of Pittsburgh Marathon, Inc.
	200 Lothrop Street
	Pittsburgh, PA 15213-2582
	Tel. (412) 647-7866
	Fax (412) 647-7320
	http://www.upmc.edu/pghmarathon
Date:	May 2, 1999; 2000 date TBA
Start Time:	8:30 a.m.
Time Course Closes:	2:30 p.m.
Number of Finishers:	1,830 in 1998
Course:	Near loop
Certification:	USATF
Course Records:	Male: (open) 2:12:02; (masters) 2:20:30
	Female: (open) 2:36:12; (masters) 2:54:11
Elite Athlete Programs:	Yes
Cost:	$29/39
Age groups/Divisions:	≤19, 20-24, 25-29, 30-34, 35-39, 40-44, 45-49,
	50-54, 55-59, 60-64, 65-69, 70+
Walkers:	No
Requirements:	None
Temperature:	50° - 63°
Aid/Splits:	20 / every mile

HIGHLIGHTS Once referred to as "hell with the lid off" because its billowy smokestacks produced a perpetual dusk, Pittsburgh bears little resemblance to that description today, and the City of Pittsburgh Marathon showcases much of the city to prove it. Starting in shiny downtown with its numerous architectural landmarks, the race crosses the Allegheny, Monongahela, and Ohio Rivers before the striking finish at the three rivers' nexus. On the way, runners encounter Pittsburgh's diversity, from the Golden Triangle, to working-class Lawrenceville, to well-to-do Shadyside. Community support of the marathon has grown tremendously, so that now, with marathon organizers' assistance, each community holds a unique, marathon-day festival to commemorate the race and support the runners. The Pittsburgh Marathon also appeals to runners looking to improve their time, and the race will use the ChampionChip timing system in 1999. In 1998, many of the United States' elite runners will be on hand as Pittsburgh hosts the Track and Field Men's National Marathon Championship for the second consecutive year.

RACE HISTORY   The brainchild of Larry Kuzmanko, the Pittsburgh Marathon started in 1985 with about 1,800 runners. Over the years, the primary sponsorship has changed from USX, to Giant Eagle food stores, to the current University of Pittsburgh Medical Center. In 1988, the marathon served as the U.S. Women's Olympic Marathon Trials won by Margaret Groos in 2:29:50. The City of Pittsburgh took over the event in 1990, and its mayor, Tom Murphy, regularly participates.

COURSE DESCRIPTION   The Pittsburgh Marathon's near loop course crosses the city's famous three rivers cutting through 12 distinct and diverse neighborhoods. The convenient layout places the start and finish within a half mile of each other. The race starts in front of the City-County Building in the midst of downtown's gleaming high rises. The course, completely closed to traffic, heads along Grant Street (passing the well-known USX tower), then onto Liberty Avenue for the first mile. A slight upgrade faces the runners at mile 2 as they pass through the Strip District, a historic waterfront area of fresh produce, vegetables, and seafood. Running into the working-class community of Lawrenceville, the course passes the neighborhood's tribute to WWI, the Doughboy statue, before returning to the Strip District for miles 3 and 4. The runners cross the Allegheny River by way of the 16th Street Bridge, passing the fabled Heinz Factory at mile 5. Upon turning off the bridge, runners go through the flat North Side for miles 6 and 7, passing the famous Mexican War streets. A slight downgrade greets runners as they prepare to leave the North Side. Runners encounter a spectacular view of the Golden Triangle as they cross the Ohio River via the West End Bridge. As they turn off the bridge, runners have a slight downgrade for .25 miles until mile 8 on Carson Street. On this street, runners go through Pittsburgh's South Side for miles 8 to 11, passing historic Station Square at mile 9. They encounter boisterous spectators at the array of antique shops, bookstores, coffee houses, neighborhood bars, and restaurants along Carson Street between miles 10 and 11. Leaving the South Side, runners cross the last of the city's three rivers, the Monongahela, by way of the Birmingham Bridge. At the end of the bridge, runners face their one significant hill, climbing about 200 feet over .75 miles along Forbes Avenue leading to Oakland. At the top of the climb, they find a flat stretch for miles 12 to 13 as they pass the University of Pittsburgh Medical Center and the university. The runners travel on relatively flat Fifth Avenue entering unique Shadyside with its huge Victorian mansions, art galleries, and upscale restaurants and shops. The course passes by Mellon Park turning onto Penn Avenue. Relatively flat from miles 15 to 19, the course travels through the neighborhoods of Point Breeze, historic Homewood/Brushton, and East Liberty. Facing some slight rolling hills, runners pass through Highland Park from miles 19 to 22. At mile 22, runners receive an overwhelming greeting from the citizens of Bloomfield, who traditionally have a weekend-long series of events culminating with the race. The large, predominantly Italian, community fills the streets to encourage runners on their final stretch. The course returns to Lawrenceville and the Strip District for miles 23 to 25 with a gradual downgrade. At mile 25, runners enter the Golden Triangle via Penn Avenue, passing historic Heinz Hall and the Benedum Center. The turn onto Liberty Avenue leads to the finish at scenic Point State Park at the confluence of Pittsburgh's three rivers.

CROWD/RUNNER SUPPORT   Enjoying the warm support of the city's residents, the Pittsburgh Marathon traditionally draws between 100,000 to 200,000 spectators around the course. Prior to 1996, a few of the neighborhoods the course bisects would schedule a festival to coincide with marathon race day. Marathon organizers have since developed a matching funds program to assist all twelve communities in hosting a race-day festival to showcase their individual neighborhood and to support the runners. In another nice touch, the Pittsburgh Post-Gazette includes all race registrants in the race-day newspaper. Many spectators attend the race with the list in hand and look for the names of the approaching runners to yell their encouragement. Pittsburgh also boasts some of the top medical assistance of any race, with approximately 800 to 900 medical volunteers. Medical personnel staff all 20 aid stations.

RACE LOGISTICS The start and finish lie within a ten-minute walk of all major downtown hotels. Runners staying outside of downtown can find plenty of convenient parking in the area. Marathoners can shower at the Downtown YMCA for a $4 fee.

ACTIVITIES On Friday and Saturday of marathon weekend, a Marathon and Fitness Expo is held in conjunction with packet pick-up and late registration. The expo takes place at the PPG Wintergarden on Stanwix Street between Third and Fourth Avenue, a five-minute walk from the Westin William Penn Hotel, the headquarters hotel. Although you may retrieve your packet on race morning, there is no race-day registration. The race hosts a pasta party the evening before the marathon for about $10. After the marathon, attend the post-race party at the Westin William Penn Hotel, starting at 1:00 p.m. The awards ceremony begins at 2:00 p.m. All race registrants are eligible for the prize raffle at the post-race party, including two complimentary airline tickets to Hawaii.

AWARDS Every runner receives a marathon T-shirt, and finishers receive medallions and official results certificates (sent in mid-July). All registrants also receive souvenir program/results booklets in August. The top three runners in each age group are sent award plaques. Elite runners compete for approximately $100,000 in prize money.

ELITE RUNNERS INFORMATION The City of Pittsburgh Marathon recruits elite runners (men under 2:20 and women under 2:45). Depending on their credentials, elites are eligible for travel, lodging, expenses, and race entry. The top 10 American male finishers earn the following prize money: $20,000, $10,000, $7,000, $5,000, $4,000, $3,000, $2,500, $2,000, $1,500, and $1,000. The top five women's finishers receive $6,000, $3,000, $1,500, $1,000, and $500. The top five masters runners and the top five Pennsylvania residents earn: $1,000, $500, $250, $150, and $100. The top three Pittsburgh residents receive: $1,000, $500, and $250. For the 1998 U.S. Men's Marathon Championship, the U.S. Champion will win $100,000 if he breaks the American race record (2:12:57). If he does not break the record, he receives $20,000. The prize money structure is likely to change if Pittsburgh does not serve as the national men's championship after 1998.

ACCOMMODATIONS The Westin William Penn Hotel, 530 William Penn Place (800-228-3000), serves as the headquarters hotel ($100). The other downtown hotel that offers discounts to runners is the Ramada Plaza Suites at $85/95 (800-225-5858).

RELATED EVENTS/RACES Race weekend kicks off with the Children's Mini-Marathon held at Point State Park on the day before the marathon. Events include a 6.2 yard Diaper Derby for tots aged 1 to 2; a Tot Trot (26.2 yards) for kids 3 to 6; and a Fun Run/Walk for children 7 to 12. All children's events require pre-registration. On marathon day, the race holds a 5K Run/Walk (the only 5K in the U.S. to use the ChampionChip). Teams of four runners can run the marathon relay, starting with the full marathoners, with 8.9, 5.3, 7.7, and 4.3-mile legs. Teams can participate in one of several divisions, Corporate, Neighborhood Groups, Running Clubs, College, or High School. Team members must provide their own transportation to the relay exchange points.

AREA ATTRACTIONS While in Pittsburgh, catch a Pittsburgh Pirates baseball game at Three Rivers Stadium. Regular attractions include the view from Mount Washington up the Duquesne Incline; the Andy Warhol Museum; the Carnegie Art Museum and Natural History Collection; the hands-on Carnegie Science Center; the Children's Museum; the Pittsburgh Zoo; Station Square; and the National Aviary.

VANCOUVER INTERNATIONAL MARATHON

OVERALL: 90.8

COURSE BEAUTY: 8+

COURSE DIFFICULTY: 5- (SEE APPENDIX)

APPROPRIATENESS FOR FIRST TIMERS: 9

RACE ORGANIZATION: 9+

CROWDS: 6

RACE DATA

Overall Ranking: 18
Quickness Ranking: 66
Contact: Vancouver International Marathon Society
P.O. Box 3213
Vancouver, B.C., Canada, V6B 3X8
Tel. (604) 872-2928
Fax (604) 872-2903
E-mail: vim@istar.ca
http://www.wi.bc.ca

Date: May 2, 1999; May 7, 2000
Start Time: 7:15 a.m.
Time Course Closes: 12:15 p.m.
Number of Finishers: 2,585 in 1997
Course: Loop
Certification: B.C. Athletics & AIMS
Course Records: New course in 1998
Elite Athlete Programs: Yes
Cost: US$38/40/60/75
Age groups/Divisions: ≤19, 20-24, 25-29, 30-34, 35-39, 40-44, 45-49, 50-54, 55-59, 60-64, 65-69, 70+
Walkers: No
Requirements: None
Temperature: 44° - 65°
Aid/Splits: 13 / mile 1 & halfway

HIGHLIGHTS Spectacularly located, Vancouver seduces visitors with seafaring charm, natural beauty, and a risqué air. The Vancouver International Marathon, our highest-rated Canadian race, captures all this and more, wafting along parkland, skyline, and shoreline. A new course debuted in 1998, eliminating the big climbs up Lion's Gate Bridge and the Second Narrows Bridge and the unsightly areas in north Vancouver. Instead, the new course sticks to Vancouver proper and South Vancouver which provides a more attractive venue. Like many West Coast marathons, VIM attracts a large number of Japanese runners, lending an international complexion to the race.

COURSE DESCRIPTION Vancouver's partially closed course starts on Pacific Blvd. sandwiched between B.C. Stadium, Plaza of Nations, and General Motors Place, home of the NBA's Vancouver Grizzlies. The largely flat first 3 miles circumnavigate False Creek, traveling through mostly commercial South Vancouver, including the futuristic ball of Science World and bustling West 2nd Avenue. Runners cross the Burrard Street Bridge at 5K, rising just over 100 feet to the apex at 3.8 miles where the high-rise apartment buildings of downtown appear. The race now angles back to the start/finish, giving your entourage another chance to wish you luck. Then it's on to Chinatown, historic Gastown, and the cosmopolitan business district. With the Coast Mountains rising to the north, runners enter gorgeous Stanley Park, Vancouver's urban forest, near mile 12. Filled with fragrant cedars and the occasional sleepy raccoon, the park has several hills during the 3-mile loop through its leafy confines. The course exits onto downtown Vancouver's south side for an enjoyable flat, wide pass of beaches, parks, and ocean views. Near mile 16 you cross the Burrard Street Bridge for the second time. Now the race shifts gears, passing through West Coast neighborhoods for a 6-mile out and back of beautiful homes, funky shops, and more beaches and parks. After crossing the Burrard Street Bridge for the third and final time near mile 24, you are thankful for the nice downgrade to mile 25, and the flat final mile to the finish at B.C. Place.

CROWD/RUNNER SUPPORT Thirteen aid stations carrying water and electrolyte replacement drinks support the runners along the course. About 40,000 spectators dot the route, with the most dense concentrations at the start/finish area and Stanley Park. Runners enjoy on-course entertainment at several points during the race.

RACE LOGISTICS B.C. Place lies near 20 or more downtown hotels, so most visitors will not require transportation to the start/finish area. If you need to drive to the start, plenty of pay parking exists at B.C. Place Stadium and nearby streets. The race does not provide shuttle bus service, so plan ahead to ensure you are not scrambling on race morning.

ACTIVITIES Pick up your race packet at the City Square Shopping Centre, 12th Avenue and Cambie Street, on Friday or Saturday before the race. There is no race-day registration or packet pick-up. You can also stop by the Lifestyle and Fitness Expo. The traditional carbo-load dinner (US$10) starts at 4:00 p.m. Saturday afternoon at the Holiday Inn Downtown. After the marathon, head to the awards ceremony and post-race social.

AWARDS Each marathon finisher receives a T-shirt, medal and certificate. The top three age-group winners receive trophies. VIM offers $7,000 in prize money, and Canadian runners are eligible for travel awards.

ELITE RUNNERS INFORMATION On a case-by-case basis, VIM offers transportation, lodging, meal allowances, and/or entry fee waivers to top marathoners. Prize money goes to the top three finishers, with $2,000 for first, $1,000 for second, and $500 for third. Top Canadian and B.C. finishers may also earn awards to overseas sister events.

ACCOMMODATIONS The Holiday Inn Downtown, 1110 Howe Street (604-684-2151), serves as the headquarters hotel. The Hyatt Regency is also convenient at 655 Burrard Street (604-683-1234). Otherwise, call the Vancouver Housing Bureau (800-224-0659) for help in finding the right accommodations for your budget and taste.

RELATED EVENTS/RACES For those souls not ready to tackle the marathon, Vancouver offers a half marathon and a 5K walk. About 2,000 runners participate in the half marathon, which starts with the marathon.

AREA ATTRACTIONS Call Tourism Vancouver (604-682-2000) for information on what's going on in Vancouver around marathon time. Cosmopolitan Vancouver offers many sights and activities, including Stanley Park, Chinatown, Gastown, and Robsonstrasse for shopping.

VANCOUVER

BRITISH COLUMBIA, CANADA

First SUNDAY in MAY

MARATHON
HALF MARATHON
5 MILER

A flat, fast course surrounded by beautiful snow capped mountains, lush parklands and the waters of the Pacific Ocean.
Starts and finishes in the heart of the finest city in North America.
The people of Vancouver are awaiting to welcome you on the first Sunday in May.

1999 MARATHON ENTRY FEE: Received before		1999 HALF MARATHON ENTRY FEE: Received before	
Dec. 31/98	$ 50Cdn./$ 36US	Dec. 31/98	$ 35Cdn./$ 26US
April 1st/99	$ 60Cdn./$ 45US	April 1st/99	$ 40Cdn./$ 30US
April 24	$ 75Cdn./$ 58US	April 25	$ 40Cdn./$ 30US
At packet pick-up $ 99Cnd./$ 75US		At packet pick-up $ 60Cnd./$ 38US	

Fees shown above are for May 1999 Vancouver International Marathon.
For 2000 and beyond, contact the marathon office at one of the addresses below.

For more information contact us at:
VIM, PO Box 3213, Vancouver, BC, V6B 3X8, Canada
or phone: (604) 872-2928, fax: (604) 872-2903
email: vim@istar.ca
See us on the web at: www.wi.bc.ca

RACE OF CHAMPIONS MARATHON

OVERALL: 74.3

COURSE BEAUTY: 8

COURSE DIFFICULTY: 5-

APPROPRIATENESS FOR FIRST TIMERS: 6+

RACE ORGANIZATION: 8+

CROWDS: 1-

RACE DATA

Overall Ranking: 108
Quickness Ranking: 73
Contact: Peter Stasz
c/o Fast Feet
231 Elm Street
West Springfield, MA 01089
(413) 734-0955

Date: May 2, 1999; May 7, 2000
Start Time: 8:00 a.m.
Time Course Closes: 1:00 p.m.
Number of Finishers: 75 in 1998
Course: Loop
Certification: USATF
Course Records: Male: (open) 2:29:48
Female: (open) 3:03:00
Elite Athlete Programs: No
Cost: $15/20
Age groups/Divisions: NA
Walkers: No
Requirements: None
Temperature: 60° - 80°
Aid/Splits: 12 / mile 13.1

HIGHLIGHTS   One of the United States' most historic marathons, the Race of Champions blasted out of the blocks with two wins by Boston Marathon great John Kelley in 1963 and 1964. The race assumed notoriety in 1967 as the "Holyoke Massacre." Designated as the trials to select the U.S. Pan American Games marathon team and the U.S. National Marathon Championships, the 1:00 p.m. race featured 90° temperatures that claimed over half the field. Even with the elite group of U.S. runners, the ultimate survivor struggled in at 2:40:04. Now run on a pleasant new (since 1991) course, the ROC continues as a small, rural race through Holyoke in eastern Massachusetts. Runners with a keen sense of running's past may want to share in ROC's history.

COURSE DESCRIPTION   Starting at Mt. Tom Ski Area, the race proceeds immediately uphill for several hundred yards, then drops sharply at .5 miles down the beautiful wooded hill. At mile 1, runners cut to Whiting Reservoir which they circle 2 2/3 times on a mostly flat dirt road (about 10 miles). Climbing a moderate hill while leaving the scenic reservoir, runners detour briefly on a rough road before reaching the country homes on Southampton Street. After a moderate .33-mile rise, the course rolls downhill to the halfway point on Rock Valley Road. A short, gentle incline to 13.7 miles precedes the dirt road from 14 until 15. Turning right on residential Pomeroy Street, runners face another dirt/gravel road from mile 16 to 16.5. Beginning to circumscribe Mt. Tom, the course is mostly flat on East Street and unshaded Northampton Street. Near mile 24, the route ascends gently then becomes rather steep after turning onto the ski area access road for the last half mile.

CROWD/RUNNER SUPPORT There are no crowds to speak of in this rural race other than the volunteers at the aid stations every two miles. The stations carry water and electrolyte replacement drink.

RACE LOGISTICS You will need to drive to the start; plenty of parking exists in the ski area parking lot. After the race, rather than hobbling up the steep hill on stiff legs, take the shuttle bus the three-quarters mile back to the start.

ACTIVITIES Enjoy the post-race chicken feast at the Mt. Tom Ski Area as you swap race heroics with fellow runners and family. Other refreshments are also provided.

AWARDS The first 100 entries receive T-shirts. Overall and masters winners receive merchandise prizes.

ACCOMMODATIONS The Holiday Inn Holidome, 245 Whiting Farms Road, Holyoke (413-534-3311), serves as the headquarters hotel. Other hotels include: Susse Chalet, 1515 Northampton Street, Holyoke (413-536-1980); Mt. Tom Motor Court, Rt. 5N, Holyoke (413-534-3429); Riviera Motel, 671 Northampton Street, Holyoke (413-536-3377); and Holiday Inn Springfield, 711 Dwight Street, Springfield (413-781-0900).

AREA ATTRACTIONS The primary tourist attraction in Springfield is the Basketball Hall of Fame. Boston lies about 100 miles east of Springfield.

WILD WILD WEST MARATHON

OVERALL: 84.7

COURSE BEAUTY: 10-

COURSE DIFFICULTY: 8+ (SEE APPENDIX)

APPROPRIATENESS FOR FIRST TIMERS: 1

RACE ORGANIZATION: 9

CROWDS: 1

RACE DATA

Overall Ranking: 53
Quickness Ranking: 103
Contact: Donna Bonnefin
Lone Pine Chamber of Commerce
P. O. Box 749
Lone Pine, CA 93545
Tel. (760) 876-4444
Fax (760) 876-9205
E-mail: lpcc@qnet.com
http://www.lone-pine.com

Date: May 2, 1999; May 7, 2000
Start Time: 7:00 a.m.
Time Course Closes: 1:00 p.m.
Number of Finishers: 162 in 1998
Course: Loop
Certification: None
Course Records: Male: (open) 2:52:45
Female: (open) 3:20:42
Elite Athlete Programs: No
Cost: $30
Age groups/Divisions: ≤19, 20-29, 30-39, 40-49, 50-59, 60-69, 70+
Walkers: No
Requirements: None
Temperature: 40° - 90°
Aid/Splits: 10 / none

HIGHLIGHTS   As the United States' third oldest trail marathon behind Pikes Peak and Catalina Island, the Wild Wild West Marathon features a challenging loop starting in Lone Pine, California (220 miles east of Los Angeles) and traversing the eastern Sierra foothills. A favorite among ultra runners, the route includes several steady climbs and moderate declines at altitudes between 4,000 and 6,000 feet. Despite the hills, elevation, and typical heat (85° by high noon), the spectacular scenery may be worth the discomfort. Striking vistas, the snow-capped eastern Sierras, and the expansive Owens Valley are just a few of the sights along the way. In fact, the area should look familiar to you. This is the site for many Western movies from Roy Rogers in the 1930s to James Garner and Mel Gibson (*Maverick*) in the 1990s. The race enjoys a cult-like following as most of the 150 plus (whether looking good, bad, or ugly at the finish), return the following year.

COURSE DESCRIPTION   The loop course starts at the Tuttle Creek Campground (about 4,500 feet) and includes about 3,600 feet of up and down and a few creek crossings. The first third of the course runs mostly uphill on fairly steep jeep roads and trails contouring and climbing to the highest point at 6,600 feet at the intersection of Whitney Portal Road and Hogback Road (8.5 miles). A long, winding 6-mile descent on a wide hard-packed dirt road leads to the north end of the famed Alabama Hills, the low point of the course at 14.5 miles. Winding and rolling Movie Flat road takes runners southbound through this unique geologic formation of huge rounded oblong rocks. The final 8 miles of the race run comparatively flatter leading to the finish at Tuttle Creek Campground. Many wildflowers, including red Indian Paintbrush, lavender Lupine and Mojave Asters, and yellow Desert Dandelions, bloom along the course. Also, don't be surprised if you see bear, Tule elk, deer, bobcats, badger, raccoons, coyotes, and skunks.

CROWD / RUNNER SUPPORT Other than the finish line, there is no spectator involvement in the race. You will, however, receive course support in the form of 10 aid stations along the way. The stations stock water, sport drink, fruit, pretzels, and other snacks. Many runners carry water bottles and/or fanny packs with personal supplies. The course is controlled as much as possible but there is essentially no radio communication support.

RACE LOGISTICS Everyone provides his or her own transportation. The race start is about 5 miles from Lone Pine. The parking is a bit limited right at the start/finish area in the upper part of Tuttle Creek Campground. Otherwise there are no parking problems. About 10 to 20 percent of the field actually stay at Tuttle Creek Campground.

ACTIVITIES The Lo-Inyo Elementary School in northeast Lone Pine serves as the registration site on Saturday between 5:00 p.m. and 7:00 p.m. The school also hosts the pasta party held in conjunction with registration. For less than a fist full of dollars ($6) you can have all the tasty pasta, salad, and bread you want. A post-race picnic and award ceremony starts around 1:00 p.m. at the city park at the north end of town.

AWARDS Every runner receives a T-shirt, and finishers earn ceramic medallions. The top three age-group finishers receive mugs fashioned by a local artist.

ACCOMMODATIONS Several hotels lie within five miles of the starting area including: Best Western Frontier (800-528-1234); Portal Motel (800-531-7054); Mt. Whitney Motel (800-845-2362); and National 9 Trails Inn (800-862-7020). If you want to get a little extra sleep on race morning, you can camp for free at the start area in the Tuttle Creek Campground.

RELATED EVENTS / RACES A 10-mile run starts with the marathon, running on the first 4 miles and the last 2 miles of the marathon course. There is also a 3-mile guess-your-time race which starts 20 minutes after the marathon.

LAKE GENEVA MARATHON

OVERALL: 80.8

COURSE BEAUTY: 9

COURSE DIFFICULTY: 7-

APPROPRIATENESS FOR FIRST TIMERS: 5+

RACE ORGANIZATION: 8+

CROWDS: 1

RACE DATA

Overall Ranking: 83
Quickness Ranking: 95
Contact: Frank Dobbs
Lake Geneva Marathon
P.O. Box 1134
Lake Geneva, WI 53147
(414) 248-4323

Date: May 8, 1999; May 13, 2000 (Day before Mother's Day)
Start Time: 8:00 a.m.
Time Course Closes: 1:00 p.m.
Number of Finishers: 195 in 1998
Course: Loop
Certification: USATF
Course Records: Male: (open) 2:33:36
Female: (open) 2:56:14
Elite Athlete Programs: No
Cost: $25/30
Age groups/Divisions: ≤17, 18-24, 25-29, 30-34, 35-39, 40-44, 45-49,
50-54, 55-59, 60-69, 70+
Walkers: Yes (5:00 a.m. start)
Requirements: None
Temperature: 55° - 70°
Aid/Splits: 9 / none

HIGHLIGHTS A getaway for wealthy Chicagoans, gorgeous Lake Geneva sparkles sapphire blue like its Swiss Alps cousins. Taking advantage of this spectacular setting in southeastern Wisconsin's glaciated hills, race director Frank Dobbs holds the tough, charming Lake Geneva Marathon that has runners returning year after year. The marathon traces the lake, heads into the surrounding farm country, passes through some spectacular neighborhoods, and finishes on an ancient Indian path. The last lake in the United States to have full mail service by boat, Lake Geneva makes a wonderful destination for a relaxing weekend or week along its serene shores.

COURSE DESCRIPTION Lake Geneva's loop course, open to local traffic, starts in downtown Lake Geneva on the lakefront bridge at the sound of a stern-wheel boat whistle. The course warms you up almost immediately with a steep, 400-yard hill through Lake Geneva's residential area. By mile 1.2, runners head downhill to the lakefront for a spectacular view of Lake Geneva. Once runners reach the lake at 1.4, they face another good hill to 1.9. Rolling away from the lake, the course then heads toward the surrounding farm country (miles 4 to 14). At mile 2.8, the course starts downhill to 3.2 where it becomes flat until 3.6. Facing a slight upgrade to the 4-

mile mark, runners then encounter slight rollers until 8.5 miles. The course passes through the tiny town of Zenda near mile 7. Perhaps the fastest mile on the course occurs from mile 8.5 to 9.5, a perfectly flat stretch leading to a good climb from 9.5 to 9.8. The course returns to slightly rolling until a down and up from 14.2 to 14.5 and 14.5 to 14.7. Runners sharply descend through a residential neighborhood to the lakefront at Fontana and the finish line for 25K runners. A beautiful, inspirational view greets runners here, which is good because the most difficult and scenic part of the race lies ahead. As the course winds along the lakefront, a tough uphill occurs from mile 16 to 16.3, followed by a welcomed downhill (16.3 to 16.8) that may rest searing lungs for the second difficult climb from 16.8 to 17.1. Runners roll past the beautiful George Williams College Golf Course before the course turns residential through the Village of Williams Bay. The route passes Yerkes Observatory at mile 18.5 and soon thereafter travels along the lakeshore for a brief spell. Facing another uphill from 20 to 20.4, runners take a short jaunt along the highway from 21.6 to 23, mostly a slight incline or rolling. At mile 23.7, the course drops into a gorgeous, wooded area with pastures and palatial homes. This section includes some challenging rolling hills. After another steep downhill from 24.9 to 25.1 into another neighborhood, the course picks up an ancient Indian trail for the dash to the finish line at Library Park on the lake.

CROWD/RUNNER SUPPORT Spectator turnout for most resort community marathons is light, and Lake Geneva is no exception. The miles are marked on the pavement; bring your watch since there are no split timers.

RACE LOGISTICS There is plenty of parking near the start/finish in Lake Geneva. The loop marathon course means that transportation is not a concern. Runners completing the 25K can opt to enjoy the beautiful trip from their finish at Fontana to Lake Geneva aboard a stern-wheel boat. On windy days, however, seasick prone runners may want to stick with the school bus.

ACTIVITIES On Friday evening, you can pick up your race packet or register late at the pasta dinner at Celebration on Wells Restaurant, 422 Wells Street, Lake Geneva. You may also retrieve your packet or register early race morning in Library Park. After the race, hang out in Library Park for the Jaycees brats and beer party, and enjoy the spectacular view of Lake Geneva. Following the awards ceremony, prizes donated by area merchants are presented in a raffle drawing. You can shower at the YMCA Health Club at 203 Wells Street.

AWARDS Every marathon and 25K entrant receives a Lake Geneva sweatshirt. The top three age-group finishers take home pottery awards, and the overall winners are awarded large pieces of pottery, merchandise, and paintings.

ACCOMMODATIONS There are plenty of lodging options in Lake Geneva from luxurious resorts to more modest motels. Among the resorts are: The Abbey in Fontana (414-275-6811); The Geneva Inn, N2009 State Road 120, on the marathon course (800-441-5881); and the Grand Geneva Resort and Spa (800-558-3417). Other options include: Budget Host Hotel, 1060 Wells Street (800-264-5678); Elizabethian Inn, 463 Wrigley Drive, Lake Geneva (414-248-9131); Harbor View Motel, 76 Johnson Street, Williams Bay (414-245-5036); Alpine Motel, 682 Wells Street, Lake Geneva (414-248-4264); Pederson Victorian B&B, 1782 Hwy. 120 North, Lake Geneva (414-248-9110); Roses—A B&B, 429 S. Lake Shore Drive (414-248-4344); Strawberry Hill B&B, 1071 Jenkins Drive, Fontana (414-275-5998); and The Watersedge of Lake Geneva, W4232 West End Road, Lake Geneva (414-245-9845).

RELATED EVENTS/RACES Runners not quite ready for the grueling marathon can opt for the popular 25K which avoids the nastiest hills on the course, or take a leg on a three-person marathon relay. Runners in the 25K get the added treat of riding the stern-wheel boat back to the start/finish area. Alternatively, friends and family can join in the 5K run/walk which begins just after the marathon/25K start. The 5K finishes in Library Park.

AREA ATTRACTIONS While Lake Geneva is a place to relax and enjoy the beautiful lake, you may want to take one of the many boat tours, have a leisurely round of golf at one of the six area courses, take a horseback or carriage ride, or go hiking.

FOREST CITY MARATHON

OVERALL: 78.4

COURSE BEAUTY: 8+

COURSE DIFFICULTY: 3+

APPROPRIATENESS FOR FIRST TIMERS: 7+

RACE ORGANIZATION: 9-

CROWDS: 2

RACE DATA

Overall Ranking:	95
Quickness Ranking:	43
Contact:	Price Waterhouse Forest City Marathon
	Runners' Choice
	207 Dundas Street
	London, Ontario, Canada N6A 1G4
	(519) 672-5105
	E-mail: tvcc@sympatico.ca
Date:	May 9, 1999; May 14, 2000
Start Time:	8:00 a.m.
Time Course Closes:	1:00 p.m.
Number of Finishers:	600 in 1998
Course:	Out and back
Certification:	Athletics Canada and USATF
Course Records:	Male: (open) 2:28:16; (masters) 2:34:22
	Female: (open) 2:59:55; (masters) 2:59:55
Elite Athlete Programs:	No
Cost:	$35 Cdn.
Age groups/Divisions:	≤19, 20-24, 25-29, 30-34, 35-39, 40-44, 45-49, 50-54, 55-59, 60-64, 65+
Walkers:	No
Requirements:	None
Temperature:	38° - 68°
Aid/Splits:	14 / mile 1, clock at 13.1

HIGHLIGHTS Considered a microcosm of Canada, London, Ontario attracts great attention from product test marketers. Like mid-America, if something sells in London, it generally sells well throughout Canada. One of the city's own products, the Forest City Marathon, fits snugly in this category. With its attractive course through the Forest City (so named because of its 50,000 trees), quality race organization, and worthy cause (Thames Valley Children's Center for kids with physical disabilities), it's no wonder that the race field has nearly doubled in only five years. Not surprising given the city's test market status, every Forest City entrant receives a marathon opinion survey. One respondent quipped, "To improve the race, you would have to pay me money to come and run in it. Oh, wait, maybe dancing girls, yeah, belly dancing girls." With or without the dancing girls, the Forest City Marathon should continue to grow along with its reputation.

COURSE DESCRIPTION The Forest City Marathon's modified out-and-back course starts outside J.W. Little Memorial Stadium, home of the powerful University of Western

Ontario Mustangs football team. The race winds through the paved streets of the university campus for the first 1.9 miles and proceeds through one of London's most exclusive neighborhoods. Runners face a gradual 300-yard hill in mile 1, followed by a quarter-mile downgrade. From 3.75 to 5, the course travels through Old London North, home to many turn-of-the-century "old wealth" houses. The course tours the flat north section of London until mile 10, before returning to the university for 1.5 miles. After a short 1.5-mile jaunt on London's bike path system, the course becomes a true out-and-back through downtown streets before reentering the bike path at the Terry Fox Parkway (mile 14). For the next 4 miles, runners trace the picturesque Thames River through Greenway Park and Springbank Park, a combined 150-acre green space surrounding Storybook Gardens, home to Slippery the Seal and his friends. Runners turn around at mile 18, retracing their steps along the Thames to the university campus. The race finishes on the track inside Little Memorial Stadium before a good, enthusiastic crowd.

CROWD/RUNNER SUPPORT   Although scattered about the course, most spectators position themselves near University Drive, where the marathon and 10K courses converge; of course, the stadium finish draws a nice crowd as well. The volunteers managing the frequent aid stations provide tremendous encouragement along the route. More motivation comes from fellow runners, especially as you pass each other on the out-and-back second half of the race. If you're concerned about splits, signs are posted every 2K.

RACE LOGISTICS   Runners need to drive to the start at the University of Western Ontario. Park on the right at the bottom of the short hill on Huron Drive. You will see the stadium and start/finish areas to your left. Runners may change or shower at the university's Thames Hall.

ACTIVITIES   Register or pick up your race packet at the Runners' Expo at Station Park Inn, 242 Pall Mall, on Saturday from 1:00 a.m. to 6:00 p.m. If you miss Saturday's registration, race-day registration lasts until one hour before the start. Following your race, join the many children of the Thames Valley Children's Center for the festive post-race celebration complete with food, drink, live entertainment, and perhaps most important, a free massage. An awards ceremony and prize drawing begin at 12:30 p.m.

AWARDS   All marathoners receive T-shirts, and each marathon finisher receives a commemorative medal and ticket for the prize drawing held during the awards ceremony. The top three overall men and women receive $350, $175, and $100, respectively. Masters prize money for men and women extends three places, $200, $100, and $75, respectively. Age-group winners earn running shoes, while 2nd and 3rd place finishers receive other merchandise prizes. If that's not enough, medals are awarded to the top three in all categories.

ACCOMMODATIONS   The Station Park Inn, 242 Pall Mall (519-642-4444), serves as the official race headquarters and offers a special marathon rate of about $80. Otherwise, try: Delta London Armouries, 325 Dundas Street (800-268-1133 or 519-679-6111); Radisson Hotel—London Centre, 300 King Street (519-439-1661); or Lamplighter Inn, 591 Wellington Road (519-681-7151).

RELATED EVENTS/RACES   Forest City offers a marathon team event for up to six-member teams. Each member runs the marathon, and the four fastest age/gender-graded times are aggregated for the final results. The team event involves no additional cost but team members must preregister and submit all entries together. For those preferring shorter distances, a 10K loop through residential streets commences at 9:00 a.m., followed by a 2K winding through the university campus, starting at 9:15 a.m.

AREA ATTRACTIONS   While not quite the attraction as its overseas counterpart, this London does offer some fun activities without the jet lag. Fool yourself and take a city tour on an authentic red, double-decker bus. Stop in at Storybook Gardens, a children's attraction, or Labatts, an adult's attraction and one of Canada's best breweries.

NATIONAL CAPITAL MARATHON

OVERALL: 86.7

COURSE BEAUTY: 9

COURSE DIFFICULTY: 3+

APPROPRIATENESS FOR FIRST TIMERS: 9-

RACE ORGANIZATION: 9

CROWDS: 4

RACE DATA

Overall Ranking: 38
Quickness Ranking: 38
Contact: National Capital Marathon
P.O. Box 426 Station A
Ottawa, Ontario, Canada, K1N 8V5
Tel. (613) 234-2221
Fax (613) 234-5880
E-mail: ncm@synapse.net
http://www.sirius.on.ca/running/ncm.html

Date: May 9, 1999; May 14, 2000
Start Time: 8:30 a.m.
Time Course Closes: 1:30 p.m.
Number of Finishers: 1,050 in 1998
Course: Two loops
Certification: Athletics Canada
Course Records: Male: (open) 2:26:02; (masters) 2:30:39
Female: (open) 2:52:03; (masters) 3:11:09
Elite Athlete Programs: Yes
Cost: $45
Age groups/Divisions: ≤19, 20-24, 25-29, 30-34, 35-39, 40-44, 45-49,
50-54, 55-59, 60-64, 65-69, 70+
Walkers: No
Requirements: None
Temperature: 60°
Aid/Splits: 14 / every 5K

HIGHLIGHTS   Unless you run on your toes, you'll be "heel-toeing through the tulips" in Canada's capital city of Ottawa during the National Capital Marathon. The haven of the Dutch royal family during World War II, Ottawa was rewarded with 100,000 tulip bulbs in 1945 and 20,000 replenishments every year thereafter. On top of the thousands of colorful tulips, majestic parliament buildings, scenic parkways, and pristine neighborhoods characterize the two-loop course. Held on Mother's Day, NCM celebrates by presenting every woman finisher with a rose.

COURSE DESCRIPTION   Starting near Ottawa's Confederation Park and RMOC Plaza, NCM's sparkling course wastes no time in passing some of the city's greatest land-marks. The route glides past the historic Lord Elgin Hotel and the architecturally impressive Chateau Laurier before swinging south on Colonel By Drive. Runners quickly reach the historic Rideau Canal, and continue along its edge for nearly 5 miles. This section essentially runs flat with the exception of small inclines at miles 4 and 5 where the course passes the canal's upper locks.

National Capital Marathon

Leaving the canal, runners head mostly downhill during mile 6 followed by a short rise into Vincent Massey Park. A quick loop through the wooded park brings you back to Heron Road and a gentle incline for about .2 miles before the route heads north on Prince of Wales Drive. The next mile runs flat as you travel through the Experimental Farm. A downhill near mile 9.25 brings runners to Dow's Lake. The course flows around the boat-swollen lake before returning to picturesque Rideau Canal. The next 3.5 miles hug the canal passing beautiful tulip displays before returning to the start of the second loop.

CROWD/RUNNER SUPPORT NCM attracts some 10,000 spectators throughout the course with most gathering around the start/finish area in downtown Ottawa. Participants from the other races and scores of aid station volunteers provide excellent encouragement for your effort.

RACE LOGISTICS You'll find NCM hassle-free on race morning if you stay at the official race hotel or one of several downtown hotels within walking distance of the start/finish. If you're driving to the race, parking is plentiful. Also, the race provides a sweats check at the start.

ACTIVITIES The pre-race check-in and race expo at RMOC Plaza, located between Laurier Street W and Lisgar Street at the Rideau Canal, takes place on Saturday 9:00 a.m. to 4:00 p.m. and Sunday 7:00 a.m. to 8:00 a.m. After the race, unless you're extremely thirsty, enjoy some solid refreshments before heading to the beer tent (sorry, not free). A Sports Active Expo is held for sponsors and merchants to exhibit and sell their products. An awards ceremony, live music and dance show round out the day's festivities.

AWARDS Every runner receives a T-shirt, while finishers receive medallions and certificates. The top three overall competitors receive prize money, $1,500, $750, and $500, respectively. Age-group awards extend three deep, with winners generally receiving merchandise. All female finishers receive roses for Mother's Day. The morning after the race, see your name published in the *Ottawa Citizen*. Results are also mailed to marathon participants.

ELITE RUNNERS INFORMATION Previous winners and elite runners, at the discretion of the race director, may receive some expense money and accommodations.

ACCOMMODATIONS The Radisson Hotel, 100 Kent Street (800-333-3333), serves as the official race hotel offering a special marathon rate. Other nearby hotels include: Lord Elgin, 100 Elgin Street (613-235-3333); Journey's End Hotel, 290 Rideau Street (613-789-7511); Chateau Laurier, 1 Rideau Street (613-241-1414); Capital Hill Motel & Suites, 88 Albert Street (613-235-1413); Parkway Motor Hotel, 475 Rideau (613-232-3781); Days Inn Roxborough-Ottawa City Center, 123 Metcalfe Street (613-237-9300); Aristocrat Apartment Hotel, 131 Cooper Street (613-232-9471); and Chateau Cartier, Aylmer, Quebec (800-807-1088).

RELATED EVENTS/RACES NCM sees to it that everyone has a chance to exercise by hosting several events over the weekend. Saturday evening brings an 8K in-line skate race starting at 6:00 p.m. and a 10K run at 6:30 p.m. Point to point, both courses travel from the Central Experimental Farm to RMOC Plaza, site of the marathon finish. Race day includes an in-line skate marathon that takes skaters on the same course that runners later follow. A half marathon starts with the marathon at 8:30 a.m. Finally, a 5K and 2K run/walk leaves at 8:45 a.m. taking participants on Queen Elizabeth Driveway along the Rideau Canal.

AREA ATTRACTIONS North America's largest tulip display has turned into one of Ottawa's largest celebrations, the Spring Tulip Festival. Don't miss the festivities which include live music, street dancing, hot air balloon rides, craft fairs, boat rides, and fireworks. Other must sees are the collection of fine art at the National Gallery of Canada and the re-creation of a rain forest at the National Museum of Civilization.

CAPITAL CITY MARATHON

OVERALL: 84.3

COURSE BEAUTY: 8+

COURSE DIFFICULTY: 4 (SEE APPENDIX)

APPROPRIATENESS FOR FIRST TIMERS: 9-

RACE ORGANIZATION: 9

CROWDS: 3+

RACE DATA

Overall Ranking: 56
Quickness Ranking: 57
Contact: Capital City Marathon
P.O. Box 1681
Olympia, WA 98507
(360) 786-1786

Date: May 16, 1999; May 21, 2000
Start Time: 7:30 a.m.
Time Course Closes: 1:30 p.m.
Number of Finishers: 600 in 1998
Course: Loop
Certification: USATF
Course Records: Male: (open) 2:28:03; (masters) 2:28:03
Female: (open) 2:43:18; (masters) 3:00:45
Elite Athlete Programs: No
Cost: $35/50
Age groups/Divisions: ≤19, 20-24, 25-29, 30-34, 35-39, 40-44, 45-49,
50-54, 55-59, 60-64, 65-69, 70+
Walkers: No
Requirements: None
Temperature: 52° - 65°
Aid/Splits: 12 / mile 20

HIGHLIGHTS There seems to be a special bond between runners and beer, so what better place for a marathon in the Pacific Northwest than Olympia, home of Olympia Brewery? The Capital City Marathon's course provides views of beautiful Capitol Lake, Budd Inlet, the State Capitol building, and on clear days, Mt. Rainier and the Olympic Mountains. Well-organized, Capital City hosts several shorter events that should keep the whole family busy. Afterward, head to the Olympia Brewery to celebrate your achievement in true runners' style.

COURSE DESCRIPTION Passing through primarily rural and residential areas, Capital City's loop course starts near the State Capitol building. After a gentle 100-yard downgrade followed by an easy rise to 5th Street, runners reach the most scenic stretch of the route on Deschutes Parkway along beautiful Capitol Lake and its Canadian geese residents, with wooded hills to their right. A little after mile 2, runners reach the most significant upgrade on the course, 170 feet over 2 miles. During this span, the route parallels Interstate-5, separated by a high sound barrier until the right on Capitol Blvd. at mile 3.1. Turning commercial near 3.9, the course quickly jaunts over Interstate-5. At mile 4.3, runners turn on Littlerock Road, going very slightly uphill through a rural community. The course hits Airindustrial Way at the 6-mile mark, passing the small rural airport at 7.4 miles. Back on Capitol Blvd. at 7.6, the course heads back toward downtown, passing the Olympia Brewery at 9.9 miles, followed by a good, 100-yard uphill. The route then becomes chiefly residential, rolling slightly by mile 11. Runners face a tough, 70-foot climb from mile 13 to 13.5 on Boulevard Road. More noticeably rolling, the course goes mostly through rural subdivisions and residential neighborhoods until it reaches Capitol Way near mile 25. From there, it's a nice downhill finish through downtown Olympia to Sylvester Park.

CROWD / RUNNER SUPPORT   Runners find the best crowd support during the last two miles of the marathon. Although particularly light on the Littlerock Road-Airindustrial Way-Capitol Blvd. loop, support does scatter along the rest of the course. Over 600 volunteers help the runners, with most at the 12 aid stations. Portable toilets are located every five miles on the course, and a medical aid station sits at mile 22.

RACE LOGISTICS   The race does not provide transportation to the start, but if you are staying at the race headquarters hotel, this is no problem since it lies only a short walk from the start. Clothing storage is available; look for the marked vehicle.

ACTIVITIES   On Saturday afternoon, register, pick up your race number, and browse trade exhibits from 12:00 p.m. to 5:00 p.m. at Olympia Center. You may register on race morning at the start area. You can also tour the marathon course for no charge in a 20-person van. Tours start at noon on Saturday. The race also hosts a pasta dinner on Saturday evening from 6:00 p.m. to 8:00 p.m. at the Olympic Center. After the marathon, savor food, refreshments, music, and the awards ceremony in Sylvester Park. Massage is available for a suggested $10 donation on a first-come, first-served basis.

AWARDS   Finishers earn long-sleeve T-shirts and commemorative medals. Age-division awards range from three to ten deep. Age-group winners receive special awards, while others receive medals. Awards are also presented to the top overall, masters, international, and inspirational runners.

ACCOMMODATIONS   The Ramada Inn—Governor House, 621 Capitol Way (800-356-5335), serves as the headquarters hotel. The Ramada is four-and-a-half blocks from the start. Also within walking distance of the start are: Best Western Aladdin Motel, 900 Capitol Way S (800-528-1234); Golden Gavel, 909 Capitol Way S (360-352-8533); and Golden Carriage, 1211 Quince Street SE (360-943-4710). Other possibilities include: Quality Inn, 2300 Evergreen Park Drive SW (800-562-5635); Comfort Inn, 4700 Park Center Avenue NE (360-456-6300); Capital Inn, 120 College Street SE (360-493-1991); Tyee Motel, 500 Tyee Drive SW (360-352-0511); and Best Western Tumwater Inn, 5188 Capitol Blvd. S (360-956-1235).

RELATED EVENTS / RACES   Capital City hosts a number of related events on marathon race day. The Capital City Half Marathon (8:00 a.m.) and the D.A.R.E. Kid's Run (8:20 a.m.), a one-mile run for children 6 to 13, start at 5th and Columbia Streets. The Capital City Five Miler (8:15 a.m.) begins at the marathon start.

AREA ATTRACTIONS   Make sure to tour the Olympia Brewery if you are a beer drinker. You can also wander through the State Capitol building and its surrounding grounds. Within a couple of hours of Olympia are Olympic National Park, Mt. Rainier National Park, and Seattle.

COEUR D'ALENE MARATHON

OVERALL: 82.4

COURSE BEAUTY: 9

COURSE DIFFICULTY: 4-

APPROPRIATENESS FOR FIRST TIMERS: 7

RACE ORGANIZATION: 9-

CROWDS: 1+

RACE DATA

Overall Ranking: **68**
Quickness Ranking: **51**
Contact: **Coeur d'Alene Marathon**
P.O. Box 2393
Coeur d'Alene, ID 83816
(208) 665-9393

Date: **May 23, 1999; May 21, 2000**
Start Time: **7:00 a.m.**
Time Course Closes: **12:00 p.m.**
Number of Finishers: **500 in 1998**
Course: **Loop**
Certification: **USATF**
Course Records: **Male: (open) 2:27:58**
Female: (open) 2:55:21
Elite Athlete Programs: **No**
Cost: **$30**
Age groups/Divisions: **≤19, 20-24, 25-29, 30-34, 35-39, 40-44, 45-49,**
50-54, 55-59, 60-64, 65-69, 70+
Walkers: **No**
Requirements: **None**
Temperature: **60°- 70°**
Aid/Splits: **13 / every 5 miles**

HIGHLIGHTS   You won't see the reputedly world's largest floating boardwalk or the world's only floating golf green (both Coeur d'Alene attractions) during this old-fashioned marathon, but you will discover why the popularity of this northern Idaho resort town is soaring. As Idaho's premier running event, the Coeur d'Alene Marathon offers a wonderful tour of the area, including thick evergreen forests, deep blue lakes, beautiful golf courses, and a fashionable city center along the lakefront.

COURSE DESCRIPTION   At an average elevation of 2,300 feet, Coeur d'Alene's loop course starts and finishes at North Idaho College in the heart of downtown. The race travels through evergreen-covered countryside, open fields, past three lakes, two golf courses, through several rural subdivisions and the city center and park. Although basically flat, the course contains one significant hill at the 9-mile point.

CROWD/RUNNER SUPPORT   For a city of only 60,000, Coeur d'Alene attracts an impressive 6,000 spectators throughout the course. Volunteers at 13 aid stations provide additional encouragement. Although race temperatures are normally ideal, organizers make sure you properly warm up by placing clothing drop boxes at each mile. Portable toilets are located at miles 5, 6.5, 11.24, 16, and 21.

RACE LOGISTICS   Coeur d'Alene starts and finishes within walking distance of downtown lodging. Plenty of parking is available for those arriving by car on race morning.

ACTIVITIES   Race packet pickup and Mini-Trade Fair take place on Saturday from 12:00 p.m. to 6:00 p.m. in the foyer of the gymnasium at North Idaho College. A deluxe shuttle bus takes course-conscious runners through the route from 1:00 p.m. to 3:00 p.m. leaving from the campus gymnasium. You will be back in plenty of time if you want to hit the $6 all-you-can-eat carbo dinner from 6:00 p.m. to 8:00 p.m. at Trinity Lutheran Church, 812 N. 5th Street. After the race, enjoy food, beverages and war stories while you wait for the awards ceremony which starts at 12:15 p.m.

AWARDS   All finishers receive long-sleeve mock turtleneck T-shirts and medals. Overall and division winners receive plaques.

ACCOMMODATIONS   Some lodging options include: The Riverbend Inn in Post Falls, Idaho, 4105 W. Riverbend Avenue (208-773-3583); the four-star Coeur d'Alene Resort, 2nd and Front Street (208-765-4000); Bennet Bay Inn featuring theme rooms with full-size jacuzzis, 5144 Coeur d' Alene Lake Drive (208-664-6168); and Holiday Inn Express, 2209 East Sherman Avenue (208-765-3200).

RELATED EVENTS/RACES   Coeur d'Alene holds a half marathon which starts concurrently with the marathon. The 13.1-mile loop follows the full marathon for over 5 miles, changes course, and then rejoins the marathon from the 19-mile marker to the finish. Race organizers encourage marathon walkers by providing an early start time of 5:00 a.m.

AREA ATTRACTIONS   Before or after the race, visit the four-star Coeur d'Alene Resort, walk along the endless floating boardwalk, or treat yourself to a memorable round of golf on the beautiful resort course. For a stunning view of Lake Coeur d'Alene, hike 2 miles up Tubbs Hill. If you prefer a closer lake view, rent a canoe or take a popular boat cruise.

Rock 'n' Roll Marathon

Overall: 82.3

Course Beauty: 8

Course Difficulty: 3- (see appendix)

Appropriateness for First Timers: 7

Organization: 7+

Crowds: 4

RACE DATA

Overall Ranking: **72**

Quickness Ranking: **32**

Contact: **Rock 'n' Roll Marathon**
c/o Elite Racing
5452 Oberlin Drive, Ste. B
San Diego, CA 92121
Tel. (619) 450-6510
Fax (619) 450-6905
http://www.rnrmarathon.com

Date: **May 23, 1999; 2000 date TBA**

Start Time: **6:45 a.m.**

Time Course Closes: **2:00 p.m. (finish line open for 8 hours)**

Number of Finishers: **15,746 in 1998**

Course: **Point to point**

Certification: **USATF**

Course Records: **New Course**

Elite Athlete Programs: **Yes**

Cost: **$65**

Age groups/Divisions: **16-19, 20-24, 25-29, 30-34, 35-39, 40-44, 45-49,**
50-54, 55-59, 60-64, 65-69, 70-79, 80+

Walkers: **Yes**

Requirements: **16 years old**

Temperature: **62° - 70°**

Aid/Splits: **26 / every mile verbally and digital clocks**

HIGHLIGHTS The inaugural Rock 'n' Roll Marathon in 1998 probably should have been called the Blues Marathon. While a rocking success at the gate, many runners ended up hot, thirsty, and not terribly inspired by the perceived handful of bands that were playing along the route (hence runners were singing the blues). For the record, the main complaints were a lack of water at the aid stations, a late start, an apparent paucity of music, and a course that didn't meet runners' aesthetic expectations. The race organizers, to their credit, have admitted the many problems and vow a much improved experience for runners in the future. The question is how many will show up for the subsequent acts after the rough first act? Still, the course remains fairly fast, although the revised route will be a bit hillier than the inaugural version, starting in beautiful Balboa Park and passing along coastal areas of San Diego. Unfortunately, it also includes a long, barren stretch on the Pacific Highway (although runners only have to experience it once on the new course). In all likelihood, 1999 will be a watershed year for the Rock 'n' Roll Marathon. It will either earn it's name and shimmy into the future, or fade like a one-hit wonder band. Organizers insist that the race will eventually belong in the Rock 'n' Roll Hall of Fame.

COURSE DESCRIPTION The Rock 'n' Roll Marathon begins in the west end of Balboa Park and goes north for 1 mile, turning right on University Avenue through the community of Hillcrest. At mile 2, runners then head south on Park Blvd., gradually descending 200 feet for the next two miles through the heart of Balboa Park. Miles 4 through 6 loop through the hip Gaslamp district and downtown before taking runners to shady Highway 163 on a 150-foot upgrade for 2 miles. The highway soon turns into the typical thoroughfare, going down for 1.5 miles to a left turn onto Friars Road in Mission Valley (mile 10). Reaching Sea World Drive (mile 12), the course loops around Mission Bay (mile 12 to mile 21), passing Sea World, Crown Point, and Mission Bay Park. The loop around Mission Bay runs mostly flat with a few bumps on overpasses. Returning towards downtown on boring Pacific Highway, the course enters the former Naval Training Center at mile 25, and finishes on a palm tree-lined road along San Diego Bay. The course still features a net elevation loss of over 200 feet, but watch out for the 150-foot rise between miles 6 and 8.

CROWD/RUNNER SUPPORT Each mile is supposed to be accompanied by a rock band and cheerleading squad. Of course, this didn't appear to happen in 1998, but we expect it to improve in the future. The music should attract some crowd support. Runner aid was not a strong point in 1998, but organizers probably will drain the Colorado River if they have to to make sure runners have enough water.

RACE LOGISTICS Many hotels are located within walking distance of the start area. However, be aware that the start and finish lie about one-and-one-half miles from each other. Race organizers transport your sweats to the finish for you to claim.

ACTIVITIES In conjunction with the packet pick-up, a Sports and Fitness Expo, featuring live rock 'n' roll music in the lobby, happens Thursday, noon to 7:00 p.m., Friday 10:00 a.m. to 7:30 p.m., and Saturday 9:00 a.m. to 6:00 p.m. at the Golden Hall - San Diego Concourse, located at Third Avenue and B Street. Late registration is available at the expo if the runner limit has not been exceeded. Though the finish line signals the end of your run, the beat goes on for the rock 'n' roll bands during the huge post-race celebration at Horton's Plaza. Billed as a hard day's night celebration, a concert with a headlining rock band puts the finishing chords on a memorable weekend. In 1998, the bands were Huey Lewis, Pat Benatar, and the Lovin' Spoonful.

AWARDS Every finisher receives a T-shirt and medal. Top runners split a total prize purse of $100,000. At the time of this writing, prize money breakdown and age-group awards had not been determined.

ELITE RUNNERS INFORMATION RNRM offers transportation and lodging to elite runners. Contact Mike Long at Elite Racing (tel. 619-450-6510; fax 619-450-6905).

ACCOMMODATIONS Several hotels near the start and finish offer special race rates. Among them are: U.S. Grant, 326 Broadway (800-237-5029); Hyatt Regency, 1 Market Place (800-233-1234); and Westin, 910 Broadway Circle (800-228-3000). For other hotel options call the marathon office at (619-450-6510).

AREA ATTRACTIONS After Richard Nixon shunned San Diego at the last minute and awarded Miami with the 1972 Republican National Convention, a few overly sensitive San Diegan's began an informal public relations campaign to protect the city's image. "San Diego - America's Finest City" became the rallying slogan. Most visitors won't argue. San Diego boasts some of Southern California's best beaches including Mission Beach, Pacific Beach, and La Jolla. You can see Shamu and his orca friends at Sea World, the city's most popular attraction. One of the best zoos in the world, the San Diego Zoo houses over 3,200 animals and 6,000 plants. Head to the Gaslamp District downtown to find your evening meal and entertainment.

Rock 'n' Roll Marathon

MADISON MARATHON

OVERALL: 86.5

COURSE BEAUTY: 9

COURSE DIFFICULTY: 4

APPROPRIATENESS FOR FIRST TIMERS: 9

RACE ORGANIZATION: 9

CROWDS: 4

RACE DATA

Overall Ranking:	40
Quickness Ranking:	55
Contact:	Madison Marathon, Inc.
	P.O. Box 14513
	Madison, WI 53714-0513
	Tel. (608) 256-9922
	Fax (608) 241-2591
	E-mail: kmack@mailbag.com
	http://www.madison-marathon.com
Date:	May 30, 1999; May 28, 2000
Start Time:	7:30 a.m.
Time Course Closes:	3:45 p.m.
Number of Finishers:	1,225 in 1998
Course:	Near loop
Certification:	USATF
Course Records:	Male: (open) 2:23; (masters) 2:42
	Female: (open) 2:54; (masters) 3:05
Elite Athlete Programs:	No
Cost:	$35/40
Age groups/Divisions:	≤19, 20-24, 25-29, 30-34, 35-39, 40-44, 45-49,
	50-54, 55-59, 60-64, 65-69, 70+
Walkers:	Yes
Requirements:	None
Temperature:	53° - 64°
Aid/Splits:	25 / every mile

HIGHLIGHTS Hip Madison, Wisconsin, home of the large and respected University of Wisconsin and the State Capitol, exudes an eclectic manner unusual for a city of this size. Pinched between two lakes, Madison offers a picturesque and vibrant setting for the youthful Madison Marathon. The marathon makes full use of Madison's resources, taking in the Capitol, the university, Lake Mendota, Lake Monona, and area parks. The marathon organizers try hard to put on a runner-friendly event, with 25 aid stations, five separate races, and a scenic course.

COURSE DESCRIPTION The Madison Marathon's course begins in Capitol Square, near the State Capitol building. A quick downhill leads runners to Johnson Street, past coffee houses and bookstores. With some very gentle slopes, the course heads along mostly residential Pennsylvania and Packers Avenues. Near mile 5, runners skirt Warner Park and then get a nice view of the Lake Mendota shoreline while heading down Woodward Drive. The first noticeable uphill grade comes near mile 6.5, entering the historic and picturesque Village of Maple Bluff.

The next couple miles pass the area's beautiful lakefront homes (including the Governor's Mansion near mile 8). Proceeding south on Sherman Avenue, runners enjoy a great view of Lake Mendota while negotiating a few rolling hills. After following the shoreline downhill to James Madison Park, runners experience the greatest inclines—two good, .2-mile hills between mile 9.5 and 11. Now back downtown, State Street (home to street vendors and historic shops) leads runners to the University of Wisconsin campus. The next 4 miles run through the campus, mostly bordering Lake Mendota. Near mile 14.5, the course circles Camp Randall Stadium (home of the Wisconsin Badgers football team) then continues south toward Vilas Park and Lake Wingra. Running past Vilas Park, racers enter the historic and revitalized Monroe Street neighborhood near 16.5 miles, then forge into the UW arboretum (mile 19) before returning to Vilas Park (mile 22). After circling Lake Monona, the race finishes in Olin Park on the northeast shore of Lake Monona.

CROWD/RUNNER SUPPORT Approximately 10,000 spectators come out for the race, most gathering at the start/finish, Governor's Mansion area, State Street, Vilas Park, and the relay exchange points. Each of the 25 aid stations generously offers water, electrolyte replacement, energy bar samples, Vaseline, and sunscreen. Medical assistance is available at six locations on the course, and portable toilets are located at the relay exchange points and at a few selected places later in the race.

RACE LOGISTICS You have a few of options for getting to the start on race morning. First, you may park at the Dane County Expo Center (near the finish) for $3.50 and take the free shuttle bus to the start. Second, you can hunt for a parking place near Capitol Square. If you park downtown, you must find your own way back after the race. If staying at the official race hotel, Marriott Madison West, catch one of their shuttle buses between 6:00 a.m. and 6:55 a.m. The race will transport your sweats from the start to the finish area.

ACTIVITIES Pick up your race packet Friday from 12:00 p.m. to 8:00 p.m. and Saturday from 9:00 a.m. to 5:00 p.m. at the Health and Fitness Expo held at the Madison Marriott West. During the day Saturday, you can take a bus tour of the marathon course for $5. A children's 1K ,3K and Diaper Dash take place from the hotel at 2:00 p.m. Later in the afternoon, the race holds a pasta party (about $10) complete with door prizes and a featured speaker. After the marathon, get kneaded for free by massage therapists and/or relax and soak tired muscles in one of three spas. Once you can walk again, gather up some food among the many food stalls to replenish some energy, and then enjoy the finish line festival, with live music and more substantial food for purchase.

AWARDS All marathon finishers receive long-sleeve T-shirts and medals. The overall male and female winners receive airline tickets, while the top three in each age group receive plaques.

ACCOMMODATIONS The Marriott Madison West, 1313 John Q. Hammons Drive (608-831-2000), is the official race hotel offering special marathon rates. Others with special marathon rates include: Best Western, 2424 University Avenue (608-2323-8778; Howard Johnson Plaza Hotel, 525 W. Johnson Street (608-251-5511; and Crown Plaza, 4402 East Washington Avenue (608-244-4703).

RELATED EVENTS/RACES Five-person teams can enter the marathon relay, running legs averaging 5 miles. Buses transport team members to the relay exchange zones and then to the finish. The half marathon starts in Capitol Square and ends on the University of Wisconsin's campus. Both the marathon relay and the half marathon start with the marathon. Shorter distance runners may consider the 10K Road Race or the 5K Run/Walk. Both start at 8:00 a.m. at Capitol Square and finish in Olin Park.

AREA ATTRACTIONS Two institutions mark Madison life, state government and the university, and both are worth a visit. The State Capitol building is topped by the only granite dome in the United States. Places of interest on the campus include the Olbrich Botanical Gardens at 3330 Atwood Avenue; Memorial Union Terrace overlooking Lake Mendota, 800 Langdon Street; and for ice cream lovers, Babcock Hall, 1695 Linden Drive. The Madison Art Center exhibits contemporary art at 211 State Street. On Saturday mornings, check out the Farmer's Market on Capitol Square.

MED-CITY MARATHON

OVERALL: 76.3

COURSE BEAUTY: 8+

COURSE DIFFICULTY: 4

APPROPRIATENESS FOR FIRST TIMERS: 7+

RACE ORGANIZATION: 9

CROWDS: 2

RACE DATA

Overall Ranking:	106
Quickness Ranking:	59
Contact:	Med-City Marathon
	1417 14th Avenue NE
	Rochester, MN 55906
	(507) 282-1411
	E-mail: medcity@millcomm.com
	http:///www.millcomm.com/~adoering/medcity
Date:	May 30, 1999; May 28, 2000
Start Time:	8:00 a.m.
Time Course Closes:	2:00 p.m.
Number of Finishers:	351 in 1998
Course:	Loop
Certification:	USATF
Course Records:	Male: (open) 2:29:40; (masters) 2:43:28
	Female (open) 3:01:56; (masters) 3:01:56
Elite Athlete Programs:	No
Cost:	$25/30
Age groups/Divisions:	≤29, 30-39, 40-49, 50-59, 60+
Walkers:	No
Requirements:	None
Temperature:	45° - 65°
Aid/Splits:	11 / mile 13.1

HIGHLIGHTS Attracting thousands of ailing people from all parts of the globe, the renowned Mayo Clinic medical facility has long been Rochester, Minnesota's claim to fame. Thanks to the newly established Med-City Marathon, however, the collective health of Rochester's visitors is improving (though many folks question the mental health of marathoners). Benefitting the Rochester Special Olympics, the race features a scenic tour of the city's pleasant mix of bike paths and rural and urban streets. And, of course, you won't get away without passing a few medical facilities before the finish. In fact, "Pass the Mayo, do you have the Mustard?" has become the race's slogan.

COURSE DESCRIPTION Providing a pleasant citywide tour, Med-City's course starts in Soldiers Memorial Field. Heading north for a 2-mile downtown loop, runners pay their respects to Methodist Hospital and the Mayo Clinic before returning to the attractive upper-class neighborhood surrounding Memorial Parkway. Around 3 miles, the route joins one of the course's many bike paths for 1 mile, then cuts quickly through a residential area before rejoining the bike path near 5.2 miles. At mile 6, the route turns right entering the beautiful wooded confines of Mayowood Road. Although mostly flat to rolling on Mayowood Road, a steeper upgrade occurs around 8 miles as the route slowly makes its way toward Lake George. Back on the bike path at 10.4 miles, the course passes Lake George at 11 miles continuing toward Soldiers Memorial Field and downtown. Runners pass the Mayo Building at mile 14 while following the bike path bordering the Zumbro River. Runners circle Silver Lake from 15 to 17 miles, then proceed south to Slattery Park. Another bike path, between miles 19 and 21, deposits runners to Pinewood Road. After a one-mile stretch through a middle-class residential area, the route rejoins the bike path as runners pass each other going opposite directions. Returning downtown, the course passes Mayo Park and Civic Center just after 25 miles and finishes adjacent to the flag pole in Soldiers Memorial Field.

CROWD / RUNNER SUPPORT Although scattered throughout the course, most spectators congregate near the aid stations and the start/finish area in Soldiers Memorial Field. Corporate-sponsored aid stations compete for the best aid station award voted on by the runners.

RACE LOGISTICS The race is limited to 750 marathoners so enter early. If you're staying at the Kahler Hotel, a complimentary shuttle service takes you to and from the start/finish. Otherwise, you need to drive to the start, where plenty of parking is available. Shuttle buses take relay runners to the exchange zones.

ACTIVITIES Race organizers mail packets to runners registering at least one week prior to the event. Otherwise, register late at Heritage Hall in the Kahler Hotel, 20 Southwest Second Avenue (800-533-1655) on Saturday from 10:00 a.m. to 6:00 p.m. After the race, replenish yourself with refreshments while awaiting the awards ceremony starting at noon. To honor all involved with the race, a post-race party complete with music and cash bar runs from 5:00 p.m. to 9:00 p.m. at the Kahler Hotel penthouse.

AWARDS Every finisher receives a T-shirt and medallion. The first overall male and female and division winners earn plaques, and 2nd and 3rd place runners receive medals. The big winner at the event is the official charity; in three years the race has raised over $16,000 for Special Olympics Minnesota.

ACCOMMODATIONS In addition to the Kahler, the following hotels offer special rates and late checkout for the marathon: Clinic View Inn and Suites, 101 E. Center Street (507-289-8646); and Holiday Inn Downtown, 220 S. Broadway (507-288-3231).

RELATED EVENTS / RACES If you want to participate in the Med-City experience but don't want to run 26.2 miles, consider joining a relay team. Choose between a two and four-person relay, both of which start with the marathon at 8:00 a.m. Kids can keep occupied with the Conoco Kids Classic—a fun run covering the last 1.2 miles of the marathon course.

AREA ATTRACTIONS If you have time, visit the Mayowood Mansion and Plummer House and Gardens. Antique shopping or picnicking at Silver Lake are other options.

VERMONT CITY MARATHON

OVERALL: 93

COURSE BEAUTY: 9

COURSE DIFFICULTY: 4+ (SEE APPENDIX)

APPROPRIATENESS FOR FIRST TIMERS: 9-

RACE ORGANIZATION: 10-

CROWDS: 6+

R A C E   D A T A

Overall Ranking: 11
Quickness Ranking: 61
Contact: Andrea Riha
Key Bank Vermont City Marathon
P.O. Box 152
Burlington, VT 05402
Tel. (800) 880-8149 or (802) 863-8412
E-mail: RUNVT@together.NET

Date: May 30, 1999; May 28, 2000
Start Time: 8:05 a.m.
Time Course Closes: 1:00 p.m.
Number of Finishers: Limit 2,000 runners (fills early)
Course: Near loop
Certification: USATF
Course Records: Male: (open) 2:18:03; (masters) 2:22:52
Female: (open) 2:38:32; (masters) 2:47:28
Elite Athlete Programs: Yes
Cost: $40/50
Age groups/Divisions: 16-24, 25-29, 30-34, 35-39, 40-44, 45-49, 50-54,
55-59, 60-64, 65-69, 70+
Walkers: No
Requirements: 16 years old
Temperature: 48° - 68°
Aid/Splits: 17 / digital clocks at miles 1, 3, 9, halfway, and 16.5

HIGHLIGHTS   Personal recommendations often lead to our greatest experiences—the corner Italian restaurant, that foreign film treasure from Mexico, and the Vermont City Marathon. The success of VCM is owed mainly to contented runners passing the word on to their friends. Word of mouth has created a 20% increase in participants each year, so that now, the race must cap entrants to 2,000 marathoners and 600 relay teams. Not surprisingly, Vermont City boasts one of the highest repeat runner rates in North America. What's its secret? For starters, location. Burlington radiates beauty with the Adirondack Mountains reflecting off gorgeous Lake Champlain. The marathon skirts the shoreline for several miles, providing spectacular views. Also, very few cities embrace a marathon quite like Burlington. Banners line the street, restaurants hang race posters, and residents wear marathon buttons. The city's largest annual event, VCM sports an incredible 1,200 volunteers for 5,000 runners, a number that translates into superb organization and happy participants. Next to Boston, Vermont City ranks as our favorite spring marathon on the East Coast.

RACE HISTORY Most people agree that autumn is the nicest time of year in New England. No mystery then why most marathon race directors in the area hold their race during this time. The trees radiate color, the weather usually cooperates, and Boston is long gone. Not deterred by Boston, VCM organizers believed that an alternative to Boston was just what the New England spring racing schedule needed. Therefore, in 1989, the VCM was born, its name reflecting that it is a city course rather than a race through the woods.

COURSE DESCRIPTION The marathon starts in Battery Park, the site of famous artillery exchanges in the Revolutionary War, and finishes at Waterfront Park on the shore of Lake Champlain. Run entirely within the city of Burlington, the course travels through the Downtown Marketplace, the surrounding Hill Section, and the Old and New North Ends. Beginning with a 3.3-mile loop around the downtown area, a gentle incline greets the runners between .8 and 1.3 miles. At 1.5, runners proceed down a sharp, short decline after a right turn on Beach Street. From here, the course returns to the downtown area and Church Street with a gradual hill from 2.5 to 2.9 miles. Upon leaving town, the route continues to a divided 6.6-mile, out-and-back section on the closed Northern Connector Highway (Beltline). Although still early in the race, this is a difficult section due to the severe camber of the road, absence of crowd support, and lack of protection from the elements. Moderate inclines and declines occur from 6 to 6.5 and from 9 to 9.5 miles. Returning downtown, the course heads south for a 6.6-mile loop through mostly residential Burlington, Oakledge Park and along the waterfront with the picturesque Adirondacks in the background. Runners are welcomed back to downtown by hundreds of spectators, the Taiko drummer corps, and a challenging hill between mile 16 and 16.5 which takes the runners conveniently past the Radisson Hotel. The race proceeds slightly downhill on North Avenue from mile 16.5 to 21.5 with a short, steep down and up from mile 17 to 17.5 and a sharp .125-mile downhill at mile 18. The final 4.7 miles trace the mostly flat to slightly downhill bike trail paralleling Lake Champlain to the finish in Waterfront Park. Overall, the course drops 100 feet.

CROWD/RUNNER SUPPORT For a town of Burlington's size (40,000), the marathon attracts an impressive crowd of 10,000 spectators. Most of the bystanders take advantage of the spectator-friendly course layout by hovering near Battery Park, which the race passes several times. Fifteen excellent aid stations are located throughout the course along with several musical groups providing entertainment along the way, most notably the Taiko drummers at the foot of the course's toughest climb.

RACE LOGISTICS The start and finish are close to each other and to the race hotel, so transportation is not a concern. We recommend staying at the Radisson due to its proximity to the start/finish and to capture more of the race flavor. If you arrive by car, ample free parking is available.

ACTIVITIES VCM hosts a two-day Sports & Wellness Expo and packet pick-up beginning on Friday from 4:00 p.m. to 9:00 p.m. and Saturday from 9:00 a.m. to 6:00 p.m. VCM also offers various seminars throughout the day on Saturday. Try not to miss the "Mile by Mile Preview," an excellent slide show and discussion of the course. Runners, family, and friends are invited to enjoy an all-you-can-eat pasta party for a modest price, featuring a special guest speaker. The party always sells out, so purchase your tickets early. If you miss the pasta party, don't worry; nearby Church Street is loaded with great restaurants to meet your carbo-loading needs. After the race, runners are treated to complimentary food, drinks, massages and live music. The awards ceremony is held in Waterfront Park at 1:00 p.m.

AWARDS Every marathon runner receives a T-shirt and hospitality booklet. Finishers are presented with uniquely Vermont medallions, certificates by professional calligraphers, and results booklets. Division awards of Vermont pottery extend three deep, and prize money is awarded to top open and masters runners. Additionally, the first Vermont resident to cross the finish line receives a cash prize.

ELITE RUNNERS INFORMATION VCM has a modest budget to recruit elite runners (men under 2:20 and women under 2:55). Transportation, hotel accommodations, entry and expenses are provided. Open prize money is offered to sixth place with the overall winner receiving $1,300, $650 for second, $325 for third, $200 for fourth, and $100 for fifth and sixth. Masters prize money extends to third place with $300 for the winner, $200 for second, and $100 for third.

ACCOMMODATIONS Try to stay at the Radisson Hotel Burlington which functions as VCM headquarters. The scenery from the upper lakeview rooms will make you loathe to leave. The Radisson is located at 60 Battery Street (800-333-3333). Other hotels offering special marathon rates include the Sheraton Burlington Hotel and Conference Center, 870 Williston Road (800-677-6576); and the Holiday Inn, 1068 Williston Road, South Burlington (800-799-6363).

RELATED EVENTS/RACES Runners not ready to tackle the marathon may consider the marathon relay, run simultaneously on the same course. The unique, 5-leg relay consists of 3.3, 6.6, 6.6, 4.1 and 5.6-mile legs, with teams consisting of 2 to 5 members with each member running at least one complete leg. Any one member may run up to four legs, in any order. In 1997, 609 teams entered the marathon relay, competing for the most creative team name.

AREA ATTRACTIONS Art loving runners will want to check out the Festival of Fine Art which coincides with race weekend. Over 25 Vermont artists open their studios to the public. Maps are available from Art's Alive (802-864-1557). History buffs may want to tour Revolutionary War hero Ethan Allen's homestead. For great lake views, take a scenic ride on Lake Champlain aboard the Ethan Allen, a 500-passenger, triple-deck cruise ship. Or spend a few hours strolling along Church Street with its trendy shops, nice restaurants, and street entertainers.

GHOST TOWN MARATHON

OVERALL: 81.2

COURSE BEAUTY: 9

COURSE DIFFICULTY: 6

APPROPRIATENESS FOR FIRST TIMERS: 5

RACE ORGANIZATION: 8+

CROWDS: 1+

RACE DATA

Overall Ranking: **77**
Quickness Ranking: **88**
Contact: **Governor's Cup**
P.O. Box 451
Helena, MT 59624
(406) 444-8261

Date: **June 5, 1999; June 3, 2000**
Start Time: **7:00 a.m.**
Time Course Closes: **1:00 p.m.**
Number of Finishers: **200 in 1998**
Course: **Point to point**
Certification: **USATF**
Course Records: **Male: (open) 2:20:35; (masters) 2:34:42**
Female: (open) 2:53:29; (masters) 3:12:44
Elite Athlete Programs: **No**
Cost: **$25/27**
Age groups/Divisions: **≤19, 20-29, 30-39, 40-49, 50-59, 60-69, 70+**
Walkers: **No**
Requirements: **None**
Temperature: **30° - 75°**
Aid/Splits: **10 / none**

HIGHLIGHTS A potluck of races, the Governor's Cup offers an event to suit everyone's interest and condition. Originally conceived to migrate from town to town in Montana, the Governor's Cup sits firmly entrenched in Helena's prairie soil. The challenging marathon—part dirt wagon trails, part asphalt—starts in the ghost town of Marysville and finishes in downtown Helena. With plenty of big sky all around, the open Ghost Town Marathon course loses 1,243 feet despite a 350-foot elevation gain in the final three miles.

COURSE DESCRIPTION Set in a broad valley framed by forested mountains, the Ghost Town Marathon starts in Marysville, Montana, at an elevation of 5,400 feet. Located in Montana's old gold mining country, this ghost town with its weather-worn buildings, was named after the first resident white woman, Mrs. Mary Ralston. The first 6 miles go generally downhill along the original horse and buggy trail. After reaching Lincoln Road, runners detour on a 1.4-mile loop (still a dirt road) beginning at the Silver City Bar. Once done, the course hits pavement for the first time on Birdseye Road leading to Helena. Miles 8 through 12 contain some tough uphill climbs, followed by a generally descending course. At about mile 18, the course ducks into the Montana National Guard and Fort Harrison complexes. Runners hit a 1-mile dirt stretch near the old Kessler Brewery around the 23-mile mark, and then hit Helena. Gaining about 300 feet over the final 3.5 miles, runners reach the finish line on Park Avenue in downtown Helena, elevation 4,157 feet.

CROWD/RUNNER SUPPORT You wouldn't expect a lot of spectators at the "Ghost Town" Marathon, and you're not disappointed. Except at the relay exchange points and the aid stations, spectators outside of Helena are definitely ghost-like. The finish line, however, is a different story, with thousands of race fans cheering on the participants. The aid stations, located approximately every 3 miles, carry water and minor first-aid supplies.

RACE LOGISTICS Since cars are not allowed on the course, park in the garage at Park Avenue and 6th in downtown Helena and catch the race bus just above the parking garage. The marathon buses leave at 5:45 a.m. It can be chilly in Marysville so make sure to take some warm-up clothing to the start. The race will return the clothing to you in the finish area.

ACTIVITIES If you preregister, your race number and T-shirt will be mailed to you. If you register late, or you need to register in person, go to the race headquarters at the Visitor and Commerce Center on Sixth Avenue and Cruse in downtown Helena to retrieve your race number. On race morning, you can pick up your race number, but you may not register. On Friday evening at the Cathedral of St. Helena, attend the Carboload Spaghetti Feed. The awards ceremony starts around noon, and refreshments are also available. Plans for other events have not been finalized.

AWARDS Each entrant receives their choice of a short-sleeve or long-sleeve T-shirt, polo shirt, or sweatshirt. The top three places in each age-group receive medals, and the top male and female overall and masters finishers receive specially crafted awards.

ACCOMMODATIONS Perhaps most convenient to race-day activities is the Park Plaza (406-443-2200). Other hotels in Helena include: Holiday Inn Express (406-449-4000); Shilo Inn (406-442-0320); Comfort Inn (406-443-1000); Days Inn (406-442-3280); Motel 6 (406-442-9990); Colonial Inn (406-443-2100); Super 8 (406-443-2450); Budget Inn Express (406-443-1770); Appleton B&B (406-449-7492); and Sanders B&B (406-442-3309).

RELATED EVENTS/RACES The Governor's Cup consists of a series of events, including: a four-person marathon relay, 20K race, 10K race, 5K race, and 400-meter Special Olympian Run. Nearly 7,000 runners participate in the Governor's Cup races, with most entering the nationally-known 5K race.

AREA ATTRACTIONS Among the activities to consider in Helena are the Gates of the Mountains boat tour, a visit to the Historical Society Museum, a train tour of Helena's historical sights, a State Capitol building tour, and a stroll through the Downtown Walking Mall.

GOD'S COUNTRY MARATHON

OVERALL: 80.5

COURSE BEAUTY: 9

COURSE DIFFICULTY: 6+ (SEE APPENDIX)

APPROPRIATENESS FOR FIRST TIMERS: 5

RACE ORGANIZATION: 9-

CROWDS: 2

RACE DATA

Overall Ranking:	84
Quickness Ranking:	92
Contact:	God's Country Marathon
	Potter County Visitors Association
	P.O. Box 245
	Coudersport, PA 16915
	Tel. (888) POTTER2
	Fax (814) 435-8230
	E-mail: potter_county@juno.com
	http://www.pavisnet.com/potter
Date:	June 5, 1999; June 3, 2000
Start Time:	8:00 a.m.
Time Course Closes:	2:00 p.m.
Number of Finishers:	102 in 1998
Course:	Point to point
Certification:	USATF
Course Records:	Male: (open) 2:25:12
	Female: (open) 2:53:14
Elite Athlete Programs:	No
Cost:	$20
Age groups/Divisions:	13-18,19-29, 30-39, 40-49, 50-59, 60+
Walkers:	No
Requirements:	None
Temperature:	55° - 80°
Aid/Splits:	12 / none

HIGHLIGHTS   Taking place in north central Pennsylvania's Potter County (nicknamed God's Country), the quarter-century old God's Country Marathon attracts approximately 100 runners. As you might imagine from the name, the race boasts a beautiful course, almost entirely through the wooded area along U.S. Route 6. Beauty aside, you may find yourself reciting a few prayers as the challenging route gains over 1,100 feet before crossing the Eastern Continental Divide near mile 17.

COURSE DESCRIPTION   The point-to-point course travels from Galeton to Coudersport along the historic and largely rural Route 6 transcontinental highway (3,227 miles from Provincetown, MA to Bishop, CA). Running along this road in Potter County is like taking a trip into north Pennsylvania's past.

After starting at Galeton High School, runners cut through this time-forgotten mountain town, head around the lake, then merge onto Route 6. The hills start early on Route 6, steadily climbing from 1,300 feet to 2,424 feet at the summit of Denton Hill (17 miles). With white pines and hemlock trees on each side, runners quickly descend for 4 miles, losing most of the previously gained elevation. Near 21 miles, the course drops into the moderately rolling hills of Sweden Valley. The last 5 miles include enough inclines to remind the runner that the work is not over, but enough elevation loss that the faint of heart can keep moving forward. Sweden Valley is more open with less tree-shaded stretches. A final downhill puts the Coudersport Town Courthouse Square into sight. At the center-of-town stoplight, the course turns right, proceeding uphill to the Coudersport Area Recreation Park and the finish around the park track. The course is very straightforward with a small diversion thrown in near mile 9 which includes a short out-and-back loop on Route 49 and a few turns near the finish.

CROWD/RUNNER SUPPORT A small number of local-yocals dot the course, while a small contingent of family and friends cheer at the finish line. Aid stations come every 2 miles supplying water, sport drink, and fruit. Route 6 is not closed for the event, making it very easy to follow the race by car.

RACE LOGISTICS The race provides bus transportation ($3) from the finish to the start line leaving at 6:20 a.m. Your spare clothing is transported to the finish.

ACTIVITIES God's Country typically has no pre-race activities. Pick up your race packet on race morning starting at 6:30 a.m. in Galeton. An awards ceremony and watermelon party take place on the CARP field.

AWARDS Every runner receives a T-shirt, and finishers receive special Potter County mementos. The top three male and female finishers earn $1,000, $500, and $250, respectively. Age-group winners usually win medals.

ACCOMMODATIONS The race maintains no official race hotel. Some choices in the area include: Hotel Crittenden, 133 N. Main St., Coudersport (814-274-8320); Coach Stop Inn, Rt. 6, Wellsboro (800-829-4130); Rough Cut Lodge, Rt. 6, Gaines (814-435-2192); Nob Hill Motel & Cabins, Rt. 6, Galeton (814-435-6738); and Laurel Inn, Coudersport (814-274-9220).

AREA ATTRACTIONS Many visitors to the area take advantage of the numerous scenic hiking and biking trails. Fishermen may want to pack their poles as 800 miles of pristine trout streams can be found in Potter County. The Pennsylvania Lumber Museum at the eastern base of Denton Hill preserves much of the lumbering history of north central Pennsylvania.

GOLD COUNTRY MARATHON

OVERALL: 84.3

COURSE BEAUTY: 9+

COURSE DIFFICULTY: 8- (SEE APPENDIX)

APPROPRIATENESS FOR FIRST TIMERS: 2

RACE ORGANIZATION: 9-

CROWDS: 1+

RACE DATA

Overall Ranking: 56
Quickness Ranking: 101
Contact: Nick Vogt
Christian Team Ministries
1025 Grange Road
Meadow Vista, CA 95722
Tel. (916) 878-0697
Fax (916) 888-6457

Date: June 6, 1999 (tentative); June 4, 2000 (tentative)
Start Time: 6:30 a.m.
Time Course Closes: 12:30 p.m
Number of Finishers: 54 in 1998
Course: Loop (Figure 8)
Certification: No
Course Records: Male: (open) 2:53:37; (masters) 3:06:22
Female: (open) 3:41:52; (masters) 3:44:19
Elite Athlete Programs: No
Cost: $30/40
Age groups/Divisions: ≤ 19, 20-29, 30-39, 40-49, 50-59, 60-69, 70-79, 80+
Walkers: No
Requirements: None
Temperature: 70° - 90°
Aid/Splits: 9 / none

HIGHLIGHTS   The 1848 gold miners lived one hundred and fifty years too soon to discover this nugget of a marathon. The Gold Country Marathon, a charming low-profile affair, staged in historic Nevada City, climbs over 2,600 feet during its figure-8 loop traversing the area's many rugged mining trails and flumes. The race's slogan, "Run for a good time, not a fast time," comes to mind as you struggle up Excelsior Ditch Camp Road and Augustine Hill (approximately 1,400 feet) from mile 15.5 to 18.5. Many top ultra runners use Gold Country to tune up for the famous Western States 100 Mile ordeal held four weeks later over neighboring terrain. In contrast to the gold strike, this event typically attracts less than 75 hearty runners who are treated to a continental breakfast before the run and full lunch afterward.

COURSE DESCRIPTION   The race starts at approximately 2,500 feet in Nevada City's Pioneer Park. The first mile heads by the balconied store fronts and gaslights of Nevada City's Victorian-styled downtown area. After joining a dirt mining road after mile 1, the next

9 miles roll up and down between 2,200 and 2,500 feet to Williams Ranch Road (10 miles). A dramatic 800-foot descent in the next 1.5 miles leads to the "Independence Trail" (the lowest point of the course at 1,450 feet) which offers gorgeous views of the Yuba River. The next 4 miles run flat, allowing you a respite before the route's biggest test, the 1,450-foot monster climb from mile 15.5 to mile 18.5. After descending 300 feet over the next 3.5 miles along Cement Hill Road and Indian Flat Road, runners retrace the first 4 miles of the course, finishing in Pioneer Park.

CROWD/RUNNER SUPPORT As with most rural races, spectator support is not one of the race's highlights. Besides the aid station volunteers located about every 3 miles, the only other areas of crowd support come in the downtown area and, of course, at the finish line.

RACE LOGISTICS Unless you are staying in downtown Nevada City, you will need to drive to the start. Sufficient parking exists near the starting area.

ACTIVITIES Pick up your race packet or register from 5:30 a.m. to 6:30 a.m. in Pioneer Park. Around 6:00 a.m. race organizers provide a continental breakfast buffet following a Sunrise Worship Service in the park's Seaman's Lodge. After finishing, enjoy a full meal while listening to live contemporary Christian music.

AWARDS Every runner receives a T-shirt, and finishers earn certificates. The top three in each age group win distinctive medals.

ACCOMMODATIONS The race does not have an official race hotel. Nearby lodging options include: Airway Motel, 575 Broad Street (530-265-2233); Northern Queen Motel, 400 Railroad Avenue (530-265-5824); National Hotel, reputedly the oldest continuously operated hotel west of the Mississippi, 211 Broad Street (530-265-4551). Several bed and breakfast and campgrounds are in the area.

RELATED EVENTS/RACES To encourage complete family participation, race organizers provide for several race day events. In addition to the marathon, participants may choose a 5K walk, 5K run, 10K run, or half marathon starting at 7:30 a.m. All races take advantage of the area's scenic country roads and historic trails.

AREA ATTRACTIONS Quaint Nevada City brims with boutiques, exceptional restaurants, and great live theatre and music. Mining museums, covered bridges and secluded swimming holes dot the area.

Taos Marathon

Overall: 78.2

COURSE BEAUTY: 8+

COURSE DIFFICULTY: 8- (SEE APPENDIX)

APPROPRIATENESS FOR FIRST TIMERS: 4+

RACE ORGANIZATION: 8+

CROWDS: 1-

RACE DATA

Overall Ranking: **97**
Quickness Ranking: **99**
Contact: **Marathon de Taos**
c/o Bruce Gomez
P.O. Box 2245
Taos, NM 87571
(505) 776-1860
http://www.taosnet.com\emanvelli\marathon-Taos

Date: **June 6, 1999; June 4, 2000**
Start Time: **6:00 a.m.**
Time Course Closes: **12:00 p.m.**
Number of Finishers: **99 in 1998**
Course: **Loop**
Certification: **USATF**
Course Records: **Male: (open) 2:34:17**
Female: (open) 3:25:40
Elite Athlete Programs: **No**
Cost: **$25/30**
Age groups/Divisions: **18-29, 30-39, 40-49, 50-59, 60+**
Walkers: **No**
Requirements: **None**
Temperature: **50° - 80°**
Aid/Splits: **17 / none**

HIGHLIGHTS   A magnet for artists from Georgia O'Keeffe to R.C. Gorman, Taos perches high in the mountains. Its adobe buildings, boundless horizons, and crystalline air rouse the creativity of those inclined to stark beauty. Despite being held for seventeen years, Taos attracts only 250 people to its five races. For the most part, runners lag behind artists in discovering this lofty retreat; most high-altitude seekers seem to congregate in Albuquerque to the south or Boulder to the north. Its remote, mountain location is certainly a prime explanation, although skiers have been shushing down its slopes for years. The challenging marathon, which reaches 7,200 feet, includes a debilitating hill at 12.5 miles.

COURSE DESCRIPTION   Starting outside Taos center at 6,950 feet, the marathon goes north on Taos Pueblo Road on a gentle decline for 200 yards with the mountains ahead of you. After 1 mile, runners make a sharp left through pastures and grassy fields. Turning onto Hwy. 64, runners face a gentle incline from mile 1.7 to 4.6 past the commercial outskirts of

Taos with fields on the left and the mountains toward the right. A moderate uphill hits from mile 5.3 to 5.9, followed by a gradual decline from 5.9 to 6.3 characterized by high desert scrub brush. Mostly flat from mile 6.3 to 9.7, the course takes a steep, curving plunge from 9.7 to 11.4, losing 600 feet. Passing through an adobe residential area, the course flattens briefly allowing runners to recover their legs before embarking on the difficult ascent to Arroyo Seco. The climb begins at mile 12.5 and is mercifully over by 13.2, but in that .75 miles runners have climbed 600 feet to an elevation of 7,100 feet. After several curves, the route flattens briefly before gradually ascending about 100 feet from mile 13.8 to 16. Rolling to 19, the town and surrounding mountains soon come into view as you begin the easy descent into Taos. A gentle incline at mile 24.8 precedes the journey through residential and commercial areas of Taos leading to the finish in Kit Carson Park.

CROWD/RUNNER SUPPORT Minimal crowds come out for the marathon, mostly race volunteers, friends and family of runners, and some residents in the neighborhoods along the course. The aid stations, located every 3 miles to mile 12, then every mile thereafter, carry water, electrolyte replacement, and energy bars. Runners can catch their own splits from the miles marked on the ground.

RACE LOGISTICS A small town, Taos is not difficult to get around, if a bit crowded near the town center. You need to find your own way to the start, located about a half mile from the town center. The start and finish are within walking distance of each other.

ACTIVITIES Saturday evening, the race expects to hold a pasta/pizza party at an undetermined location. There is no race-day registration. A post-race massage is available for a donation. You also have a chance to win one of the many random merchandise prizes.

AWARDS All runners get to wear home Taos Marathon T-shirts. Overall and age-group winners receive special prizes.

ACCOMMODATIONS Possible accommodations in Taos include: Best Western Kachina Lodge (505-758-2275); Holiday Inn Don Fernando de Taos, 1005 Paseo Del Pueblo (505-758-4444); Quality Inn, 1043 Paseo Del Pueblo (505-758-2200); Rancho Ramada Inn de Taos, 615 Paseo Del Pueblo (505-758-2900); Taos Civic Plaza, 121 Civic Plaza Drive (505-758-5792); Taos Inn, 125 Paseo Del Pueblo (505-758-2233); and El Pueblo Lodge, 412 Paseo Del Pueblo (505-758-8700).

RELATED EVENTS/RACES The Taos extended family of races includes several events for so few runners. A Marathon Relay for 5-member teams runs concurrently with the marathon (4 legs of 5 miles each, and one leg of 6.2 miles). At 7:00 a.m., a half marathon, 5K run, and 5K walk begin at the marathon start.

AREA ATTRACTIONS Made for browsing, Taos boasts numerous art galleries and curio shops. Also, stop by the still active Taos Pueblo.

STEAMBOAT MARATHON

OVERALL: 86.4

COURSE BEAUTY: 9+

COURSE DIFFICULTY: 5+ (SEE APPENDIX)

APPROPRIATENESS FOR FIRST TIMERS: 6

RACE ORGANIZATION: 9

CROWDS: 1-

R A C E   D A T A

Overall Ranking: 41
Quickness Ranking: 83
Contact: Special Events Coordinator
Steamboat Springs Chamber Resort Association
P.O. Box 774408
Steamboat Springs, CO 80477
(970) 879-0882
E-mail: info@steamboat-chamber.com
http://www.steamboat-chamber.com

Date: June 6, 1999; June 4, 2000
Start Time: 7:30 a.m.
Time Course Closes: 1:00 p.m.
Number of Finishers: Limited to 500
Course: Point to point
Certification: USATF
Course Records: Male: (open) 2:23:59
Female: (open) 2:54:59
Elite Athlete Programs: Yes
Cost: $35/40
Age groups/Divisions: ≤19, 20-29, 30-39, 40-49, 50-59, 60+
Walkers: No
Requirements: None
Temperature: 35° - 74°
Aid/Splits: 8 / every 2 miles

HIGHLIGHTS Famous as a winter playground, Steamboat Springs equally entices in the summer when the Steamboat Marathon runs. Green mountains. Waving aspen. Rustling rivers. Pure air. All make Steamboat one of the most compelling marathons on the continent. You won't find hoopla here. You won't find throngs of screaming spectators. And, you won't find air, at least a lot of it. Steamboat starts in tiny Hahns Peak Village, elevation 8,128 feet and ends in downtown Steamboat Springs, elevation 6,728 feet, making it a challenge for lowlanders even though most of the course runs downstream. You will find exhilarating nature which soothes your searing lungs. After the marathon, enjoy hot springs, fishing, horseback rides, air balloon flights, river rafting, and golf.

COURSE DESCRIPTION Wonderfully scenic, high altitude, moderately difficult, and point-to-point, the Steamboat course loses 1,400 feet from start to finish. The course begins in Hahns Peak Village, passes alpine ranches, Sleeping Giant mountain, and the Elk River on its way to downtown Steamboat Springs. Despite the significant elevation loss, several hills, made even more difficult by the thin air, tax runners. The open course runs on a narrow, country road, so beware the hurried fisherman on his way to the daily catch.

From the start, the setting treats runners to sweeping mountain vistas and meadows as they head down a gradual decline for the first half mile. Runners soon warm up on a modest incline between mile .6 and 1.2 that steepens near the crest, and then head sharply downhill past ranch land to the 2-mile mark. The next .75 miles roll slightly downhill. Then you face the first real hill on the course, a moderate, 1-mile incline, followed by an acute, sweeping downhill to the 10K point. This hill screams, fully testing your quadriceps muscles. You get a chance to recuperate over the next several miles: mostly flat from mile 6.2 to 6.8, slight upward slant from mile 6.8 to 7, and then gently down to mile 8.7. From 8.7 to 11.4, the course rolls slightly until you hit another moderate climb from mile 11.4 to 12.2. The Sleeping Giant mountain reclines to your right, and the Elk River tumbles down below. The next 10 miles roll easily down the mountain, until a short but abrupt climb at mile 22.5. A downhill to the turn onto Highway 40 leads toward downtown Steamboat at 24.5. A short, easy rise to 24.7 precedes a downward slope until a slight incline from mile 26 to the Courthouse lawn finish.

CROWD/RUNNER SUPPORT A small mountain resort, Steamboat doesn't attract many spectators to its marathon course but compensates with its scenery.

RACE LOGISTICS The extremely narrow road up Hahns Peak and the scarce parking once there make the free shuttle service extremely attractive. Shuttles leave from the parking lot at 8th and Oak Streets in downtown Steamboat between 6:00 a.m. and 6:15 a.m. There are also shuttle buses from the Sheraton to 8th and Oak. The race transports any personal belongings from the start to the finish area.

ACTIVITIES Pick up your race packet on Friday or Saturday on race weekend at Christy Sports in Central Park Plaza. You can attend the pasta dinner the night before the marathon. The dinner features a guest speaker (Gwyn Coogan in 1998) and all the food you can eat (about $12). After the race, soak in the famous Steamboat Springs Hot Springs. Immediate race results are generally handed out at the finish line. The awards ceremony and random drawing are held in the finish area at noon.

AWARDS All entrants receive T-shirts, and finishers also corral finisher's medals. Top age-group runners receive special awards.

FIRST TIMERS INFORMATION A challenging race for the novice marathoner, Steamboat's altitude, sparse crowds, relatively few aid stations, and pounding course make it less than ideal for the beginner. On the other hand, the beauty of the area doesn't hurt. If you are a first-timer training for Steamboat, we suggest you try to include some downhill training to accustom your quads to the pounding of running sharp downhills and some altitude training. While you could complete the race without these, you will be in better shape afterwards with them.

ELITE RUNNERS INFORMATION Steamboat offers inducements to elite runners. The criteria vary, so you need to contact race organizers to see if you qualify for elite status. Men with sub 2:30 times and women with sub 2:50 times will likely qualify. For those who are awarded elite status, the race offers lodging, expenses, and free entry. And, of course, a great weekend in Steamboat Springs.

ACCOMMODATIONS Call Steamboat Central Reservations (800-922-2722) to arrange your accommodations in Steamboat. They can take care of just about any lodging requirement to fit most budgets.

RELATED EVENTS/RACES In addition to the marathon, three other events for friends and family kick off on Sunday. The half marathon starts at the marathon midpoint (elevation 6,990 feet) and ends in downtown Steamboat. A 10K run and fitness walk over rolling hills begins at 8:00 a.m. Starting and finishing at the courthouse in downtown Steamboat Springs,

the 10K attracts many celebrity runners. Finally, the race holds a free, half-mile fun run for children starting at 11:15 a.m. at the courthouse.

GRANDMA'S MARATHON

OVERALL: 92.4

COURSE BEAUTY: 9-

COURSE DIFFICULTY: 2+ (SEE APPENDIX)

APPROPRIATENESS FOR FIRST TIMERS: 9

RACE ORGANIZATION: 10

CROWDS: 5

RACE DATA

Overall Ranking:	13
Quickness Ranking:	11
Contact:	Scott Keenan
	Grandma's Marathon
	P.O. Box 16234
	Duluth, MN 55816
	Tel. (218) 727-0947
	Fax (218) 727-7932
	E-mail: grandmas@grandmasmarathon.com
	http://www.grandmasmarathon.com
Date:	June 19, 1999; June 17, 2000; June 16, 2001
Start Time:	7:30 a.m.
Time Course Closes:	1:30 p.m.
Number of Finishers:	5,694 in 1998
Course:	Point to point
Certification:	USATF
Course Records:	Male: (open) 2:09:37
	Female: (open) 2:29:36
Elite Athlete Programs:	Yes
Cost:	$35/40
Age groups/Divisions:	12-18, 19-34, 35-39, 40-44, 45-49, 50-54, 55-59,
	60-64, 65-69, 70+, grandmother, wheelchair
Walkers:	No
Requirements:	12 years old
Temperature:	50˚ - 65˚
Aid/Splits:	15 / miles 5, 6.2, 10, halfway, 15, 20, 25 & 26

HIGHLIGHTS   What's this? A race for all the blue-haired, little old ladies of the world? Hardly. You don't have to be a grandma to run, but if you are, you can vie for the top Grandma award. Grandma's has earned a reputation as fast, exceptionally well organized, and a celebration. The race has attained cult-like status among marathon runners, possibly because of the odd name and Duluth location. The community really gets behind the race making Grandma's a BIG DEAL. And, event organizers have plenty of other activities to keep the family occupied. Kids love the Aerial Lift Bridge, reputedly one of only two left in the world. Straight and scenic in many places, the course rolls along the shores of Lake Superior. Few races match Grandma's in overall excellence for the runners and their families.

RACE HISTORY   Sadly, Grandma's is not named for that rocking chair planted, sweater-making, bespectacled woman we all remember so fondly. Rather, the race gets its name from its original sponsor, Duluth-based Grandma's Saloon and Deli. The race was started by a group of Duluth runners in 1977 and had 150 entrants. Since then, Grandma's has grown into one of the top races in the country, with more than 7,000 runners. Because of its popularity, organizers limit entries at 7,500.

COURSE DESCRIPTION Grandma's runs on a point-to-point course beginning in Two Harbors, MN and ending in Duluth's Canal Park. The completely closed course follows Old Highway 61 along the shore of Lake Superior, the largest freshwater lake in the world,

rolling lazily most of the way over newly resurfaced asphalt. The rural start turns more residential around mile 2. On the right are heavy woods. The first real hill on the course hits from mile 5.3 to 5.6, then it's an easy downhill. The course soon loses its residential quality and by mile 9.5 you are running right next to Lake Superior. Houses still pop up, and by mile 12, you pass some envy-worthy homes. The course continues to roll until mile 22, location of infamous Lemon Drop Hill which is actually two short hills to mile 22.4. Though not particularly difficult, Lemon Drop Hill could hit tired runners hard. Luckily, the thick crowds push you up the hill, and as you veer onto Superior Street, downtown Duluth emerges. Entering downtown after mile 24, you run on cobblestones and bricked streets. Just after 25, you make the turn toward the harbor, trudge up an overpass, wind through renovated Canal Park, and finish within a stone's throw of the Aerial Lift Bridge.

CROWD / RUNNER SUPPORT The Duluth community looks forward to the Grandma's celebration every year. An old train runs parallel to the marathon course to help spectators follow the race. Onlookers are mostly scattered, though, until roughly the 19-mile mark as runners approach downtown. Then the crowds become quite sizeable growing thicker and thicker as you near Canal Park. While every race claims it has great volunteers, Grandma's truly does. The 15 aid stations are very ably handled. Water, electrolyte replacement drink, sponges, and ice are all available at the stations.

RACE LOGISTICS The race provides bus transportation to the start at Two Harbors. Buses leave from a number of area hotels and the Duluth Convention Center from 5:15 a.m. to 6:00 a.m. You could provide your own means to the start, but it is not recommended due to limited parking. The race gladly transports your belongings to the finish.

ACTIVITIES On Friday, the Health and Fitness Expo kicks off at the Duluth Entertainment Convention Center (DECC), where you pick up your race packet and attend the free presentations by noted running experts. Also on Friday afternoon, take a bus tour of the marathon course. Buses leave from the DECC at noon, 2:00 p.m., and 4:00 p.m. Friday evening, make sure you join in the all-you-can-eat Michelina's spaghetti dinner at DECC from 11:00 a.m. to 9:00 p.m. Afterward, get jazzed-up by the live entertainment under the Big Top in Canal Park. Following the marathon, relax at one of the most festive post-race parties around, with live entertainment, a beer tent, and awards ceremony. All-in-all, Grandma's has just about the best activities in the country.

AWARDS All marathon finishers receive T-shirts and medallions. The top three runners in most age groups win special awards, as do the top local runner and grandmother. There is also $64,500 in prize money up for grabs as well as incentives.

ELITE RUNNERS INFORMATION Speedsters can negotiate with the race director for entry, transportation, food expenses, and possibly lodging, depending on just how speedy you are. Prize money goes to the top ten male and female runners ranging from $7,000 for first to $500 for tenth. The top masters runners and wheelchair finishers also earn prize money. There are a number of incentive bonuses for open and masters men who run under 2:20 and women under 2:40. The incentive bonuses range from $500 to $10,000.

ACCOMMODATIONS The key to finding the right place to stay in Duluth is to start early. Seriously. If you procrastinate you may find yourself pitching a tent. It's probably easiest to first call the Visitors Bureau (800-4-DULUTH) since they act as Grandma's lodging clearinghouse. Most convenient to the finish area are: The Inn on Lake Superior (218-726-1111); Radisson (218-727-8981); Holiday Inn (218-722-1202); Canal Park Inn (218-727-8821); and Comfort Suites (218-727-1378). Other good bets are Fitger's Inn (800-726-2982); and the Best Western—Edgewater (800-777-7925).

RELATED EVENTS / RACES Grandma's offers two other top-flight races: the William A. Irvin 5K and the Garry Bjorklund Half Marathon. The extremely festive atmosphere surrounding the 5K held Friday evening is perfect for friends and family. On Saturday morning, the popular half marathon starts at the marathon halfway point. The half has become one of the most popular in the Midwest, reaching its 3,500 runner limit one week after entry forms become available.

MAYOR'S MIDNIGHT SUN MARATHON

OVERALL: 85.5

COURSE BEAUTY: 9

COURSE DIFFICULTY: 5- (SEE APPENDIX)

APPROPRIATENESS FOR FIRST TIMERS: 9+

RACE ORGANIZATION: 9-

CROWDS: 1+

RACE DATA

Overall Ranking: 46
Quickness Ranking: 72
Contact: John McCleary
Anchorage Sports & Recreation
P.O. Box 196650
Anchorage, AK
(907) 343-4474

Date: June 19, 1999; June 17, 2000
Start Time: 8:00 a.m.
Time Course Closes: 4:00 p.m.
Number of Finishers: 2,700 in 1998
Course: Point to point
Certification: USATF
Course Records: Male: (open) 2:24:48
Female: (open) 2:48:16
Elite Athlete Programs: No
Cost: $32/35
Age groups/Divisions: 10-14, 15-19, 20-24, 25-29, 30-34, 35-39, 40-44,
45-49, 50-54, 55-59, 60-64, 65-69, 70+
Walkers: Yes
Requirements: None
Temperature: 55° - 70°
Aid/Splits: 10 / none

HIGHLIGHTS   Alaska, the last frontier, is quickly becoming the first frontier for many marathoners. The main lodestone, Mayor's Midnight Sun Marathon, pulls in the runners with its trademark Alaskan scenery, including the majestic Chugach Mountain Range and historic Cook Inlet. Enjoyed predominantly by locals until 1994, MMS's popularity changed when the Leukemia Society's Team in Training, a national fundraising and first-time marathoner training program, added the race to its marathon agenda. The largest Team in Training destination in the country, MMS's field has mushroomed from a long-standing few hundred runners to over 1,800 in 1996. With TNT's involvement, MMS boasts the largest percentage of first-time marathoners of any marathon in North America. What better place for a marathon adventure than the adventure capital of the world?

RACE HISTORY   Named to commemorate the summer solstice and honor the area's two mayors, the Mayors' Midnight Sun Marathon began in 1974 with 71 entries and 36 finishers. Realizing a politician's normal penchant for ego boosting, race organizers smartly named the race Mayors' Marathon to gain support for services, permits, and police patrol from the city and borough of Anchorage. The name soon changed to Mayors' Midnight Sun Marathon, and upon unification of city services, the apostrophe moved to reflect a singular mayor.

C O U R S E   D E S C R I P T I O N   Mayor's Midnight Sun Marathon's attractive, point-to-point course navigates through Anchorage from the striking Chugach Mountains to the historic Cook Inlet. It runs on a variety of surfaces, from paved bike trail, to road, to gravel road, to wooded trail, and back to bike trail and road. Including an uphill gain of 500 feet and downhill loss of 600 feet, the course boasts the possibility of spotting porcupines, moose, bears and other wildlife. Starting at Bartlett High School in east Anchorage (elevation 220 feet), the course travels northeast paralleling wooded Glenn Highway for 4 mostly flat miles on a paved bike path. After crossing the highway at mile 4, the course continues southwest on Arctic Valley Access Road for 3 miles of rolling hills before turning southeast on flat Arctic Valley Road passing the military guardhouse and Ship Creek. With the grand Chugach Mountains on the left, the course heads northeast on a dirt/gravel roadway and intersects the historic Oilwell Tank Trail at mile 9. The next 6 miles provide a shaded, meandering trail through an urban forest marked with several short but steep uphills and one long, gradual uphill from the half-marathon point to mile 14 (the highest point on the course at 500 feet). An enthusiastic aid station and a quick glimpse of downtown Anchorage greet the runners at 15 miles as the course turns right and heads downhill to Tudor Road, one of Anchorage's main thoroughfares. Jaunting briefly through a residential neighborhood on Checkmate Street, runners then return to another scenic bike path leading toward Westchester Lagoon (elevation 15 feet) at mile 25. On a clear day, a glance to the right reveals magnificent Mt. McKinley which provides inspiration for the challenging 400-yard hill awaiting at mile 25.5. Another short pass through a residential area precedes the finish on the West High School track.

C R O W D / R U N N E R   S U P P O R T   Although a smattering of spectators position themselves along the course, the rural nature of the race limits most of the support to the start and finish areas. The spectacular and peaceful scenery, however, more than makes up for the small number of spectators. Well-manned aid stations are found every 2-3 miles. Keep your eyes peeled between 18 and 19 miles for a generous, unofficial aid station on Checkmate Street. Last year, family members handed popsicles to marathon competitors, and other residents cooled runners with garden hoses.

R A C E   L O G I S T I C S   Since hotels are not located near the start/finish, you need to arrange transportation to the race. Fortunately, the race provides transportation from a number of hotels throughout Anchorage. Buses also transport runners from the finish back to their hotels. In addition, an equipment shuttle truck transports belongings to the finish.

A C T I V I T I E S   With the exception of a course tour, provided by local runners the day before the event, and loud, upbeat music played at the starting area, MMS has no pre-race activities. This should be of little concern as you will find plenty to do with your time, perhaps taking in one of the many solstice celebrations found city wide. Awards ceremonies occur directly upon the conclusion of each event.

A W A R D S   Sweatshirts and medallions are awarded to marathon finishers. Overall and age-group winners are awarded plaques or trophies. A special award, known as the Visitor's Cup, is presented to the best performance by an out-of-state female and male. The Anchorage Daily News newspaper publishes race results the following day. Official race results are mailed 4 to 6 weeks after the event.

A C C O M M O D A T I O N S   There is no official race hotel for the marathon. Some hotels in the area involved with the marathon transportation system include: Regal Alaskan Hotel, 4800 Spenard Road (907-243-2300); Best Western Barratt Inn, 4616 Spenard Road (907-243-3131); Super 8 Motel, 3501 Minnesota Drive (907-276-8884); Comfort Inn, 111 W. Ship Creek

Avenue (907-277-6887); Days Inn, 321 E. Fifth Avenue (907-276-7226); and Inlet Tower, 1200 L Street (907-276-0110).

RELATED EVENTS/RACES In addition to the marathon, MMS features other events. A marathon walk takes place on the same marathon course and begins one hour before the run. One hour after the marathon start, a half marathon and 5.6 miler start and finish at West High School, finish site for the marathon. Assuring that there is something for everyone, race organizers have added a 1.6-mile youth run for kids ages 8 to 13. The course loops around Westchester Lagoon with the start/finish at West High School.

AREA ATTRACTIONS Anchorage and the surrounding area offer plenty to see and do. If the marathon does not fulfill your physical activity quota, Kincaid Park, the Tony Knowles Coastal Trail and Chugach National Forest, all within arms length of Anchorage, offer excellent hiking, climbing, fishing, kayaking, and mountain biking. More sedate entertainment takes the form of sightseeing while cruising south on the Seward Highway. Keep your eyes peeled for whales at Beluga Point and Dall sheep on the steep cliffs near Windy Point. Also along the highway, is the Alyeska Ski Resort and its 60 passenger tram which provides a panorama of the Girdwood area. Twenty minutes further south sits Portage Glacier, the state's most popular tourist attraction. Take a walk along Portage Lake for a close-up look at countless, floating icebergs, or get to the glacier itself aboard a tour boat. Back in Anchorage, a must-see is the Museum of History and Art which depicts 10,000 years of Alaskan history. Finally, celebrate your marathon finish at one of the scores of solstice parties happening around town.

MANITOBA MARATHON

OVERALL: 74.6

COURSE BEAUTY: 8-

COURSE DIFFICULTY: 4

APPROPRIATENESS FOR FIRST TIMERS: 7

RACE ORGANIZATION: 9-

CROWDS: 3-

RACE DATA

Overall Ranking:	107
Quickness Ranking:	59
Contact:	Shirley Lumb
	Manitoba Marathon Foundation
	200 Main Street
	Winnipeg, Manitoba, Canada R3C 4M2
	(204) 925-5751
Date:	June 20, 1999; June 18, 2000
Start Time:	7:00 a.m.
Time Course Closes:	12:30 p.m.
Number of Finishers:	523 in 1998
Course:	Loop
Certification:	MRA, Athletics Canada
Course Records:	Male: (open) 2:13:53; (masters) 2:24:27
	Female: (open) 2:38:08; (masters) 2:45:30
Elite Athlete Programs:	Yes
Cost:	$55
Age groups/Divisions:	16-19, 20-24, 25-29, 30-34, 35-39, 40-44, 45-49, 50-54, 55-59, 60-64, 65+
Walkers:	No
Requirements:	None
Temperature:	75°
Aid/Splits:	25 / mile 1

HIGHLIGHTS If you're looking for a way to celebrate fitness, family, friendship and fun on Father's Day, consider the Manitoba Marathon in Winnipeg. Offering all this and more, the MM fundraises for local charitable projects. Everyone has an opportunity to participate as this event features four races in addition to the marathon—bringing together over 6,700 runners in all. What better way to spend Dad's Day than to pay tribute to health and posterity?

COURSE DESCRIPTION You'll appreciate the enthusiasm of the Winnipeg community as you make your way from the start at the University of Manitoba through the flat, loop course. Winnipeg residents typically come out to praise participants and happily shower them with water. The marathon course takes you down many main arteries of the city. Traveling down Wellington Crescent, you pass many stately old homes through beautiful Assiniboine Park (a shady respite from the summer sun) and the Legislative Buildings as you wind your way to the finish line at University Stadium. If you hate hills, be thankful, for they are virtually nonexistent on this course:

the maximum elevation variance is barely over 10 feet with most of the course at 770 feet.

CROWD/RUNNER SUPPORT   Since the Manitoba Marathon has a long history in the Winnipeg community, the marathon has become a very popular event for spectators, participants and volunteers alike. Watch at the intersections for course marshals and their antique cars. Water, medical staff, sponges, portable toilets and lubrication are part of what to expect at each station. Splits are provided only at the first-mile mark so bring your watch if you're tracking your pace. Runners worried about completing the entire distance will be interested in Manitoba's "exit with dignity" program, allowing runners to drop out at any point, turn in their tags, and catch a complimentary bus back to the finish area. A certificate attesting to the distance completed is then mailed to the participant.

RACE LOGISTICS   Transportation is not provided to the start/finish so plan ahead! For those with cars, there is plenty of parking within a short walk of the start.

ACTIVITIES   Race kits may be picked up at the race headquarters hotel during the two-and-a-half weeks prior to race day. There is no race-day registration or packet pickup. Join runners and volunteers at the Pasta Fest held Friday night. As a marathon participant, you're entitled to free admission to the dinner, held from 5:30 p.m. to 8:00 p.m. at the Winnipeg Convention Centre. If you didn't get enough to eat at the Pasta Fest, you have a second opportunity to fill up at the Carbo Brunch held Saturday morning at the International Inn. Listen to well-known running gurus share their expertise and experiences with you as you make your way through your meal. Tickets are available at the race headquarters. After you exit the finish chute, the pancake breakfast at University Stadium awaits you and your family. Here, you have an opportunity to share your race day stories and compare times with other competitors. What's more, at an affordable price, you can treat everyone to a Father's Day feast!

AWARDS   The Manitoba Marathon salutes top finishers with $10,000 in total prize money. The top Manitoban male and female finishers are recognized, and the Rick McLennan Memorial Trophy is awarded to the first Manitoban breaking a three-hour finish for the first time. Medals are mailed to all 1st, 2nd, and 3rd place finishers in each age group.

ELITE RUNNERS INFORMATION   Ten thousand dollars in prize money is divided between the top three overall and the first masters finishers as follows: 1st—$2,500; 2nd—$1,200; 3rd—$800; and masters—$500. The race also offers course record bonus money.

ACCOMMODATIONS   The official hotel is the International Inn (204-786-4801), adjacent to the International Air Terminal. Or, if you prefer less expensive accommodations about 100 yards from the start line, try the University of Manitoba, St. Andrews College (204-474-8895). Don't delay setting up reservations—this event attracts thousands of runners and space fills quite quickly.

RELATED EVENTS/RACES   If you're with those who wish to participate in less laborious activities, guide your guests to the Marathon Relay (team of 5 over 26.2 miles), the Super Run (2.6 miles), the Half Marathon (13.1 miles) or the 10K Walk. All of these events are featured on race day, and friends or family members can register at the headquarters if they've missed the preregistration deadline.

AREA ATTRACTIONS   In Winnipeg, check out the Forks Market located downtown on the banks of the Red and Assiniboine Rivers, featuring river walks, a children's museum, restaurants, and craft shops. Get a taste of life in central Canada's fur trading past at Ft. Garry, reachable by riverboat, double decker bus, or car. Perhaps spend an afternoon at Assiniboine Park and Zoo, located on the marathon course. Other Winnipeg staples include the Winnipeg Art Gallery, Captain Kennedy House, Leo Maude Sculpture Gardens, Oak Hammock Marsh, and the Winnipeg Mint.

CALGARY MARATHON

OVERALL: 82.4

COURSE BEAUTY: 8

COURSE DIFFICULTY: 3

APPROPRIATENESS FOR FIRST TIMERS: 8

RACE ORGANIZATION: 9

CROWDS: 3-

RACE DATA

Overall Ranking:	**68**
Quickness Ranking:	**34**
Contact:	**Heather McRae**
	Stampede Run-Off
	P.O. Box 296, Station M
	Calgary, Alberta, CANADA T2P 2H9
	Tel. (403) 264-2996
	Fax (403) 265-0640
Date:	**July 4, 1999; July 2, 2000**
Start Time:	**7:00 a.m.**
Time Course Closes:	**12:30 p.m.**
Number of Finishers:	**711 in 1998**
Course:	**Loop**
Certification:	**Athletics Alberta**
Course Records:	**Male: (open) 2:23:49**
	Female: (open) 2:45:59
Elite Athlete Programs:	**Yes**
Cost:	**$50/65/75**
Age groups/Divisions:	**18-29, 30-34, 35-39, 40-44, 45-49, 50-54, 55-59, 60-64, 65+**
Walkers:	**No**
Requirements:	**18 years old**
Temperature:	**50° - 57°**
Aid/Splits:	**14 / every mile and every 5K; projected finish times at 15K and 30K**

HIGHLIGHTS Lovers of things Western will want to consider the Calgary Marathon. Held during the world-famous Calgary Exhibition and Stampede, the marathon assumes much of its cowboy flavor—the Carbo Chow Down, Stampede Breakfast, and white cowboy hats for the winners. Mostly flat, the marathon takes in the wonderful Calgary Zoo, the Bow River and a number of residential communities.

RACE HISTORY The Calgary Marathon carries through a long tradition in Calgary, site of the 1988 Winter Olympics. In 1963, the nascent Calgary Marathon—then-named the Alberta and Western Canada Marathon Championship—hosted a meager nineteen participants. Its fate was forever changed, however, in the following year when Calgary hosted the Canadian Marathon Championship and the trials for the Tokyo Olympics. The Calgary Marathon joined the Stampede 10K and the Mayor's Fun Run/Walk in 1989 to become the Stampede Run-Off. To date, the event has raised over $250,000 for the Alberta Children's Hospital Foundation.

COURSE DESCRIPTION Calgary's rolling, out-and-back course runs through the scenic Bow River Valley; the only changes in elevation occur at roadway overpasses and underpasses. The race starts in downtown Calgary on 11th Street and 7th Avenue SW, immediately in front of the Calgary Science Centre and historic Mewata Armoury, and heads east through the city center. The course crosses the Bow River and continues east to loop through the Calgary Zoo. Runners go up a short rise (about 50 feet) to cross Memorial Drive and swing through Bridgeland, Calgary's Italian district. At 5 miles, the course heads west on Memorial Drive, paralleling the tree-lined Bow River, and takes a short loop through the West Hillhurst community. Crossing over the Crowchild Trail near 10 miles, runners loop through Parkdale, a quiet, shady community, before passing under the TransCanada Highway and through the community of Montgomery. At the halfway point, the course crosses the Bow River into Bowness, heading down the main avenue through this former suburb. The race loops past the old Bowness High School and then takes in the western section of the community below Canada Olympic Park. With the ski jumps of the 1988 Winter Olympics looming overhead, runners turn for home on a straight, flat stretch along the Bow River to 14th Street. An overpass draws runners to the finish line in Mewata Stadium, one block west of the start line.

CROWD/RUNNER SUPPORT Most spectators congregate near the bridge at 10K, in the neighborhoods at four relay exchange points on the marathon course, and at the finish.

ACTIVITIES The Calgary Marathon holds the Runners' Fitness Fair the two days preceding the race at the Southern Alberta Institute of Technology (SAIT). There, you have an opportunity to visit health and fitness-related exhibits, purchase merchandise, pick up your race package, or register late. Course tours are available on Saturday at 9:00 a.m., noon, and 3:00 p.m., for a $1 fee. Another event you shouldn't miss is the all-you-can-eat Carbo Chow Down ($20), a buffet held Saturday evening at the Southern Alberta Institute of Technology. All finishers can gather at the Stampede Breakfast for a monumental pancake spread, a part of Calgary's great Stampede tradition. A number of activities are available to entertain participants of all ages. Additional tickets are available at the breakfast for $3. Post-race awards begin at 2:00 p.m., closing out the weekend of activities.

AWARDS In the finish area, the first overall finishers are honored. In keeping with its Western theme, marathon winners are crowned with a white cowboy hat! Prize draws are held, including the drawing for a trip to Vancouver. Each runner receives a long-sleeve T-shirt, and all finishers are awarded medals at the finish line. Certificates for all finishers, as well as age-group medals, trophies, and draw prizes are presented at the Post Race Whoop Up. Trophies are awarded to the fastest overall, first-time marathoners, masters overall (40-49), masters B (45-49), and seniors (50-59).

ELITE RUNNERS INFORMATION Complimentary entry and some expense coverage are available for those with PRs faster than the course record. Fastest overall runners receive $500 for first place, $250 for second, and $175 for third. A $500 bonus is handed out to the first runner to break the existing course records.

ACCOMMODATIONS Limited low-cost accommodation is available at the Southern Alberta Institute of Technology. Call Linda (403-284-8012) to book a room. You can also contact the Calgary Convention & Visitors' Bureau (800-661-1678) for more information regarding accommodations. Book early as this is the peak tourist season in Calgary, and rooms fill quickly.

RELATED EVENTS/RACES If you have family or friends who aren't prepared for 26.2 miles, the 10K Road Race and 5K Family Walk are options.

AREA ATTRACTIONS You'll have no problem finding activities at the Calgary Exhibition & Stampede. Food, entertainment, rodeos, and chuckwagon races are among the possibilities. If you seek the outdoors, Calgary lies one hour away from the majestic Canadian Rockies.

GRANDFATHER MOUNTAIN MARATHON

OVERALL: 85.3

COURSE BEAUTY: 9+

COURSE DIFFICULTY: 7

APPROPRIATENESS FOR FIRST TIMERS: 5

RACE ORGANIZATION: 8

CROWDS: 2

RACE DATA

Overall Ranking:	49
Quickness Ranking:	98
Contact:	Grandfather Mountain Marathon
	Harry Williams/Jim Deni
	Department of Psychology
	Appalachian State University
	Boone, NC 28607
	(704) 265-3479
Date:	July 10, 1999; July 8, 2000
Start Time:	7:00 a.m.
Time Course Closes:	12:00 p.m.
Number of Finishers:	325 in 1997
Course:	Point to point
Certification:	None
Course Records:	Male: (open) 2:34:51
	Female: (open) 3:01:54
Elite Athlete Programs:	No
Cost:	$20/25
Age groups/Divisions:	≤19, 20-24, 25-29, 30-34, 35-39, 40-44, 45-49,
	50-54, 55-59, 60+
Walkers:	No
Requirements:	None
Temperature:	50° - 60°
Aid/Splits:	11 / none

HIGHLIGHTS   Kilts, bagpipes, and log throwing may seem mismatched with marathons and out of place in North Carolina, but at the Grandfather Mountain Marathon they come together in a boisterous mix of athletics and pageantry. Starting in Boone, NC, the race (celebrating its 32nd anniversary in 1999) winds through the scenic Blue Ridge Mountains before culminating in MacRae Meadows to the shrill sound of bagpipes and 15,000 cheering spectators attending the world's second largest Scottish Highland Games.

COURSE DESCRIPTION   Grandfather Mountain's point-to-point course starts in Kidd Brewer Stadium on the Appalachian State University campus in Boone. After dashing through the campus, the course enters the country including a section of the Blue Ridge Parkway. Winding through Blue Ridge Mountain forests, the mostly paved course (the course contains 3 miles of gravel) climbs from 3,333 feet to 4,279 feet. After two flat miles, runners roll through the mountains before twisting and turning uphill for the last 4 miles to the finish at MacRae Meadows.

CROWD / RUNNER SUPPORT As a runner, you're probably accustomed to delayed gratification. Keep this in mind as you trudge up and down the lonely Grandfather Mountain course anticipating the finish line scene amidst the Highland Games. Volunteers at 11 aid stations provide water and encouragement along the way. If you need something other than water during the race, be sure to make your own arrangements.

RACE LOGISTICS Located 80 miles west of Winston-Salem, Boone is a 2-hour drive from both the Charlotte Airport and the Piedmont Triad International Airport in Greensboro. Family and friends are encouraged to attend the 6:00 a.m. meeting on Saturday morning for special instructions about accessing the course and parking permits. Finish-line parking (for a fee) may be an adventure because of the Highland Games, so car pooling is highly recommended. The race director provides a bus to transport your gear from the start to the finish. If you need to return to the start, the same bus leaves after 1:00 p.m.

ACTIVITIES Packet pickup takes place Friday from 1:00 p.m. to 4:00 p.m. at Kidd Brewer Stadium at Appalachian State University. A pre-race Spaghetti Feast and Marathon Clinic, called "Enduring the Mountain," runs from 6:00 p.m. to 7:30 p.m. Race-day registration extends from 6:00 a.m. to 6:50 a.m. at which time all runners must report to the starting line for last minute instructions. Following the race, enjoy food, beverages, and Highland Games music and entertainment while waiting for the race results and awards scheduled for 12:15 p.m. under the marathon tent.

AWARDS All finishers receive T-shirts, while the top three male and female finishers receive special awards presented by both the GMM committee and the Highland Games. Age-group awards extend three places.

ACCOMMODATIONS Although Boone, Linville and neighboring towns offer many lodging options, July is high-tourist season so make early reservations. Possibilities near the start in Boone include: Cabana Motel, 782 Blowing Rock Road (704-264-2487); Elk Motel, 321 Blowing Rock Road (704-264-6191); Elliott Inn, 358 E. King Street (704-264-9002); High Country Inn, 1785 Hwy. 105 (704-264-1000); Perkins Park Inn, 1905 E. King Street (704-264-3638); and Red Carpet Inn, 862 Blowing Rock Road (704-264-2457). Accommodations near the finish include: Linville Resorts Inc., 175 Linville Hwy. (704-733-9241); Prixie Motel, Linville (704-733-2597); Linville Falls Motel, Linville Falls (704-765-2658); and Park View Motor Lodge, Linville Falls (704-765-4787).

AREA ATTRACTIONS If you have some time, there are many entertainment options in the area. After enjoying the kilts, bagpipes and unique athletic competitions of the Scottish Highland Games, stroll through some of the many antique and arts and crafts shops scattered about the area. If you're not afraid of heights, enjoy the view below as you walk across The Mile High Bridge over Linville Gorge. Nature lovers also should catch the beautiful Linville Falls.

SAN FRANCISCO MARATHON

OVERALL: 93.6

COURSE BEAUTY: 10-

COURSE DIFFICULTY: 5+ (SEE APPENDIX)

APPROPRIATENESS FOR FIRST TIMERS: 9-

RACE ORGANIZATION: 9

CROWDS: 5-

RACE DATA

Overall Ranking:	8
Quickness Ranking:	81
Contact:	Providian San Francisco Marathon
	120 Ponderosa Court
	Folsom, CA 95630
	Tel. (916) 983-4622
	Fax (916) 983-4624
	http://www.sfmarathon.com
Date:	July 11, 1999; July 9, 2000
Start Time:	7:00 a.m.
Time Course Closes:	1:00 p.m.
Number of Finishers:	3,697 in 1998
Course:	Point to point
Certification:	USATF
Course Records:	Male: (open) 2:17:34
	Female: (open) 2:40:32
Elite Athlete Programs:	No
Cost:	$45/55/70
Age groups/Divisions:	≤18, 19-24, 25-29, 30-34, 35-39, 40-44, 45-49,
	50-54, 55-59, 60-64, 65-69, 70+
Walkers:	No
Requirements:	None
Temperature:	50° - 60°
Aid/Splits:	12 / every 2 miles

HIGHLIGHTS Held in one of the world's great cities and starting on earth's most famous span, the San Francisco Marathon has made tremendous strides the past two years. With over 4,000 runners in 1998, the marathon is poised to become one of the top destination marathons in North America. After all, the San Francisco Marathon sports an exciting and spectacular course over the Golden Gate Bridge, through the Presidio, Marina District, Fisherman's Wharf, North Beach, Chinatown, Financial District, Haight-Ashbury, Golden Gate Park, and Sunset District—the ultimate tour of San Francisco! While challenging, the course avoids many of the city's most egregious hills. With a bit more progress promoting the race, both within the city and the country, and in attracting top runners, San Francisco should crest the hill and again emerge as one of the country's best.

COURSE DESCRIPTION San Francisco's beautiful, point-to-point course begins on the Marin County side of the Golden Gate Bridge. With only two of the bridge's six lanes dedicated to the runners, anticipate a crowded and slow first mile. On a clear morning, the bridge

offers incomparable views of San Francisco's skyline ahead and Alcatraz to the left. Upon crossing the bay, the course drops 225 feet in 2.25 miles, going through the scenic Presidio, a 200-year-old former military base. Runners then enter the Marina District, passing the Palace of Fine Arts, the Exploratorium, and the red-brick buildings of Ghirardelli Square. The course climbs approximately 50 feet between mile 4 and 5 and drops 50 feet from mile 5 to 6. At mile 6, you head up Columbus Street, the heart of North Beach, home to many of the city's great Italian restaurants, rising another 50 feet to mile 7. Telegraph Hill and Coit Tower sit to your left. Heading straight into bustling, vibrant Chinatown, the course falls 50 feet once again to mile 8. The route then quickly touches the Financial District before proceeding down the Embarcadero, temporary home to the large ships docking in the harbor. Around mile 11, the course goes past the warehouses and cheap clothing outlets of the Mission District. At the half-marathon point, runners hit the toughest part of the course—a 200-foot climb in just over a mile. Coming in stages, the climb begins on Guerrero and ends on Haight Street. Here, runners pass sidewalk cafes and bargain shopping in the world's hippie capital. You then start downhill into gorgeous Golden Gate Park, one of San Francisco's true wonders. The downhill trek through the park reaches land's end at the Great Highway near 18.5 miles. After a short jaunt along the ocean just before the 19-mile mark, the course begins to climb about 100 feet to 20 miles at Sunset Boulevard. The race then leaves the park to go up and back for 3 miles on Sunset, giving you a nice, flat break before completing the climb through Golden Gate Park (another 100 feet) to the finish inside Kezar Stadium, former home of the San Francisco 49ers. Watch out for that last hill just before the stadium. While not long or difficult in normal circumstances, it has caused more than a few tears in the past.

CROWD/RUNNER SUPPORT   The San Francisco Marathon still needs to bring out more residents to cheer on the runners. Still, city dwellers and tourists provide pockets of support along the course, particularly in the Marina District, along Columbus Street, in Chinatown, in Haight-Ashbury, and in Golden Gate Park.

RACE LOGISTICS   The fantastic Golden Gate Bridge start means that all runners must use the race-provided transportation. No cars or spectators are allowed at or near the starting line. Buses leave from the race headquarters hotel and from Kezar Stadium in Golden Gate Park beginning at 5:00 a.m. The race provides limited shuttle service from the finish back to the race hotel. Just be prepared for a wait.

ACTIVITIES   On Friday and Saturday of race weekend you can attend the Sports and Fitness Expo held with packet pick-up and late registration at Pier 35, a large warehouse near well-known Pier 39 on Fisherman's Wharf. You may not register on race day. The pasta dinner dishes out on Saturday evening. After the race, struggle up the stairs to reach the refreshments and snacks in Kezar Stadium.

AWARDS   Every entrant gets to wear home a San Francisco Marathon T-shirt, and finishers under 6 hours also get to drape a nice medal around their neck. Age-group awards (generally engraved marble paperweights) go three deep in each division. Top runners compete for $35,000 in prize money, with $10,000 for first, $5,000 for second, and $2,000 for third.

ACCOMMODATIONS   The San Francisco Marriott at 4th and Mission Street (415-896-1600) serves as the headquarters hotel. Other convenient hotels include: The Parc Fifty Five Hotel, Market at Fifth (415-392-8000); Hyatt Regency San Francisco, 5 Embarcadero Center (415-788-1234); the Grand Hyatt San Francisco on Union Square (415-398-1234); Ramada Limited Downtown, 240 7th Street (415-861-6469); Ramada Inn at Union Square, 345 Taylor Street (415-673-2332); Best Western Carriage Inn, 140 7th Street (415-552-8600); Best Western Canterbury Hotel, 750 Sutter Street (415-474-6464); Days Inn Downtown, 895 Geary Street (415-441-8220); Holiday Inn, 1500 Van Ness Avenue (415-441-4000); and Donatello Hotel on Post (415-441-7100).

RELATED EVENTS / RACES   Your non-marathoning family and friends can join in the San Francisco 5K which starts in Kezar Stadium and winds through Golden Gate Park, or organize a team for the marathon relay. San Francisco 5K runners may register on race day. Your friendly four-legged friends might enjoy the Alpo Dog Walk.

AREA ATTRACTIONS   One of the world's great destination cities, San Francisco beckons with its incredible setting, colorful neighborhoods, eccentric population, world-class dining, and activities to suit any taste. Don't miss Golden Gate Park, loaded with interesting things to do and see, such as the Japanese Tea Gardens, a romantic picnic, or an outdoor performance. After making the Fisherman's Wharf circuit, make sure you check out some of San Francisco's myriad neighborhoods—exclusive Nob Hill, the beautiful Marina District, Italian North Beach, frenzied Chinatown, Japantown, wacky Haight-Ashbury, or industrial/arty SOMA (south of Market). For a cross-cultural experience, or culture shock depending on your point-of-view, stroll the Castro District, center of San Francisco's infamous gay community. If you need a break, head across the Golden Gate Bridge to artistic Sausalito. If you really need a break, trek up gorgeous Mt. Tamalpais (about 20 minutes north of SF), hit the beach at Santa Cruz (about 90 minutes south of SF), hike at Point Reyes National Seashore (about 45 minutes north), or head to the wine region of Sonoma and Napa Valleys (about 45 minutes north). A visitor could literally spend weeks in the area and not come close to exhausting the possibilities.

MOSQUITO MARATHON

OVERALL: 78.4

COURSE BEAUTY: 9

COURSE DIFFICULTY: 10+ (SEE APPENDIX)

APPROPRIATENESS FOR FIRST TIMERS: 1

RACE ORGANIZATION: 8-

CROWDS: 0

RACE DATA

Overall Ranking: **95**
Quickness Ranking: **110**
Contact: **Jay Jones**
Leadville Mosquito Marathon
500 E. 7th Street
Leadville, CO 80461
(719) 486-2202 or (800) 933-3901

Date: **July 17, 1999; July 15, 2000**
Start Time: **7:00 a.m.**
Time Course Closes: **4:00 p.m.**
Number of Finishers: **121 in 1998**
Course: **Loop**
Certification: **None**
Course Records: **Male: (open) 4:02:08**
Female: (open) 5:15:56
Elite Athlete Programs: **No**
Cost: **$35/45/50**
Age groups/Divisions: **≤29, 30-39, 40-49, 50+**
Walkers: **No**
Requirements: **High altitude and/or marathon experience recommended**
Temperature: **20° - 60°**
Aid/Splits: **3 / none**

HIGHLIGHTS   This mosquito bites! Actually, mosquitoes are the least of your concerns at the Leadville Mosquito Marathon, named for a recurring obstacle on the course—Mosquito Pass. Quite simply the toughest marathon in North America, Mosquito runs above 11,000 feet for 80% of the race. Heap onto that between 5,500 and 6,500 feet of climbing in paper-thin air. Did we mention the fixed-rope drop over the snow cornice near mile 15? Or, the fact that race organizers require toting a map? Obviously not for the novice, Leadville appeals to those runners seeking an extreme experience to challenge their minds and bodies. Leadville also attracts ultramarathoners wanting a tune up for longer trail runs, including the Leadville 100 miler at the end of August.

COURSE DESCRIPTION   Race organizers alter the Mosquito Marathon course yearly, depending on snow conditions and their whim. Be assured that the race will run on a variety of surfaces, including Jeep roads, rocky single-track trails, paved roads, and cross country with no trail. During one half-mile section of ridge called "hands-on saddle," runners with shaky balance could spend as many as two hours negotiating the irregular large rocks. Expect at least 2 to 4 miles of snow, possibly including the fixed-rope drop over the snow cornice. The race starts in Leadville at 10,150 feet, the lowest point on the loop course. The elevation profile depicts the 1996 course which contained about 800 fewer feet of vertical climbing than usual. Even with fewer uphills, the course included a 2,000-foot climb (from 11,500 feet to 13,500 feet) in 2 miles, and two 1,000-foot ascents in less than 2 miles. About 70% of the race takes place above timberline. In these higher elevations, you must be prepared for whipping winds, snow, rain, and sun, possibly all in the same race.

CROWD / RUNNER SUPPORT   Crowds here are a misnomer. Your support consists of your handlers and the race volunteers. The race sets up three aid stations, at approximately miles 8, 13, and 18.7, where water, food, medical aid, and phones are available. You must pack your own food and water to get you from one aid station to the next. Consider wearing some type of ankle protection against the rocks, and you should also consider leg protection for the snow. A hat and windbreaker will also be beneficial for the upper elevations.

RACE LOGISTICS   Unlike most marathons, getting to the start at 6th and Harrison in Leadville is the least of your concerns. You must sign in on race morning even if you already have your bib number so they know you are out on the course. Pre-race orientation starts at 6:45 a.m., and the race begins at 7:00 a.m. The race has two cutoff times, which means you must reach the designated points by a certain time, or you will be forced to withdraw from the race. The cutoff time for reaching aid station #1 at 8 miles is 9:30 a.m. and for aid station #2 at 13 miles is 11:30 a.m. It is possible that an injured runner will ask you to turn around or go ahead to summon help from the nearest aid station. This is simply the nature of these mountain races.

ACTIVITIES   You can pick up your packet or register at Club Lead, 500 E. 7th Street in Leadville on Friday from 6:00 p.m. to 8:00 p.m. You may register on race day at Hard Rock Park near the start from 5:45 a.m. to 6:45 a.m. as long as the total 300 runner limit (for both races) has not been reached. Nurse your aching body at the post-race picnic; the awards ceremony starts at 3:00 p.m. with the chance to win many random prizes.

AWARDS   Every early-registered runner receives a race shirt, as do the first 25 entrants who missed the postmark cutoff date. The top three in each age group receive ribbons with the age-group winners also receiving merchandise prizes, such as trail running shoes, clothing, and ski passes. The top finishers in each age division receive rosette ribbons.

ACCOMMODATIONS   Leadville offers a number of lodging choices: Wood Haven Manor, 807 Spruce Street (800-748-2570); Grand West Village Resort (800-691-3999); Leadville Country Inn (719-486-2354); The Delaware Hotel (800-748-2004); Mountain Hideaway (800-933-3715); Timberline Motel (800-352-1876); The Apple Blossom Inn (719-486-2141); Twin Lakes Nordic Inn (719-486-1830); and Club Lead with simple rooms and bunks (719-486-2202). Others are given on the entry brochure.

RELATED EVENTS / RACES   Runners still on this side of sanity may want to test the mountain waters with about 100 other borderline cases by first trying the 15 Mile Short Race. The short race contains about 3,000 feet of climbing on dirt roads past Lake Isabelle to the summit of Mosquito Pass at 13,200 feet and back to Leadville. The top men finish in about 2:20 and the top women in about 2:45.

AREA ATTRACTIONS   The Leadville area contains outstanding recreational activities, including mountain biking, white water rafting, hiking, and trail running. Visitors also can head to nearby Vail (35 miles) and Aspen (60 miles).

University of Okoboji Marathon

Overall: 77.6

COURSE BEAUTY: 9+

COURSE DIFFICULTY: 5-

APPROPRIATENESS FOR FIRST TIMERS: 6

RACE ORGANIZATION: 7+

CROWDS: 0+

RACE DATA

Overall Ranking: 101
Quickness Ranking: 75
Contact: University of Okoboji Marathon
Box 7933
Spencer, IA 51301 - 7933
Tel. (712) 338-2424
Fax (712) 338-4322

Date: July 17, 1999; July 15, 2000
Start Time: 6:00 a.m.
Time Course Closes: 11:00 a.m.
Number of Finishers: 106 in 1998
Course: Loop
Certification: USATF
Course Records: Male: (open) 2:23:07
Female: (open) 2:57:43
Elite Athlete Programs: No
Cost: $15/20
Age groups/Divisions: ≤19, 20-29, 30-39, 40-49, 50-59, 60-69, 70+
Walkers: No
Requirements: None
Temperature: 73°
Aid/Splits: 8 / miles 1, 2 & 3

HIGHLIGHTS   Most people have never heard of Okoboji, nor know that it houses a famous university which hosts a marathon every year. Okoboji lies in the beautiful Iowa Great Lakes area and features West Lake Okoboji, heralded by National Geographic as one of the most beautiful blue water lakes in the world. The lake serves as the centerpiece of the University of Okoboji Marathon which takes runners in and out of the surrounding resort areas. With its beautiful course, small field, and low-key race management (remember it's a vacation resort), Okoboji harkens back to the days when running a marathon was a novel endeavor. The marathon is but one of many festivities tied into homecoming weekend at the University of Okoboji—the most famous nonexistent university in the world.

RACE HISTORY   The story of the University of Okoboji Marathon is directly connected to the founding of the University of Okoboji by a group of lakes-area residents and sports enthusiasts. "We were always playing tennis, or softball, or something," says one of the founders,

Herman Richter, "and we used to kid each other, 'What's going on at Camp Okoboji tomorrow?'" The group began talking about their private club so much that they printed their own University of Okoboji T-shirts which became an instant hit with local residents and Okoboji's large tourist population. The usual university souvenirs (bumper stickers, pennants, sweatshirts) followed for this nonexistent school that offers only two courses of study—recreation and running. The university quickly evolved into a fundraising organization which sponsors several events each year including the marathon. The race has grown from forty runners in its inaugural year in 1978 to its current average of just over one hundred. And don't worry, the marathon, unlike the university, really does exist.

COURSE DESCRIPTION   The Okoboji Marathon begins at Pikes Point State Park on the upper northeast side of West Okoboji Lake. In a clockwise manner, the course circles the lake and runs through resort areas passing million-dollar homes on oak tree-lined roads. After completing one loop of the lake, the course retraces the first 5.5 miles and ends on the waterfront at Arnold's Park at the lake's southeast end. Lake Okoboji lies at approximately 1,400 feet so elevation is not a concern. Held on a smooth, asphalt road, the race contains only two noticeable inclines near the 2-mile mark (100 yards) and 10-mile mark (200 yards).

CROWD/RUNNER SUPPORT   Most of the race spectators concentrate at the start in Pikes Point State Park and at the finish in Arnold's Park. In addition to family and friends of the marathoners, the spectator base is enhanced by the other events that directly follow the marathon. Since the race course is not closed to traffic, spectators can easily follow their favorite runner throughout the event. With the exception of a handful of early bird fishermen, don't expect to experience overwhelming crowd support through the resort areas until later in the morning.

RACE LOGISTICS   Shuttle buses are provided from the finish line to the starting area. In addition, runners who park at the starting line may catch a shuttle bus back to the start after completing the race. The race will transport warm-up clothing from the start to the finish.

ACTIVITIES   Again, this is a no frills race which offers none of the pomp and circumstance that many other races provide. Take advantage of the peaceful setting that Okoboji offers to relax and center yourself for race day. Runner's packets can be picked up at the Three Sons Clothing Store in Milford on the Friday before the race from 10:00 a.m. to 8:00 p.m. Packets may also be picked up on race day at the start in Pikes Point State Park. Race-day registration is available until 15 minutes prior to the start. After finishing, relax at the waterfront while you enjoy music, food and drinks. An awards ceremony gets under way at 11:00 a.m.

AWARDS   Race T-shirts displaying the coveted U of O emblem are presented to each participant. Overall winners and top division finishers receive special awards.

ACCOMMODATIONS   Virtually all of the lakeshore cabins, inns and motels provide excellent accommodations and easy access to the start and finish areas. Some worth noting include: Beaches Resort, 15109 215th Avenue, Spirit Lake (712-336-2230); Crescent Beach Lodge, 1620 Lakeshore Drive, Wahpeton (712-337-3351); and Crow's Nest Resort, 304 Lake Drive, Arnold's Park (712-332-2221). Camping is available at the White Oaks Campground, 1508 4th Street, West Okoboji (712-332-5114).

RELATED EVENTS/RACES   Okoboji hosts a festival of races on marathon day including a half marathon, 10K run and triathlon. Be advised that the 10K and half marathon start at separate locations.

AREA ATTRACTIONS   If you have not used all of your energy in the marathon, there are plenty of things to do around the lakes. Swimming, fishing, golfing, and boat cruising are some considerations. Strolling through the many area antique shops and Indian museums or exploring the amusement park are other options. If you're a scuba diver, bring your gear. Homecoming weekend features a contest held for divers to search the bottoms of the lakes for the most unusual items in several different categories. Better yet, just plain relaxing may be the ticket, and there are few better places for it than Okoboji and its peaceful surroundings.

DESERET NEWS MARATHON

OVERALL: 87.7

COURSE BEAUTY: 9

COURSE DIFFICULTY: 7

APPROPRIATENESS FOR FIRST TIMERS: 7-

RACE ORGANIZATION: 8

CROWDS: 7-

RACE DATA

Overall Ranking: 31
Quickness Ranking: 97
Contact: Deseret News Marathon
Salt Lake County Recreation
2001 S. State Street, #S-4900
Salt Lake City, UT 84190
(801) 468-2560
http://www.desnews.com/run/

Date: July 24, 1999; July 24, 2000
Start Time: 5:00 a.m.
Time Course Closes: 11:00 a.m.
Number of Finishers: 763 in 1998
Course: Point to point
Certification: USATF
Course Records: Male: (open) 2:16:57
Female: (open) 2:45:35
Elite Athlete Programs: Yes
Cost: $25/28/30
Age groups/Divisions: ≤11, 12-14, 15-18, 19-24, 25-29, 30-34, 35-39, 40-44, 45-49, 50-54, 55-59, 60-64, 65-69, 70+, Clydesdale (M) 200+ lbs., (F) 140+ lbs.
Walkers: No
Requirements: None
Temperature: 50° - 75°
Aid/Splits: 17 / every mile

HIGHLIGHTS When Brigham Young descended the Wasatch Mountains on July 24, 1847, he looked out over the Salt Lake Valley below and exclaimed, "This is the place!" for his Mormon settlers. When you run the Deseret News Marathon and lope down Emigrant Trail, you may very well agree. With spectacular scenery, the end of July is perhaps the best time to visit Salt Lake City outside of ski season. Part of the Days of '47 festivities, the DNM helps celebrate the state holiday commemorating those Mormon settlers. The challenging marathon course retraces the steps of these first pioneers down into the valley. Faster runners finish in front of 200,000 screaming onlookers waiting for the start of the Days of '47 Parade, one of the largest in the country. After the race, join in the Founder's Day festivities.

COURSE DESCRIPTION The Deseret News Marathon starts at 5,880 feet in the beautiful Wasatch Mountains and follows much of the same trail carved from the wilderness by the ill-fated Donner Party of 1846 and Mormon Pioneers who entered the Salt Lake Valley on

July 24, 1847. Runners battle altitude and several tough climbs on this challenging course. The first 1.5 miles are a gradual to steep downhill. Runners then have a quick uphill, followed by a .3-mile downhill. At 1.9 miles, you begin a long, arduous 377-foot climb to the turnaround at the 6-mile mark. Watch your fellow runners go by as you retrace your steps to just past 8 miles, make a sweeping right turn, and climb another 3 miles to the course's zenith, 6,227-foot Little Mountain Summit. A 3-mile downhill through a peaceful residential area, Emigration Canyon, rewards your previous hard work. The course then flattens around mile 14, but quickly goes downhill again as you run alongside a creek, past the Santa Fe Inn and Ruth's Diner at 17 miles and the "This Is The Place Monument" and Hogle Zoo just after mile 18. This area offers a nice, panoramic view of the city, the Great Salt Lake and the surrounding mountains. After a right turn on Foothill Blvd., runners face a slight upgrade for a half mile and then a sharp right turn and gradual incline through the campus of the University of Utah to approximately mile 21. It's all downhill from here traversing an older residential neighborhood and a brief steep descent to South Temple Street toward downtown Salt Lake City. A left turn of 900 East and a quick, sharp right on 100 South brings you toward the Days of '47 parade route on 200 east at the 24-mile mark. If you make the turn under the 3.5 hour mark, you'll run to the cheers and applause of nearly 200,000 spectators waiting for the 9:00 a.m. parade start. The last .75 miles are slightly uphill to the finish at Liberty Park, elevation 4,265 feet.

CROWD/RUNNER SUPPORT   The early morning and remote start mean crowds are limited for most of the race. Runners who can make it to Main Street under 3.5 hours, however, are greeted by the huge crowd—about 200,000 strong—waiting for the start of the Days of '47 Parade. Seventeen aid stations along the course carry water, electrolyte replacement drink and sponges. To avoid dehydrating as the summer day wears on, make sure to take advantage of every station.

RACE LOGISTICS   With no parking at the marathon starting line, runners must take shuttle buses to the start. Buses leave between 3:00 a.m. and 3:30 a.m. from the Delta Center downtown and the University of Utah football stadium. Shuttles return runners from the finish area to their cars parked at both parking locations starting at 7 a.m.

ACTIVITIES   Walk-in registration is available from July 15 through July 18 at all Granite Furniture locations; Salt Lake County Parks and Recreation, 2001 S. State #S-4900; and Deseret News, 30 East 100 South. Those interested in registering on July 22 or 23 must head to the official race hotel, Marriott University Park Hotel, 480 Wakara Way. A pre-race pasta party and race clinic occur the afternoon prior to the race. Enjoy live music, a sports expo, and the parade while you wait for the awards ceremony following the race.

AWARDS   Marathon entrants receive a T-shirt and free transportation to the race start. Finishers earn a medallion and certificate. The top three runners in each age and special division receive medals. Overall winners earn $1,000 for first, $500 for second, and $250 for third.

ELITE RUNNERS INFORMATION   DNM does recruit elite marathoners, but no criteria have been established. The race could offer transportation expenses, hotel accommodations, entry and prize money, depending on your credentials. Contact Scott Kerr (801-468-2560) for more information.

ACCOMMODATIONS   Marriott Park Hotel, 480 Wakara (800-637-4390), serves as the sponsoring accommodations. Otherwise, try the Little America Hotel, 500 South Main Street (801-363-6781); Shilo Inn, 206 SW Temple Street (801-521-9500); or Holiday Inn Hotel, 999 South Main Street (801-359-8600).

RELATED EVENTS/RACES   The well-known Deseret News 10K starts at the marathon 20-mile mark at 6:15 a.m. The 10K, which attracts over 2,500 runners, is generally recognized as one of the fastest in the country. Race organizers have recently added a non-competitive 5K fitness walk beginning at 6:30 a.m. at the Delta Center.

AREA ATTRACTIONS   Numerous events are held in conjunction with Founder's Day, including the parade, rodeo, art show, and fireworks display.

KILAUEA VOLCANO MARATHON

OVERALL: 87

COURSE BEAUTY: 10

COURSE DIFFICULTY: 9-

APPROPRIATENESS FOR FIRST TIMERS: 4

RACE ORGANIZATION: 9-

CROWDS: 0+

RACE DATA

Overall Ranking: 35
Quickness Ranking: 105
Contact: Jim Moberly
Kilauea Volcano Marathon & Wilderness Runs
P.O. Box 15321
Honolulu, HI 96830
Tel. & Fax (808) 735-8733
E-mail: jmoberly@lava.net

Date: July 24, 1999; July 22, 2000
Start Time: 6:00 a.m.
Time Course Closes: NA
Number of Finishers: 165 in 1998
Course: Loop
Certification: None
Course Records: Male: (open) 2:56:18
Female: (open) 3:33:41
Elite Athlete Programs: No
Cost: $40/45
Age groups/Divisions: ≤19, 20-29, 30-39, 40-49, 50-59, 60+
Walkers: No
Requirements: None
Temperature: 50° - 90°
Aid/Splits: 8 / none

HIGHLIGHTS   A race worthy of our rugged pioneer ancestors, the Kilauea Volcano Marathon runs on some of the most virgin soil on earth created by the world's most active volcano. Possibly North America's toughest certified marathon, only the hardy and adventurous should brave the sharp lava fields, the wafting sulfur, and the hilly, uneven terrain brimming the Kilauea caldera. Started in 1983 as a way to whisk park rangers into shape, the race now raises money for the Volcano Art Center which supports area artists. With this connection, you can be assured of beautiful T-shirts and original awards in addition to the incredible memories of running on top of earth's most billowiest fire pit.

COURSE DESCRIPTION   The marathon's loop course starts at the Kilauea Military Camp flagpole (elevation 4,000 feet) and heads west on a relatively calm and scenic paved road. You proceed past Hawaiian Volcanoes Observatory on the Kilauea Crater Rim and take the right fork to the Ka'u Desert Trail, a 7.1-mile stretch dropping 1,018 feet over rugged lava and uneven terrain. When you're not hopping rocks, you may be running in deep black sands. Runners pick up the Mauna Iki Trail for 6.3 miles over sharp lava fields and newer lava flows. Don't stray here as there are unstable lava tubes and bottomless pit craters. The course turns left on Hilina Pali Road, 4 miles of curvy paved road that climbs 220 feet. At the 17-mile mark, the route descends 170 feet on Chain of Craters Road; be alert for cars but rest up for the brutal uphill which approaches. Get plenty of fluids at the Mauna Ulu parking lot aid station before proceeding up the Escape Road, a 700-foot climb over 4 miles. The Escape Road is a four-wheel drive road used when lava flows interrupt traffic on Chain of Craters Road. Wild pigs, a National Park pest, have been seen here eating blackberries and ohela berries. Emerging at the incredible Thurston Lava Tube near mile 23, the course finishes on narrow trails through ohia-fern forests and blooming yellow gingers. The race merges with the ten-mile Crater Rim Trail Run course at Waldron's Ledge, which overlooks Kilauea Crater. Runners proceed on Crater Rim Trail behind the Volcano House, past the Visitor Center and the Art Center toward the Steaming Bluffs Trail. Although less than a mile to the finish, one cannot help but take in the spectacular view overlooking Steaming Bluff, enhanced by puffs of steam. The race finishes at the Kilauea Military Camp Theater.

CROWD/RUNNER SUPPORT Over 375 volunteers support the runners along the course. Aid stations, stocked with water, electrolyte replacement drink, and energy bars, lie approximately every 3 miles. Sorry, gas masks not available.

RACE LOGISTICS Unless you are staying in Hawaiian Volcanoes National Park, you will need to drive to the start. We suggest you reserve your rental car far in advance because they can be completely booked. Head to the KMC Back Gate off Highway 11 (milepost 30); Marines will show you where to park. You must have your shoes scrubbed before starting the race to avoid introducing foreign weeds into the sensitive environment, so arrive a little early. You may check your personal belongings near the T-shirt area.

ACTIVITIES Race weekend starts with the Carbo Load Dinner on Friday evening from 5:00 p.m. to 7:00 p.m. at the Kilauea Military Camp Dining Room (about $11). Runners who find their bravery dwindling can take advantage of the no-host cocktails. You may register or pick up your race number at the dinner or at the pre-race check-in starting at 5:00 a.m. on race morning. After the race, nurse your psyche with fresh Hawaiian-grown fruit, refreshments, massage, and Hawaiian entertainment. The awards ceremony starts at 10:30 a.m.

AWARDS Entrants who don't finish get to take home memories and possibly some scrapes and bruises from their trek through the lava fields. Finishers receive the distinctive Makoa finisher T-shirt. Special prizes designed by Volcano Art Center artists are awarded to the top three overall, military, and age-group winners. In all, over 200 prizes go to winners and random award recipients.

ACCOMMODATIONS The Hilo Hawaiian Hotel, 71 Banyan Drive (808-935-9361) serves as the official headquarters hotel for the Kilauea Wilderness Runs. A limited number of dormitory rooms are available at the Kilauea Military Camp (808-438-6707). The Volcano House (808-967-7321) is located in Hawaii Volcanoes National Park. Other accommodations include: Kilauea Lodge in Volcano Village (808-967-7366); Hale Ohia Cottages (800-455-3803); Kilauea Volcano Kabins (800-626-3876 or 808-967-7773); Carson's Volcano Cottage (800-845-LAVA); Country Goose B&B and Vacation Rentals (800-238-7101); and My Island B&B at Volcano (808-967-7216).

RELATED EVENTS/RACES The Kilauea Volcano Wilderness Runs, which attract 900 runners total, comprise a menu of races: the challenging 5-Mile Kilauea Caldera Run & Walk which goes down into the caldera and back out; the popular 10-Mile Rim Run which circles Kilauea Caldera; and the marathon.

AREA ATTRACTIONS Brimming with attractions, the diverse Big Island boasts Hawaii Volcanoes National Park, with the massive Mauna Loa and Mauna Kea Volcanos, and Kilauea. Be sure to explore the amazing Thurston Lava Tube lined with beautiful ferns. See the artwork supported by the marathon at the Volcano Art Center. Beaches ring the island, including Black Sand Beach formed by worn lava.

CRATER LAKE MARATHON

OVERALL: 87

COURSE BEAUTY: 10

COURSE DIFFICULTY: 8+

APPROPRIATENESS FOR FIRST-TIMERS: 3

ORGANIZATION: 9-

CROWDS: 0+

RACE DATA

Overall Ranking: 35
Quickness Ranking: 104
Contact: **Bob and Beverly Freirich**
Crater Lake Rim Runs
5830 Mack Avenue
Klamath Falls, OR 97603
Tel. (541) 884-6939

Date: **August 8, 1999 (tentative); August 13, 2000 (tentative)**
Start Time: **7:30 a.m.**
Time Course Closes: **1:00 p.m.**
Number of Finishers: **500 limit between all races**
Course: **Point to point**
Certification: **None**
Course Records: **Male: (open) 2:38:34**
Female: (open) 3:18:10
Elite Athlete Programs: **No**
Cost: **$25/35**
Age groups/Divisions: **≤12, 13-19, 20-29, 30-39, 40-49, 50-59, 60-69, 70+**
Walkers: **No**
Requirements: **None**
Temperature: **52°-75°**
Aid/Splits: **11 / none**

HIGHLIGHTS The word "crater" usually does not have a good connotation when associated with running. It is usually applied to a person who has hit the proverbial wall. Admittedly, the difficulty of the Crater Lake Marathon increases your chances of "cratering" as you follow the dormant volcano's rim from The Watchman to Lost Creek Camp. The race's brochure drives home this point by offering several testimonials from past runners saying how bad they felt during the trip around Mount Mazama. So, everyone agrees that the hills on the course kill you. In the throes of your pain, however, you are enveloped by the intense beauty of the intense blue lake, thick forests, panoramic views of valley floors, and neighboring peaks, without (for the most part) having to endure the nasty interruption of cars. The organizers package this race in a very plain wrapper; there is no pasta party, expo, race-weekend registration, or other race-related activity to speak of. This makes it just perfect for the many runners who want a challenging, gorgeous, no-nonsense marathon at a fair price and with a little space to breathe—deeply.

COURSE DESCRIPTION The Crater Lake Marathon begins at the western edge of the lake and undulates its way around the northern rim before tracing the eastern side and heading toward the Pinnacles formation. Runners leave from The Watchman (elevation 7,600 feet), a prominent observatory point adjacent to Wizard Island. Framed by rocky peaks, this scenic spot overlooks a wooded valley to the left. After rounding the bend at .5 mile, you see the jutting peaks and cliffs that mark the area as you enjoy a 400-foot downhill until mile 2. The course tucks in and out of lake view, and you get your first glimpse of the gorgeous lake at mile 1.6. The race climbs about 200 feet between miles 2 and 3. Now you go through the woods on a great downhill (with a slight bump at mile 4.7), losing approximately 700 feet to mile 6.5. This stretch features awesome lake glances at miles 4.7 and 5.3, and from mile 5.7 to mile 6. At mile 6.5, the course begins to climb past the finish line of the 6.7 mile race (which features a spectacular view) for a total of 150 feet over .4 mile. Runners can bask in the downgrade over the next 1.7 miles laced with beautiful scenery, gearing up for the 100-foot climb between miles 8.6 to 9.2. Enjoy the last brief respite—a 82-foot drop over .4 mile—before the tough climb from mile 9.6 to 13 (932 feet). You get a break just before mile 13 (where the half marathoners finish), and then the course completes an out-and-back to the Cloudcap Overlook (mile 14.5), going slightly uphill on the way out. From mile 15, runners have a tremendous downgrade leading to the left turn toward The Pinnacles at mile 19, and continuing down to Lost Creek Camp (mile 22.3). Over these 7.3 miles the course drops 1,767 feet. You turn into Lost Creek Camp, where the surface turns from pavement to dirt/crushed cinders, and complete a 2-mile out and back on Grayback Road, climbing 470 feet out and dropping the same amount back. Tired runners finish at Lost Creek Camp (elevation 5,980 feet).

CROWD/RUNNER SUPPORT   Since the course is closed to traffic for most of the race, spectator access to the course is limited. The much-needed aid stations start at mile 3, and then are spaced approximately every 2 miles or so. The aid stations stock water, sport drink, and sponges. A medical team awaits at mile 6.7, and portable toilets are available at miles 6.7 and 13.

RACE LOGISTICS   Your race packet contains information on getting to the race start on the free buses. The race course is closed to vehicular traffic on a rolling schedule, which means slower runners could be relegated to the side of the road later in the race. The course is closed between the start and mile 13 for three hours, and to mile 19 for 3.5 hours. Note that traffic from Kerr Notch to Lost Creek Camp (miles 19 to 22.3) is monitored, but not closed.

ACTIVITIES   Be aware that you cannot register for the race on race weekend; you must register in advance. The event limits itself to the first 500 runners between the three races, so we suggest that you get your entry in early. Neophytes may want to head to the Steel Visitor Center at 6:00 p.m. on Friday evening before the race to watch the video "The Rim and its Runners." After the grueling race, watermelon and other munchies and drinks are available in the low-key finish area. Limited showering facilities are available at Mazama Campground near the park entrance.

AWARDS   Each race finisher receives a T-shirt and certificate. Plaques go to the age-group winners, while the second through fifth-place finishers in each age group receive ribbons. The overall race winners take home engraved tankards.

ACCOMMODATIONS   Runners on a budget may opt to stay in one of the area campgrounds, such as Lost Creek Camp or the larger Mazama Village. Sites are available on a first-come, first-served basis. You can stay inside the park at Crater Lake Lodge or Mazama Village Motor Inn. We suggest reserving your room well in advance (tel. 541-830-8700; fax 541-830-8514). If you want to stay in a larger town, we suggest Klamath Falls, about an hour drive from Crater Lake National Park. Among the choices there are: Travelodge, 11 Main Street (541-882-4494); Best Western Inn, 2627 S. 6th. Street (541-882-9665); Super 8 Motel, 3805 N Highway 97 (541-884-8880); Motel 6, 5136 S. 6th Street (541-884-2110); Quality Inn, 100 Main Street (541-882-4666); Shilo Inn Suites Hotel, 2500 Almond Street (541-885-7980); and Comfort Inn, 2500 S. 6th Street (541-884-9999).

RELATED EVENTS/RACES   Runners can opt for the still challenging 6.5-mile race or the 13-mile race. Walkers are limited to the 6.5 miler. All races start at The Watchman.

AREA ATTRACTIONS   The primary attraction at Crater Lake National Park, is of course the bright blue lake. Plenty of hiking, ranging from short, easy strolls to longer day hikes, can be found in the park. Fishing is also possible in nearby lakes and rivers.

PAAVO NURMI MARATHON

OVERALL: 77.5

COURSE BEAUTY: 8

COURSE DIFFICULTY: 6+

APPROPRIATENESS FOR FIRST TIMERS: 5+

RACE ORGANIZATION: 9-

CROWDS: 2

RACE DATA

Overall Ranking: 103
Quickness Ranking: 92
Contact: Tina Paruolo
Hurley Area Chamber of Commerce
316 Silver Street
Hurley, WI 54534
(715) 561-4334
http://www.hurleywi.com

Date: August 14, 1999; August 12, 2000
Start Time: 7:30 a.m.
Time Course Closes: 1:30 p.m.
Number of Finishers: 434 in 1998
Course: Point to point
Certification: USATF
Course Records: Male: (open) 2:19:10
Female: (open) 2:47:49
Elite Athlete Programs: No
Cost: $25/30
Age groups/Divisions: M: ≤15, 16-21, 22-29, 30-34, 35-39, 40-44, 45-49,
50-59, 60+, wheelchair
F: ≤17, 18-22, 23-29, 30-39, 40-49, 50+, wheelchair
Walkers: No
Requirements: None
Temperature: 75°
Aid/Splits: 13 / miles 5, 10, 13, 15 & 20

HIGHLIGHTS Affectionately known by locals as "The Paavo," the Paavo Nurmi Marathon (named for the Finnish distance runner who won nine Olympic gold medals during the 1920s) ranks as Wisconsin's oldest and most notorious marathon. Steeped in tradition, from its opening ceremonies—complete with an Olympic torch relay and lighting ceremony—to its delicious post-race Mojakka (Finnish-style beef stew), The Paavo relishes in such intense community support that individual miles along the course bear the names of longtime race supporters. Runners enjoy the rural hills and historic towns on the peaceful course through Iron County in northern Wisconsin. While awarding no gold medals, The Paavo's coveted T-shirts adorn runners like badges of honor for completing the grueling course, often in sweltering conditions.

COURSE DESCRIPTION The point-to-point course over rural, wooded roads travels through several small logging and mining communities. Starting in the little town of Upson on Hwy. 77, the course loops around town before turning right on Hwy. 122 at .4 miles.

Substantial rolling hills take you over Alder Creek at 1.6 miles. With a right turn onto County Road E at 2.1 miles, the road improves, rolling past a cemetery on the left before returning to Hwy. 77 on the way to the town of Ironbelt. Gently climbing from Ironbelt to 9.5 miles, you descend into the town of Pence at the 10-mile point. The route continues down to 10.6 miles with subsequent ups and downs to another iron town, Montreal, at 11.5 miles. From mile 11.5 to 12.4, the course contains a nice downhill past quaint roadside homes. At 12.6 miles, the route detours from Hwy. 77 through the town of Gile (miles 12.6 to 13.9). A short climb greets runners as they exit Gile, returning to Hwy. 77. The course remains mostly flat once on the highway from Gile at the 14-mile point until 15.4 miles and the right turn onto County Road C. After a .1-mile steep uphill, County Road C rolls across the Gile Flowage, a scenic pond flowing with birds, at 18.2 miles. Another steep uphill awaits from 19.9 to 20 miles. You'll probably be ready to shoot the smiley face leering at you from the side of the road at mile 20.3 (at least someone is smiling at this point!). At 20.5, you endure more steep rollers until a left turn at 21.4 miles onto Hwy. 51. Refreshingly flat until a slight grade from mile 23.8 to 24.1 and another from mile 25.4 to 25.8, Hwy. 51 descends into charming downtown Hurley and the Silver Street finish line in front of John Wiita Insurance.

CROWD/RUNNER SUPPORT The entire community anticipates this Iron County rite of summer, supporting The Paavo as race sponsor, volunteer, or cheerleader. Spectators are most visible in the small towns along the race route and at the finish line in downtown Hurley. The volunteers at the 13 aid stations, which lie every 3 miles to 18 then every mile, provide even more support and encouragement.

RACE LOGISTICS Buses to the start in Upson depart at 6:30 a.m. from the Ramada Inn on Hwy. 51 N, and the Citgo Station (corner of Hwy. 51 and Silver Street). If you have your own special drink, mark the bottles with your bib number and your desired aid station, drop it off at the Chamber of Commerce by 9:00 p.m. Friday night, and the race will distribute them to the aid stations of your choice.

ACTIVITIES The Hurley Chamber of Commerce, 316 Silver Street, serves as the registration and pre-race packet pickup site. You may want to hit the all-you-can-eat Paavo Spaghetti Feed from 4:00 p.m. to 7:00 p.m. at the Iron County Senior Center. Signaling the start of race weekend, the torch relay and lighting ceremony take place in the parking lot of Tom's North Pride Foods. Be sure to speed your marathon recovery by replenishing lost calories with The Paavo's patented Mojakka and easing tight muscles with a post-race massage. At 12:30 p.m., the traditional Paavo party begins in Riccelli Park. Stick around for the music while downing a cold beer and bratwurst sold by the Hurley Lioness Club. Finally, if you didn't win an award in the race, your luck may change in the prize drawing held at 2:30 p.m. after the awards ceremony.

AWARDS Every finisher receives a coveted race T-shirt. The top 10 overall males and top five overall females receive an award plus free entry to next year's race. The top age-group finishers receive trophies, with second and third place receiving medals.

ACCOMMODATIONS No hotel officially hosts the marathon. However, hotels near the finish include: Ramada Inn, Hwy. 51 and Silver Street (715-561-3030); Starlite Motel/Bar and Grill, near downtown Hurley (715-561-3085); and Silver Street Motel, on Silver Street (715-561-4684).

RELATED EVENTS/RACES Share the pain with your friends in the increasingly popular 5-person and 2-person marathon relays. Each team must provide its own transportation to each relay station.

AREA ATTRACTIONS The marathon coincides with the annual Iron County Heritage Festival which features arts and crafts fairs, ethnic cuisine, a parade, history tours, concerts, and dances. While you're in Iron County, visit the Plummer Mine headface located off Hwy. 77 between Pence and Iron Belt; Copper Peak, the only ski flying hill in the Western Hemisphere, offering a breathtaking view of the Gogebic range; or the "Pines and Mines" Mountain Bike Trail with over 200 miles of mapped and marked trails.

MARATHON BY THE SEA

OVERALL: 86.1

COURSE BEAUTY: 8-

COURSE DIFFICULTY: 5- (SEE APPENDIX)

APPROPRIATENESS FOR FIRST TIMERS: 8

RACE ORGANIZATION: 10-

CROWDS: 4+

RACE DATA

Overall Ranking: **43**
Quickness Ranking: **69**
Contact: **Mike Doyle**
Marathon By The Sea
c/o Canada Games Aquatic Centre
50 Union Street
Saint John, New Brunswick, Canada E2L 1A1
Tel. (506) 658-4715; Fax (506) 658-4730
E-mail: aquatics@nbnet.nb.ca
http://www.aquatics.nb.ca
Date: **August 15, 1999; August 13, 2000**
Start Time: **8:00 a.m.**
Time Course Closes: **2:00 p.m.**
Number of Finishers: **524 in 1998**
Course: **Loop**
Certification: **Run NB and Athletics NB**
Course Records: **Male: (open) 2:35:02**
Female: (open) 2:58:11
Elite Athlete Programs: **No**
Cost: **$34.50/46**
Age groups/Divisions: **≤19, 20-29, 30-34, 35-39, 40-44, 45-49, 50-54,**
55-59, 60-64, 65-69, 70+
Walkers: **Yes**
Requirements: **None**
Temperature: **49° - 62°**
Aid/Splits: **12 / none**

HIGHLIGHTS What happens when you grow tired of traveling long distances to find a fun, vacation-like marathon? Most people appease themselves with shorter races. A few energetic souls like Mike Doyle simply create a marathon in their own backyards. And in Mike's case, a very successful one. In only four years, St. John, New Brunswick's Marathon by the Sea has doubled in size, drawing over 500 marathoners in 1998. It's not hard attracting large numbers when no other marathon in North America offers more bang for the buck. And the bang resounds even louder as race organizers continue striving to impress. This urban/rural marathon features the following (all included in your entry fee): pre-race Spa Party at the impressive Canada Games Aquatic Centre; oceanfront pasta dinner; pre-race massage; post-race BBQ with musical entertainment; 4" x 6" finish line photograph; day care; and runners lounge where finishers can sit down and have a cool drink while watching their buddies finish on the big screen television showing live finish coverage. All of this takes place during the Festival by the Sea Celebration, a ten-day citywide performing arts extravaganza.

COURSE DESCRIPTION Marathon By The Sea's diverse, loop course incorporates many parts of downtown Saint John before exiting west through older, attractive residential neighborhoods, industrial areas and forest, all preceding the return to the city center finish. After the start alongside the Canada Games Aquatic Centre, a quick left turn reveals a short stint through a warehouse district and an immediate .75-mile hill which becomes relatively steep for the last 200 yards. From 1 to 2.3 miles, the course rolls through a downtown residential district on a notably cambered street. After another short hill at 2.3, the course goes flat to downhill through a commercial area to 4.1 miles. A short grade followed by a .25-mile hill leads to a quick downhill to the Harbour Bridge at 4.9 miles. From the bridge, the course continues mostly uphill to another residential area at 5.8 miles and then to the tree-lined neighborhood of West Saint John after mile 7. By the 8-mile mark, the course flattens to 9.8 where a mild 300-yard hill greets runners. Continuing through a light industrial/motel district after the 10-mile mark, the route goes slightly downhill along a wooded highway to the U-turn at mile 16. The course returns gradually uphill to mile 19 where it enters Hwy. 1 heading back toward downtown Saint John. Miles 19 to 22.3 are predominately downhill after which runners face a challenging climb from 23.4 to 24 miles. After sharply descending, the course goes up over the Harbour Bridge at mile 25, providing a welcome view of downtown Saint John and the finish line.

CROWD/RUNNER SUPPORT Embracing the race more and more each year, locals offer vocal support primarily in the residential areas, Harbour Bridge, and at the finish. Live musical entertainment hits the course for the first time in 1999. Twelve aid stations along the course provide additional support for the runners. But watch out for Shakey Evidence, the most notorious cheater in Saint John history. He uses any means to win.

RACE LOGISTICS Since the start/finish line is conveniently located within walking or jogging distance from area hotels, race morning involves little transportation hassle. To ease race-morning stress further, the race provides day care for a limited amount of children. The kids can glide down a cool water slide in the Aquatic Centre or participate in a plethora of fun activities.

ACTIVITIES Race packet pickup occurs at the Aquatic Centre, 50 Union Street, Friday from 4:00 p.m. to 8:00 p.m., Saturday from 10:00 a.m. to 6:00 p.m., and race day from 6:00 a.m. to 7:30 a.m. Race-day registration is available. The race offers free course tours on Saturday between 10:00 a.m. and 4:00 p.m. On Saturday night, eat at the free outdoor pasta party overlooking the harbor. Cries of sore muscles on the starting line fall on deaf ears as the race provides free, pre-race massages. Massages are available after the race as well, and an awards ceremony takes place as soon as results are available. To round out race weekend, attend the post-race BBQ, with music, at the Aquatic Centre. All race activities culminate in time for participants to take in the main stage performances conducted by the Festival by the Sea.

AWARDS Every runner receives the following goodies: T-shirt, finisher's medallion, race certificate, and a 4 x 6-inch finish-line photograph. The top three open and masters runners receive special awards as do the top three finishers in each age group. However, slow runners won't want to miss the awards ceremony as a generous random drawing takes place for dozens of valuable items including running shoes, watches, and gift certificates.

ACCOMMODATIONS The Delta Brunswick Hotel, 39 King Street (800-268-1133 from Canada) and (800-877-1133 from the U.S.) serves as the official race hotel offering a special rate of about $80/night. Other nearby hotels include: Saint John Hilton, One Market Square (800-561-8282). Keddy's Fort Howe Hotel, Main and Portland Streets (800-561-7666), lies less than one-half mile from the start/finish as does the Howard Johnson Hotel, 400 Main Street, Chesley Drive (800-475-4656).

RELATED EVENTS/RACES Added in 1999, the Friendship 5K Breakfast Run gives out-of-towners a chance to mingle with members of the local running club and other participants while warming up their legs the day before the marathon. Race day includes a five miler and half marathon both starting concurrently with the marathon.

PIKES PEAK MARATHON

OVERALL: 83.9

COURSE BEAUTY: 9

COURSE DIFFICULTY: 10

APPROPRIATENESS FOR FIRST TIMERS: 3

RACE ORGANIZATION: 9+

CROWDS: 1-

RACE DATA

Overall Ranking: 60
Quickness Ranking: 109
Contact: Pikes Peak Marathon
P.O. Box 38235
Colorado Springs, CO 80937
Tel. (719) 473-2625
Fax (719) 687-2135

Date: August 22, 1999; August 20, 2000
Start Time: 7:00 a.m.
Time Course Closes: 5:00 p.m.
Number of Finishers: 800 limit, usually filled by late May
Course: Out and back
Certification: None
Course Records: Male: (open) 3:16:39; (masters) 3:56:18
Female: (open) 4:15:18; (masters) 4:26:59
Elite Athlete Programs: No
Cost: $45/60
Age groups/Divisions: 16-19, 20-24, 25-29, 30-34, 35-39, 40-44, 45-49, 50-54, 55-59, 60-64, 65-69, 70-74, 75-79, 80-84, 85+
Walkers: No
Requirements: 16 years old & must have completed either the Pikes Peak Ascent, an ultramarathon, or a marathon
Temperature: 42° - 80°
Aid/Splits: 6 / at summit

HIGHLIGHTS Once considered an impossibility by its namesake Zebulon Pike, ascending and descending Pikes Peak has become a mid-August tradition for the 800 adventurists in the Pikes Peak Marathon. Known as "America's Ultimate Challenge®," our second-most difficult destination marathon climbs an imposing 7,815 feet in 13.32 miles from Manitou Springs to the summit (14,110 feet). Once there, the thin air and glorious view of the plains, and west to the Sangre de Cristo Mountains, and the Continental Divide leave you breathless. The very same view inspired Kathy Lee Bates to write "America the Beautiful" with "Purple Mountain's Majesty" referring to Pikes Peak. If you're thinking about running Pikes Peak, don't delay your entry. With its cult-like following, the race fills extremely early, usually in May.

RACE HISTORY The first annual race up and down Pikes Peak occurred on August 10, 1956. Race originator Dr. Arne Suominen, of Del Ray Beach, Florida, had two distinct reasons for establishing the event. First, he wanted to commemorate the 150th anniversary of the discovery of America's most famous mountain by Zebulon Montgomery Pike. Second, as a former Finnish marathon champion and harsh critic of tobacco, he wanted to prove that smoking reduced one's physical endurance. By challenging smokers and nonsmokers to race Pikes Peak, he was confident of proving his point. With the assistance of race director Rudy Fahl, who continued as the race director until 1980, thirteen runners including Suominen accepted the challenge. As it turned out, not one of the three smokers who entered the race finished. Suominen, indeed, proved his point, and in so doing, started one of the most infamous marathons in the world.

COURSE DESCRIPTION Although the average grade to Pikes Peak summit is 11%, it varies drastically including, believe it or not, some downhill portions. Don't get too excited on the downhills though, as the rule of the trail states that for every downhill section there is an immediate steep climb. Most runners can expect to come within a few minutes of their best road marathon time during the 13.4-mile ascent. Adding 25% to your best road half-marathon time gives you a good estimate of your time for the 12.9-mile descent.

Starting in front of the Manitou Springs City Hall (elevation 6,295 feet), the course travels along Manitou Avenue before turning left on Ruxton Avenue at approximately .5 miles. After passing Miramont Castle on the right, the route continues up a small hill. At the Cog Railway around 1.5 miles, a gravel road replaces the asphalt, marking the beginning of the steepest section of the course lasting almost a half mile before hitting the wild flowers and switchbacks of Barr Trail. Known as the Ws, the 13 switchbacks on Mount Manitou turn more than 90°, and the last rewards you with the first view of Pikes Peak since the start. The Ws end around 3 miles, but more switchbacks and a short downhill lead you to a natural rock arch at about 5.5 miles. Just beyond the arch, there is a brief flat section. Six steep switchbacks bring you to a welcomed flat to downhill stretch as you leave Mount Manitou for Barr Camp (mile 7). The downhill ends at the "1/2 Mile to Barr Camp" sign, and that half mile is extremely challenging. Barr Camp (10,200 feet) marks the beginning of what many runners describe as the toughest section of the course; from here it's all uphill. The terrain soon turns rocky as you make your way past the sign to the Bottomless Pit at the 8-mile mark. From here, 15 switchbacks, each one longer than the last, take you to the A-Frame (11,500 feet) at 10.5 miles. The "3 Miles to Summit" sign signals you will soon be above tree line. Several switchbacks take you to the east face of Pikes Peak. With two miles to go, the trail crosses the east face of Pikes Peak straight to The Cirque (13,200 feet) at nearly 12 miles. Becoming quite rocky, the course winds to the Sixteen Golden Stairs—the 16 rocky switchbacks near the summit. After scrambling up the stairs, you head right to a short flat to downhill section before hitting the next series of switchbacks. These take you past a sign honoring the memory of Fred Barr, the builder of the Barr Trail. Two switchbacks and a few rocky zigzags after the sign and you've made it to the summit! Now it's time to catch your breath and retrace your steps to the finish on Manitou Avenue in front of Soda Springs Park just beyond the corner of Ruxton Avenue.

CROWD/RUNNER SUPPORT Since few spectators are crazy enough to climb the mountain to cheer you on, most of the crowd support is limited to the start and finish areas. Additional support comes in the form of aid stations along the route and race personnel at the summit. Six aid stations (which runners pass both going up and coming down) cling to the mountain at the following locations: Manitou Incline—2.4 miles; French Creek—4.3 miles; Barr Camp—7.6 miles; A-Frame—10.2 miles; The Basin—12.8 miles; and the summit—13.4 miles. The rest of the time it's just you, nature, and 799 other runners challenging the mountain.

RACE LOGISTICS If you want a hassle-free race morning, try to stay in Manitou Springs. Most motels are within walking distance to the start line, affording you a satisfying shower soon after finishing. Pikes Peak maintains several time cutoffs at specific points on the route. Runners must reach these points by the indicated times or they will be pulled from the race: Barr Camp by 10:15 a.m., A-Frame by 11:30 a.m., and the summit by 1:30 p.m.

ACTIVITIES Race packets are available for pick-up the week of the race (location and times provided with your confirmation of entry). On Friday and Saturday nights, the Manitou Springs Kiwanis Club holds a pre-race pasta party in Schryver Park for $10 per person. The awards ceremony begins at 2:15 p.m. in Soda Springs Park.

A W A R D S   All entrants receive long-sleeve T-shirts, and finishers receive medals. The top three male and female runners in each age group earn awards, with the top 10 overall finishers receiving special prizes.

A C C O M M O D A T I O N S   Although Pikes Peak has no official race hotel, accommodations abound in the Manitou Springs and Colorado Springs area. But, don't procrastinate; August is high-tourist season so rooms go fast. Some options near the race include: Santa Fe Motel, 3 Manitou Avenue (719-475-8185); Red Wing Motel, 56 El Paso Blvd. (719-685-9547); Park Row Lodge, 54 Manitou Avenue (719-685-5216); and El Colorado Lodge, 23 Manitou Avenue (719-685-5485). You can also contact the Manitou Springs Chamber of Commerce (800-642-2567) or Colorado Springs Visitors Bureau (800-368-4748) for lodging and tourist information.

R E L A T E D   E V E N T S / R A C E S   On Saturday, the day before the marathon, the Pikes Peak Ascent is held. The race is limited to 1,800 runners and, like the marathon, fills in May.

A R E A   A T T R A C T I O N S   If you're impatient and don't want to wait for race day to admire the summit view, reserve a seat on the Pikes Peak Cog Railway, the effortless way to the top. Another natural wonder, Garden of the Gods City Park, contains 300-million-year-old natural formations accessible by a 45-minute tram tour. The U.S. Olympic Training Center provides a different kind of wonder in the form of state-of-the-art athletic training techniques and equipment, with athletes to match. A 75-minute tour of the Center will fuel your training fire. If you're not toured out, head to the United States Air Force Academy and jaunt through its grounds.

MONSTER TRAIL MARATHON

OVERALL: 78.8

COURSE BEAUTY: 9

COURSE DIFFICULTY: 10- (SEE APPENDIX)

APPROPRIATENESS FOR FIRST TIMERS: 2

RACE ORGANIZATION: 8

CROWDS: 0+

R A C E   D A T A

Overall Ranking:	91
Quickness Ranking:	108
Contact:	John McMurray
	Monster Trail Marathon
	625 Highland Road
	Ithaca, NY 14850
	Tel. & Fax (607) 257-3592
Date:	August 29, 1999; August 27, 2000
Start Time:	7:00 a.m. - 8:30 a.m.
Time Course Closes:	None
Number of Finishers:	92 in 1997
Course:	Double out and back
Certification:	None
Course Records:	Male: (open) 3:27:00
	Female: (open) 3:47:35
Elite Athlete Programs:	No
Cost:	$12/18/22, add $7 for optional "Trail Monster" T-shirt
Age groups/Divisions:	None
Walkers:	No
Requirements:	None
Temperature:	60°
Aid/Splits:	7 / none

HIGHLIGHTS   If you're looking to qualify for Boston, look no further—at this entry that is. One glance at the course elevation profile, amusingly compared to Boston's, and you'll see that lack of USATF certification is not the only reason that qualifying is out of the question. Classified as the toughest marathon in the East, Monster features 5,560 feet of total climbing. Although you won't run a PR, you can still enjoy a beautiful run through hardwoods, hemlocks, and plantations of red pines, white pines, spruce, and tamarack along the double-out-and-back on the North Country National Scenic Trail and the Finger Lakes Trail. Since the Monster does not discriminate in its prey, the race handicaps runners to eliminate age and gender differences.

RACE HISTORY   A 500-year-old Iroquois Indian legend tells how a "Forest Monster" chased the Indian brave Jost-du-it out and back twice along the present course. An incredibly accurate sundial recorded his time for the 26.2 miles at 3:26:59. Jost-du-it quickly vanished, presumably eaten by the "Forest Monster." Unlike his cousin whose similar disappearance led to signs reading Watch Out For Falling Rock, Jost-du-it was basically forgotten until 1989 when the Finger Lakes Running Club organized the Virgil Forest Monster Marathon in his honor.

COURSE DESCRIPTION   The course profile does not lie; the Monster is not a friendly one. Starting and finishing at The Rafters restaurant on Route 392, the course consists of two out-and-backs on wooded trails with a total climb of 5,560 feet. The course follows Route 392 to Tone Road before joining the Finger Lakes Trail at .85 miles. Allowing your knees and chin to become well acquainted, the route climbs 800 feet in 1.5 miles to a course high of 2,134 feet. At 3 miles, you reach the Greek Peak summit and an aid station at 3.2 miles. Although remaining hilly, the course continues losing elevation to the turnaround and second aid station at 6.55 miles. After a quick refueling, it's back to The Rafter restaurant and one more out-and-back.

CROWD/RUNNER SUPPORT   Believe it or not, race organizers have a hard enough time attracting runners to the race. Due to the nature of the course, crowd support is limited to the start and finish area. However, the volunteers at the aid stations along the way provide full "banquet" spreads and tremendous encouragement.

RACE LOGISTICS   Since the race starts and finishes at the same location, your main concern is finding your way there. This is a sex/age group handicap race meaning start times are based on a formula to eliminate age and gender differences. Theoretically, this practice places every runner on equal footing, with 70-year-old females sprinting to the finish, neck and neck, with 25-year-old males.

ACTIVITIES   As with most trail races, Monster places most emphasis on the race itself. Nevertheless, a pre-race pasta feed takes place Saturday night at The Rafters restaurant from 5:30 p.m. to 8:00 p.m., where you can also pick up your race packet. To top off your glycogen stores, coffee, juice and muffins are available race morning. After finishing, enjoy more food and drink.

AWARDS   In keeping with the tongue-in-cheek nature of the race, only "joke" awards are presented to those who outrun the Monster.

ACCOMMODATIONS   Monster does not have an official race hotel. Many hotels are available in the Courtland-Ithaca area, but call early as the race occurs on Labor Day weekend. Some hotels in Courtland include: Marathon Three Bear Inn, Exit 9 on I-81 (607-849-3258); Courtland Motor Court, 393 Tompkins Street (607-753-3351); and Courtland Super 8, Exit on I-81 (607-756-5622). In Ithaca try: Best Western University Inn, E. Hill (607-272-6100); Holiday Inn, 222 S. Cayuga Street (607-272-1000); Ramada Inn Ithaca Airport, 2310 N. Triphammer Road (607-257-3100); Sheraton Inn, 1 Sheraton Drive (607-257-2000); Econo Lodge, 2303 N. Cayuga Street (607-257-1400); or Springwater, Route 366 2 miles east of Cornell University (607-272-3721).

RELATED EVENTS/RACES   If one trip up and back over Virgil Mountain summit is enough for you, try the accompanying half marathon. For marathoners reluctant to let the Forest Monster chase them for a second out-and-back, race officials allow them to stop midway with the half marathoners.

AREA ATTRACTIONS   If you have some time, enjoy more of the area's natural beauty by staying at one of the state's parks in the Ithaca area. Buttermilk Falls and Robert H. Treman State Parks offer swimming, hiking and wonderful waterfalls. Wine-drinking runners must visit New York state's most acclaimed wine region on the nearby Cayuga Trail along Route 89 between Seneca Falls and Trumansburg. Do some wine tasting, and buy a bottle or two to complement your campside cooking.

SILVER STATE MARATHON

OVERALL: 85.3

COURSE BEAUTY: 9

COURSE DIFFICULTY: 6- (SEE APPENDIX)

APPROPRIATENESS FOR FIRST TIMERS: 7

RACE ORGANIZATION: 9

CROWDS: 1

RACE DATA

Overall Ranking:	49
Quickness Ranking:	85
Contact:	Valentine Pisarski
	Silver State Striders
	2358 Camelot Way
	Reno, NV 89509
	(702) 849-0419
	http://silverstatemarathon.com
Date:	August 29, 1999; August 27, 2000
Start Time:	6:00 a.m.
Time Course Closes:	11:30 a.m.
Number of Finishers:	240 in 1997
Course:	Loop
Certification:	USATF
Course Records:	Male: (open) 2:37:58
	Female: (open) 3:04:00
Elite Athlete Programs:	No
Cost:	$20/25/35
Age groups/Divisions:	≤19, 20-29, 30-39, 40-49, 50-59, 60-69, 70+
Walkers:	No
Requirements:	None
Temperature:	44° - 75°
Aid/Splits:	14 / mile 1

HIGHLIGHTS Tucked back in the beautiful Washoe Valley at the foot of the Sierra Nevada mountains, the Silver State Marathon quietly holds a wonderful event unbeknownst to the rest of the running world, but one of our favorites. Mere miles from Lake Tahoe, the course wraps around Washoe Lake and moves through an incredible arch of pine trees during the Franktown Loop. Finishers are treated to the best medallions in North America, which would fit nicely in the dollar slot machines in nearby Reno. Do not be tempted.

COURSE DESCRIPTION In 1998, Silver State unveiled a new, combination rural road and trail course. Varying between 5,035 feet and 5,245 feet, the loop route (around Washoe Lake) starts in Bowers Mansion Regional Park and proceeds north in the dawn on old highway 395. After a 55-foot hill awakes runners at mile 1, the course crosses U.S. Highway 395 (mile 2) and then parallels the highway before darting down a short, steep hill just prior to mile 3. This section is on a dirt road for about a mile and returns to U.S. Highway 395 near mile 4. Again paralleling U.S. 395 for just over a half mile, the course turns off-road into the Little Washoe Lake State Park, heads up a 60-foot climb passing mile 5, and then continues through the park on an asphalt and then dirt road to mile 6. The next 9.5 miles meander flat through Scripps State Wildlife Management Area and Washoe Lake State Park on dirt and asphalt surfaces. Your progress may be slowed a bit with heavy sand for about a third of a mile after mile 12. Runners exit the park at mile 15.6 onto East Lake Blvd. and skirt the Wildlife Mitigation Viewing Area at 17.3 miles. Passing under U.S. 395 at 18.5 miles, runners return on old highway 395 preparing for the looming 200-foot climb up LeMond Hill. At mile 20.1, you enter the gorgeous Franktown Loop, enveloped by a canopy of towering pine trees to mile 23.1. Bidding farewell to the beautiful loop, runners cruise down a dirt ranch road for .7 miles, experiencing a 100-foot drop in elevation. A left turn onto old 395 has you heading for the final 2.4 miles to the main gate into Bowers Mansion Regional Park.

CROWD/RUNNER SUPPORT   The aid stations and the finish area provide the bulk of the crowd participation for the race. The 14 aid stations offer water, electrolyte replacement drink, and petroleum jelly in case you're rubbed the wrong way. Roving aid stations are available to the heavy footed.

RACE LOGISTICS   All runners must find their own way to the start. Since parking is limited in Bowers Mansion Regional Park, try parking alongside highway 395. Slower runners may start at 5:00 a.m., but they should bring their own fluids since early aid stations may not be set up.

ACTIVITIES   Late registration and packet pick-up take place at the Reno Super 8 Motel, 5851 South Virginia Street in Reno, from noon until 7:00 p.m. on Saturday. Although discouraged, packets can be retrieved on race morning at the park entrance, but there is no race-day registration. An outstanding post-race picnic is held in the park, featuring free beer, food, music, massages, barbeque, and a raffle. Runners and their families can take advantage of the volleyball court, swimming pool, showers, picnic tables among the pines, and large expanses of grass to relax and reflect on the day.

AWARDS   Every participant receives a marathon T-shirt. Each finisher receives an encased solid copper medallion draped in a silver and blue ribbon. Minted on the silver dollar press at the Carson City Mint, the medal is the only non-government piece stamped with the official U.S. Government "CC" marking. Solid silver medals are presented to the top three age-group finishers. The top three overall runners receive gold-plated solid silver medals, solid silver medals, and solid nickel silver medals, respectively.

ACCOMMODATIONS   The Super 8 Motel and Convention Center, 5851 South Virginia Street, Reno (800-797-7366) serves as the host hotel. Runners can stay in either Reno or Carson City since both are convenient to the start. In Carson City try: Best Western Trailside Inn, 1300 N. Carson Street (702-883-7300); Days Inn, 3103 N. Carson Street (702-883-3343); Motel 6, 2749 S. Carson Street (702-885-7710); or Super 8 Motel, 2829 S. Carson Street (702-883-7800). In Reno try: Best Western Continental Lodge, 1885 S. Virginia Street (702-329-1001); Comfort Lodge, 844 S. Virginia Street (702-786-6700); Holiday Inn Casino, 111 Mill Street (702-329-0411); or Motel 6, 1901 S. Virginia Street (702-827-0255).

RELATED EVENTS/RACES   The Silver State events menu also includes a half marathon, 10K run, and 10K walk. The two runs start at 7:00 a.m., and the 10K walk starts at 7:10 a.m. Finishers in each of these events receive the famous commemorative medal from the Carson City Mint.

AREA ATTRACTIONS   The area bursts with attractions and activities. Night owls will relish the casinos and shows in Reno, offering plenty of opportunities to blow some money. Nature enthusiasts will appreciate the region's proximity to Lake Tahoe and just about every outdoor activity imaginable. Historic Carson City and Virginia City are less than 20 miles away.

ERIESISTIBLE MARATHON

OVERALL: 80.9

COURSE BEAUTY: 9-

COURSE DIFFICULTY: 4- (SEE APPENDIX)

APPROPRIATENESS FOR FIRST-TIMERS: 7+

ORGANIZATION: 8+

CROWDS: 3-

RACE DATA

Overall Ranking:	81
Quickness Ranking:	50
Contact:	Eriesistible Marathon
	PO Box 8311
	Erie, PA 16505-0311
	Tel. (814) 456-0621
	Fax (814) 459-8381
	E-mail: rfgodzwa@velocity.net
	http://www.erie.net/~runerie
Date:	Generally second or third Sunday in September
	[No future dates set at publication time]
Start Time:	8:00 a.m.
Time Course Closes:	1:30 p.m.
Number of Finishers:	NA
Course:	Loop
Certification:	USATF
Course Records:	Race does not know course records
Elite Athlete Programs:	No
Cost:	$30/40
Age groups/Divisions:	≤19, 20-24, 25-29, 30-34, 35-39, 40-44, 45-49, 50-54, 55-59, 60+
Walkers:	No
Requirements:	None
Temperature:	53° - 70°
Aid/Splits:	varies / varies

HIGHLIGHTS A nice mix between city running and sandy state park, the Eriesistible Marathon starts in downtown Erie and spends about half of its time along the shores of Presque Isle Bay and Lake Erie. This small, but well-organized race, comes at the start of the fall marathon season, which makes it a good choice for runners who want to pack two marathons into their autumn race schedule. Very flat for most of the race, the course includes one tough hill near mile 21 as you approach the city. You will have to decide for yourself whether the Eriesistible Marathon really is irresistible to you.

COURSE DESCRIPTION The Eriesistible Marathon leaves from the Avalon Hotel at 10th and State Street in downtown Erie. Runners head east on a 5K loop through downtown, turning left on East Avenue (after mile 1) and another left on E. 6th Street. The course then proceeds west through residential neighborhoods, heading out of town on W. 6th Street, with a nice downhill between mile 7 and 8. Miles 8 to 21 loop scenic Presque Isle State Park, a completely flat,

3,200-acre sandbox between Lake Erie and Presque Isle Bay. As runners climb 150 feet (mile 21), they retrace their steps along W. 6th Street, before ducking into the exclusive neighborhood around South Shore Drive (mile 23). After running around the Bayview overlook, with its nice view of the bay and Presque Isle, the route heads back downtown, circling Perry Square to the finish.

CROWD/RUNNER SUPPORT The marathon does not have consistent aid station placement or split times from year to year. Organizers promise that both occur frequently along the course. The aid stations carry water and sport drink. Most of the crowd support comes in the first six miles and last four miles of the marathon.

RACE LOGISTICS Runners can shower after the race at the Downtown YMCA, 10th and Peach Streets. Bring your own soap and towel.

ACTIVITIES You may pick up your race packet or register late at the Avalon Hotel on Saturday from noon until 6:00 p.m., or on race morning from 6:30 a.m. to 7:30 a.m. The Avalon Hotel also hosts the carbo load dinner on Saturday evening, 5:00 p.m. to 8:00 p.m. The awards ceremony kicks off at Sabella's of Union Station, 14th and Peach, at 2:00 p.m. A pasta buffet dishes out at Sabella's from 1:30 p.m. to 3:00 p.m.

AWARDS Every participant receives a long-sleeve sweat shirt; finishers also receive a medal after they cross the finish line, and results booklets and finisher's certificates in the mail. The top age-group finishers get awards, as do the top 3 overall runners and first masters runners. The Rich Martino Memorial Award is given to the top male and female first-time marathoners.

ACCOMMODATIONS The Avalon Hotel, West 10th Street & State Street (800-822-5011), serves as the official host hotel. Other hotels nearby include: Holiday Inn Downtown, 18 West 18th Street (800-544-0689 or 814-452-4682); Erie Downtowner Inn, 205 W. 10th Street (814-456-6251); Midtown Motel, 14 W. 26th Street (814-455-7529); and Bel-aire Hotel, 2800 W. 8th Street (814-833-1116). Some motels off of Interstate 90 are: Motel 6, exit 6 (814-864-4811); Comfort Inn, exit 6 (814-866 6666); Econo lodge, exit 6 (814-866-5544); Days Inn, exit 7 (814-868-8521); Red Roof Inn, exit 7 (814-868-5246); and Super 8 Motel, exit 7 (814-864-9200).

RELATED EVENTS/RACES If you feel like running a half marathon, find a friend and enter the marathon relay. Both members run 13.1 miles, and the race provides transportation to and from the exchange point. Fitness-types can join in the non-competitive 5K fun run/walk, and children ages 2 through 12 may want to do the Kids Run.

AREA ATTRACTIONS Presque Isle State Park, one of the area's biggest attractions, offers swimming, picnicking, and sunbathing on warmer days. You may want to see if the Erie Playhouse has a play on during your visit, or try the Roadhouse Theatre. Erie has lots of museums: Erie Art Museum, Erie History Center at Discovery Square, Erie Maritime Museum, and the reconstructed Flagship Niagara. Families should visit the ExpERIEnce Children's Museum at Discovery Square or the amusement park, Waldameer Park and Water World. Nature lovers may want to see the wildflowers at the Erie National Wildlife Refuge. And, of course, Niagara Falls is only a short drive away.

U.S. AIR FORCE MARATHON

OVERALL: 81.2

COURSE BEAUTY: 8+

COURSE DIFFICULTY: 5- (SEE APPENDIX)

APPROPRIATENESS FOR FIRST-TIMERS: 8+

ORGANIZATION: 9+

CROWDS: 4-

RACE DATA

Overall Ranking: **77**
Quickness Ranking: **70**
Contact: **Thomas Fisher**
United States Air Force Marathon
88 SPTG/SV
5215 Thurlow Street, Suite 2
Wright-Patterson AFB, OH 45433
Tel. (800) 467-1823 or (937) 787-4350
Fax (937) 656-1000
http://afmarathon.wpafb.af.mil
Date: **September 18, 1999; September 23, 2000**
Start Time: **7:30 a.m.**
Time Course Closes: **3:30 p.m.**
Number of Finishers: **1,668 in 1997**
Course: **Loop**
Certification: **USATF**
Course Records: **Male: (open) 2:28:34; (masters) 2:35:00**
Female: (open) 2:55:04; (masters) 3:43:15
Elite Athlete Programs: **No**
Cost: **$35/40**
Age groups/Divisions: **≤19, 20-24, 25-29, 30-34, 35-39, 40-44, 45-49,**
50-54, 55-59, 60-64, 65-69, 70+, wheelchair
Walkers: **Yes (if can finish in 8 hours)**
Requirements: **None**
Temperature: **49°-68°**
Aid/Splits: **25 / verbal splits every mile**

HIGHLIGHTS   This is the race for all of you lovers of flying machines. Complete with aircraft flyovers, a finishing stretch in a row of airplanes, an awesome finisher's medal depicting an Air Force plane, and historic Wright brothers sites, the Air Force Marathon gives you a strong dose of all things related to flight. You may not quite be flying along the moderately challenging course, however, with good climbs near miles 1, 19, and 22. The race supports you extraordinarily well, with water stations every mile and plenty of energy bars, gel, and fruit. The inaugural race in 1997 celebrated the Air Force's 50th Anniversary in supersonic style, and the marathon deserves to become a long standing Air Force tradition. After all, there are plenty of runners who love to fly.

COURSE DESCRIPTION   The challenging loop course starts with an artillery blast at the Air Force Museum on Wright Patterson Air Force Base (elevation 790 feet). The course climbs 160 feet in the first 1.5 miles while passing hangars and static display aircraft. Runners then begin the 100-foot downhill to mile 3.5, going by the Air Force Institute of Technology (mile 2) and the Wright Memorial (mile 3), which unfortunately is hidden from view. The race soon proceeds on Old State Route 4, with several ups and downs, passing through Wright State University. Between miles 7 and 8 you scoot by the headquarters of the Air Force Materiel Command showcasing two F-4 aircraft. Following Skeel Avenue, the route passes by the historic Foulois House (named after the Major General who piloted the first dirigible balloon purchased by the U.S. Government) and Arnold House (named for the Air Force's only 5-star general), after mile 9. Runners now begin the approximately 6-mile circumnavigation of Patterson Field (miles 9 to 15), checking out the flight line, display aircraft, and jets taking off and landing. Runners traverse Huffman Prairie between miles 18 and 19, site of the Wright brothers' 1904 hangar and the world's first flying and landing field. By mile 19.5, runners retrace their steps of the first 6.5 miles of the race. Remember the tough hill as you re-enter the base. Aircraft fly overhead as you loop the flight-line, leading to the finish beneath a dramatic row of aircraft at the Air Force Museum.

CROWD/RUNNER SUPPORT The Air Force Marathon gives runners outstanding support during the race. Approximately 10,000 spectators cheer you on, with most congregating at the relay exchange points and the finish area. In addition, the race provides water stations and portable toilets every mile on the route. Eleven of the stations also offer sport drink and medical assistance, and about seven stations offer Power Bars, PowerGel, or fruit. After the race, runners have free access to showers and changing facilities. A military band is also on hand.

RACE LOGISTICS Plenty of parking exists at the Air Force Museum, the race start and finish, and the expo site.

ACTIVITIES Browse the expo and pick up your race packet at the USAF Museum on Thursday, 10:00 a.m. to 4:30 p.m., or Friday, 10:30 a.m. to 7:30 p.m. You can also retrieve your packet on race morning from 5:00 a.m. to 6:00 a.m. The Pasta Dinner dishes out on Friday evening from 5:00 p.m. to 7:30 p.m. at the Air Force Museum. Tickets are $8. Aircraft perform flyovers throughout race day.

AWARDS Every runner receives a T-shirt and patch, while finishers receive one of the popular collector's medals depicting a different Air Force plane each year. The top 3 age-group finishers are mailed awards, and the top male and female overall, masters (40+), grandmasters (50+), and wheelchair winners receive special awards. All finishers receive an unofficial results postcard one week after the race, and an official certificate in November.

ACCOMMODATIONS The USAF Marathon does not have an official race hotel. Some nearby options include: Red Roof Inn, 2580 Colonel Glenn Highway, Fairborn (tel. 937-426-6116); Hampton Inn-Fairborn, 2550 Paramount Place (tel. 937-429-5505); Fairfield Inn-Fairborn, 2500 Paramount Place (tel. 937 427-0800); Homewood Suites, 2750 Presidential Drive, Fairborn (tel. 937-429-0600); Holiday Inn, 2800 Presidential Drive, Fairborn (tel. 937-426-7800); and Dayton Marriott Hotel, 1414 S. Patterson Blvd. (tel. 937-223-1000).

RELATED EVENTS/RACES Groups of four runners can compete in the marathon relay, with legs of 5 miles, 7 miles, 8 miles, and 6.2 miles. Relay categories include: coed, male open, female open, masters (40+), and military. The race transports team members to and from the relay exchange points. There is also a marathon team competition. Teams consist of five members, each running the full marathon, with all five finishing times counting toward the team score.

AREA ATTRACTIONS The U.S. Air Force Museum houses 200 aircraft, 20,000 other items of historical interest, and an IMAX theater. Also on Wright-Patterson AFB, you will want to visit the Wright Memorial situated on a 100-foot bluff overlooking Huffman Prairie, site of the Wright brothers' first full circle in powered flight. Other popular sites in the area include the Oregon District and Young's Dairy Farm.

EQUINOX MARATHON

OVERALL: 80

COURSE BEAUTY: 9-

COURSE DIFFICULTY: 10- (SEE APPENDIX)

APPROPRIATENESS FOR FIRST TIMERS: 2

RACE ORGANIZATION: 9-

CROWDS: 0+

RACE DATA

Overall Ranking:	87
Quickness Ranking:	107
Contact:	Steve Bainbridge
	Running Club North
	P.O. Box 84237
	Fairbanks, AK 99708
	(907) 452-8351
Date:	September 18, 1999; September 16, 2000
Start Time:	8:00 a.m.
Time Course Closes:	6:00 p.m.
Number of Finishers:	450 in 1997
Course:	Loop
Certification:	None
Course Records:	Male: (open) 2:41:30
	Female: (open) 3:25:19
Elite Athlete Programs:	No
Cost:	$15/25/35/50
Age groups/Divisions:	12-19, 20-29, 30-39, 40-49, 50-59, 60+
Walkers:	Yes
Requirements:	None
Temperature:	35°
Aid/Splits:	8 / none

HIGHLIGHTS   The fourth most challenging marathon in North America, the Equinox Marathon appeals to those runners looking to test the limits of their strength and endurance, climbing about 4,500 feet from start to finish. Held just outside the middle of nowhere in Fairbanks, Alaska, Equinox runs mostly on trails, some of which could be covered with snow during the race. The race has been run every year for 36 years, except for 1992 when the race was "officially" canceled due to over 2 feet of snow on the course. Some local hard-core runners still "unofficially" ran the race. On clear days, Ester Dome's summit offers rousing views of the surrounding area if you can lift your head from your knees.

COURSE DESCRIPTION   Equinox's loop course starts at the University of Alaska Fairbanks' athletic field. As a little taste test of the delights ahead, the race immediately heads up the 200-foot, college ski hill to warm up chilled runners. Hitting the densely forested ski trails north of the campus, the course reaches the second major hill at mile 2, a 300-foot incline over a mile. This hill is followed by a sharp downhill and another 300-foot climb near mile 4. Runners pass the Musk Ox Farm at mile 5, soon getting their first glimpse of Ester Dome. Continuing on the heavily wooded ski trail, runners begin the excruciating 1,800-foot climb over three miles to Ester Dome's summit by mile 9. In the higher elevations, runners should be prepared to encounter snow and wind. Once runners reach the summit, they begin a roller coaster, 5.5-mile out-and-back over hills and down valleys. Runners get no time to recover because at 17 miles, the course practically falls off a cliff, dropping 1,700 feet in four miles. Becoming slightly less unpleasant on the Aspen Trail between 18 and 20, good downhillers can make up some time. The dirt trails give way to pavement near mile 21 as runners enter the final section of the race. Around 23.5, runners can spot the satellite dish on top of UAF's Geophysical Institute signaling the end is near. Just to show who's the boss, race organizers throw in a final 100-foot climb over the UAF ski trail at mile 25, making the approaching finish line taste that much sweeter.

CROWD/RUNNER SUPPORT The two relay exchange points and the eight aid stations provide the biggest areas of support for the runners. Consider packing your own provisions to provide the energy necessary to complete the brutal course.

RACE LOGISTICS Runners must find their own way to the start, although there is plenty of parking at the university.

ACTIVITIES The day before the marathon, claim your race package and attend the pre-race Pasta Party ($7) at the Pump House Restaurant & Saloon, 1.3 Mile Chena Pump Road. Pick up your race packet or register late on race morning at UAF Patty Center Gym. After the marathon ordeal, replenish a little sugar at the dessert buffet held with the awards ceremony in the Wood Center.

AWARDS All entrants receive Equinox Marathon T-shirts, and runners finishing under 10 hours earn Equinox Marathon patches. The top three in each age division receive medals, and the top five overall winners earn trophies.

ACCOMMODATIONS Accommodations are available at the Fairbanks Princess Hotel, 4477 Pikes Landing Road (800-426-0500); Fairbanks Hotel, 517 Third Avenue (888-329-4685); Westmark Fairbanks, 813 Noble Street (907-456-7722); or Super 8 Motel, 1909 Airport Way (907-451-8888). Fairbanks has countless bed & breakfast inns. Among them are: Alaska 7 Gables B&B (907-479-0751); Fairbanks B&B (907-452-4967); Chena River B&B (907-479-2532); and Joan's (907-479-6918). For other B&B reservations call the Fairbanks Association of Bed & Breakfasts (907-452-7700).

RELATED EVENTS/RACES Runners not crazy enough to run the marathon can hike it or assemble a relay team of three members, either single sex or mixed. Relay runners complete legs of 8.5, 8.6, and 9.2 miles. Team members must provide their own transportation to the relay exchange areas.

AREA ATTRACTIONS While in Fairbanks, check out the Dog Mushing Museum above the Alaska Public Lands Information Center at Courthouse Square. Also, browse the surprisingly good University Museum at UAF. Then, hurry to Denali National Park, home of Mt. McKinley, before it closes for the season to view amazing wildlife and gorgeous scenery. Make sure to reserve your tour bus and lodging ahead of time.

WALKER NORTH COUNTRY MARATHON

OVERALL: 78.5

COURSE BEAUTY: 9

COURSE DIFFICULTY: 4+ (SEE APPENDIX)

APPROPRIATENESS FOR FIRST TIMERS: 7

RACE ORGANIZATION: 9-

CROWDS: 1-

RACE DATA

Overall Ranking:	93
Quickness Ranking:	64
Contact:	Barb Iverson
	Walker North Country Marathon
	P.O. Box 1440
	Walker, MN 56484
	(218) 547-3327
	E-mail: golfisme@paulbunyan.net
Date:	September 18, 1999; September 16, 2000
Start Time:	9:00 a.m.
Time Course Closes:	3:00 p.m.
Number of Finishers:	110 in 1998
Course:	Loop
Certification:	USATF
Course Records:	Male: (open) 2:37:53
	Female: (open) 3:01:20
Elite Athlete Programs:	No
Cost:	$18
Age groups/Divisions:	≤14, 15-19, 20-24, 25-29, 30-34, 35-39, 40-44, 45-49, 50-54, 55-59, 60-64, 65-69, 70+
Walkers:	No
Requirements:	None
Temperature:	38° - 60°
Aid/Splits:	13 / none

HIGHLIGHTS Patterned after a German Black Forest festival celebrating life and land, the Walker North Country Marathon in northern Minnesota provides heartening views of remote forests, tranquil lakes and rolling farmlands for which Minnesota's famous. Run along a portion of the National Scenic Trail in the Chippewa National Forest, the course resonates with autumn's hues. Unique awards, handcrafted by local artists, further showcase the area's beauty.

COURSE DESCRIPTION Run on grass, gravel, dirt, and pavement, Walker North Country's loop course starts near the Walker-Hackensack-Akeley High School overlooking Walker Bay. After descending 75 feet to Main Street in the first half mile, runners turn south following State Hwy. 371 for the next 7.5 miles passing forest, lakes and an occasional home or business. Leaving the highway near 8 miles, the race veers onto the North Country Trail, a broad, grassy pathway. With several short steep hills, the difficult and scenic trail twists and turns the next 9 miles. At this stage, runners may take exception to the race's calling card, "The Celebration of Life and Land that is Northern Minnesota." At 16.6 miles, the route turns west onto the paved Heartland State Trail following an old railroad grade for approximately 1.5 miles. Minnesota's nickname, "Land of 10,000

Lakes," comes to mind as the race easily rolls through lake country to the finish. Around 18 miles, the course moves to a dirt road for 1.5 miles before briefly rejoining the North Country Trail and returning to the Heartland Trail at mile 21. The next 4.5 miles traipse mostly downhill to Walker where a challenging 75-foot rise in the last half mile leads to the finish line at Ostlund Field.

CROWD / RUNNER SUPPORT   Except for the occasional couple in a canoe, runners are on their own as far as crowd support. The largest cheering section congregates near the start/finish with the crowd enhanced by the 10K runners. Thirteen aid stations provide medical personnel, first aid supplies, emergency communications, water and electrolyte replacement (fluids only at 3.5 and 8.8 miles).

RACE LOGISTICS   Plenty of parking is available at the start/finish area at WHA High School. A shuttle service takes relay runners to and from the relay exchange points. Relay participants exchange a wristband in the transition area and turn it in at the finish. Showers are available in the school gym.

ACTIVITIES   All race activities take place at WHA High School. Race packet pickup takes place on Friday between 4:00 p.m. and 7:00 p.m. You can also pick up your packet on race day from 7:00 a.m. to 8:30 a.m. Carb up at the Spaghetti Feed Friday night from 5:00 p.m. to 8:00 p.m. After the race, stay for refreshments before the awards ceremony.

AWARDS   All participants receive T-shirts, and finishers earn specially designed medallions, part of a continuing series. Overall male and female winners and division winners receive art pieces crafted by local artists.

ACCOMMODATIONS   Although the race maintains no official race hotel, numerous motels and campgrounds exist in the popular resort community of Walker. Some of them include: AmericInn, Hwy. 371N, N Walker (218-547-2200); Tianna Farms Bed and Breakfast, Walker (218-547-1306); Chase on the Lake Lodge, Leech Lake (218-547-1531); Lakeview Inn, Hwy. 371E, E Walker (218-547-1212); Northwoods Beach Motel, Walker (218-547-1702); and Pioneer Inn Motel, Walker (218-547-1366). If you prefer to camp, consider the Acorn Hill Resort on Leech Lake (218-547-1015); or Shores Leech Lake Campground and Marina (218-547-1819). For more information contact the Leech Lake Area Chamber of Commerce (800-833-1118).

RELATED EVENTS / RACES   Walker North also conducts a 10K run/walk starting at 9:15 a.m. Traveling along portions of the Heartland Trail and past scenic Lake May, the race finishes with the famous half-mile uphill onto Ostlund Field. In 1995, race officials added Minnesota's only 2-Person Marathon Relay which starts with the marathon.

AREA ATTRACTIONS   Camping, hiking, fishing and boating head the area's entertainment.

BURNEY MARATHON

OVERALL: 78.8

COURSE BEAUTY: 9

COURSE DIFFICULTY: 7-

APPROPRIATENESS FOR FIRST TIMERS: 6

RACE ORGANIZATION: 8+

CROWDS: 1-

RACE DATA

Overall Ranking:	91
Quickness Ranking:	96
Contact:	Don Jacobs/Jim Crockett
	Burney Lions Club
	P.O. Box 217, Dept. M
	Burney, CA 96013-0217
	Tel. (530) 335-2825/335-3866
	Fax (530) 335-5476
	E-mail: dilligas@c-zone.net
Date:	September 19, 1999; September 17, 2000
Start Time:	8:00 a.m.
Time Course Closes:	1:00 p.m.
Number of Finishers:	38 in 1998
Course:	Point to point
Certification:	USATF
Course Records:	Male: (open) 2:33:35; (masters) 3:00:04
	Female: (open) 3:19:40; (masters) 3:35:25
Elite Athlete Programs:	No
Cost:	$25/30
Age groups/Divisions:	≤9, 10-14, 15-19, 20-24, 25-29, 30-34, 35-39, 40-44, 45-49, 50-54, 55-59, 60-64, 65-69, 70+
Walkers:	No
Requirements:	None
Temperature:	38° - 70°
Aid/Splits:	12 / first five miles

HIGHLIGHTS   A small mountain town provides the setting for the Burney Classic Marathon, a weekend of scenic running and family entertainment. Tucked away in the wilderness beyond Redding in Northern California, Burney offers a panoramic view of Mt. Shasta and Mt. Lassen. Though serene, the course challenges with an average elevation of 3,100 feet and plenty of hills over the first half. Looking for ways to attract more visitors to the beautiful Intermountain area, Race Director Don Jacobs and the Burney Lions founded the race in 1990. The beautiful Burney course leaves you wondering why the race hasn't grown over its brief history. Along with the marathon, the Burney Chamber of Commerce hosts a weekend of activities starting Saturday with a chili cookoff, crafts fair, live music, raffle and microbeer tasting. Race day includes a 5K, 10K, and half marathon. Though spectators are sparse and attendance is modest, the natural beauty and small town allure are enough to entice even the most competitive marathoner to Burney.

COURSE DESCRIPTION   Surrounded by spectacular mountain peaks, this well-kept secret (until now) of a course journeys by expansive ranches and enchanting forests. Beginning behind the make-shift, start-line garden hose, the point-to-point route runs predominantly uphill for the first half with steep sections from mile 5.8 to 6.4 and mile 10 to 10.8. A steep downhill from mile 11.4 to mile 12 allows you to recuperate and enjoy a wonderful panorama before climbing to 12.6 miles. A precursor to the faster second half, a nice downhill occurs from mile 12.6 to 14. Rolling to mile 14.7, the route falls to mile 16.5 followed by a few rollers to the 17-mile mark. A left turn on Cassell Road at 17.3 miles takes runners through flat cattle ranches to the 20-mile mark. Here, runners turn right on Hwy. 89, climbing a short but steep hill before turning left at 20.9 miles. Veering onto the uneven dirt/gravel terrain of Mountain View Road, the route runs flat to slightly downhill with scattered pine trees to the right and open fields and distant mountains on the left. At 24.2 miles, the race rises sharply to 24.5, flattens briefly, and then continues up to mile 24.9. The final 1.3 miles travel downhill to the Burney High School track where the announcer has plenty of time to work on name pronunciation for each of the 38 periodic finishers.

CROWD/RUNNER SUPPORT With the exception of two or three bodies at each of the 10 aid stations, the course affords you virtual solitary appreciation of its beauty. Before becoming too lonely, however, you may join or pass some half marathoners who started at the marathon halfway point 75 minutes after the marathon start. You may also pass 10K and 5K runners over the final miles of the race. If you're a Gatorade drinker, note that not all aid stations want you to "Be like Mike."

RACE LOGISTICS If you're traveling by airplane, the nearest airports to Burney are located in Redding and Reno. Make your lodging arrangements early as accommodations are limited, and hunting season begins the next week. On race morning, one school bus is all that is needed to transport the field of runners to the start. The bus leaves at 7:00 a.m. from Burney High School. After the half-hour ride, you depart the bus knowing almost each one of your competitors.

ACTIVITIES Pick up your race packet Friday from 1:00 p.m. to 5:00 p.m. or on Saturday from 9:00 a.m. to 1:00 p.m. at Charles Pillion's Accounting and Tax Service, 37104 Main Street. Otherwise, race packets are available at Veterans Hall during the Spaghetti Feed starting at 4:30 p.m. Be careful not to tire yourself the day before the race during all of the town festivities. Enjoy a post-race steak barbecue and plenty of beverages while awaiting the awards ceremony (almost everyone wins an award).

AWARDS Every runner receives a T-shirt, the top male and female in each division win medals, and second and third place division finishers receive rosette ribbons. The top three overall finishers receive $500, $200, and $100, respectively, while the first through third masters runners receive $250, $125, and $75.

ACCOMMODATIONS Several small hotels lie on Main Street (Hwy. 89), only a few blocks away from the finish at Burney High School. Among them are: the newly refurbished Burney Motel, 37448 Main Street (530-335-4500); Clark Creek Lodge, Hwy. 89 (530-335-2574); Green Gable Motel, 37385 Main Street (530-335-2264); Shasta Pines Motel, 37386 Main Street (530-335-2201); and Sleepy Hollow Lodge, 36898 Main Street (530-335-2285).

RELATED EVENTS/RACES If 26.2 miles is further than you want to run, consider the accompanying half marathon, 10K or 5K. All races run on sections of the marathon course. The half marathon begins at 9:15 a.m. from the marathon halfway point. The 10K and 5K feature out-and-back courses leaving from Burney High School at 10:00 a.m. and 10:15 a.m., respectively.

AREA ATTRACTIONS Burney Falls State Park and Mt. Lassen National Park spoil the outdoor lover. You can't go wrong with hiking, mountain biking, fishing or plain sightseeing.

DUTCHESS COUNTY MARATHON

OVERALL: 77.9

COURSE BEAUTY: 8

COURSE DIFFICULTY: 3+

APPROPRIATENESS FOR FIRST TIMERS: 7+

RACE ORGANIZATION: 9

CROWDS: 2-

RACE DATA

Overall Ranking:	99
Quickness Ranking:	42
Contact:	Irvin Miller
	Dutchess County Classic
	11 Manor Drive
	Poughkeepsie, NY 12603-3712
	(914) 473-2568
	E-mail: immiller1@juno.com
	http://www.pojonews.com/dcclassic
Date:	September 19, 1999; September 17, 2000
Start Time:	9:30 a.m.
Time Course Closes:	3:00 p.m.
Number of Participants:	106 in 1998
Course:	Two loops
Certification:	USATF
Course Records:	Male: (open) 2:33:13; (masters) 2:38:54
	Female: (open) 2:51:14; (masters) 3:08:59
Elite Athlete Programs:	No
Cost:	$25/30
Age groups/Divisions:	19-29, 30-39, 40-49, 50-59, 60+
Walkers:	No
Requirements:	None
Temperature:	70°
Aid/Splits:	7 / none

HIGHLIGHTS Many small marathons in North America get by on their requisite charm, offering few of the extras that runners expect in bigger affairs. Nothing wrong with that. However, if you like charm and appreciate special treatment (and who doesn't), consider the Dutchess County Classic held near Poughkeepsie, NY. A classic overachiever, Dutchess County does many little things that make a big difference. On top of a course featuring the picturesque scenery of the Hudson Valley, the race compiles a one-of-a-kind post-race yearbook with photographs of participants accompanied by an analysis of each runner's race (without the aid of the CHAMPI-ONCHIP). The professional singing of the National Anthem, permanent, artistic mile markers, and one of the most attractive race T-shirts anywhere, are a few of Dutchess County's attributes.

COURSE DESCRIPTION Dutchess County's double-loop country course travels through three towns, over several streams, and past schools, churches and historic homes. Starting at Wappinger Recreation Park in Wappinger, the course follows a mostly flat, rural route until two miles where it passes the Sons of Italy Joe DiMaggio Lodge and Van Wyck Junior High School. Here, runners enter a pleasant neighborhood for approximately 1 mile before returning to rural surroundings. At mile 4, the first of the course's two hills appears, lasting about .25 miles. After flattening briefly, the hill continues rising to the town of LaGrange. After the 5-mile mark coming off the upgrade, the course continues flat past the Karl Ehmer Farm and estate on the right and the Kinkead Farm located after the 6-mile mark. Between the two farms, runners pass the rock cut geological landmark while moving slightly uphill. From mile 7, the course continues flat and open until nearly the 9-mile mark when runners may encounter heavy traffic exiting the Presbyterian Church. A steep, .1-mile uphill greets runners after 9 miles (it can feel more like a mountain during the second loop) followed by a flat, narrow road through woodsy surroundings which most runners consider the loneliest part of the course. A slight, almost undetectable downhill lies after 11 miles, becoming flat by mile 12. Here, the scenic Secor Farm features a field of blazing sunflowers before the route returns to Wappinger Recreation Area and the start of the second loop.

CROWD / RUNNER SUPPORT   DCC's rural nature means few spectators line the course. Most of the cheering comes at the halfway point as many of the 5K and half marathoners cheer on the marathon runners. Volunteers at the five aid stations offer additional support. To bolster community involvement, the Poughkeepsie Journal typically devotes several pages to DCC coverage before and after the race.

RACE LOGISTICS   Several hotels lie in the vicinity but none within walking distance of the start; however, adequate parking areas exist around the start/finish area. Absolutely no vehicle parking is allowed on Robinson Lane in front of the park.

ACTIVITIES   Race packet pickup takes place at the Wappinger Recreation Area on Robinson Lane on race day from 7:30 a.m. to 9:15 a.m. Following the race, enjoy individual food bags, beverages, rousing disc jockey music, and an awards ceremony.

AWARDS   Runners preregistering up to a week before the event are guaranteed T-shirts. Additionally, each marathon finisher receives a medal, gloves, water bottle, certificate, food and a results booklet mailed after the race. The unique results booklet includes: a record of your position at different mile points along the course; the names of the runners that passed you or that you passed between the checkpoints; an analysis of the data and recommendations for future race strategy. In other words, if you go out too fast at DCC, you'll suffer in more ways than one. Overall and age-group winners receive trophies, and medals are awarded up to tenth place in some categories. The first local male and female runners receive clocks.

ACCOMMODATIONS   Although the race maintains no official hotel, the area contains plenty of lodging choices. Some of your options include: Econo lodge of Poughkeepsie, 418 South Road (914-452-6600); Best Western Inn and Conference Center, 679 South Road (914-462-4600); Holiday Inn Express, 341 South Road (914-473-1151); and Days Inn of Poughkeepsie, 418 South Road (914-454-1010).

RELATED EVENTS / RACES   For runners not wanting to go the entire distance, the half marathon runs concurrently with the marathon, while the 5K begins at 9:15 a.m.

AREA ATTRACTIONS   After the race, visit some of the area's historical sights including West Point Military Academy, FDR Historical site, Vanderbilt Mansion and other mansions along the scenic Hudson River. Treat yourself to a relaxing stay at one of the area's excellent bed and breakfasts after imbibing in some of the selections at the local wineries.

CLARENCE DEMAR MARATHON

OVERALL: 91.3

COURSE BEAUTY: 9+

COURSE DIFFICULTY: 2+

APPROPRIATENESS FOR FIRST-TIMERS: 9-

ORGANIZATION: 9

CROWDS: 4

RACE DATA

Overall Ranking: 16
Quickness Ranking: 16
Contact: Clarence DeMar Marathon
P.O. Box 6257
Keene, NH 03431
(877) 526-2379

Date: September 26, 1999 (tentative); September 24, 2000 (tentative)
Start Time: 8:00 a.m.
Time Course Closes: 1:00 p.m.
Number of Finishers: 400 in 1998
Course: Point to point
Certification: USATF
Course Records: Male: (open) 2:17:05
Female: (open) 2:33:56
Elite Athlete Programs: No
Cost: $18/30 (plus $12 for a T-shirt)
Age groups/Divisions: ≤39, 40-49, 50-59, 60+
Walkers: No
Requirements: None
Temperature: 58°
Aid/Splits: 12 / none

HIGHLIGHTS Named for the 7-time champion of the Boston Marathon, the Clarence DeMar Marathon competes for the best small marathon in North America award. DeMar grew up near the finish line in Keene, New Hampshire and later bought a homestead by the Keene Airport (which the race passes at mile 22). That the gritty DeMar came from beautiful New Hampshire may be surprising at first, then one must only think of the tough winters in northern New England. Happily, the marathon runs at the beginning of the fall foliage season, and the first 7 miles of the race are stunning, especially the stretch on Surry Road. While the final 19 miles cannot live up to the first 7, they do click by in relative rapidity, except for the harsh hill at mile 18. The race drops a net of 420 feet, with most of the downhill coming in the first 10 miles. While you may not be running as fast as DeMar did, you will at least be running in his quick footsteps.

COURSE DESCRIPTION The Clarence DeMar Marathon starts at Town Hall in tiny Gilsum, New Hampshire (elevation 900 feet). Quickly merging onto Route 10, the course heads into the country for some of the most scenic 7 miles of any marathon in the country. Proceeding on a nice downhill, runners turn right on completely closed Surry Road across the Stone Arch Bridge near .7 mile. As it runs through the surrounding forest, the course encounters its first rise at mile 1.5 where it winds along a gurgling stream. Soon the race begins to undulate down past a beautiful meadow and canopies of trees. Just before mile 5, the course turns left onto larger Route 12A (which is not completely closed), still following the stream. By mile 7, runners reach the edge of Surry (mile 7 to 8), passing the odd farm and houses. A nice downhill occurs from 8.4 to 10.5 as the race enters Keene. Passing through the outskirts of Keene, runners turn right onto Hurricane at mile 13.3 as they tour several residential neighborhoods. The course crosses busy Route 9 near mile 16 entering Swanzey. Proceeding gently downhill through a nice wooded area, runners reach the largest climb on the course, a tough rise from 17.7 to 18.3. After reaching the apex, the road drops steeply through the Yale Forest. Sawyer's Crossing Covered Bridge, red and barn-like, comes at mile 19.3, taking runners to Swanzey center and Monadnock Regional High School. The route turns left just before the school (mile 20) onto Route 32. After a bump at 20.6, runners head toward Keene through one of the less attractive sections of the race. Runners gratefully reach William Pond near mile 22, which also contains Keene Airport and a farm once owned by Clarence DeMar himself. Crossing Route 12, the route rolls onto Route 101 (mile 24). Now on the homestretch to central Keene (with a quick tour of a residential neighborhood), you finally reach Main Street which leads to Keene State College for the scenic finish in front of the library (elevation 480 feet).

CROWD/RUNNER SUPPORT The marathon places 12 aid stations along the course, five of which carry sport drink in addition to water. Spectators certainly do not mass the route, but clumps of support pop up in the residential neighborhoods and in Keene.

RACE LOGISTICS Gilsum is miniscule so there is very little parking there. (Besides, there are no buses after the race to return you to the start.) Instead, park near the finish line in Keene and ride one of the race buses from Spaulding Gymnasium at Keene State College to the start. The last bus leaves at 7:15 a.m. on Sunday. You can leave your sweats in a bag in Gilsum for pick-up at the finish.

ACTIVITIES Pick up your race packet at the Keene State College (KSC) Dining Commons between 5:00 p.m. and 6:00 p.m. on Saturday, or race morning at Spaulding Gymnasium (next door to the Dining Commons) between 6:00 a.m. and 7:15 a.m. Carbo load at the pasta dinner (about $8) in KSC Dining Commons from 6:00 p.m. to 8:00 p.m. on Saturday. A guest speaker usually addresses the feeding runners. After the race, feel free to shower inside Spaulding Gymnasium and get a massage. Then you should be ready for the awards ceremony around 12:30 p.m.

AWARDS If you want a T-shirt, you need to fork over an additional $12 above the race entry fee. Race finishers do receive certificates and results. Trophies go to the overall winners and the winners of each division. The next four finishers in each division receive plaques.

ACCOMMODATIONS The marathon does not have an official hotel. Some motels in the area include: Best Western Sovereign Hotel, Keene (603-357-3038); Super 8 Motel, Keene (603-352-9780); Days Inn, Keene (603-352-7616); Valley Green Motel, Keene (603-352-7305); and Wright Mansion Inn, Keene (603-355-2288). In Brattleboro, VT (about 30 minutes from Keene), try: Super 8 Motel (802-254-8889); Days Inn (802-254-4583); Quality Inn (802-254-8701); Colonial Motel (802 257-7733); or Econo Lodge (802-254-2360).

AREA ATTRACTIONS The end of September marks the beginning of the fall foliage season in New England. Tourists come from all over to view the firebrand trees while hiking, bicycling, canoeing, or driving their cars.

EAST LYME MARATHON

OVERALL: 77.9

COURSE BEAUTY: 9-

COURSE DIFFICULTY: 5

APPROPRIATENESS FOR FIRST TIMERS: 7-

RACE ORGANIZATION: 8+

CROWDS: 1-

RACE DATA

Overall Ranking: **99**
Quickness Ranking: **80**
Contact: **Way Hedding**
East Lyme Marathon
P.O. Box 186
East Lyme, CT 06333
(203) 739-2864

Date: **September 26, 1999; September 24, 2000**
Start Time: **8:30 a.m.**
Time Course Closes: **No time limit**
Number of Finishers: **NA**
Course: **Loop**
Certification: **USATF**
Course Records: **Male: (open) 2:23:56**
Female: (open) 2:48:51
Elite Athlete Programs: **No**
Cost: **$25**
Age groups/Divisions: **≤29, 30-39, 40-49, 50-59, 60+**
Walkers: **Yes**
Requirements: **None**
Temperature: **60°**
Aid/Splits: **14 / miles 1, 6 & 13**

HIGHLIGHTS Connecticut's oldest and most scenic marathon, East Lyme rolls past wooded farms, apple orchards, Rocky Neck State Park, coastline, and Black Point mansions. The cozy, relaxed ambiance makes for a serene experience. Kids can keep busy with the free timed track run.

COURSE DESCRIPTION East Lyme's completely paved, loop course promenades several of the area's most scenic back roads. Starting at East Lyme High School, the route heads northwest over winding and rolling Pataguanset Road. A small lake (at mile 1), several attractive country homes, and an occasional grazing cow characterize the rural, early miles. Two notable uphills (with corresponding downhills) occur between 1.2 and 1.8 miles on Pataguanset Road and 3 miles and 3.6 miles on Scott Road. Near 4.8 miles, the route turns left on Post Road beginning a 3-mile loop through the tree-canopied residential area of Lovers Lane and Dean Road. Around the 8-mile mark, the course turns left embarking on a nice rolling to mostly downhill stretch on Bride Brook Road. Flattening around the 11-mile mark, the course loops around Rocky Neck State Park for 3 miles before heading east another 3 miles to the exclusive Black Point residential area near 17.5 miles. Flat narrow roads, luxury homes and ocean glimpses mark the next few miles — the fastest and most scenic on the course. After a couple of quick ups and downs, the route exits Black Point near 21.5 miles, rises for a brief stint, and then heads east for .5 miles through downtown Niantic after 22 miles. At 22.5 miles, the course turns left heading north on Penn Avenue. Flat to gradually rolling for the next 3.5 miles, the race cuts through a commercial area around 24.6 miles and finishes at the high school.

CROWD/RUNNER SUPPORT Spectators spread along sections of the rural route. The 14 aid stations supply water, electrolyte replacement, diluted soda, oranges, and additional encouragement.

RACE LOGISTICS A hassle-free race, East Lyme starts and finishes within 100 yards of East Lyme High School where plenty of parking is available. Runners may take advantage of the high school's hot showers and locker rooms.

ACTIVITIES A spaghetti dinner is held on marathon eve from 6:00 p.m. to 8:00 p.m. at East Lyme High School (about $5). You can pick up your race packet or register while at the dinner or on race day from 7:00 a.m. to 8:00 a.m. Plenty of food and refreshments await the runners following the race.

AWARDS Every registered runner receives a marathon T-shirt, and marathon finishers receive high-quality medals. Merchandise prizes go to the top finishers, and the top three in each age group and overall winners receive other awards.

ACCOMMODATIONS While there is no official race hotel, several offer special rates for East Lyme Marathon entrants: Connecticut Yankee Inn (203-739-5487); Days Inn—East Lyme (203-739-3951); Howard Johnson Lodge (203-739-6921); and Motel 6 (203-739-6991).

RELATED EVENTS/RACES Non-marathoners can enter the 5K Run and Health Walk which starts immediately after the marathon. The free Children's Track Run starts at 9:30 a.m. with ribbons and refreshments for all runners.

AREA ATTRACTIONS Coastal Connecticut offers some interesting diversions, such as the USS Nautilus Submarine Museum and the Mystic Seaport. Gamblers can test their luck at the huge Fox Woods Resort Casino, or the Mohegan Sun.

FOX CITIES MARATHON

OVERALL: 86.7

COURSE BEAUTY: 8-

COURSE DIFFICULTY: 4-

APPROPRIATENESS FOR FIRST TIMERS: 10

RACE ORGANIZATION: 10-

CROWDS: 7-

RACE DATA

Overall Ranking:	38
Quickness Ranking:	44
Contact:	Community First Fox Cities Marathon
	P.O. Box 1315
	Appleton, WI 54913
	(920) 830-7259
	http://www.runningzone.com/foxcitiesmarathon
Date:	September 26, 1999; October 1, 2000 (tentative)
Start Time:	8:00 a.m.
Time Course Closes:	4:00 p.m.
Number of Finishers:	1,050 in 1997
Course:	Point to point
Certification:	USATF
Course Records:	New course
Elite Athlete Programs:	Yes
Cost:	$35/45
Age groups/Divisions:	≤19, 20-24, 25-29, 30-34, 35-39, 40-44, 45-49, 50-54, 55-59, 60-64, 65+, Cruiserweight (men 200+, women 150+), wheelchairs
Walkers:	Yes
Requirements:	None
Temperature:	46° - 65°
Aid/Splits:	22 / clocks every 5 miles, and halfway

HIGHLIGHTS The upper Midwest hosts some heavyweight marathons in early fall, including the Chicago, Detroit, Twin Cities, and Lakefront Marathons. With these well-established races, you might think that a relative newcomer like Fox Cities, held in the paper communities in eastern Wisconsin, would get overlooked in the shuffle. But it doesn't, and it shouldn't. Not only a nice marathon for runners, Fox Cities serves as a community event for local residents of seven towns that dot the Fox River. Exceptionally well organized, the race contains 22 aid stations and digital clocks every 5 miles as it crosses several decorated bridges. Though Fox Cities is an urban marathon, the fall foliage radiates along the course. Among the number of excellent fall marathons in the Midwest, Fox Cities proves itself as one of the best.

COURSE DESCRIPTION (*Note:* At press time, the 1999 race route had not been finalized. In 1998, the route varied from the original course due to bridge construction. Race organizers indicate that the route will likely mirror the original course, described below, but finish at the UW-Fox Valley Campus.)

Starting in Neenah, WI, the Fox Cities Marathon meanders along the Fox River passing through ten communities along the way, and finishes in Appleton, WI. Brilliant fall colors punctuate the entire area. The point-to-point course is entirely paved and closed to traffic. The starting line is located in Neenah's beautiful, tree-filled Riverside Park on the shores of Lake Winnebago. Mansions line the road opposite the park. Miles 1 through 7 head through commercial and residential areas of Neenah and Menasha, with runners crossing two of the seven bridges in this stretch. As you pass through Jefferson Park (between miles 3 and 4), admire the view of Lake Winnebago to your right and the slight downhill. The next 5 miles (5 through 9) offer homes in a rural setting in Appleton and include the first hill along the course. Runners climb approximately 30 feet over a 2-mile span (4 to 6); many runners will not even notice the change. Miles 9 through 17 cut through more subdivisions and residential areas on a gradual decline of 80 feet. Here, runners traverse Combined Locks and Kaukauna and experience plenty of entertainment. Between miles 15 and 16, you cross bridge number 3, slightly climbing across the river. Mile 18 marks the beginning of the most difficult section of the course as you go past Little Chute and Kimberly, home of the "wall." Runners climb 50 feet in this section, with the Washington Street bridge at 19 a particularly tough spot for some. You have a chance to recover as you head back toward Appleton before another 50-foot incline between miles 22 and 23, highlighted by the fifth bridge of the course. After mile 23, it's mostly flat through commercial areas in Appleton. You cross the last two bridges, and finish after the Oneida Skyline Bridge. You can now rejoice at having conquered the river you have been tracing for 26.2 miles!

CROWD/RUNNER SUPPORT As a bona fide community event, Fox Cities attracts thousands of spectators, more or less depending on who the Packers play that day, to cheer the runners and walkers. No part of the course is left uncovered. Costumed characters provide a humorous lift for the runners. The race also organizes hoopla along the course, with themes for aid stations and bridges, each of which is dressed-up by local civic groups and businesses for the occasion. You should have seen the Halloween station in 1998! The 22 water stations are well-stocked with water and electrolyte replacement. Medical vehicles travel the course prior to mile 13, and there are six medical aid stations after that point.

RACE LOGISTICS The race offers free shuttle buses to the start from official hotels in the area, and then back to the hotels from the finish area. Buses are also available to transport runners from the finish back to the start. The race also stores any belongings you may have at the start and transports them for retrieval at the finish area.

ACTIVITIES Fox Cities holds a Sports and Fitness Expo on Saturday from 9:00 a.m. to 7:00 p.m. at UW-Fox Valley Campus, 1478 Midway Road, Menasha. Here you can pick up your race packet and check out the latest in sports items. Note that there are no race-day entries. If you must see the course before the race, board one of the tour buses leaving from the UW-Fox Valley parking lot between 12:30 p.m. and 2:30 p.m. On Saturday evening, the traditional pasta dinner (about $7) opens at 7:00 p.m. at the UW Fox Valley Student Union. After the race, runners may opt for a well-deserved massage. The awards ceremony begins at 2:00 p.m.

AWARDS Every entrant receives a Fox Cities Marathon T-shirt, with finishers also earning medals. Age-group awards are given to the top three finishers in each division. The race offers approximately $7,000 in prize money.

ELITE RUNNERS INFORMATION The race offers free entry and lodging to selected athletes. For consideration, call the marathon office for details. The top three finishers in the open, masters, seniors, and wheelchair categories earn money.

ACCOMMODATIONS The race maintains no official event hotel. For accommodation information contact the Fox Cities Convention and Visitors Bureau (800-236-6673).

RELATED EVENTS/RACES Fox Cities is more than just a marathon. On

Saturday, there is a popular 1% Kids Marathon for children ages 14 and under. The actual distance varies depending on the age of the child. Kids receive their own race number, T-shirt, and goody bag. The 1% Marathon is held at UW-Fox Valley Campus. Then, on Sunday at 8:45 a.m. non marathoners can participate in the 5K also held on campus. Finally, the race offers a unique Marathon Relay for two to five-member teams. There are five exchange points at approximately the 5, 10, 15, and 20-mile points. Teams can decide which exchange points to utilize, depending on their number of runners. Race officials provide free transportation to/from relay exchange points. Relay team divisions are: open, corporate, credit union, and pulp and paper.

AREA ATTRACTIONS While you're in the Fox Cities area, visit a cheese factory, stroll Huidini's haunts, or take a city tour offered to the runners.

ADIRONDACK MARATHON

OVERALL: 87.1

COURSE BEAUTY: 10-

COURSE DIFFICULTY: 6 (SEE APPENDIX)

APPROPRIATENESS FOR FIRST-TIMERS: 8

ORGANIZATION: 9-

CROWDS: 3

RACE DATA

Overall Ranking: 34
Quickness Ranking: 76
Contact: Adirondack Marathon
Schroon Lake Chamber of Commerce
P.O. Box 583
Schroon Lake, NY 12870
Tel. (888) 724-7666
Fax (518) 532-7675
E-mail: info@adirondackmarathon.org
http://www.adirondackmarathon.org/
Date: September 26, 1999 (tentative); September 24, 2000 (tentative)
Start Time: 9:00 a.m.
Time Course Closes: 2:30 p.m.
Number of Finishers: 326 in 1998
Course: Loop
Certification: USATF
Course Records: Male: (open) 2:37:21
Female: (open) 3:04:22
Elite Athlete Programs: No
Cost: $35/40/45/50
Age groups/Divisions: <30, 30-39, 40-49, 50-59, 60+
Walkers: No
Requirements: None
Temperature: 60°
Aid/Splits: 12 / none

HIGHLIGHTS If we had to choose three words to describe the Adirondack Marathon, we would pick: Gorgeous, Resort, and Fall. This neophyte race runs around Lake Schroon in the Adirondack Mountains, a beautiful course that has some good climbs in the first half. The early fall scenery enhances the view as runners make their way around the lake. Afterwards, enjoy life in the peaceful resort, watching the leaves change as you prop your feet up in satisfied soreness.

COURSE DESCRIPTION The course strongly rolls with some good hills during the first half, while the second half runs mostly flat. The Adirondack Marathon begins on Main Street in Schroon Lake Village. The race quickly jogs around the school, and then rolls along Route 9 through the outskirts of the small town. Just before mile 2, runners turn right onto Alder Meadow Road which tops Lake Schroon. After passing the tiny airport, the road undulates its way between farms and soon some pretty forests. The first real hill occurs near mile 3.8, a quarter-mile rise. At mile 4, the route veers up East Shore Road, a beautiful lane with lots of shady trees under a protective canopy in places. Near mile 6, the road starts to descend for over a mile leading to a tough little hill at mile 7 (and another at 9.7 miles). Then winding down until mile 10.4, the road begins to roll once again from there preceding the challenging climb around 11.2 miles to 11.6. Then runners have a great downhill until the stop sign near mile 12.3, where runners head to the right. Now runners have their first unencumbered view of the gorgeous lake and the Adirondacks behind. Now mostly flat, the course reaches the bottom of Lake Schroon near mile 16, and makes its way back to Route 9 (17.2 miles) where it heads north toward Schroon Lake Village. On the way north, runners catch several glimpses of the lake through the thick trees. The route contains a few mild rises on the way home, most of which are offset by corresponding downhills. Near mile 23.3, motels and houses begin to crop up, foreshadowing the approaching town. Upon hitting Schroon Lake Village, the course turns right and finishes at the Town Beach.

CROWD/RUNNER SUPPORT The young Adirondack Marathon has already established good support from the community, but given the extremely small population, don't expect too much noise. Besides, it doesn't fit with the surrounding serenity of the lake and countryside. The aid stations carry the usual amenities.

RACE LOGISTICS Since Schroon Lake Village is a tiny town, runners can easily get to the start on their own. Several motels are within walking distance, and many more are a short drive away.

ACTIVITIES Pick up your race packet at the Schroon Lake Central School gymnasium on Friday from 3:00 p.m. to 9:00 p.m. and on Saturday from 9:00 a.m. to 5:00 p.m. Otherwise, retrieve your number on race morning at Town Hall on South Avenue from 7:30 a.m. to 8:30 a.m. The race also hosts a pasta party on Saturday evening.

AWARDS All entrants receive a marathon T-shirt. The top 3 runners in each age group receive prizes, as do the top 3 male and female overall finishers. The race will mail results to you for a $2 charge. Otherwise, results are available on the race webpage.

ACCOMMODATIONS There is no host hotel, but the Schroon Lake area is full of motels. Here's a few to try in Schroon Lake Village: Blue Ridge Motel (518-532-7521); Chamlar Lodge & Cottages (518-532-7716); Davis Motel & Cottages (518-532-7583); Dun Roamin Cabins (518-532-7277); Rainbow Motel & Cottages (518-532-7348); and Schroon Lake Place (518-532-7649).

AREA ATTRACTIONS Schroon Lake is a beautiful resort area in the Adirondack Mountains. The lake itself is the center of attention here, and you can do just about anything that one would normally do at a lake resort. There is also great hiking in the area, should you need to stretch your legs before or after the marathon.

NEW HAMPSHIRE MARATHON

OVERALL: 82.1

COURSE BEAUTY: 9+

COURSE DIFFICULTY: 6 (SEE APPENDIX)

APPROPRIATENESS FOR FIRST TIMERS: 6

RACE ORGANIZATION: 8+

CROWDS: 0+

RACE DATA

Overall Ranking: **73**
Quickness Ranking: **89**
Contact: **Fred MacClean**
New Hampshire Marathon
P.O. Box 6
Bristol, NH 03222
(603) 744-2649

Date: **October 2, 1999; September 30, 2000**
Start Time: **10:00 a.m.**
Time Course Closes: **3:00 p.m.**
Number of Finishers: **220 in 1997**
Course: **Loop**
Certification: **USATF**
Course Records: **Male: (open) 2:33:54**
Female: (open) 3:12:00
Elite Athlete Programs: **No**
Cost: **$20**
Age groups/Divisions: **≤39, 40+**
Walkers: **No**
Requirements: **None**
Temperature: **50° - 65°**
Aid/Splits: **14 / none**

HIGHLIGHTS   The deep golden ponds and lakes sparkling throughout central New Hampshire lured Hollywood to the region to shoot the famous movie with Kathryn Hepburn and Henry Fonda. One of the purest and deepest of them all, Newfound Lake, serves as the centerpiece of the New Hampshire Marathon, with about 16 rolling miles set around the lake. The fiery leaves at water's edge make for inspiring beauty, and you will welcome every morsel of motivation to get through the difficult course.

COURSE DESCRIPTION   The New Hampshire Marathon's course wraps around Newfound Lake in a modified out-and-back configuration that traces the lake's eastern shore out and its western shore back. The race, run in the shoulder of country roads, starts near central Bristol, NH on Lake Street (Route 3A) immediately in front of Newfound Memorial Middle School. Runners go north on Route 3A through a brief commercial area, climbing from .3 miles to mile 2. After running along the river, you reach Newfound Lake at 2.5 miles, where you climb to mile 2.8 and then have a gentle descent to 3.4. From the start to mile 4, the course gains about 250 feet. The course undulates to the 8-mile mark, with a tough 100-foot rise from 8 to 8.6. Turning left on North Shore Road at 8.5 miles, the route continues on this road until the turnaround at Sculptured Rocks (14 miles). A sharp downhill lies from 8.9 to 9.3; enjoy it because another stiff ascent awaits from 9.6 to mile 10, followed by a corresponding downhill. The course flattens or gently rolls through the town of Hebron before turning uphill from 12.8 to 13.8. A brief downgrade leads to the turnaround, with runners coming back the same way until West Shore Road at 16.8. Back along the lake, West Shore Road contains a good hill from 17.5 to 17.8, then mostly rolls with a few nice downhills thrown in. The area offers some great views of Newfound Lake. By the time the race returns to Route 3A just after mile 24, it is mostly a gentle downgrade to the finish through Bristol in Kelley Park.

CROWD/RUNNER SUPPORT The 14 aid stations inject some enthusiasm into runners in the sparsely populated Bristol area. Some spectators do scatter along the course, particularly in Hebron village, with its quaint village green and gazebo, and at the Inn on Newfound Lake (mile 6), where people gather on the porch to watch the race and enjoy the view. Every mile is marked, so those of you with watches can catch your split times.

RACE LOGISTICS Most runners will need to drive to the start, but plenty of parking exists at Newfound Memorial Middle School, opposite the race start. Additional parking is located at the elementary school a block to the east on School Street.

ACTIVITIES On Friday evening, the Masonic Hall hosts a pasta dinner ($5) from 5:00 p.m. to 7:30 p.m. Pick up your race package on marathon morning at Newfound Memorial Middle School. You may register on race morning, but if you want a T-shirt it will cost you extra (about $5) to cover shipping costs. After you run, enjoy a free massage, shower, refreshments, and bluegrass concert.

AWARDS Every early-registered entrant receives a New Hampshire Marathon T-shirt, and finishers sport medals. Approximately $2,500 in prize money is awarded to the top five open and masters finishers, with overall winners receiving $500.

ACCOMMODATIONS The race does not have an official host hotel. Most of the lodging in the area consists of small motels or private cottages. Among those in the vicinity are: Bungalo Village Cottages and Motel, West Shore Drive, Bristol (603-744-2220); Cliff Lodge, HC 60, Bristol (603-744-8660); Lakeside Cottages, 68 Lake Street, Bristol (603-744-3075); Pleasant View B&B, Hemphill Road, Bristol (603-744-5547); The Inn on Newfound Lake, 1030 Mayhew Turnpike, Bridgewater (603-744-9111); Whip-O-Will Motel, 1755 Mayhew Turnpike, Bridgewater (603-744-2433); and Whittemore Inn, 367 Mayhew Turnpike, Bridgewater (603-744-3518). For rentals try Century 21 Country Lakes Realty, 130 Lake Street, Bristol (800-342-9767); or Greenan Realty (603-744-8144).

RELATED EVENTS/RACES The New Hampshire 10K Road Race starts with the marathon and runs on an out-and-back route over the first 5K of the marathon course. Winners receive $150 in prize money. The race also holds an informal, noncompetitive 10K Fun and Health Walk at 10:15 a.m. to benefit the Camp Mayhew Program for at-risk boys and the D.A.R.E. program.

AREA ATTRACTIONS You come to New Hampshire this time of year to relax (after the marathon) and enjoy the change of seasons. Those with some energy reserves can find plenty of hiking and canoeing.

St. George Marathon

Overall: 94

Course Beauty: 9+

Course Difficulty: 3 (see appendix)

Appropriateness for First Timers: 8

Race Organization: 10-

Crowds: 4-

RACE DATA

Overall Ranking:	7
Quickness Ranking:	33
Contact:	St. George Marathon
	Leisure Services
	86 South Main Street
	St. George, UT 84770
	Tel. (801) 634-5850; Fax (801) 634-0709
	E-mail: leisure@infowest.com
Date:	October 2, 1999; October 7, 2000
Start Time:	6:45 a.m.
Time Course Closes:	12:45 p.m.
Number of Finishers:	3,174 in 1997
Course:	Point to point
Certification:	USATF
Course Records:	Male: (open) 2:15:16; (masters) 2:22:52
	Female: (open & masters) 2:37:13
Elite Athlete Programs:	Yes
Cost:	$30
Age groups/Divisions:	Male: ≤12, 13-14, 15-18, 19-24, 25-29, 30-34, 35-39, 40-44, 45-49, 50-54, 55-59, 60-64, 65-69, 70-74, 75+, Heavyweight (200+)
	Female: ≤18, 19-24, 25-29, 30-34, 35-39, 40-44, 45-49, 50-54, 55-59, 60-64, 65-69, 70+, Heavyweight (140+)
Walkers:	No
Requirements:	None
Temperature:	37° - 80°
Aid/Splits:	13 / every 2 miles

HIGHLIGHTS A few years ago, amidst the hysteria of runners attempting to qualify for the 100th Boston Marathon, St. George garnered the reputation as the fastest marathon in the United States. Ever since then, the race has filled it's 4,000-runner limit in days. It is true that some people run fast at St. George. But not all, or even most. A couple of long, taxing uphills and sharp, quad-killing downhills do in many runners. The question is, does it matter? To our mind, no. The St. George Marathon has plenty more to offer runners than its 2,560-foot vertical drop. A distinctively beautiful, well-organized, fun community event, the race provides unique touches that runners love, such as bonfires at the start to keep participants warm. Sunrise over the barren mountains, the brilliant red rock formations of Snow Canyon, and several ancient volcanos make the scene spectacular in places. St. George also lies within an easy drive of some of America's top destinations. All of these combine to make the St. George Marathon one of America's finest, fast or not. Andre Tocco of San Pedro, California says, *"I have been going to this race for the past 14 years,* *and I have seen it grow .... But every year the quality of the race was never affected."*

COURSE DESCRIPTION The St. George Marathon runs point to point on Highway 18 from Pine Valley Road near Central, UT, to Worthen Park in St. George. Entirely closed to traffic with excellent asphalt, the course begins at an elevation of 5,240 feet and ends at 2,680 feet, an elevation loss of 2,560 feet. This impressive figure excites everyone about the speed of the race. However, the course contains two significant hills at miles 7 and 21.5, slowing down most runners.

The first small rise on the course occurs at .7 miles, then it levels out for a half mile. Runners hit a noticeable .33-mile hill, then it's mostly flat or gently downhill (except 3.2 to 3.7) to mile 5.6. You descend quickly into the town of Veyo at the 7-mile mark. Upon leaving Veyo, a challenging 1-mile climb (about 500 feet) awaits you, making you doubt talk of fast, downhill courses. The hill crests near 8 miles. You then have some time to recover on flat to slightly downhill roads to mile 9, where the road inclines gradually with some intermittent bumps to mile 12.3. The next essentially flat 2 miles become a sharp downhill from mile 13.7 to 15.4. Hope you did your downhill training! At 14.4, you negotiate a right curve and come face to face with interesting rock formations. The course flattens out from mile 15.4 to 16.7 and then declines just perceptively to 18.2. Another hill looms between mile 18.2 and 18.6, and then it's mostly downhill with a few bumps from mile 18.6 to 21.5. Just before the 20-mile mark, notice the beautiful rock formations to your right. Yet another strenuous, steep climb must be conquered between mile 21.5 and 22.1. Your legs are then hit immediately with a sharp downhill for .25 miles that eases slightly for the rest of the way to St. George at mile 23.4. Here, Highway 18 becomes Bluff Street, the main drag in St. George. Enjoy the sound of the crowds as you check out the impressive red rock bluffs overlooking the town. Bluff Street provides a nice, easy slope for a downhill finish. Before mile 25 you can see the white tip of the Mormon Temple against the red rock backdrop. At mile 25, you make a sharp left onto 300 South Street straight into Worthen Park for the finish.

CROWD/RUNNER SUPPORT The marathon is the community event in St. George. Over 1,400 volunteers cater to the runners, while the locals turn out in droves in downtown St. George. Due to limited access, relatively few spectators perch along Highway 18. The two exceptions are at Veyo, where a large and supportive crowd turns out, and at Snow Canyon (mile

15). Aid stations stock water, electrolyte replacement drink, petroleum jelly, sponges, and first aid supplies; nurses are available for medical aid. Approximately 80 portable toilets dot the course.

RACE LOGISTICS All runners must take the buses from Worthen Park to the start, unless camping in the Pine Valley area. Buses begin departing at 4:30 a.m. with the last bus leaving around 5:40 a.m. The race must bus 4,000 runners to the start, so arrive early. And remember, if you are staying in Nevada, St. George's clocks are one hour ahead. The bus ride provides an excellent opportunity to get an idea of what you're in for since it drives the course in reverse, although you can only see so much in the dark. Of course, the race transports your personal belongings from the start to the finish.

ACTIVITIES St. George sponsors a race expo on Friday, from 9:00 a.m. to 9:00 p.m. at the Smith's Auditorium, Dixie Convention Center. A pasta feed with entertainment and all-you-can-eat food and drink is also at the Convention Center ($6). The race hosts a number of running clinics, including "Marathon 101" offering advice on how to run the St. George course. Runners keep warm by bonfires near the start in the morning chill. St. George hosts an excellent post-race party in Worthen Park. Good food, fresh fruit, drinks and entertainment preface the awards ceremony. Runners can relax with a complimentary 15-minute massage after the race before viewing the results at the Recreation Center.

AWARDS All entrants receive T-shirts and race posters. Finishers earn special medallions to commemorate their achievement. Age-group awards go up to ten deep. Overall and masters winners typically receive an all-expenses paid trip to run in the Ibigawa Marathon in Japan. A Special Achievement Award recognizes a particularly exceptional effort. After completing 10 St. George marathons, you are eligible for the Ten-Year Club. Club members are entitled to special T-shirts, photos, discounts on entry fees, and a post-marathon party.

FIRST TIMERS INFORMATION St. George offers a couple of challenges for the first timer—a demanding course (see Course Description) at moderate altitude and few spectators over the first 25 miles (except for miles 7 and 15). These factors are tempered by a supportive race organization with excellent aid stations, a scenic course, a sizeable field of runners, and usually good weather conditions. Prepare yourself for the course by doing plenty of hill training (both up and down). In one of St. George's many distinctive touches, first timers are given special T-shirts, products and prizes.

ELITE RUNNERS INFORMATION St. George provides limited assistance to elite runners, possibly including entry, transportation, lodging, and/or expenses. Funds are limited, so contact Kent Perkins for more information on obtaining elite status.

ACCOMMODATIONS For accommodations in St. George, call (800-259-3343). Entry forms also have a complete listing of lodging in Washington County. Hotels in St. George fill extremely early, so many runners stay in Nevada, a 45-minute drive from St. George (remember the time difference). You shouldn't have much trouble obtaining a reservation there.

RELATED EVENTS / RACES A 2-mile Mayor's Walk from Bluff Street Park to the marathon finish line begins at 7:00 a.m. Walkers receive T-shirts, walker numbers, and post-walk refreshments, and are eligible for random drawings. The walk draws over 1,200 participants.

AREA ATTRACTIONS St. George sits within a modest drive of two completely dichotomous attractions—Zion National Park and Las Vegas. Definitely worth the short trip from St. George, Zion offers some spectacular hiking, camping, and just plain sight-seeing. Also nearby is Cedar Breaks National Monument. If you have an extra couple of days, you can also visit Bryce Canyon National Park, which lies just beyond Zion. If you feel like a little city action, Las Vegas lies just 2 hours away. Make the drive during the daylight, if you can, to admire the stunning gorge just outside of St. George on Interstate 15. The incredible bluffs envelope you in their majesty. Unforgettable!

JOHNSTOWN MARATHON

OVERALL: 81.5

COURSE BEAUTY: 9+

COURSE DIFFICULTY: 5

APPROPRIATENESS FOR FIRST-TIMERS: 6+

ORGANIZATION: 8+

CROWDS: 2+

RACE DATA

Overall Ranking: 75
Quickness Ranking: 78
Contact: Dennis Arnold, Race Director
Johnstown YMCA
100 Haynes Street
Johnstown, PA 15901
Tel. (814) 535-8381

Date: October 3, 1999; October 1, 2000
Start Time: 9:00 a.m.
Time Course Closes: 3:00 p.m.
Number of Finishers: 130 in 1997
Course: Near loop
Certification: USATF
Course Records: Male: (open) 2:22:52
Female: (open) 2:48:49
Elite Athlete Programs: No
Cost: $20/25
Age groups/Divisions: ≤19, 20-29, 30-34, 35-39, 40-44, 45-49, 50-54, 55-59, 60+, wheelchair
Walkers: No
Requirements: None
Temperature: 55°
Aid/Splits: 11 / verbal splits at miles 1, 5, 10K, halfway, 15, 20, & 25

HIGHLIGHTS   The Johnstown Marathon made its first appearance on the running scene in the mid 1970s, attracting 103 runners. Since then, the race has had a number of interesting years. In 1977, the Johnstown Flood nearly wiped out the race and scarred the course. In a poignant reminder of the devastation, runners were drenched by a heavy downpour on race day. The following year proved a little better when Steve Alpert filmed his movie "Marathon Fever" during the race. One final historical note: in 1980, 10-year-old Jennifer Amyx was the first female to cross the finish line in a remarkable 3:12:50. For today's runners, Johnstown provides a welcome relief. Its intimate size, pretty autumn foliage, and small-town warmth recall the simpler times of distance running. It also contains one of the most beautiful patches of running anywhere as it traces the 1,000-foot deep Conemaugh Gap. With these features, its not surprising that the Johnstown Marathon has hung around for so long.

COURSE DESCRIPTION   The marathon starts on Edgehill Drive in suburban Westmont. The first 5 miles take runners through the surrounding residential areas, with several rolling sections. Just before mile 5, the route turns right onto St. Clair Road (miles 5 to 7), a wooded stretch that is mostly downhill. St. Clair Road turns into Fairfield Avenue after mile 7, which passes through more residential neighborhoods, before the race leaves the city on Strayer Street. Miles 9 to 14 take runners along the western edge of the Conemaugh Gap, a 1,000-foot gorge sculpted by the waters of the Conemaugh River. This gorgeous segment is also well-traveled by cars, so make sure you stick to the right-hand side of the highway. The course then undulates its way to the eastern side of the Conemaugh Gap, where the traffic thins out a bit (miles 14 to 17). Then leaving Cramer on the Cramer Pike (PA 403), runners have a long, unprotected path that can be quite warm in sunny weather. You reenter the city after mile 21 on a mostly flat road. After crossing the bridge to Broad Street, runners head through historic Cambria City. Downtown Johnstown soon arrives, and after passing along Roosevelt Blvd., Washington Street, and Market Street, the race merges onto Main Street, finishing at the Point Stadium.

CROWD / RUNNER SUPPORT The Johnstown Marathon has aid stations every 3 miles, then every mile for the last 5 miles of the race. The aid stations carry water, sport drink, and Vaseline.

RACE LOGISTICS The race encourages runners to park downtown near the finish line, and take the Incline Plane (free) up to the race start. The Incline Plane entrance is one block from Point Stadium on Route 56 east. The marathon start is located two blocks from the top of the Incline Plane on Edgehill Drive in Westmont.

ACTIVITIES Pre-registered runners can pick up their race packets at the Pasta Dinner (free for runners) on Saturday, from 3:00 p.m. to 7:00 p.m., at the Senior Activities Center, 550 Main Street in downtown Johnstown. You may also retrieve your race packet, or register late, on race morning up to a half hour prior to the race start. After the race, the YMCA plans events for the entire family, such as Punt, Pass and Kick contests (and we all want to do this after a marathon) and Lollipop Races. There is also entertainment in the finish area.

AWARDS All entrants receive race T-shirts. Marathon finishers earn medals and certificates. Age group winners take home an award, and the top three overall finishers get U.S. Savings Bonds of $500, $250, and $100, respectively. The fastest runner under 2:22:52 (the existing course record) receives $100 cash.

ACCOMMODATIONS The Holiday Inn, 250 Market Street (two blocks from the finish line) (814-535-7777) is the official host hotel. Other reasonably-priced accommodations nearby include: Comfort Inn, 455 Theatre Drive (814-266-3678); Days Inn, 1540 Scalp Avenue (814-269-3366); Towne Manor Motel, 155 Johns Street (814-536-8771); Holiday Inn Express, 1440 Scalp Avenue (800-822-9194); Murphy Inn, Penmar Line (814-266-4800); Sleep Inn, 453 Theatre Drive (814-262-9292); and Motel 6, 430 Napoleon Place (814-536-1114).

RELATED EVENTS / RACES Shorter distance runners can compete in the marathon relay, with teams of four runners, or the 10K. There is also a 2-mile Fun Walk and an adaptive cycling marathon and 10K.

AREA ATTRACTIONS Johnstown's Inclined Plane is the world's steepest at 71.9°. At the top you have panoramic views of Johnstown and the Conemaugh Valley. The Johnstown Flood Museum chronicles the 1889 flood, one of America's most infamous disasters. The area also contains lots of beautiful scenery for walking, hiking, or bike riding.

MAINE MARATHON

OVERALL: 79.9

COURSE BEAUTY: 9-

COURSE DIFFICULTY: 6-

APPROPRIATENESS FOR FIRST TIMERS: 7-

RACE ORGANIZATION: 8+

CROWDS: 2

RACE DATA

Overall Ranking: **88**
Quickness Ranking: **86**
Contact: **Joe Teno**
c/o Maine Track Club
P.O. Box 8008
Portland, ME 04104
(207) 741-2084

Date: **October 3, 1999; October 1, 2000**
Start Time: **8:00 a.m.**
Time Course Closes: **2:00 p.m.**
Number of Finishers: **300 in 1997**
Course: **Out and back with a loop**
Certification: **USATF**
Course Records: **Male: (open) 2:35:00; (masters) 2:41:01**
Female: (open) 2:51:44; (masters) 3:14:02
Elite Athlete Programs: **No**
Cost: **$30/35**
Age groups/Divisions: **≤19, 20-29, 30-34, 35-39, 40-44, 45-49, 50-54,**
55-59, 60-64, 65+69, 70+
Walkers: **No**
Requirements: **None**
Temperature: **53°**
Aid/Splits: **12 / none**

HIGHLIGHTS The home of marathon great Joan Benoit Samuelson and boasting a beautiful craggy coast, Maine hosts one of the most easterly marathons in the United States—the Maine Marathon. The Atlantic Ocean, rural communities, and urban Portland, punctuated with fall's changing colors, dominate the scenery along the loop course. Although the route never exceeds an elevation of 180 feet, its rolling hills make it challenging for most runners.

COURSE DESCRIPTION The Maine Marathon begins adjacent to the University of Southern Maine (USM), running along flat, scenic Back Cove for 2 miles with downtown's skyline rising to your right. After traversing an on-ramp to Route 1, the course continues flat with Casco Bay to the right. Exiting Route 1 after mile 4, runners head down less busy Route 88 (miles 4 through 13). Here, the course begins to roll gently, passing through rural woodsy residential areas most of the way, with particularly beautiful homes near mile 9. A good hill awaits from mile 8.5 to mile 9.1, followed by a steep descent from 9.3 to 9.6. Two more uphills lie on this stretch from 10.5 to 11.1 and from 12.5 to 12.7. Runners enter the town of Yarmouth traversing mostly flat North Road and Leighton Road, where the street and the scenery deteriorate slightly. The course turns rolling again on West Elm Street as it goes through a middle-class neighborhood. At mile 17, the course briefly bisects an industrial area, and then returns to rolling through rural communities. Mile 18 to 18.7 is largely uphill, while miles 18.7 to 19.8 mostly undulate. Flat to mile 21.5, the course crosses a beautiful waterscape with a wonderful bridge back to the right and then contains a few short rollers. Runners face a challenging climb from mile 22.8 to 23.2, past modern homes, and then have mostly level running through Payson Park, along Back Cove, and to the finish.

CROWD/RUNNER SUPPORT   The small crowds mostly gather at the start/finish line, and residents come out of their homes at scattered parts of the course to support the runners. Otherwise, the best encouragement comes from the aid station volunteers placed approximately every 2 miles.

RACE LOGISTICS   You will need to drive to the start; parking is available at the USM on Bedford Street. The race provides a bag check service so you can leave your sweats at the start without having to return to your car.

ACTIVITIES   Race weekend gets underway on Saturday with the University of Southern Maine's Fitness Expo from 11:00 a.m. to 5:00 p.m. After picking up your race packet, stick around for the all-you-can-eat pasta party. After the race, enjoy refreshments and a well-deserved massage.

AWARDS   All preregistered runners receive Maine Marathon T-shirts. The top three finishers in each age group and the top five overall runners receive awards.

ACCOMMODATIONS   While there is no official race hotel, several in the area may offer a special rate to Maine Marathon runners. Over a dozen hotels/motels sit within one to three miles of USM. Contact the race organizers for a list.

RELATED EVENTS/RACES   On Saturday prior to the marathon, the Lifeline 5K and Kids 1K and 1 Mile Fun Run are held near USM. The Casco Bay Half Marathon (about 750 entrants) starts with the marathon on Sunday. The women's course record holder is, of course, Joan Benoit Samuelson. A four-person marathon relay (with legs of 6.5, 6.5, 6, and 7.2 miles) runs with the full marathon.

AREA ATTRACTIONS   Literature lovers may consider the Wadsworth-Longfellow House, 487 Congress Street. At the other end of the spectrum, the Portland Pirates hockey team plays at the Civic Center. For a gorgeous getaway, cruise to one of the many offshore islands, or drive south to Kennebunkport. The shopping outlets (including L. L. Bean) in Freeport lie an hours drive north.

PORTLAND MARATHON

OVERALL: 91.3

COURSE BEAUTY: 8+

COURSE DIFFICULTY: 4- (SEE APPENDIX)

APPROPRIATENESS FOR FIRST TIMERS: 10

RACE ORGANIZATION: 10

CROWDS: 6

RACE DATA

Overall Ranking:	16
Quickness Ranking:	44
Contact:	Portland Marathon
	P.O. Box 4040
	Beaverton, OR 97076
	Tel. (503) 226-1111
	Fax (503) 645-9526
	E-mail: info@portlandmarathon.org
	http://www.portlandmarathon.org
Date:	October 3, 1999; October 1, 2000
Start Time:	7:00 a.m.
Time Course Closes:	3:00 p.m.
Number of Finishers:	4,167 in 1998
Course:	Near loop
Certification:	USATF
Course Records:	Male: (open) 2:17:00; (masters) 2:26:03
	Female: (open) 2:36:39; (masters) 2:54:57
Elite Athlete Programs:	No
Cost:	$55/90 (1999); $60/100 (2000)
Age groups/Divisions:	≤19, 20-24, 25-29, 30-34, 35-39, 40-44, 45-49, 50-54,
	55-59, 60-64, 65-69, 70-74, 75-79, 80-84, 85-89, 90+,
	Clydesdale (185+ lbs.) and Bonnydale (145+ lbs.)
Walkers:	Yes
Requirements:	None
Temperature:	50° - 56°
Aid/Splits:	19 / every mile including pace

HIGHLIGHTS Just as a rose radiates with well-defined, intriguing beauty, so does the City of Roses' Portland Marathon with its incredible organization and positive attitude. Boasting twenty-six years of experience, the race is one of the premier marathon events in the United States. No stranger to adulation, Portland annually hosts the National Race Director's Conference during race weekend. What better way to learn how to produce a successful event than to watch first hand Portland's masterful organization. And, with Portland offering more running and non-running events over race weekend than any other marathon in North America, effective organization is a must. The second largest non-prize money marathon in the country (Marine Corps is larger), Portland definitely believes in its motto "Everybody is a winner." This fact is, undoubtedly, the reason why 70% of participants come from points 100 miles or further; 46 states and 15 countries in all. The race also offers friendliness all-year round. What other marathon sends Christmas cards to past participants?

RACE HISTORY   One of the many races under the auspices of the Oregon Road Runners' Club, the Portland Marathon premiered in 1972 with 173 runners. However, due to rapid growth, the marathon was forced to change courses numerous times in its formative years. Add to this the frequent shifting of the race date and race director, and Portland topped out in the late seventies with 1,219 runners, then declined to a five-year low of 481 in 1981. Ironically, that same year marked the first time the course entered the downtown area, a dream of the race's founding fathers but continually squelched by city officials. That year also signaled the beginning of a new era for the Portland Marathon. As strange as it may sound, it started when one of the 481 runners quit mid-race. Runner Les Smith, president of the ORRC, did not quit from exhaustion. He quit because he felt that race management could be doing much more for the runners. He spent the next few hours assisting at an undermanned aid station and cheering on his fellow runners all the while visualizing the transformation of Portland into a world-class marathon. After assuming the position of race director in 1984, Les completely overhauled the race. Fifteen years later, Les continues at the helm of the race that treats every runner like a champion.

COURSE DESCRIPTION   The Marathon and Marathon Walk begin and end at charming Chapman/Lownsdale/Schrunk Parks, which are actually one big park in downtown Portland. Starting at the corner of SW Madison and Fourth, the course traces a route that embraces the many faces of a beautiful and friendly city, including the scenic riverfront, historic Old Town, and various residential neighborhoods. Broad panoramas of the city and dramatic views of the Cascade Mountain Range (Mt. Hood and Mt. St. Helens) and the St. Johns Bridge, one of the most beautiful suspension bridges in the world, inspire runners. Well-marked, the race provides large signs covered by balloons to signal each mile. The first 5 miles of the course are downtown. A gentle 1-mile downhill starts the race, with the next 2.5 miles gradually gaining 140 feet. An immediate, 2-mile downhill takes runners along the waterfront. The next section, from mile 5.5 to 12, travels through the industrial northwest section of town. You hardly notice this least scenic area of the course since the music and the adrenaline rush from eyeing other runners approaching from the opposite direction easily divert your attention. Making another gradual downhill, the course heads along the flat border road of the Forest Park area through mile 15. The principal elevation gain on the course occurs over the next two miles as runners climb nearly 150 feet leading to the beautiful St. Johns Bridge. Thereafter, you run along Portland's spectacular east bluff that faces the Willamette River from mile 18 through 24. There is an elevation loss of approximately 140 feet from mile 22 to 24.5, with a slight rise as runners go over Portland's Steel Bridge. You then turn back down to Marathon Avenue which leads to Front Avenue along the waterfront to the finish. Entirely run on well-maintained asphalt, the majority of the course is closed to vehicular traffic. Because the course records are relatively slow, you might surmise that the course is slow. But, remember, fast times are partly a function of prize money, one of the few things Portland doesn't offer. Make no mistake about it, Portland is a potential PR course.

CROWD/RUNNER SUPPORT   Enthusiastic spectators, numbering upwards of 50,000, line the streets throughout the course with the greatest percentage in the downtown area for the first 5 miles and for the last 1.5 miles. Large neighborhood crowds gather between 18 and 21 miles. Various musical groups and street performers entertain along the course and appear to enjoy the event as much as the runners. Les Smith no longer has to work an aid station for the race as Portland fashions 19 of them manned by volunteers from businesses and organizations around the city. The stations compete for awards, including best organized, best decorated, and most enthusiastic. The aid stations are tremendous (some have cups with lids and straws), and depending on the weather, sponge and spray stations are also available.

RACE LOGISTICS   Because the race starts and ends near all the hotels in downtown Portland, transportation is not a concern. Clothing storage is provided starting at 6:00 a.m. and closing at 3:00 p.m. in the basement area of the Portland Building.

ACTIVITIES   Featuring more pre-race activities than any marathon in North America, the Portland Marathon offers something for the whole family, including: a golf tournament, Big Band Jazz Night, Pasta Party, National Race Director's Conference (2 days), and a Sports and Fitness Expo. A post-race party for finishers takes place in the finish area. Portland offers a novel approach to the post-race food frenzy. To prevent those at the end of the event from missing out on food, the last 400 finishers receive large, sealed plastic bags containing a plethora of goodies. Massage practitioners provide foot/leg massages in the finish area. A party open to all entrants, volunteers and their guests begins at 1:00 p.m. at the Portland Hilton, with the awards ceremony at 3:00 p.m.

AWARDS   Each finisher receives a long-sleeve T-shirt, finisher medallion, race pin, super Pacific NW fir seedling, and rose. Race certificates and post-race results are mailed to finishers at a later time. Awards go as deep as 15 depending on the number and percentage of entrants in each age division.

ACCOMMODATIONS   The Portland Hilton, 921 SW 6th Avenue downtown (503-226-1611), serves as event headquarters. Specially priced rooms are reserved for marathoners and their guests at $150 per night. Other hotels in the area include: Days Inn, 1414 SW Sixth Avenue (503-221-1611); Marriott, 1401 SW Front Street (503-226-7600); Heathman Hotel, 1009 SW Broadway (503-241-4100); and the Benson Hotel, 309 SW Broadway (503-228-9611).

RELATED EVENTS/RACES   Portland features six separate events in addition to the marathon. The fun includes a Marathon Walk, Niketown 5-miler, 10K Mayor's Walk, and Marafun Kids' run (2 miles), all of which take place on race Sunday. The Run & Shoot Summer Biathlon and 24-Hour Track Ultra Run take place on Saturday.

PORTLAND MARATHON

ENTRY FORM

Be a part of "the best organized marathon in America"!
— The Ultimate Guide to Marathon.

Future Dates: October 3, 1999 • October 1, 2000

Please read carefully before completing form. Please print clearly. Please note deadlines for sending applications and late fees. Marathon and Marathon Walk entries by mail ($50) must be postmarked on or before midnight, Sept. 10 for 1998, Sept. 9 for 1999, an Sept. 11 for 2000. Note: runners and walkers may enter in person for all events at a late fee rate at the Marathon Expo held at the Portland Hilton on the two days before the event.

(No refunds, exchanges or transfers)

(Please begin your name in the large box)   Check one box: ☐ Marathon Run ☐ Marathon Walk

1. Last Name _____ First Name _____ M.I. ____

2. Address _____

   City _____ State ___ Zip Code ____ Country _____
   (If other than U.S.)

3. Age ___ 4. Sex M ☐ F ☐ 5. Total years of school ___

6. Shirt size: S ☐ M ☐ L ☐ XL ☐ XXL ☐ (100% cotton)

7. Phone (work) ___—___—____ (home) ___—___—____

8. Best Previous Marathon Time: ___ hr. ___ min. ___ sec.

9. Predicted Time: ___ hr. ___ min. ___ sec.

10. Completed Marathons: ___

11. Completed Portland Marathons: ___

Office Use Only
UGM 1/98

Entry Fee ($55)	$_____
"Training For" Shirt ($15/$20)	$_____
Souvenir Shirt ($15/$20/$35)	$_____
Postage & Handling (see chart)	$_____
Total Enclosed:	$_____

(US Dollar amounts only: No foreign checks or money orders)

**Make checks payable to: Portland Marathon;
Mail to: P.O. Box 4040, Beaverton, OR 97076**

TRAINING FOR PORTLAND MARATHON SHIRTS
(check size)

A. S ☐ M ☐ L ☐ XL ☐ Short Sleeve $15.00
B. S ☐ M ☐ L ☐ XL ☐ Long Sleeve Crew Neck - T-Shirt $20.00

PORTLAND MARATHON SOUVENIR SHIRTS
(check size)

A. S ☐ M ☐ L ☐ XL ☐ Short Sleeve $15.00
B. S ☐ M ☐ L ☐ XL ☐ Long Sleeve Crew Neck - T-Shirt $20.00
C. S ☐ M ☐ L ☐ XL ☐ Sweatshirt $35.00

Shirt Postage & Handling Fees (Allow 5-6 weeks for delivery)		US/Canada	Foreign
	Up to $25	$6	$8
	$26-$50	$7	$10
	Over $50	$8	$12

THIS IS AN IMPORTANT LEGAL DOCUMENT. READ CAREFULLY BEFORE SIGNING. Waiver of Liability: In consideration of your accepting this entry. I, the undersigned, intending to be lega ly bound, hereby, for myself, my family, my heirs, executors, & administrators, forever waive, release & discharge any and all rights & claims for damages & causes of suit or action, known unknown, that I may have against The Portland Marathon, The Oregon Road Runners Club, The City of Portland, Multnomah County and all other political entities, the Portland Terminal RR Co and it's owners, including PDC, Union Pacific, Southern Pacific & Burlington Northern Railroads, all independent contractors & construction firms working on or near the course, all Portland Marathe Race Committee persons, Officials & Volunteers & all sponsors of the Marathon, & the related Marathon Events & their officers, director, employees, agents & representatives, successors, & assign for any and all injuries suffered by me in this event. I attest that I am physically fit, am aware of the dangers & precautions that must be taken when running in warm or cold conditions, & have su ficiently trained for the completion of this event. I also agree to abide by any decision of an appointed medical official relative to my ability to safely continue or complete the Run. I further assur and will pay my own medical & emergency expenses in the event of an accident, illness, or other incapacity regardless of whether I have authorized such expenses. Further, I hereby grant full pe mission to The Oregon Road Runners Club and/or agents hereby authorized by them to use any photographs, videotapes, motion pictures, recordings, or any other record of this event for any leg imate purpose at any time. I have read this waiver carefully & understand it.

Signature _____ Date _____

This form may be reproduced, duplicated or enlarged.

MARATHON HOTLINE: (503) 226-1111
e-mail: pdxmar@teleport.com
Or visit our websites:
http://www.teleport.com/~pdxmar
http://www.portlandmarathon.org

The Portland Hilton

*IF YOU WOULD LIKE A COPY OF OUR 16 PAGE MARATHON ENTRY BOOKLET OR AN ENTRY BOOKLET THAT ALSO DESCRIBES THE FIVE-MILER, THE MAYOR'S W. THE MARAFUN KIDS' RUN OR THE 26.2-MILE MARATHON WALK, PLEASE SEND A LEGAL SIZE SELF ADDRESSED STAMPED ENVELOPE (55¢) TO THE ABOVE ADDRE

QUAD CITIES MARATHON

OVERALL: 84.9

COURSE BEAUTY: 9

COURSE DIFFICULTY: 4-

APPROPRIATENESS FOR FIRST TIMERS: 8

RACE ORGANIZATION: 9

CROWDS: 4+

R A C E   D A T A

Overall Ranking: 51
Quickness Ranking: 47
Contact: Joe Moreno
Quad Cities Sports Commission
2021 Riverdrive
Moline, IL 61265
(309) 797-1733
http://www.qcmarathon.org

Date: October 3, 1999; October 1, 2000
Start Time: 7:30 a.m.
Time Course Closes: 1:30 p.m.
Number of Finishers: 1,282 in 1998
Course: Loop with an out and back
Certification: USATF
Course Records: Male: (open) 2:34:50; (masters) 2:53:33
Female: (open) 2:59:55; (masters) 2:59:55
Elite Athlete Programs: Yes
Cost: $30/35
Age groups/Divisions: ≤24, 25-29, 30-34, 35-39, 40-44, 45-49, 50-54, 55-59, 60-64, 65-69, 70-74, 75+
Walkers: No
Requirements: None
Temperature: 52° - 72°
Aid/Splits: 16 / every mile; digital clocks at 10K, halfway & 20 miles

HIGHLIGHTS Just when you thought the Midwest's fall marathon calendar was full, along comes the Quad Cities Marathon, run almost entirely within view of the mighty Mississippi River. Successfully debuting in 1998, the well-organized race attracted over 1,200 runners to its unique course traveling back and forth across the river through five area cities. The race enjoys fantastic community support with the residents of each city attempting to out do the others with more music and enthusiasm. Even the local television station provides live race coverage. If its first edition is any indication, we expect Quad Cities to grow dramatically in the coming years. After all, somewhere along the line they grew into five cities (we still don't understand that one).

COURSE DESCRIPTION Starting and finishing in downtown Moline, IL, the Quad Cities Marathon course winds through five cities, two states, and over several bridges. The flat loop (with an out and back at the end) runs almost entirely along the mighty Mississippi River. Within the first 1.5 miles, runners head over the I-74 Bridge, into downtown Bettendorf, IA, passing the Lady Luck Riverboat Casino on the way to neighboring Davenport. This stretch brims with breathtaking views of the Mississippi. Runners enter East Davenport near the 5-mile mark then head along the Davenport Bike and Recreational Path running within feet from the river levee. While running through LeClaire Park, you encounter the hype and hoopla of the "President's Mile" sponsored by the President Riverboat Casino. After cutting through Davenport, the route traverses the second bridge (Centennial) and arrives into downtown Rock Island, IL (near 12 miles). Looping Rock Island, runners pass the third riverboat along the course, Jumers Casino Rock Island. Another bridge crossing drops you onto scenic Arsenal Island, the largest inhabited island on the Mississippi, where you complete seven miles along the island's perimeter bike path darting through the military installation's golf course. The fourth and final bridge emerges very near the large crowds near the start/finish in Moline. Unfortunately, your work is not complete. A long stretch along River Drive takes you to boisterous East Moline. The East Moliner's and their business association pride themselves in the enthusiasm they muster up for community events. After turning around in East Moline, you pass other runners as you retrace your way back to downtown Moline and the finish at the "Mark of the Quad Cities" (the national award winning civic center). Except for the four bridge crossings, the course runs very flat with one lane closed to traffic at all times.

CROWD/RUNNER SUPPORT Several thousand spectators support the competitors on race day with most congregating at the ends of all four bridges and at the relay transition points. The village of East Davenport, the district of Rock Island, Arsenal Island, and downtown East Moline all create their own variety of hoopla and party atmosphere with bands, food and drinks, and activities for spectators. There's no avoiding the wall in this event. Race supporters erect a large wall at mile 23 where runners run through and are greeted by a large group of spectators, cheerleaders, and music. The race provides 16 aid stations with every other one supplying electrolyte replacement.

RACE LOGISTICS For the least hassle on race morning, stay at The Radisson On John Deere Commons. The hotel lies within easy walking distance of the start/finish. If driving to the race, plenty of parking is available near THE MARK.

ACTIVITIES On Friday from 3:00 p.m. to 8:00 p.m. and Saturday 10:00 a.m. to 8:00 p.m., Quad Cities hosts a Health and Fitness Expo at the River Center, 136 E. 3rd Street, downtown Davenport. Here you can pick up your race packet, register late, and browse the running-related exhibits. Free bus tours of the marathon course depart on Saturday 11:30 a.m. to 2:30 p.m. from THE MARK and the River Center. Starting at 5:00 p.m. on Saturday, join other runners for a pasta party at the River Center. After finishing the race, enjoy loads of food and beverages while listening to musical entertainment.

AWARDS Every runner receives a T-shirt, and finishers receive medals. Top open and masters runners compete for over $10,000 in prize money. Age division awards extend three deep.

ELITE RUNNERS INFORMATION The race provides accommodations and free entry to men under 2:20 and women under 2:40. Open division prize money extends ten deep, from $1,000 for first to $50 for tenth. The top three masters earn $250, $100, and $50, respectively.

ACCOMMODATIONS The official race hotels are the Radisson on John Deere Commons, 1415 River Drive, Moline (309-764-1000), and the Radisson Quad City Plaza Hotel, 111 E. 2nd Street, Davenport (319-322-2200). For further hotel information contact the Quad Cities Visitor and Convention Bureau (800-747-7800).

RELATED EVENTS/RACES No need to be a marathon runner to take part in the Quad Cities event. In 1998, a combined 2,500 individuals participated in the 5-person Marathon Relay, 5K Run/Walk, or the Mayor's Mile Fun Run.

TWIN CITIES MARATHON

OVERALL: 99.9

COURSE BEAUTY: 10

COURSE DIFFICULTY: 3- (SEE APPENDIX)

APPROPRIATENESS FOR FIRST TIMERS: 10

RACE ORGANIZATION: 10

CROWDS: 9-

RACE DATA

Overall Ranking: 2
Quickness Ranking: 19
Contact: Twin Cities Marathon
708 North First Street, Ste. CR-33
Minneapolis, MN 55401
Tel. (612) 673-0778; Fax (612) 673-0780
E-mail: tcmarathon@aol.com
http://www.doitsports.com/marathons/twincities
Date: October 3, 1999; October 8, 2000; October 7, 2001
Start Time: 8:00 a.m.
Time Course Closes: 2:00 p.m.
Number of Finishers: 5,305 in 1997 (limited to 7,600)
Course: Point to point
Certification: USATF
Course Records: Male: (open) 2:10:05; (masters) 2:15:15 (U.S. Masters Record)
Female: (open) 2:27:59; (masters) 2:35:08 (U.S. Masters Record)
Elite Athlete Programs: Yes
Cost: $40/45/50
Age groups/Divisions: ≤19, 20-24, 25-29, 30-34, 35-39, 40-44, 45-49, 50-54,
55-59, 60-64, 65-69, 70+
Walkers: No
Requirements: None
Temperature: 43° - 64°
Aid/Splits: 13 / digital clocks at miles 1, 2, 3, 4, 10, halfway, 15, 20 & 25

HIGHLIGHTS "Beautiful" and "urban" are two words that cannot often be used together to describe marathons. When applied to the Twin Cities Marathon (TCM), however, beautiful and urban are as harmonious as Minneapolis and St. Paul—they have blended into a single, inseparable phrase. More than just another pretty race, TCM is one of America's finest marathons. Gorgeous, fast, flawless, and loud, over 200,000 spectators surround the route. Toss in all of the amenities of the Twin Cities area and you have an irresistible destination marathon. Few races should be on every marathoners' must-run list; TCM is one.

RACE HISTORY The Minnesota Distance Running Association created the Land of Lakes Marathon, Twin Cities' antecedent, in 1963. The first race had a rather modest three finishers. Over the next several years Land of Lakes was held at various locations in the Twin Cities. In 1976, the race was recast as the City of Lakes Marathon and moved to a four-lap course around Lakes Calhoun and Harriet. It had 178 finishers. Then came the running boom. In 1981, City of

Lakes reached its 1,700 runner limit in only one month. That same year, St. Paul held its own marathon, the St. Paul Marathon, which attracted nearly 2,000 runners. Organizers soon realized that a race which spanned the two cities straddling the Mississippi River would be a much greater attraction than two separate events. In 1982, the modern Twin Cities Marathon was born, drawing more than 4,500 entrants—a then-record for a first-time marathon. Since then, Twin Cities has blossomed into one of America's premiere races. It has been the site of numerous national marathon championships, and is the site of the U.S. Masters Marathon Championship until 2000. More U.S. records have been set on its course than any other marathon.

COURSE DESCRIPTION   The bulk of TCM traces parkways in bursting autumn brilliance, passing four lakes, a creek, and the Mississippi River on its trek from Minneapolis to St. Paul. The course is nothing short of spectacular. The race is run entirely on asphalt and is completely closed to vehicle traffic. TCM starts at the Hubert H. Humphrey Metrodome, home of the Minnesota Twins (MLB) and Vikings (NFL). The first 1.5 miles course through downtown Minneapolis, where you encounter the world renown Guthrie Theater and the Walker Art Center and Sculpture Garden. You complete one of the route's biggest inclines, an 80-foot climb in a half mile, as you reach the first aid station at 2.5 miles. Then it's slightly downhill until just past mile 3, where you come to the first lake on the course: Lake of the Isles, site of some of the finest homes in the Twin Cities. It's also the first step on the cities' parkway system, where you will run the next 19 miles of the race. After leaving Lake of the Isles behind, you soon reach Lake Calhoun (miles 4 to 6). The sun's reflection off the lake creates an inspirational setting. Shortly after the 6-mile point, a quick 20-foot climb brings you to Lake Harriet, where you pass the Rose Garden, a popular area for spectators and the media. As you depart Lake Harriet at 7.5 miles, you may feel a bit envious knowing that the three lakes are the most popular training sites for area runners. But try to remember that they have to endure the local winters. See, it all works out in the end!

With a smile on your face, the course turns east, starting a 4.5-mile stretch on Minnehaha Parkway, a tree-lined boulevard along beautiful Minnehaha Creek. This gently rolling piece (including a good 40-foot drop) leads to lake number four on the course: Lake Nokomis. After circling Nokomis, you pass the 13.1-mile mark—you're halfway home! Then it's back to Minnehaha Parkway for the next two miles before turning north to run along the Mississippi River (miles 15 to 19).

Crossing the Mississippi at mile 19, runners may be tempted to stop to view the bank of trees in full fall colors along the river. You then head south for two miles on the river road to begin the toughest part of the course—an incline of 130 feet over a two-mile stretch up Summit Avenue and its stately mansions (miles 21 to 23). You may see the governor as you puff past his mansion; he's usually out there watching the race. It's mostly downhill from this point to the finish, with a small rise at mile 25.

Seeing St. Paul Cathedral means you've done it. As you turn the corner at mile 26, the finish line, with the state capitol as a backdrop, is an awesome and welcomed sight. Bask in the glory the last two tenths of a mile as some of the 200,000 spectators cheer your arrival.

CROWD/RUNNER SUPPORT   Over 200,000 Twin City residents come out to cheer on the runners, quite a large turnout for communities of this size. TCM is not big on hoopla, the loud and crazy entertainment that lines so many courses these days. But it is big on volunteers, with more than 4,000 people helping out along the way. Twelve aid stations speckle the course at miles 2.5, 5, and every two miles thereafter, carrying water, electrolyte replacement drink, portable toilets, and medical aid. In addition, first aid is available at every mile marker. Medical personnel will be wearing red shirts, and communications personnel (should you need a ride to the finish) will be decked out in yellow shirts. Digital clocks which show the elapsed time are located at miles 1, 2, 3, 4, 10, 13.1, 15, 20, and 25.

RACE LOGISTICS   Race organizers provide shuttle bus service to the starting line from official race hotels, and then from the finish area back to the hotels. Transportation is also available from the finish to the start following the race. The race transports your belongings from the start to the finish area.

ACTIVITIES   TCM sponsors the large, two-day (Friday and Saturday) Marketplace and Fitness Fair that attracts 20,000 people to the headquarters hotel. The fair has more than 80 exhibitor booths with hands-on exhibits, free health screenings, great deals on running gear, and hourly drawings for free merchandise and services. You must pick up your race packet at the fair as there is no race number pick-up on race day. On Saturday, attend seminars on a variety of running topics presented by Running Times magazine. On Saturday evening, devour all the pasta you can at the carbo-load party (about $10). The post-race party and awards ceremony begin at 11:30 a.m. near the finish line.

AWARDS   Every entrant receives a TCM Results Book. Finishers also receive T-shirts, medallions, and official results cards. TCM offers approximately $155,000 in prize money to at least 22 division winners. Division winners also receive merchandise awards. Masters runners make out particularly well at TCM. The first three finishers in each five-year age group, starting at age 40, receive prize money—$250 for first, $100 for second, and $50 for third—a nice, and rare, little bonus for many masters runners.

FIRST TIMERS INFORMATION   Twin Cities is one of the best marathons in the country for first timers (our only nit-pick is there could be more than 13 aid stations), with about 2,000 in the race each year. All of the conditions are optimal for a positive experience: usually cool weather, abundant company, gentle course, supportive crowds, exceptional scenery, and top-flight organization.

ELITE RUNNERS INFORMATION   TCM extends several benefits to elite runners (men under 2:20, women under 2:40), including hotel, transportation, expenses, free entry, and generous prize money. Priority is given to previous TCM participants. Open division prize money is offered to tenth place, with overall winners earning $20,000, then $12,000 for second, $7,000 for third, $5,000 for fourth, $4,000 for fifth, $3,000 for sixth, $2,000 for seventh, $1,500 for eighth, $1,000 for ninth, and $500 for tenth. The top five masters runners receive prize money from TCM ($5,000; $3,000; $2,000; $1,000; $500), and the top three masters also win prize money as part of the USATF American Masters Championship ($2,000; $1,000; $750). Contact the marathon office for more information.

ACCOMMODATIONS   The headquarters hotel for the race is the Minneapolis Hyatt Regency, 1300 Nicollet Mall (800-233-1234). The Hyatt offers special rates to marathon runners, but you must book extremely early. Several other hotels in St. Paul give runners special rates, including: Days Inn Civic Center, 175 W. Seventh Street (800-325-2525); The Saint Paul Hotel, 350 Market Street (800-292-9292); the Radisson Inn, 411 Minnesota Street (800-333-3333); the Radisson St. Paul, 11 E. Kellogg Blvd. (800-333-3333); and Embassy Suites, 175 E. Tenth Street (800-EMBASSY). If you prefer to stay near the start in Minneapolis, the following offer special rates: Regal Minneapolis Hotel, 1313 Nicollet Mall (800-522-8856); Doubletree Guest Suites, 1101 LaSalle Avenue (800-662-3232); The Marquette, 710 Marquette Avenue (800-328-4782); Minneapolis Hilton Hotel, 1001 Marquette Avenue (800-HILTONS); and Marriott City Center, 30 S. 7th Street (800-228-9290).

RELATED EVENTS/RACES   On Saturday, the day before the marathon, organizers hold a 5K Race/Walk, Kids' Half-Mile Fun Run, Toddlers' Trot, and Diaper Dash at the State Capitol grounds in St. Paul. Every participant receives a T-shirt and post-race refreshments. In addition, every child who enters receives a "Number 1" bib and ribbon. You may register at the Fitness Fair, or on race day.

AREA ATTRACTIONS   If you need more sports while in the Twin Cities, attend a Minnesota Vikings game. It is possible that the Twins will still be playing, if they make the playoffs. On the cultural side, see the Guthrie Theater, Walker Art Center, Minnesota Orchestra, St. Paul Chamber Orchestra, or the St. Paul Science Museum. Or, if you need to shop, check out the country's largest shopping center, The Mall of America, about 20 minutes from either city.

It's the annual running of the most scenic 26.2 urban miles in the country

It's more than 7,500 runners coursing along 26.2 miles of winding parkways, stunning foliage, blue lakes, and the majestic Mississippi River. It's a weekend packed with events, including a health and fitness expo, a 5K race, and a Kid's Half-Mile Fun Run. It's the lightning-fast course for the USA Track & Field Masters' Championship. It's over 200,000 colorful fans and 4,000 volunteers.

It's the Annual Twin Cities Marathon.

Minneapolis–St. Paul, Sunday, October 3, 1999, 8:00 A.M.
Minneapolis–St. Paul, Sunday, October 8, 2000, 8:00 A.M.

The Most Beautiful Urban Marathon in America©

For more information, contact TCM, 708 N. 1st Street, Minneapolis, MN 55401 (612) 673-0778.

http://www.doitsports.com/marathons/twincities

WINEGLASS MARATHON

OVERALL: 88.9

COURSE BEAUTY: 9

COURSE DIFFICULTY: 2+ (SEE APPENDIX)

APPROPRIATENESS FOR FIRST TIMERS: 8+

RACE ORGANIZATION: 9

CROWDS: 4

RACE DATA

Overall Ranking:	26
Quickness Ranking:	16
Contact:	Greater Corning Area Chamber of Commerce
	Wineglass Marathon
	P.O. Box 117
	Corning, NY 14830-0900
	(607)936-4686
	http://www.pennynet.org/wineglas.htm
Date:	October 3, 1999; October 8, 2000
Start Time:	9:00 a.m.
Time Course Closes:	3:00 p.m.
Number of Finishers:	485 in 1997
Course:	Point to point
Certification:	USATF
Course Records:	Male: (open) 2:22:52; (masters) 2:42:09
	Female: (open) 2:49:46; (masters) 2:49:46
Elite Athlete Programs:	Yes
Cost:	$30/40/50
Age groups/Divisions:	14-24, 25-29, 30-34, 35-39, 40-44, 45-49, 50-59, 60+
Walkers:	No
Requirements:	14 years old
Temperature:	40° - 60°
Aid/Splits:	16 / mile 1 & halfway

HIGHLIGHTS New York's Finger Lakes clasp the Wineglass Marathon like a goblet of fine Cabernet as fall's burnt red and orange hues sprinkle the surrounding hills. The region, famous for its incredible gorges, tasty wine, and glass making, plays generous host to this rural marathon with big-time amenities. Generous corporate sponsorship makes terrific awards possible, such as $4,500 in prize money, crystal trophies, commemorative glass medallions, and local wine. Designed to maximize the chances for a tailwind, the rolling course boasts a net elevation loss of 200 feet.

COURSE DESCRIPTION The point-to-point Wineglass Marathon course starts at Philips Lighting, just north of Bath. Adrenaline and a 40-foot drop over the first mile should get you going as you travel through Bath, while flat miles 2 through 4 should allow you to get into a good rhythm. With a 40-foot uphill lying from mile 4.75 to mile 5, the next 4 miles proceed through the countryside to Savona (mile 9). During this stretch, the course falls 90 feet, but includes two small hills. Upon leaving Savona, runners continue through the countryside while the course gradually descends 40 feet over the next 4 miles. Runners reach the halfway point in Campbell, home of Polly-O String Cheese, and then it's back to nature. Runners ascend about 30 feet just beyond mile 14, before gradually losing 80 feet in elevation as they reach Coopers Plains (mile 18.2). Painted Post lies only a short distance from Coopers Plains; after a brief, 25-foot hill, runners enter a local park and tour a residential neighborhood. A bike path (mile 22.5) leads runners through the village of Riverside and into Corning, providing a flat journey to the finish line. Once in Corning, runners proceed through several neighborhoods before hitting the downtown area. At mile 25.4, they turn onto historic Market Street and then proceed several blocks before turning left to Centerway Square. After passing through Riverfront Park and across the Chemung River, the finish line lies just ahead at the Corning Glass Center.

CROWD/RUNNER SUPPORT   Runners encounter particularly energetic crowds in the numerous small towns dotting the route, while cheerleaders and bands entertain you in downtown Bath. The countryside between the towns leaves runners to their own thoughts. The course is a convenient one for family and friends to follow your progress in a car, allowing them to inspire you at several points. The 16 aid stations offer water and electrolyte replacement.

RACE LOGISTICS   The race provides bus transportation from the finish line near Corning Inc. Center to the start on race morning. Buses leave from 6:30 a.m. to 8:00 a.m. and cost $6. If your friends can't drop you off at the start, you need to drive to the finish and take the bus. The race transports your gear from the start for you to pick up in the finish area.

ACTIVITIES   Race weekend starts on Saturday from 2:00 p.m. to 5:00 p.m. with the Runners Expo, packet pickup, registration, and a visit by a noted running personality, held in Bath/Hammondsport, NY. Immediately following the expo, the Pasta Party goes from 5:00 p.m. to 8:00 p.m. in Bath. The dinner costs $6 and includes live music, door prizes, and carbos. After you finish the race, cool down with refreshments and food. If you want to clean up, showers are available at the Corning YMCA next to the Glass Center. Free massages are also available. The awards ceremony starts around 1:30 p.m.

AWARDS   All marathon runners receive T-shirts, and finishers also take home long-sleeve finisher's T-shirts, commemorative glass medallions, finisher's certificates, and Souvenir Wineglass Editions of Runner's Gazette. Age-group awards go to the top 10% of age-group finishers and include local wine and champagne. Approximately $4,500 in prize money goes to the top overall and masters runners.

ELITE RUNNERS INFORMATION   The race offers free lodging and race entry to elite runners, generally those with times under the current course record. Overall winners earn $1,000, Steuben Crystal, and champagne, with $500 for second, $250 for third, and $125 for fourth. Masters winners take home $250 and Steuben Crystal, with $125 for second.

ACCOMMODATIONS   There is no official race headquarters hotel. In Corning try: Comfort Inn (607-962-1515); or Radisson Hotel Corning (607-962-5000). In Bath try Old National Hotel (607-776-4104). In Painted Post try: Hampton Inn (607-936-3344); Econo Lodge (607-962-4444); or Holiday Inn (607-962-5021).

RELATED EVENTS/RACES   Wineglass also holds a Merrill Lynch Team Relay in conjunction with the marathon, with teams of three runners completing legs from 8 to 9 miles. Starting at 9:15 a.m., the relay offers male, female, and mixed divisions in open and masters age groups. The race transports runners from the start line to the relay exchange points.

AREA ATTRACTIONS   Apart from the scenic beauty of the area, visit the fascinating Corning Glass Center, the third largest tourist attraction in New York state. You can also tour area wineries (over 20), possibly catching them during the harvest season, and browse the Rockwell Museum of Western Art.

HARTFORD MARATHON

OVERALL: 83.5

COURSE BEAUTY: 8

COURSE DIFFICULTY: 4- (SEE APPENDIX)

APPROPRIATENESS FOR FIRST TIMERS: 9-

RACE ORGANIZATION: 10-

CROWDS: 4

RACE DATA

Overall Ranking: 64
Quickness Ranking: 46
Contact: Beth Shluger
Hartford Marathon Foundation
221 Main Street
Hartford, CT 06106
Tel. (860) 525-8200
Fax (860) 724-7317
E-mail: eatrun@erols.com
http://www.hartfordmarathon.com

Date: October 9, 1999; October 14, 2000
Start Time: 8:00 a.m.
Time Course Closes: 2:00 p.m.
Number of Finishers: 840 in 1997
Course: Out and back
Certification: USATF
Course Records: Male: (open) 2:16:59; (masters) 2:36:07
Female: (open) 2:36:53; (masters) 3:00:18
Elite Athlete Programs: Yes
Cost: $30/35/40/45
Age groups/Divisions: 16-19, 20-29, 30-39, 40-49, 50-59, 60-69, 70+
Walkers: No
Requirements: None
Temperature: 41° - 65°
Aid/Splits: 25 / every two miles with six digital clocks

HIGHLIGHTS The Greater Hartford Marathon features five different races sandwiched between some of the best tasting pre- and post-race parties in North America. The pre-race pasta party showcases over two dozen of the city's finest restaurants serving up their favorite pasta dishes. As one of the fastest courses in New England, Hartford features a dramatic start and finish near the golden-domed State Capitol building while treating runners to a memorable stretch along a beautiful country road dotted with 17th century homes, pumpkin farms, and stunning autumn foliage.

COURSE DESCRIPTION A loop course (completely closed to traffic), Hartford starts downtown in Bushnell Park amongst the golden-domed State Capitol building and landmark Memorial Arch. After a short tour of downtown, including a stint on the brick-covered pedestrian walkway of Pratt Street, the route crosses Founders Bridge spanning the Connecticut River—the most difficult upgrade on the course—at the 2-mile mark. After a brief stretch on a bike path beside the Connecticut River, the course loops around an office park before heading north through a business/commercial area on Rt. #5/Main Street. Gently rolling past a middle-class neighborhood on King Street, the course veers left onto Old Main Street at mile 7. For the next 11 miles, Old Main Street, with its impressive 17th century homes, rural pumpkin farms and colorful autumn foliage, hosts the most scenic area of the course, heading slightly downhill to the turnaround at 12.5 and slightly uphill back. After a pleasant stint along the bike path, runners return over Founders Bridge at mile 22. The course meanders through an industrial/warehouse area which ushers in the finish under the grand Memorial Arch.

CROWD/RUNNER SUPPORT Nearly 15,000 spectators cheer the marathoners, with most, including participants from the related races, stationing themselves near the start/finish area where they can see the runners several times. In addition, over 700 volunteers ensure that each marathoner is supported along the course. Twenty-two musical bands, en route, is another encouraging feature.

RACE LOGISTICS The start /finish in Bushnell Park lies within walking distance of downtown hotels. If you're arriving by car on race morning, sufficient parking is available.

ACTIVITIES In conjunction with the packet pickup & late registration, a Health & Fitness Expo featuring health screening, sport vendors, and running clinics takes place under the Big Top in Bushnell Park beginning Friday from 11:00 a.m. to 8:00 p.m. Race-day packet pickup and late registration extend from 6:00 a.m. to 8:00 a.m. under the tent in Bushnell Park. The Pasta Party, one of the finest in North America, gets underway at 5:30 p.m. at Aetna, 151 Farmington Avenue. Hartford's finest restaurants prepare their favorite sauces for this carbo fest (about $10). The party-like atmosphere continues after the race with the Post-Race Picnic, including food, drink (micro-brewed beer!), music, magicians, clowns, awards, and Sports Expo in Bushnell Park from 10:00 a.m. to 2:00 p.m. Before you start dancing to the music, take advantage of the free massages offered to runners on a first-come, first-served basis.

AWARDS All marathon entrants receive T-shirts. Finishers are awarded commemorative medals and certificates. Top runners vie for over $22,000 in prize money, and top age groupers earn merchandise prizes. Individual result postcards are mailed to all finishers within ten days of the race. Results of all races are mailed to registered runners within 45 days.

ELITE RUNNER INFORMATION Males under 2:30 and females under 2:45 receive complimentary entries and consideration for transportation and accommodations. Open prize money extends to ninth place with the following breakdown: $4,000, $2000, $1,000, $750, $500, $250, $125, $75 and $50, respectively. The winner collects an additional $1000 if he/she breaks the course record. Masters prize money stretches three deep: $500, $250, and $100, respectively.

ACCOMMODATIONS The Sheraton Hartford Hotel, 315 Trumbull Street (860-728-5151) serves as headquarters of the marathon, lying two blocks from the race start. Other nearby hotels include: Ramada Inn Capitol Hill, 440 Asylum Street (860-246-6591); Super 8 Motel, 57 West Service Road (860-246-8888); Susse Chalet, 185 Brainard Road (860-525-9306); Holiday Inn—East Hartford, 363 Roberts Street (860-528-9611); Ramada Inn East Hartford, 100 East River Drive (860-528-9703); or Wellesley Inn, 333 Roberts Street (860-289-4950).

RELATED EVENTS / RACES Race day provides several options for would-be runners. If you're a team player, enter the marathon relay consisting of 2 to 5 runners tackling any combination of 5 legs varying in length from 3.8 to 6.2 miles. A highly competitive half marathon begins with the marathon at 8:00 a.m. The Kids K, a .7-mile, noncompetitive run for children aged 3 to 7, begins at 8:45 a.m. Youngsters aged 8 to 11 run 1.4 miles around Bushnell Park. The Java Jolt 5K run takes place at 8:15 a.m. and starts in Bushnell Park. With so many options, no one is left out!

AREA ATTRACTIONS If the events surrounding the marathon are not enough, take in one or more of the fall festivals in the area. Those desiring a little culture should visit the Wadsworth Atheneum, 600 Main Street, the oldest public art museum in the country, featuring collections of Monet, Renoir and Degas. Literary buffs may want to tour the homes of Mark Twain and Harriet Beecher Stowe, both of whom wrote their most famous works in the area.

LAKEFRONT MARATHON

OVERALL: 84.3

COURSE BEAUTY: 8+

COURSE DIFFICULTY: 3- (SEE APPENDIX)

APPROPRIATENESS FOR FIRST TIMERS: 8

RACE ORGANIZATION: 9

CROWDS: 3+

RACE DATA

Overall Ranking: 56
Quickness Ranking: 30
Contact: The Lakefront Marathon
c/o Badgerland Striders
9200 W. North Avenue
Milwaukee, WI 53226
(414) 783-5009
http://www.runningzone.com/lakefront

Date: October 10, 1999; October 8, 2000
Start Time: 8:00 a.m.
Time Course Closes: 1:00 p.m.
Number of Finishers: 1,100 in 1997
Course: Point to point
Certification: USATF
Course Records: Male: (open) 2:14:09
Female: (open) 2:39:15
Elite Athlete Programs: No
Cost: $32/35/40/45
Age groups/Divisions: 18-24, 25-29, 30-34, 35-39, 40-44, 45-49, 50-54,
55-59, 60-64, 65+, Clydesdale
Walkers: No
Requirements: None
Temperature: 43° - 64°
Aid/Splits: 10 / every mile, digital clocks at 1, 5, 10, halfway,
15 & 20

HIGHLIGHTS   You will find much more than beer in Milwaukee. The U.S. Beer Capital houses a large ethnic population with their accompanying cuisines, a terrific summer of festivals, and an excellent fall marathon—the Lakefront Marathon. Despite the packed autumn marathon season in the Midwest, Lakefront manages to draw more than 1,000 runners. Mostly paralleling the shore of Lake Michigan, the point-to-point course finishes downtown in South Urban Park and offers a reasonable shot at a PR.

COURSE DESCRIPTION   Traveling through rural countryside and quiet northshore neighborhoods, Lakefront starts at Grafton High School (26 miles north of downtown Milwaukee). Heading east, the course presents a slight downhill before climbing the steepest hill (Hwy. 43 overpass) at 1.2 miles. Hwy. 60 then becomes Uleo Road which leads to two short hills at 1.7 miles. Turning right, the course goes south on rolling to downhill Hwy. C. Cornfields and llama farms on the right and views of Lake Michigan on the left provide scenic variety. By mile 4.5, the route parallels Hwy. 43, running very close to Lake Michigan while continuing flat until a .1-mile hill at 7.1. Runners continue on long, straight stretches, filing by lovely lakefront homes. A gradual rise occurs from 9.5 to 9.8 miles, and near mile 10.7, runners tour a new subdivision. Be alert for a few sharp turns before the course changes from open-road running to a one-lane, coned course. From mile 15 to 24, the course features some of Milwaukee's finest homes, many of which are palatial lakeshore estates. During this stretch, the race goes downhill near 18.2 miles, before rising at 20.6. Runners have a great view of Lake Michigan from mile 23 to 23.4 accompanied by a steep downhill. The mostly flat final 2.5 miles bring runners through McKinley Marina and the finish line in South Urban Park.

CROWD / RUNNER SUPPORT The Lakefront Marathon doesn't pass through any highly populated areas, so most of the crowds are centered around the four relay exchange points and the finish (with the exceptions being miles 15 and 21.5). The ten aid stations feature cups with lids and straws, water, electrolyte replacement, and petroleum jelly. Digital clocks show the elapsed time at six points on the course, and split timers call out at every other mile.

RACE LOGISTICS Runners may park at the Milwaukee Art Museum and take the free race shuttle to the start. Buses leave between 6:00 a.m. and 7:15 a.m. Runners with friends or family along can drive directly to the start at Grafton High School, but note that there is no bus transportation back to the start after the race. Organizers transport your sweats to the finish for you to reclaim.

ACTIVITIES Pick up your race packet on Saturday from 10:00 a.m. to 6:00 p.m. at the Milwaukee Hilton, 509 W. Wisconsin Avenue (north of I-794 at 5th and Wisconsin), and breeze through the small expo. You may also retrieve your packet or register at Grafton High School on race morning. After the race, munch on fruit, cookies, veggies, and cheese, while washing it down with good ol' Milwaukee beer (soda or water if you prefer).

AWARDS All marathon entrants collect colorful, long-sleeve sweatshirts and official results programs mailed at a later date. Each finisher also gets a medal hung around his neck in the finish chute. Age-group awards go three deep in most divisions and two deep in a few of the less-populous ones.

ACCOMMODATIONS The Milwaukee Hilton, 509 W. Wisconsin Avenue (414-271-7250), serves as the official race hotel. Other possibilities include: Exel Inn (414-961-7272); Hilton Inn (414-962-6040); Holiday Inn (414-273-2950); Manchester East (414-351-6960); Hyatt Regency (414-276-1234); Park East Hotel (414-276-8800); Residence Inn (414-352-0070); Sheraton Inn (414-355-8585); and Super 8 Motel (414-481-8488).

RELATED EVENTS / RACES Get in on the action by running the marathon relay for five-member teams. Relayers run legs of 5, 5.7, 4.3, 5, and 6.2 miles. Divisions include Male, Female, Mixed (at least two females), and Corporate. The race provides bus transportation from the start to each of the relay exchange points and from the exchange points to the finish.

AREA ATTRACTIONS You must tour one of the many beer factories—Miller Brewery is located at 4251 W. State Street, and Pabst Brewing Company is at 915 W. Juneau Avenue. Friday nights in Milwaukee mean fish fry. Go to just about any restaurant to join in the tradition. Top it off with some frozen custard. Sneak a peek in the Pettit National Ice Center, 500 S. 84th Street, where some local runners do their winter training.

MOUNT RUSHMORE MARATHON

OVERALL: 84.9

COURSE BEAUTY: 9

COURSE DIFFICULTY: 2- (SEE APPENDIX)

APPROPRIATENESS FOR FIRST-TIMERS: 8+

ORGANIZATION: 9

CROWDS: 1+

RACE DATA

Overall Ranking: 51
Quickness Ranking: 7
Contact: Lynn Von Wald
Rapid City Convention & Visitors Bureau
P.O. Box 747
Rapid City, SD 57709
(800) 487-3223 or (605) 343-1744
http://www.rapidcitycvb.com

Date: October 10, 1999; October 8, 2000
Start Time: 9:00 a.m.
Time Course Closes: 3:00 p.m. (traffic control ends)
Number of Finishers: 239 in 1997
Course: Point to point
Certification: USATF
Course Records: Male: (open) 2:20:31
Female: (open) 2:39:25
Elite Athlete Programs: No
Cost: $35/40
Age groups/Divisions: ≤19, 20-24, 25-29, 30-34, 35-39, 40-44, 45-49,
50-54, 55-59, 60-69, 70+, wheelchair
Walkers: No
Requirements: None
Temperature: 45° - 60°
Aid/Splits: 20 / none

HIGHLIGHTS The noble busts of four great American presidents provide the easily-recognized name of the Mount Rushmore International Marathon, but perhaps it is the luge-course route that really marks this race. The 2,180 feet of vertical drop has runners reaching for the brakes in some places, but unlike an Olympic luge run, this race does contain several hills, especially until mile 17. It also contains some beautiful scenery as it chisels through the Black Hills National Forest. Speaking of those famous hills, division winners receive Black Hills gold rings which provide a fittingly noble respite from the usual plaques or trophies.

COURSE DESCRIPTION The Mount Rushmore International Marathon begins in a mountain meadow surrounded by large stands of distant pines (elevation 5,461 feet), just south of Custer Crossing Campground on US 385. With a seasonal wind from the northwest, runners head southeast on an asphalt highway (US 385) that ribbons through a cluster of tall trees. Although facing a slight incline, runners see no houses, businesses, or any signs of development lining the highway. Passing through gaps in the hillsides, you may spot an occasional deer or ground squirrel. The course descends about 400 feet just prior to the 6-mile mark, where a brief, challenging climb of 150 feet awaits. Another flowing descent (with a few rollers) of 700 feet takes runners through the next 6 miles. While the pine forests tend to thin out from time to time and houses become more evident in this section, runners catch glimpses of buffalo and cattle grazing in pastures divided by wandering trout streams. Between miles 6 and 8, the route turns to the east on SD 44 and the descent becomes more pronounced, as does the narrowness of the canyon highway cutting through the Black Hills National Forest. Slight challenges of elevation appear from place to place, but a refreshing downslope is never more than a few hundred feet ahead. Near mile 11, Rapid Creek makes its first appearance, only to disappear in canyons and reappear around following bends. Just beyond Big Bend, the creek is out of sight for the next 8 miles or so, but the steepness of the canyon walls, formed by the ravages of millennia of floods, entertain the runners until a 100-foot climb wakes them up in mile 17. From then on, the real downhill begins. Over the next five miles, runners immediately descend 1,150 feet into the outskirts of Rapid City. This track has three distinct downhills. The first is a gradual decline, the second is a steeper downgrade that drives toes into the tips of shoes, and the third is shorter, but even steeper, with the flatland hidden around a distant curve. Entering Rapid City, runners pass through a canyon where the creek reappears on the far side of a trout fish hatchery, followed by picture-perfect Canyon Lake Park. Then, just as your spirits drop from the long city boulevard, a quick turn to the north takes you into the final stretch and Fitzgerald Stadium for the finish line (elevation 3,281 feet).

CROWD/RUNNER SUPPORT The marathon doesn't gather much in the way of crowds until it nears the finish and in Fitzgerald Stadium. There are aid stations every 2 miles until mile 10, and every mile thereafter. The aid stations carry sport drink, water, minor medical supplies, and sponges.

RACE LOGISTICS The race provides bus transportation from the finish at Fitzgerald Field to the start. Runners with family tagging along can also get dropped off at the start.

ACTIVITIES Pick up your race packet on Saturday from 9:00 a.m. to 7:00 p.m. in Room 101 of the Rushmore Plaza Civic Center, 444 Mt. Rushmore Road North. You will surely want to attend the buffet-style pasta dinner at Mount Rushmore on Saturday evening from 6:00 p.m. to 8:00 p.m. (about $7 per person). At 8:00 p.m. Mount Rushmore is flooded by light in the special ceremony.

AWARDS Each participant receives a long-sleeve T-shirt. Medals go to all finishers. If you are lucky enough to win your division you will receive a Black Hills gold ring.

ACCOMMODATIONS The race does not have an official host hotel, but many options exist in Rapid City: Best Western Inn, 1901 W. Main Street (605-343-6040); Best Western, 2505 Mt. Rushmore Drive (605-343-5383); Comfort Inn, 1550 N. Lacrosse Street (605-348-2221); Days Inn, 125 Main Street (605-343-5501); Days Inn, 1570 Rapp Street (605-348-8410); Econo Lodge, 625 E. Disk Drive (605-342-6400); Holiday Inn, 505 N. 5th Street (605-348-4000); Holiday Inn, 750 Cathedral Drive (605-341-9300); Motel 6, 620 Latrobe Avenue (605-343-3687); Radisson Hotel, 445 Mt. Rushmore Drive (605-348-8300); Ramada Inn, 1721 N. Lacrosse Street (605-342-1300); and Super 8 Motel, Mt. Rushmore Drive & Cleveland (605-342-4911).

RELATED EVENTS/RACES There are plenty of alternative races for runners of all stripes. For the super-long-distance folks, there is a 50-mile ultramarathon. Bands of 5 runners can enter the marathon relay in either single sex or coed divisions. Finally, on Saturday, the YMCA sponsors a non-competitive 5-Mile Run and Walk.

AREA ATTRACTIONS The three-day Columbus Day weekend should leave some time for you to explore the Rapid City area while there for the marathon. After the obligatory pilgrimage to Mount Rushmore, you have quite a few other options: Badlands National Park, Black Hills National Forest, Jewel Cave National Monument, Wind Cave National Park, Devils Tower, Custer State Park, Crazy Horse Memorial, and Deadwood.

ROYAL VICTORIA MARATHON

OVERALL: 90.4

COURSE BEAUTY: 9

COURSE DIFFICULTY: 4 (SEE APPENDIX)

APPROPRIATENESS FOR FIRST TIMERS: 8+

RACE ORGANIZATION: 9

CROWDS: 4

RACE DATA

Overall Ranking: 20
Quickness Ranking: 55
Contact: Victoria Marathon Society
c/o #182-911 Yates Street
Victoria, B.C. Canada V8V 4X3
(604) 382-8181
E-mail: rvm@islandnet.com
http://www.islandnet.com/~rvm

Date: October 10, 1999; October 8, 2000
Start Time: 8:00 a.m.
Time Course Closes: 12:00 p.m.
Number of Finishers: 2,100 in 1997
Course: Modified out and back
Certification: B.C. Athletics
Course Records: Male: (open) 2:19:31
Female: (open) 2:42:32
Elite Athlete Programs: No
Cost: $55
Age groups/Divisions: ≤29, 30-34, 35-39, 40-44, 45-49, 50-54, 55-59,
60-64, 65-69, 70+; Walkers; Teams: Open, Masters,
Husband & Wife
Walkers: No
Requirements: None
Temperature: 50° - 65°
Aid/Splits: 17 / miles 1, 5, 10K, halfway, 15, 30K, 20 & 25.2

HIGHLIGHTS   A truly unique marathon experience in North America awaits you on Vancouver Island, northwest of Seattle by car and ferry. The elegant and beautiful Royal Victoria Marathon, held in quaint, seaside Victoria, British Columbia, will delight and transport you to the Old World's heart. Victoria, a British enclave of pubs and afternoon tea, enchants visitors with its immaculate gardens, monumental air, and English manner. That marvelous setting, a healthy dose of ocean views, and typical Canadian hospitality unite to produce one of marathoning's rising stars.

COURSE DESCRIPTION   Containing no serious hills, RVM's modified out-and-back course rolls for much of its 26.2 miles posing a challenge for many runners. The race starts alongside the B.C. Parliament Building, a monumental, gray stone structure that lends a decidedly British air to the city. After a downhill start passing famous, stately Empress Hotel, the course heads along Wharf Street, bordering Victoria's beautiful harbor. The first 2.3 miles proceed through downtown Victoria, passing shops, restaurants, and hotels with some long, gentle ups and downs.

Runners then come up behind Beacon Hill Park, enter it by mile 2.8, and enjoy the gardens while passing through it. As you leave the park (mile 3.5), the ocean greets you until 4.3 when you traverse residential Oswego Street to the scenic Inner Harbor at mile 5. Following the line of hotels around the point, runners hit the shoreline at mile 6 and hug the coast for 2.3 miles. About mile 6.2, runners begin a gentle 60-foot incline to the 7-mile mark and then descend to mile 8. Ross Bay at 7.8 offers a great vantage to Hollywood Cove's hillside homes overlooking the ocean. Winding through residential Oak Bay from 8.3 to 11.4, the course rolls, rising about 50 feet. You're back along the water by 11.5 miles, passing expensive houses and entering the exclusive and scenic Royal Victoria Golf Course at 12.2. Runners roll through the golf course and reach RVM's halfway point at the marina on Oak Bay. The next five miles are mostly flat through an upscale neighborhood until you return to the marina (mile 18) and face the 50-foot climb to the golf course. Runners retrace their steps the rest of the way and finish in front of the Parliament Building at the Inner Harbor.

C R O W D / R U N N E R   S U P P O R T   As the race grows, Victorians turn out in larger numbers to cheer the runners. While onlookers still speckle most of the route, the start/finish area and Oak Bay attract good crowds. Runners pass aid stations 17 times. Besides carrying the usual water and electrolyte replacement drink, aid stations, after mile 16, also provide PowerBars to energy-flagged runners.

R A C E   L O G I S T I C S   The small downtown area and the proximity of several hotels to the Inner Harbor make race-morning transportation unnecessary for many runners. If you stay further out, you must provide your own means to the start, but abundant, free parking exists in the area.

A C T I V I T I E S   On Friday or Saturday, runners may pick up their race packets at the headquarters hotel. Otherwise, retrieve your packet on the legislative grounds near the start on race morning. Bus tours of the marathon course depart Saturday afternoon and cost $5. On Saturday evening, attend the pasta dinner for about $20. After the marathon, stop by the free post-race social at the Harbour Towers, featuring a video of the race, finishers' certificates, and race results.

A W A R D S   Early registrants receive original design sweatshirts, with finishers earning RVM medals engraved with the shirt design and certificates. Age-group awards go up to 10 deep depending on the number of entrants in each category. All runners are eligible for several raffle prizes, including a trip to the London Marathon. A one-ounce gold coin goes to the runner who sets a new course record.

A C C O M M O D A T I O N S   Located about four blocks from the RVM start, the Harbour Towers, 345 Quebec Street (800-663-5896), serves as the sponsoring hotel, offering marathoners special rates of about $100 per night. Other lodging possibilities include: Ocean Point Resort, 45 Songhees Road (800-667-4677), about $100 a night; The Coast Victoria Harbourside Hotel, 146 Kingston Street (800-663-1144), about $110; Clarion Hotel Grand Pacific, 450 Quebec Street (800-663-7550), about $110; Quality Inn Harbourview, 455 Belleville Street (800-663-7550), about $90; Dashwood Seaside Manor, #1 Cook Street (800-667-5517); Dominion Hotel, 759 Yates Street (800-663-6101); Hotel Douglas, 1450 Douglas Street (800-332-9981); Strathcona Hotel, 919 Douglas Street (604-383-7137); and Green Gables Inn, 850 Blanshard Street (800-661-4115). For cheaper accommodations, try one of Victoria's many bed & breakfast inns, most of which lie outside downtown.

R E L A T E D   E V E N T S / R A C E S   RVM welcomes walkers to stride the full marathon. Royal Victoria sponsors an 8K run beginning at 8:30 a.m. on Sunday. Early registered 8K runners receive original shirts, and all 8K entrants participate in the random drawing for a trip for two on Air BC. Kids may do the Children's 1K Run for Charity, beginning at 9:30 a.m.

A R E A   A T T R A C T I O N S   A great tourist city, charming Victoria contains numerous attractions for marathoners. Flower lovers will delight in the hanging flower baskets throughout the city and world-renowned Butchart Gardens. The British-like Old Town area contains scores of pubs, shops, and restaurants. Join in an English tradition and take afternoon tea at the Empress Hotel, or stroll the Inner Harbor and Beacon Hill Park.

STEAMTOWN MARATHON

OVERALL: 86.8

COURSE BEAUTY: 8+

COURSE DIFFICULTY: 2- (SEE APPENDIX)

APPROPRIATENESS FOR FIRST-TIMERS: 8+

ORGANIZATION: 9

CROWDS: 5

RACE DATA

Overall Ranking: 37
Quickness Ranking: 4
Contact: Steamtown Marathon
Pennsylvania's Northeast Territory Visitors Bureau
100 Terminal Road, Suite 216
Wilkes/Barre International Airport
Avoca, PA 18641
(800) 229-3526 or (717) 457-1320
http://www.visitnepa.org/marathon/

Date: October, Sunday before Columbus Day
Start Time: 8:00 a.m.
Time Course Closes: 2:00 p.m.
Number of Finishers: **806 in 1997**
Course: **Point to point**
Certification: **USATF**
Course Records: **Male: (open) 2:22:33; (masters) 2:49:37**
Female: (open) 2:49:37; (masters) 3:28:47
Elite Athlete Programs: **No**
Cost: **$35/45**
Age groups/Divisions: **18-24, 25-29, 30-34, 35-39, 40-44, 45-49, 50-54,**
55-59, 60-69, 70+, wheelchair (half marathon)
Walkers: **No**
Requirements: **18 years old**
Temperature: **42° - 61°**
Aid/Splits: **13 / digital clocks at 10K & halfway**

HIGHLIGHTS   Powered by Gatorade and oxygen, runners roll through the northeastern Pennsylvania countryside like a runaway locomotive in the Steamtown Marathon (for the first 15 miles at least when runners descend about 950 feet). This Pullman of marathons chugs along as one of America's most promising young races. It boasts a few scenic views from a runner's window seat, strong and growing community support in the 15 towns in which it makes a call, and efficient conducting from the race organization. With these characteristics, the marathon surely will not ride the steam train into oblivion, but instead it has a confirmed booking on the bullet train to marathon success.

COURSE DESCRIPTION   The point-to-point course leaves from Forest City High School on Susquehanna Street, heading downhill along the steepest pitch of the race. Runners take a sharp right turn onto Main Street (Route 171), and pass through the central business district and several blocks of neatly maintained older homes. After enjoying the great crowd support in Forest City, runners enjoy the beautiful fall scenery along Route 171 as they head downhill through Fell Township toward Carbondale. Main Street Carbondale features City Hall, businesses, large crowds, banners, and cheerleaders. Miles 9 through 12 weave through the small communities of Carbondale Township, Mayfield, and Jermyn Boroughs. During these mostly flat miles, runners pass through several older neighborhoods. Near mile 13, runners turn onto Main Street in Archbald Borough (which they follow for the next 4 miles), lined with older homes and businesses. This mostly rolling section contains one tough hill. At mile 17, competitors turn left into Mellow Park in Jessup Borough, making a half-mile sweep past the athletic fields and the banks of the Lackawanna River. After some more residential neighborhoods, runners can anticipate the good crowd waiting for them in downtown Olyphant Borough. As they near Olyphant, competitors cruise downhill across a set of railroad tracks and parallel to an industrial area. At 19.5 miles, the course heads right onto Lackawanna Avenue leading to Olyphant's historic central business district. Pay attention as you enter mile 20 on Main Avenue in Dickson City; this section is the busiest from a traffic standpoint. Just before mile 21, the route turns left into the Dickson City Industrial Park where runners pass several industrial buildings before entering yet another residential area. Miles 21 to 23 features a straightaway that takes runners underneath Interstate 81 and past an undeveloped area near the Lackawanna County Recycling Center. At mile 23, runners enter the Green Ridge section of Scranton—by far the most difficult part of the course. From miles 23.5 to 24.3, runners must fight their way up a tough climb that weaves through the tree-lined streets of Green Ridge, featuring many stately homes. Finally the course levels and after several more blocks through the pretty streets of Green Ridge, runners turn left onto N. Washington Avenue where the outline of downtown Scranton appears. Runners pass the rowdy crowd at Andy Gavin's pub, go through an older commercial district, and then tackle the final incline of the course near the big boat of Cooper's Seafood Restaurant. Entering downtown Scranton at Vine Street, competitors pass several prominent landmarks, including the Lackawanna Junior College, the Scranton Public Library, the Scranton Cultural Center, and City Hall. William Haggerty, a 79-year-old runner from Dunmore, PA said that surviving the hills of Green Ridge to get to the homestretch in downtown Scranton, "was like moving from purgatory to heaven." A modest downhill takes runners the final two blocks to the finish at historic Lackawanna County Courthouse Square.

CROWD/RUNNER SUPPORT The crowd support along the Steamtown Marathon course is quite good, particularly in the 15 towns runners pass through. Expect an especially large crowd in the homestretch in downtown Scranton. The race features 13 aid stations, with water and sport drink available. Portable toilets are placed at several points on the course, as well as at the start and finish lines. If you must bail from the race, an orange sag wagon will eventually pick you up.

RACE LOGISTICS Parking near the start at Forest City High School is limited, but you can be dropped off there. Otherwise, park near the Lackawanna County Courthouse in Scranton, and take the race-provided bus (from Spruce Street and Adams Avenue) to the start. Buses depart between 5:30 a.m. and 6:45 a.m. at 5-minute intervals. The race hands out clothing bags at the starting line; pick up your warmups at the finish line.

ACTIVITIES Retrieve your race packet and breeze through the expo at the Atrium of the Fleet Pennsylvania Services' building on Saturday between 11:00 a.m. and 6:00 p.m. The race provides directions in your confirmation letter. On Saturday evening, 4:30 p.m. to 8:30 p.m., inhale your carbos at the Pasta Party in the lodge of the Montage Ski Resort. After the race, head back to the resort for the free Post-Race Party from 5:00 p.m. to 9:00 p.m.

AWARDS Each runner receives a long-sleeve T-shirt. Medals go to all finishers. Age-group awards range from 3 to 5 deep. Top runners compete for approximately $10,000 in prize money, with the top 7 male and female runners receiving: $1,500, $1,000, $500, $400, $300, $200, and $100, respectively. The top 3 masters finishers earn $300 for first, $200 for second, and $100 for third.

ELITE RUNNER INFORMATION   Runners who meet the B standard for the U.S. Olympic Marathon Trials (2:22 for men and 2:50 for women), qualify for elite status at Steamtown Marathon on a case-by-case basis. Elites receive a free entry and possibly some lodging assistance.

ACCOMMODATIONS   Contact the Visitor's Bureau (800-229-3526) for the latest information on hotel accommodations for the Steamtown Marathon. Some possibilities are: Ramada, 300 Meadow Avenue (717-344-9811); Best Western, 320 Franklin Street (717-346-7061); Courtyard, Exit 51 off I-81 (717-969-2100); Hampton Inn, Exit 51 off I-81 (717-342-7002); Days Inn, 4130 Birney Avenue (717-457-6713); Econo Lodge, 1175 Kane Street (717-348-1000); Quality Inn, 1946 Scranton Carbondale Hwy (717-383-9979).

RELATED EVENTS/RACES   Wheelchair racers can participate in the wheelchair-only half marathon, and children can run the Kids' Mini-Marathon.

AREA ATTRACTIONS   Forest City (the start venue) hosts an October Street Fair on Friday and Saturday of race weekend featuring games, food, music, and antique dealers. Definitely visit the marathon's namesake, Steamtown National Historic Site. Steamtown houses one of the world's largest collections of steam locomotives and related memorabilia and is sure to be a huge hit with the kids.

CANADIAN INTERNATIONAL MARATHON

OVERALL: 86.1

COURSE BEAUTY: 8-

COURSE DIFFICULTY: 3- (SEE APPENDIX)

APPROPRIATENESS FOR FIRST TIMERS: 9-

RACE ORGANIZATION: 9+

CROWDS: 5-

RACE DATA

Overall Ranking: 43
Quickness Ranking: 15
Contact: Jay W. Glassman
The Canadian International Marathon
240 Heath Street West, Suite 802
Toronto, Ontario, Canada M5P 3L5
Tel. (416) 972-1062
Fax (416) 972-1238
E-mail: marathon@netcom.ca
http://www.RunToronto.com
Date: October 17, 1999; October 15, 2000
Start Time: 9:00 a.m. (7:00 a.m. for walkers)
Time Course Closes: 2:00 p.m.
Number of Finishers: 3,123 in 1997
Course: Point to point
Certification: AIMS, Athletics Canada, & Ontario Roadrunners Ass'n
Course Records: Male: (open) 2:20:33; (masters) 2:27:45
Female: (open) 2:37:52; (masters) 2:52:06
Elite Athlete Programs: No
Cost: $35/45/50; $45/55/70 Cdn.
Age groups/Divisions: 18-24, 25-29, 30-34, 35-39, 40-44, 45-49, 50-54, 55-59, 60-64, 65-69, 70+, wheelchair
Walkers: Yes (but must finish in 7 hours)
Requirements: 18 years old
Temperature: 50° - 60°
Aid/Splits: 15 / mile 1 & every 5K

HIGHLIGHTS The maturing Canadian International Marathon offers a relatively quick course through perhaps Canada's most exciting city, Toronto. The race features a new route for 1998, cutting off about 4 miles from the loop at its top end, and then detouring through mostly residential areas in its middle section. The course still travels down Yonge Street, Toronto's main thoroughfare, for several miles. Runners take in Toronto's financial district, St. Lawrence Market, and the Ontario Legislature toward the end of the race. The recent upheaval in the Canadian marathon scene (with the demise of the Toronto Marathon in 1995 and the cancellation of Montreal in 1997) only bolsters CIM's future.

COURSE DESCRIPTION CIM's new course starts with an 8-mile loop through North York. Like before, the race begins on Yonge Street (reputed to be the longest street in the world) just north of Mel Lastman Square. Runners head south .6 miles to Sheppard Avenue and turn right, rolling through residential streets before heading north on Dufferin Street through G. Ross Lord Park. At Steeles Avenue, the course turns back toward Yonge Street, passing parks interspersed with shopping malls and apartment complexes. Back on Yonge Street, the route gradually descends past Mel Lastman Square (8 miles) continuing under the Highway 401 overpass. At Hogg's Hollow, near the halfway point, runners face the largest hill on the course, a tough 100-footer. Once over the hump, the course turns downhill once again. As the race continues on Yonge Street, it turns west on Chaplin to Oriole Parkway. Here it passes Upper Canada College, one of Canada's most exclusive boy's schools, before scurrying through upscale Forest Hill. Following Winston Churchill Park, runners go by pre-WWI Casa Loma, Canada's largest home. After proceeding down Davenport to Belmont (which turns into Aylmer Avenue), the course follows the scenic and forested Rosedale Valley Road to Bayview Avenue. The course meanders along the Don River Valley, before turning onto Front Street, marked by abandoned factories and warehouses. As the city approaches, runners pass the historic St. Lawrence Market, Gooderham, Worts Flatiron Building, and the trendy stores and restaurants of the area. Front Street gives way to Wellington Street through the heart of Toronto's financial district. Turning on University Avenue, you encounter cheering crowds while passing stately Osgoode Hall Provincial Courts, hospitals, and finish after a brief loop around the top of Queen's Park, home to the Ontario Legislature.

CROWD/RUNNER SUPPORT Approximately 35,000 supporters come out for the marathon. You also receive a warm reception by the 20 to 30 entertainment stations stretched along Yonge Street. The new 9:00 a.m. start should even boost audience attendance. You won't go unassisted at aid stations as typically over 800 volunteers offer their help, handing out water, sports drink, fruit, medical assistance, and transportation every 5K, then more frequently in the last 15K of the race. The course is marked every kilometer and every 5th mile.

RACE LOGISTICS Public transportation starts at 9:00 a.m. on Sundays so you need to find some other way to the start. Parking is provided if you plan to drive. Otherwise, shuttle buses depart the host hotels starting at 7:00 a.m. Take the bus from the finish area back to your hotel or to Mel Lastman Square. The marathon also provides a bag check at the start; your bag will be waiting for you at the finish.

ACTIVITIES Pick up your race packet, register, and attend the Runners' Expo on Thursday, Friday or Saturday preceding the marathon at the Delta Chelsea Inn (see below for address) from 10:00 a.m. to 7:00 p.m. Out-of-town runners may retrieve their packets on race morning at Mel Lastman Square. A free feast is provided for runners the evening before the marathon (non-runners may attend for $10). A workshop is also held to orient newcomers to the course and to talk about running generally. Food and refreshments are plentiful at the finish line in Queen's Park, and showers and a changing room are available at nearby Hart House.

AWARDS Every entrant takes home a Canadian International Marathon T-shirt. All full and half marathoners receive medals as they cross the finish line, and certificates of completion are mailed later. Overall winners receive merchandise.

ACCOMMODATIONS The official race hotels are the Holiday Inn On King, 370 King Street West (800-263-6364); and The Delta Chelsea Inn, 33 Gerrard Street West (tel. 416-595-1975; fax 416-585-4366). Reserve your room early because it can be difficult to find last-minute accommodations in Toronto on race weekend. Other hotels to try include: Sheraton Centre Toronto Hotel & Towers, 123 Queen Street West (416-361-1000); Toronto Hilton, 145 Richmond Street West (416-869-3456); or Royal York, 100 Front Street West (416-386-2511).

RELATED EVENTS/RACES Also featured are a half marathon, the Canadian Wheelchair Marathon Championships, and a corporate/school/military marathon challenge (for teams of up to eight runners). The fast half marathon runs along the lower part of the marathon course.

AREA ATTRACTIONS Renowned as one of the most culturally diverse cities on the planet, Toronto offers a dizzying array of activities, including an extremely active theater scene and excellent museums. Catch the tremendous view from the 553-meter CN Tower, the tallest freestanding building in the world. Hockey fans should visit the Hockey Hall of Fame and then catch a Maple Leafs game. Even if the Blue Jays are not playing, check out the amazing Sky Dome with its retractable roof.

DETROIT INTERNATIONAL MARATHON

OVERALL: 82.4

COURSE BEAUTY: 8+

COURSE DIFFICULTY: 2+

APPROPRIATENESS FOR FIRST TIMERS: 9-

RACE ORGANIZATION: 10-

CROWDS: 3-

RACE DATA

Overall Ranking: 68
Quickness Ranking: 16
Contact: Detroit Free Press/FlagStar Bank
P.O. Box 44405
Detroit, MI 48244-0405
(313) 393-7749

Date: October 17, 1999; October 15, 2000
Start Time: 8:00 a.m.
Time Course Closes: 1:30 p.m.
Number of Finishers: 2,572 in 1997
Course: Point to point
Certification: USATF
Course Records: Male: (open) 2:13:07; (masters) 2:19:25
Female: (open) 2:34:55; (masters) 2:45:21
Elite Athlete Programs: Yes
Cost: $27/37/42
Age groups/Divisions: ≤19, 20-24, 25-29, 30-34, 35-39, 40-44, 45-49,
50-54, 55-59, 60-64, 65-69, 70+
Walkers: No
Requirements: None
Temperature: 42° - 57°
Aid/Splits: 25 / every mile

HIGHLIGHTS The Detroit Free Press/Flag Star Bank International Marathon may surprise you. Boasting one of the fastest courses and most unique starts in North America, Detroit begins in Windsor, Ontario and makes a dramatic entrance into the United States via a well-ventilated traffic-free, one-mile tunnel beneath the Detroit River. The pounding echo of runners' feet inspires you for the long journey ahead. Although the race lacks the prestige of its October marathon neighbors (namely Twin Cities and Chicago), Detroit deserves serious consideration when making your marathon plans.

COURSE DESCRIPTION The Detroit Marathon starts at Jackson Park in Windsor, Ontario, and loops around retail and residential areas before descending into the Detroit/Windsor Tunnel at the 5-mile mark. Closed to vehicles and well-ventilated, the tunnel offers a surreal running experience. After a moderate quarter-mile climb, runners leave the tunnel and enter downtown Detroit to the roar of the large crowd. From here, the course proceeds eastward past business districts and ethnic neighborhoods to Belle Isle Park near the halfway point. Designed by Frederick Olmstead, designer of New York's Central Park, and built near the turn of the century, Belle Isle hosts 5.4

miles of the marathon. Leaving the park shortly past 18 miles, the race heads back toward downtown, eventually hitting Woodward Avenue (formerly an Indian trade trail and the oldest road in Michigan) around 22 miles. After a short out and back on Woodward Avenue and a small loop near the Civic Center, the race finishes near the gleaming Renaissance Center in Hart Plaza. Flat and fast, Detroit's course contains only three small uphills which occur at the tunnel exit and the entrance and exit to Belle Isle Park.

CROWD/RUNNER SUPPORT Though growing in recent years, Detroit's crowd participation is still smallish by big city marathon standards. The majority of the 25,000 spectators cheer at the Detroit/Windsor tunnel exit and the finish in Hart Plaza. To the race organizers' credit, aid stations are located every mile, and one dozen "morale stations" with entertainment and cheering spectators support your effort.

RACE LOGISTICS The race provides bus transportation to the start from the Westin Hotel at the Renaissance Center. The Westin is conveniently located near the finish line, where ample parking is available.

ACTIVITIES Detroit holds a Health & Fitness Expo at the Westin beginning Friday from 12:00 p.m. to 8:00 p.m. and continuing Saturday from 9:00 a.m. to 7:00 p.m. The site for race packet pickup, the expo also hosts running clinics and the usual sports-related vendors. There is no late registration since all entries must be inspected by customs and immigrations before anyone can cross the Canada - U.S. border. In fact, the entry deadline is always set two weeks prior to race day to help expedite the process. A pre-race pasta dinner begins at 5:00 p.m. Saturday evening. A brief awards ceremony for top finishers follows the event at Hart Plaza.

AWARDS Every marathon entrant receives a T-shirt which may be picked up at the expo or at the finish line after the race. All finishers receive medals and finisher certificates. The latter are mailed to marathoners 3-4 weeks after the race. Finish times of marathoners are published in the Monday Detroit Free Press, which can be mailed to runners for a $5 fee. Age-group awards extend as deep as 12 depending on the number of entrants in the division. Top division finishers are awarded plaques, mailed after the race.

ELITE RUNNERS INFORMATION Male runners under 2:22 and female runners under 2:50 qualify for elite status and may receive some expense money and lodging assistance. Overall male and female winners earn $8,000. Second through ninth place finishers earn $2,000, $1,500, $1,000, $750, $500, $250, $100, and $50, respectively. Masters prize money stretches four deep: $1,000, $500, $250, and $100, respectively.

ACCOMMODATIONS The Westin Hotel in Detroit's Renaissance Center (313-568-8200), serves as the host hotel. Conveniently located near the finish line, the hotel offers a package that includes a complimentary breakfast on race morning. Other nearby hotels include the DoubleTree Hotel, 333 E. Jefferson Avenue (312-222-7700); and The Atheneum Suite Hotel, 1000 Brush Avenue (313-962-2323).

RELATED EVENTS/RACES Race day includes the Old Navy Fun Run Race Day 5K starting at Hart Plaza, finish location for the marathon. The 5K begins at 9:00 a.m.,allowing plenty of time for participants to complete the run and then cheer the marathoners at the finish line.

AREA ATTRACTIONS Have you known anyone to vacation in Detroit? Neither have we. However, the city is not completely devoid of entertainment. The Henry Ford Museum lies in nearby Dearborn. Also of historical significance is the Motown Museum on W. Grand Blvd. The nation's largest movie theater hall, the Fox, stands on Woodward Ave. Belle Isle Park, located three miles from downtown on the marathon course, holds many attractions, including a small zoo, aquarium and nature center. Sports fans may see the Wolverines of the University of Michigan or the Detroit Lions of the NFL, both of which play in neighboring towns. Another option involves heading across the Detroit River to the clean, charming Canadian city of Windsor, Ontario. Windsor, which recently legalized gambling, maintains a casino in an old art gallery and a riverboat casino on the Detroit River.

HUMBOLDT REDWOODS MARATHON

OVERALL: 87.6

COURSE BEAUTY: 10

COURSE DIFFICULTY: 2 (SEE APPENDIX)

APPROPRIATENESS FOR FIRST TIMERS: 8+

RACE ORGANIZATION: 9-

CROWDS: 1-

RACE DATA

Overall Ranking:	32
Quickness Ranking:	12
Contact:	Humboldt Redwoods Marathon
	P.O. Box 4989
	Arcata, CA 95518-4989
	Tel. (707) 443-1220
	Fax (707) 443-2553
	E-mail: spowers@northcoast.com
Date:	October 17, 1999; October 15, 2000
Start Time:	9:00 a.m.
Time Course Closes:	2:00 p.m.
Number of Finishers:	356 in 1997
Course:	Two out and backs
Certification:	USATF
Course Records:	Male: (open) 2:22:23
	Female: (open) 2:46:16
Elite Athlete Programs:	No
Cost:	$30/40
Age groups/Divisions:	≤18, 19-24, 25-29, 30-34, 35-39, 40-44, 45-49, 50-54, 55-59, 60-64, 65-69, 70-74, 75-79, 80-84, 85-89, 90-94, 95-99, 100+, wheelchair
Walkers:	Yes (but must move to side of road after 2:00 p.m.)
Requirements:	None
Temperature:	45˚ - 60˚
Aid/Splits:	10 / miles 1, 5, 10, 15, 20 & 25

HIGHLIGHTS   Noble, old growth redwood groves provide a protective canopy almost every step of the way in one of North America's best small races, the Humboldt Redwoods Marathon. The ultimate nature lover's race, Humboldt's fast course offers the perfect setting for inspired running and tranquil introspection as you weave among the creaking giants. The filtered light cascades down runners like worshipers in an outdoor cathedral. After the race, explore the rugged beauty of California's northern coast and surrounding parks.

COURSE DESCRIPTION   The Humboldt Redwoods Marathon starts and finishes at the Dyerville Bridge on the Avenue of the Giants (a Hwy. 101 alternative scenic route). After crossing the south fork of the Eel River, the race immediately enters a canopy of centuries-old redwoods that recedes only for a quarter mile at 2.2 and 10.6. The mostly flat, extremely fast, completely closed first half contains some gentle ups and downs that impart an interesting illusion. *"The first half seems downhill both out and back! Really fast,"* says Jeff Hildebrandt of Roseville,

California. Returning to the Dyerville Bridge at mile 13, runners proceed left down Bull Creek Road for the second out and back passing through Rockefeller Forest. Monitored by CHP pilot cars, this section of the course is narrower, quieter, and more winding and rolling, gaining about 150 feet from mile 14 to 20 and losing the same amount from mile 20 to the finish.

CROWD/RUNNER SUPPORT Other than the thousands of ancient redwoods witnessing your quest, spectators are pretty much limited to the start, halfway, and finish. In addition to the usual water and electrolyte replacement drink, the aid stations near miles 17 and 22 carry energy bars and fruit to help get you through the final miles. Portable toilets are located at every aid station.

RACE LOGISTICS The undeveloped race site in Redwoods State Park means facilities in the area are fairly limited. You will need to drive to the start since lodging is scattered throughout the area. If you are traveling north on Highway 101, take the Founder's Tree exit, while southbound travelers should take the second Redcrest exit. You immediately hit upon the staging area and monitors will direct you to the parking location. Try to arrive before 8:00 a.m. to avoid traffic hassles.

ACTIVITIES Runners can register late on Saturday afternoon at the Burlington Campground Visitor's Center or on race day near the start area. On late Saturday afternoon, attend a slide show and discussion of the course at the Visitor's Center. Saturday evening you can attend the Weott American Legion's Spaghetti Feed ($5), an all-you-can-eat affair. After the race, there are refreshments, a raffle, and awards ceremony.

AWARDS Marathon entrants receive T-shirts, finishers earn medallions, and the top three in each age group receive special medals. The overall winners are awarded merchandise prizes, and the top three overall, top two masters, and top seniors take home commemorative awards.

ACCOMMODATIONS The race sponsor hotel is Carter House Victorians, 301 L Street, Eureka (about 40 miles from the start) (707-444-8062). Possibilities in Fortuna (about 24 miles from the start) include: the Best Western Country Inn, 1528 Kenmar Road (800-528-1234); Holiday Inn Express, 1859 Alamar Way (800-465-4329); and Super 8 Motel, 1805 Alamar Way (800-800-8000). In Scotia (about 15 miles from the start) try the Scotia Inn, 100 Main Street (707-764-5683). In Eureka (about 40 miles from the start) try the: Eureka Inn, 7th and F Streets (707-442-6441); Comfort Inn, 2014 4th Street (800-424-6423); Red Lion Inn, 1929 4th Street (800-547-8010); Carson House Inn, 4th and M Streets (800-772-1622); and Motel 6, 1934 Broadway (707-445-9631). See the Avenue of the Giants Marathon entry on page 75 for more accommodations.

RELATED EVENTS/RACES You may want to run in the super-fast Humboldt Redwoods Half Marathon which covers the first half of the full marathon course. The popular half, the USATF Pacific Association Half Marathon Championship, regularly attracts over 1,000 entrants and runs concurrently with the marathon. In addition, $4,000 in prize money is offered to the top half marathon finishers (must be USATF Pacific Association members to receive prize money).

AREA ATTRACTIONS Spend some time wandering amongst the redwoods, such as the Founder's Grove Nature Trail for starters. If you have the energy and time, we highly recommend driving north to Prairie Creek Redwoods State Park (south of Klamath) and hiking the incomparable Fern Canyon Trail with 50-foot precipices covered by immense ferns.

TOWPATH MARATHON

OVERALL: 80.9

COURSE BEAUTY: 9+

COURSE DIFFICULTY: 2+

APPROPRIATENESS FOR FIRST TIMERS: 8

RACE ORGANIZATION: 9-

CROWDS: 1-

RACE DATA

Overall Ranking:	81
Quickness Ranking:	23
Contact:	Pacific Sports
	c/o Towpath Marathon
	1900 E. 9th Street, Loc. 7000
	Cleveland, OH 44114
	Tel. (216) 575-3439; Fax (216) 575-3167
	E-mail: pacific@multiverse.com
	http://www.pacificLLC.com
Date:	October 17, 1999 (tentative); October 15, 2000 (tentative)
Start Time:	9:00 a.m.
Time Course Closes:	NA
Number of Finishers:	775 in 1997
Course:	Loop
Certification:	USATF
Course Records:	Male: (open) 2:27:59
	Female: (open) 2:50:42
Elite Athlete Programs:	No
Cost:	$35
Age groups/Divisions:	≤19, 20-24, 25-29, 30-34, 35-39, 40-44, 45-49, 50-54, 55-59, 60-64, 65-69, 70+; Clydesdale (M: 200+; F: 140+)
Walkers:	No
Requirements:	None
Temperature:	55°
Aid/Splits:	14 / none

HIGHLIGHTS Nestled between Cleveland and Akron, the Cuyahoga Valley National Recreation Area hosts a wonderful marathon largely undiscovered by the outside world—the Towpath Marathon. Run on the Towpath Trail along the historic Ohio & Erie Canal and the Cuyahoga River, the race treats runners to the ultimate running surface, a soft path of crushed limestone. The trail envelopes runners with exploding orange and gold leafed trees. Leonard Fisher of Dublin, OH, a 15-marathon veteran, calls Towpath, *"The most beautiful course I've run."* The event benefits the Ohio Canal Corridor, a nonprofit organization whose mission is to create a legacy park system along the historic Ohio and Erie Canal from Cleveland to Zorr.

COURSE DESCRIPTION The only marathon held in a United States National Park, Towpath features a flat, loop course starting at Brandywine Ski Area. After one mile of pavement running, you meet the Towpath Trail where it intersects with Highland Road. Here, you are greeted by the spectacular fall colors that accentuate the twisty, cushioned trail. Constructed in

1825, the Towpath Trail served as the path that mules and horses used to pull canal boats along the canal. Notice the old locks along the canal, many of which are hidden by overgrowth. The race finishes at the historic Boston Store Area.

CROWD/RUNNER SUPPORT As you would expect, this rural race does not draw large crowds, but the enthusiastic race volunteers provide much needed support. Friends and family can also access the route at several points along the canal to support you.

RACE LOGISTICS Parking is available at the race start (Brandywine Ski Area). There is limited parking at the finish line (Boston Mills Ski Area) and the surrounding areas. A shuttle service transports people to and from the ski areas.

ACTIVITIES You can pick up your race packet on Saturday from 10:00 a.m. to 4:00 p.m at the small expo held at the Cleveland Athletic Club, 1118 Euclid Avenue in downtown Cleveland. Race day registration goes from 6:30 a.m. to 8:30 a.m. at the start area. The race offers post-marathon refreshments and free massages for spent legs.

AWARDS All marathoners receive a T-shirt, and finishers earn an official finisher's pin (with a year bar to attach) and medallion. Overall and age-group awards extend three deep.

ACCOMMODATIONS The Holiday Inn Hudson (330-653-9191) serves as the race hotel, offering special rates to marathon participants. Otherwise we suggest trying the following options within the Cuyahoga Valley National Recreation Area: the Historic Wallace farmhouse, now the Inn at Brandywine Falls, 8230 Brandywine Road (216-467-1812); or the Stanford House Hostel, an American Youth Hostel Association member which accepts adults as well. Located at 6093 Stanford Road (216-467-8711), the hostel offers simple lodging and food preparation facilities.

RELATED EVENTS/RACES Friends can join forces and enter the marathon relay, consisting of two- and four-person teams. Teams may be unisex or coed. Additionally, a 5K run was added in 1998.

AREA ATTRACTIONS The area offers numerous opportunities for hiking, bike riding, and bird watching. Football fans can dissect the Pro Football Hall of Fame in nearby Canton, and music lovers may want to check out the new Rock and Roll Hall of Fame in Cleveland. Cleveland also offers a variety of professional sports.

CAPE COD MARATHON

OVERALL: 89.4

COURSE BEAUTY: 9+

COURSE DIFFICULTY: 6-

APPROPRIATENESS FOR FIRST TIMERS: 8

RACE ORGANIZATION: 9

CROWDS: 3-

RACE DATA

Overall Ranking:	25
Quickness Ranking:	84
Contact:	Courtney & Carolyn Bird
	Cape Cod Marathon
	P.O. Box 699
	West Falmouth, MA 02574
	Tel. (508) 540-6959
	Fax (508) 548-0617
	http://www.capecodmarathon.com
Date:	October 31, 1999; October 29, 2000
Start Time:	8:00 a.m.
Time Course Closes:	1:00 p.m.
Number of Finishers:	536 in 1997
Course:	Loop
Certification:	USATF
Course Records:	Male: (open) 2:17:35; (masters) 2:30:49
	Female: (open) 2:37:06; (masters) 3:02:29
Elite Athlete Programs:	No
Cost:	$35/40
Age groups/Divisions:	14-39, 40-49, 50-59, 60-69, 70+
Walkers:	No
Requirements:	14 years of age
Temperature:	45° - 60°
Aid/Splits:	10 / miles 1, 5, 10, 15, 20 & 25

HIGHLIGHTS Windswept coast, cranberry bogs, pulsing lighthouses, and clapboard homes provide the backdrop for New England's most charming marathon, the Cape Cod Marathon. Offering spectacular scenes, fall in the Cape often treats runners to fair weather for race day. After completing the challenging course and reloading at the post-race meal, head to the race directors' home for an evening of beer, snacks, and camaraderie. Such personal touches make for an experience that few marathons can match.

COURSE DESCRIPTION Cape Cod's loop course, open to residential traffic, starts at Village Green in downtown Falmouth, a wonderfully quaint town of wood and brick shops and restaurants. By .3 miles, the course enters a beautiful residential community before tracing Falmouth harbor (with a short, steep hill at 2.7) and fronting the coast until near mile 4. Here, the course turns inland through a scenic residential area, crossing one of the area's numerous finger inlets. Runners go down a short hill at 7.6, leading to cranberry bogs, woods, and farm land in rolling terrain. On Thomas Landers Road, from about mile 11 to 13, the course gains 70 feet over rolling hills. The course goes gently down from 13 to 13.5 and then rolls again as it becomes more residential. From mile 15.2 to 15.5, runners go up newly-paved Old Palmer Road and then drop from 15.8 to 16.1. As the course heads south toward Woods Hole, the rolling hills become more pronounced. At mile 20, a tough, .33-mile hill greets runners as they pass a nicely manicured golf course. Following part of the Falmouth Road Race course, runners enter Woods Hole at mile 21, go past the harbor, along the shore, and around Nobska Point and its lighthouse at mile 22. The short uphill provides spectacular views for runners. The course has a few steep rollers left before leveling off after 23.5 as it hugs the Vineyard Sound shore until mile 25.3. The course then turns up, away from the water, briefly cutting through a residential section before arriving downtown for the finish at Village Green. Though not closed to traffic, the course utilizes secondary roads and is monitored by the police and numerous volunteers.

CROWD/RUNNER SUPPORT   Since the course goes through several residential areas, the race attracts good crowds for a small community, about 4,000 to 5,000 people. Portable toilets are available at the second, third, and fourth relay exchange points. A medical team roams the course as does a sag wagon for race victims.

RACE LOGISTICS   Held in a small town, the race neither requires nor offers transportation to the start. Many accommodations are within walking distance of the start/finish. There is plenty of parking at the Lawrence School.

ACTIVITIES   The Lawrence School on Lakeview Avenue serves as pre-race headquarters for most race activities. On Friday evening and Saturday afternoon, pick up your race packet, register late, or get info on things to do in the area. Since moving to an 8:00 a.m. start in 1998, the race no longer allows race-day registration. The race does not have an organized pasta party, but does cooperate with several local restaurants for pasta specials and free beer. Let one of the race massage therapists work out the kinks from the challenging course. Afterwards, enjoy a great meal of pasta, clam chowder, salad, juice, and soda in the school cafeteria. The awards ceremony starts at 1:00 p.m. in the school gym. After the mess at the school is cleaned up, head to the home of race directors Courtney and Carolyn Bird for a post-race party of free beer and leftover race tidbits.

AWARDS   Every marathoner receives a Cape Cod Marathon long-sleeve T-shirt, and finishers receive medallions and certificates. A random drawing is held for various merchandise. Trophies and merchandise prizes go to the top age-group finishers, with the overall open and masters winners competing for about $7,000 in prize money.

ACCOMMODATIONS   The Quality Inn—Falmouth, 291 Jones Road (800-854-1507), is the official race hotel. Located about a half mile from Village Green, the inn offers specials rates to Cape Cod runners. Also convenient are: Ramada on the Square, 40 North Main Street (508-457-0606); Elm Arch Inn, Elm Arch Way (508-548-0133); Inn at One Main Street, 1 Main Street (508-540-7469); Capt. Tom Lawrence House, 75 Locust Street (508-540-1445); Village Green Inn, 40 West Main Street (508-548-5621); and Palmer House Inn, 81 Palmer Avenue (508-548-1230). B&Bs dot the entire area, and the race can provide additional suggestions.

RELATED EVENTS/RACES   The five-leg marathon relay runs concurrently with the marathon. Teams of two to five members run legs of 3, 6.5, 5.5, 5.8, and 5.4 miles. Each member can run from one to four legs in any order.

AREA ATTRACTIONS   You can avoid the tourist mob on the Cape by visiting in the fall at marathon time. For unspoiled beaches, head to the Cape Cod National Seashore. Visit one of the many historic towns, such as Provincetown, Sandwich, and Truro. You can also explore the offshore islands, Martha's Vineyard and Nantucket. If you prefer your action a little faster, head north to Boston, about 90 minutes away.

CHICAGO MARATHON

OVERALL: 99.3

COURSE BEAUTY: 8+

COURSE DIFFICULTY: 1+

APPROPRIATENESS FOR FIRST TIMERS: 10

RACE ORGANIZATION: 10

CROWDS: 9+

RACE DATA

Overall Ranking: 4
Quickness Ranking: 1
Contact: The LaSalle Banks Chicago Marathon
P.O. Box 10597
Chicago, IL 60610-0597
Tel. (888) 243-3344 or (312) 243-3274
Fax (312) 243-5652
http://www.ChicagoMarathon.com

Date: October 24, 1999; 2000 TBA
Start Time: 7:45 a.m.
Time Course Closes: 1:15 p.m.
Number of Finishers: 17,093 in 1998
Course: Loop
Certification: USATF
Course Records: Male: (open) 2:06:54
Female: (open) 2:21:21
Elite Athlete Programs: Yes
Cost: $50/60
Age groups/Divisions: ≤19, 20-24, 25-29, 30-34, 35-39, 40-44, 45-49,
50-54, 55-59, 60-64, 65-69, 70+
Walkers: Yes
Requirements: None
Temperature: 53°
Aid/Splits: 14 / digital clocks every mile and at 5K

HIGHLIGHTS   Chicago's dead population notoriously arises at opportune times; John F. Kennedy could have attested to that after the 1960 presidential election! Not limited to Chicago politics, however, resurrection extends to Chicago sports—Michael Jordan, the Bulls, the 1998 Cubs, and the Chicago Marathon. Sponsorship problems forced the cancellation of the 1987 race, but Chicago has regained its place as one of the country's top, big-city marathons; and if you like big cities, Chicago is a must. The city of big shoulders' impressive architecture, skyline, lakefront, sports, entertainment, history, and culture make it a destination town *par excellence*. Our fastest-rated race, Chicago's lightning course (North American records for male and females have been established here) tours numerous ethnic neighborhoods that most visitors never see. With the exception of the disqualified women's winner from 1992, rarely will you hear a negative comment about the extremely well organized Chicago Marathon. Alive and well, Chicago is yours to enjoy.

COURSE DESCRIPTION Taking runners through many of the city's most historic and diverse neighborhoods, the Chicago Marathon's loop course passes through Lincoln Park, Old Town, Greektown, Little Italy, Pilsen, Chinatown, Bridgeport and the Gap District. Starting in Grant Park, site of famous Buckingham Fountain, near the shore of beautiful Lake Michigan, runners head north traveling past the Hard Rock Café, Planet Hollywood and other chic restaurants and night spots during the three miles in the River North area. Continuing north, the route heads through Lincoln Park past the Lincoln Park Zoo and Diversey Harbor. Coffee shops, bookstores, and restaurants characterize the Lakeview area between miles 6 and 8. Heading south from Lakeview, runners return to Lincoln Park passing the world-renowned dance and blues clubs and international restaurants on Clark Street. Still early in the race, your sense of humor should still be intact as you pass the great comedy clubs in Old Town Chicago around 8 miles. After cruising past The Loop (shoppers' paradise), Merchandise Mart, City Hall, and Sears Tower near mile 11, the course heads west, crossing the Chicago River into Greektown. After hitting the halfway point in Little Italy, expect great spectator support, including music and dancing as the route enters Pilsen, Chicago's largest Hispanic area, around mile 18. The rainbow tour proceeds, cutting through Chinatown's Lion and Dragon dancers at mile 19. Bridgeport, the mayor's neighborhood, Comiskey Park, home of the White Sox, and the Southside, home of Bad Bad Leroy Brown, lie between miles 22 and 23. Heading east toward Lake Michigan, runners enter the supportive Gap District, a large black community, near the 23-mile mark. The next two miles head north on Lakeshore Drive and pass McCormick Place before hitting Columbus Drive. The beautiful view of the Chicago skyline should ease your effort up the short climb at mile 25. After passing Soldier Field and the Field Museum, you finish down the broad lanes of Columbus Drive in Grant Park.

CROWD/RUNNER SUPPORT Chicago's legendary sports-town image extends to the marathon; over 600,000 onlookers line the streets or hang out of apartment windows encouraging the marathoners. The 14 aid stations stretch an entire block in places, while numerous musical groups entertain. The course layout makes it very easy for spectators to view the race from several spots along the way. In fact, onlookers can watch the start, saunter six blocks, and cheer at the ten-mile mark.

RACE LOGISTICS Convenient Grant Park makes arriving at the start relatively hassle free with the major hotels nearby. If you're arriving by car, you'll find ample parking in the area.

ACTIVITIES Chicago features a two-day Health and Fitness Expo and race registration at the Chicago Hilton & Towers. The expo includes over 150 exhibitors displaying the latest products and services from the sports, health and fitness industries. Runners may register or pick up their packets at the expo on Friday between 10:00 a.m. and 8:00 p.m. and Saturday from 9:00 a.m. to 7:00 p.m. A spectacular pasta carbo-load dinner is held on Saturday night from 6:00 p.m. to 8:00 p.m. at the Chicago Hilton & Towers. The dinner includes a three-course, sit-down meal, special guest appearances by celebrity runners, and a drawing for prizes. Runners, family, and friends are welcome, but seating is limited. After the race, a great post-race finishers party takes place at a local hot spot with free food, wine, and beer.

AWARDS Every marathoner receives a race T-shirt, goody bag, official race results booklet and entry into the post-race party. Participants finishing under 5:30 receive medallions, results cards and finisher's certificates. Age-group winners receive special prizes which are mailed soon after the event. Elite runners compete for $350,000 in prize money.

ELITE RUNNERS INFORMATION Chicagoan's have come to expect big-time sports with big-time players. Chicago Marathon organizers realize this and actively recruit some of the top names in marathoning. The race executive director holds complete discretion in conferring elite status. To be considered for expense money, you must contact Carey Pinkowski between January 1st and September 15th. A fast course and $350,000 in prize money, including generous time incentive bonuses, do not hurt Chicago's recruitment efforts. Prize money goes 10 deep in Open Divisions and five deep in Masters Divisions. Open winners earn $55,000, $25,000 for second, $20,000 for third, $15,000 for fourth, $10,000 for fifth, $5,000 for sixth, $4,000 for seventh, $3,000 for eighth, $2,000 for ninth, and $1,000 for tenth. The top five Americans receive additional awards from $10,000 to $1,000. Masters winners take home $1,500, down to $550 for third. Time bonuses are awarded to any male runners under the qualifying times, ranging from $1,000 for a sub 2:13 to $100,000 for a world record. For women, the times range from sub 2:33 ($1,000) to a world record ($100,000).

ACCOMMODATIONS The Chicago Hilton and Towers, 720 S. Michigan Avenue (800-445-8667), only two blocks from the start/finish line, acts as the official race hotel. It offers special rates to marathon runners, but don't procrastinate. Other convenient hotels with special marathon rates include: Best Western Grant Park, 1100 S. Michigan Avenue (312-922-2900); Holiday Inn Chicago City Center, 300 E. Ohio Street (312-787-6100); River North Hotel, 125 W. Ohio Street (312-467-0800); Congress Plaza Hotel, 520 S. Michigan Avenue (312-427-3800); and the Sheraton Chicago, 301 E. North Water Street (312-464-1000).

RELATED EVENTS/RACES Race weekend begins Saturday with the Youth Run open to children 5 to 14 years of age. Starting at 11:00 a.m. in Grant Park, the course loops Buckingham Fountain on Chicago's spectacular lakefront. For those not bitten by the marathon bug, Chicago offers a popular 5K Run starting at 8:15 a.m. on race day. If you're running the marathon, consider recruiting a few friends or co-workers and enter the Team Challenge. For an extra fee, corporate or open teams of three to five members compete in this uniquely scored event. Team members are scored according to their place within their age group, relative to the number of finishers in that division. The top three performances are then added together, and the team with the lowest total points wins.

AREA ATTRACTIONS Spicy Chicago offers something for everyone: architecture, art galleries, museums, fine restaurants, Chicago Pizza, theaters, night clubs, blues music, sports, ethnic neighborhoods, shopping, and the lakefront beach. Save a little race energy, and allow time to take in some of the attractions.

RUN CHICAGO

The LaSalle Banks Chicago Marathon®

For an application or information contact:

The LaSalle Banks Chicago Marathon, P.O. Box 10597, Chicago, IL 60610-0597
Phone: (312) 243-0003   Toll-Free: 1-888-243-3344 (U.S. only)
Internet: www.chicagomarathon.com

Credit: Michael Gustafson

MARINE CORPS MARATHON

OVERALL: 96.6

COURSE BEAUTY: 10-

COURSE DIFFICULTY: 3+

APPROPRIATENESS FOR FIRST TIMERS: 10

RACE ORGANIZATION: 10-

CROWDS: 5+

RACE DATA

Overall Ranking:	6
Quickness Ranking:	36
Contact:	Marine Corps Marathon
	P.O. Box 188
	Quantico, VA 22134-0188
	Tel. (800) RUN-USMC or (703) 784-2225
	Fax (703) 784-2265
	E-mail: marathon@quantico.usmc.mil
	http://www.marinemarathon.com
Date:	October 24, 1999; October 22, 2000
Start Time:	8:30 a.m.
Time Course Closes:	3:30 p.m.
Number of Finishers:	13,957 in 1997
Course:	Loop
Certification:	USATF
Course Records:	Male: (open) 2:14:01
	Female: (open) 2:37:00
Elite Athlete Programs:	No
Cost:	$45
Age groups/Divisions:	≤19, 20-24, 25-29, 30-34, 35-39, 40-44, 45-49,
	50-54, 55-59, 60-64, 65-69, 70+
Walkers:	No
Requirements:	None
Temperature:	49° - 68°
Aid/Splits:	20 / miles 1, 3, 5, 10, 15, 20, 22 & 24

HIGHLIGHTS Nicknamed "The People's Marathon®" and "Marathon of the Monuments," the Marine Corps Marathon has established itself as one of the country's finest marathons. As the name implies, the U.S. Marine Corps hosts this Washington, D.C. classic, drawing about 16,000 runners, about half of whom are first timers. The Marines execute the race splendidly, from race organization to providing encouragement along the course. Topping most other marathons in North America for first timers (Oprah ran her first marathon here), Marine Corps also provides a great race for veterans. The course tours the nation's capital, passing Arlington Cemetery, Georgetown, the Kennedy Center, Lincoln Memorial, Jefferson Memorial, U.S. Capitol, Washington Monument, Union Station, and Smithsonian Museums. The Washington, D.C. location and the Marines' dedication combine for an unbeatable destination marathon.

COURSE DESCRIPTION MCM's closed course starts and finishes near the Marine Corps War Memorial marked by the Iwo Jima Monument in Arlington, VA. The marathon first passes through sobering Arlington National Cemetery where many of the nation's great soldiers and John F. Kennedy are buried. Then it's past the Pentagon, the world's largest office building (after mile 1), Pentagon City, a large shopping mall (mile 2), and the mostly commercial surrounding areas between miles 2 and 3. During miles 4 to 6, runners wind around the Pentagon before returning to Arlington Cemetery (near mile 7). The course passes the starting area and the high-rise office buildings of Rosslyn, VA, at mile 8. At this point, the heart of the MCM course begins. Runners enter Key Bridge after mile 8 on a slight incline. Crossing the bridge, the stone spire of prestigious Georgetown University looms above you. Runners exit Key Bridge onto M Street, one of fashionable Georgetown's main thoroughfares. The course then cuts down to scenic Rock Creek Parkway, skirting the Potomac River, and passing the bright white Kennedy Center just after mile 10. Around 10.7 miles, the course turns left past the Lincoln Memorial to the famous Mall (miles 10.7 to 13 and 14.7 to 17.7). At about 11.5 miles, runners can glimpse the White House beyond the Ellipse on the left and the towering Washington Monument on the right. During mile 12,

the course heads by many of the Smithsonian Museums, and mile 13, runners have an excellent view of the U.S. Capitol. Then, with a slight incline, it's on to Union Station (about 13.5 miles) before circling the Capitol and returning down to the Mall on the opposite (south) side. At mile 17.5, look across the Tidal Basin for a nice view of the Jefferson Memorial. Completely flat, miles 18 to 22.5 are run in scenic East Potomac Park, around Hains Point. The course crosses the 14th Street Bridge (mile 23) with a gentle incline, and then it's past the now very familiar Pentagon as runners retrace their steps to finish, on an incline, at the Iwo Jima Monument.

CROWD/RUNNER SUPPORT Most of MCM runs in the historic sections of Washington, so the course doesn't pass through many residential neighborhoods. Despite this, local spectators turn out in surprisingly good numbers at several points. Nearly 10,000 spectators pack the start/finish area, and large numbers also turn out along the Key Bridge. Particularly strategic, the Mall attracts many onlookers as they can cheer for their favorite runner three times. Right before the 14th Street Bridge is another prime spectator spot, since it is scenic and near accessible parking. Friends and family can take the Metro to several of these and other points on the course to support their runner. Helpful, polite, and enthusiastic, the Marines along the course provide the best inspiration (besides your fellow runners). Tall, 12-foot yellow poles with large mile indicators mark the course.

RACE LOGISTICS Several hotels have shuttle buses to the start. Check with race officials for the most recent list. If you have a car, you can park in the Pentagon's North and South parking lots and then take a shuttle from there to the start (6:30 a.m. to 8:30 a.m.). The Metro now opens at 6:30 a.m. on marathon morning, so take the Orange or Blue Line to the Rosslyn stop or the Blue Line to the Arlington Cemetery stop. The race has a bag drop for your belongings. After the race, meet your family in the post-race linkup area, marked by red banners indicating first letters of your last name.

ACTIVITIES Runners can pick up their race packets at the Hyatt Regency Crystal City Hotel on Thursday from 4:00 p.m. to 8:00 p.m., Friday from 10:00 a.m. to 10:00 p.m., or Saturday from 8:00 a.m. to 10:00 p.m. There is no race-day packet pick-up or registration. On Friday and Saturday, attend the runner's expo and symposium. On Saturday night, the Hyatt hosts a pasta dinner (about $10). After the race, hang out at the post-race party with refreshments, drink, and fruit. The awards ceremony is held on the west steps of the War Memorial at 1:00 p.m.

AWARDS Every entrant receives a T-shirt, and finishers receive medals, certificates and results books. Over 400 trophies are awarded in individual and 11 team categories. MCM presents Middendorf Trophy replicas to the overall winners. Among the categories of awards are: age-groups (men up to 10 places and women up to 5 places), wheelchair, first Virginia, Maryland, and Washington, D.C. residents, U.S. military, U.S. Marine Corps, Canadian military, Clydesdale, and retired military.

ACCOMMODATIONS The Hyatt Regency Crystal City Hotel, 2799 Jefferson Davis Highway (703-418-1234), serves as the race headquarters hotel (about $110). Also convenient are the: Holiday Inn Key Bridge, 1850 N. Fort Myer Drive, Rosslyn (703-522-0400); Sheraton Crystal City, 1800 Jefferson Davis Hwy., Arlington (800-862-7666); Sheraton National Hotel, Columbia Pike & Washington Blvd. in Arlington (703-521-1900); and the Courtyard Marriott, 2899 Jefferson Davis Hwy. (800-847-4775). The race provides a complete list of hotels offering special rates to MCM runners.

RELATED RACES MCM sponsors the Special Olympics Mini Marathon, where athletes from around the country compete in 5K, 10K, and unified road races after the marathon start.

SILICON VALLEY MARATHON

OVERALL: 87.9

COURSE BEAUTY: 8+

COURSE DIFFICULTY: 2 (SEE APPENDIX)

APPROPRIATENESS FOR FIRST TIMERS: 9-

RACE ORGANIZATION: 10-

CROWDS: 4-

RACE DATA

Overall Ranking:	29
Quickness Ranking:	8
Contact:	Tom Bradley
	First Wave Events
	P.O. Box 1785
	Capitola, CA 95010
	Tel. (831) 477-0965
	Fax (831) 477-0964
	E-mail: Tom@Firstwave-Events.com
	http://www.svmarathon.com
Date:	October 31, 1999; October 22, 2000
Start Time:	7:30 a.m.
Time Course Closes:	1:30 p.m.
Number of Finishers:	972 in 1997
Course:	Loop
Certification:	USATF
Course Records:	Male: (open) 2:18:59; (masters) 2:43:42
	Female: (open) 2:39:20; (masters) 2:53:18
Elite Athlete Programs:	Yes
Cost:	$45/55
Age groups/Divisions:	≤19, ,20-24, 25-29, 30-34, 35-39, 40-44, 45-49,
	50-54, 55-59, 60-69, 70+
Walkers:	No
Requirements:	None
Temperature:	52° - 68°
Aid/Splits:	25 / every mile

HIGHLIGHTS   The Silicon Valley Marathon logged onto the marathon Internet with an impressive 1997 Version 1.0. with nearly 1,000 runners. Our eighth-fastest marathon, Silicon Valley processes several key components for fast times—a lightening fast course, aid stations every mile, split timers each mile indicating pace and projected finish time, a start/finish area within steps of several downtown hotels, and, of course, the ChampionChip computer timing system. Spectators also can speed around the course as the city's VTA light rail system virtually parallels the entire course. As the race matures and more companies spring up along the race route, expect to see more high tech displays in addition to the "virtual wall" (mile 20) and the Jumbo Tron located at the finish. And to add to your memory, the race presents you with one of the most unique finisher's medal containing a real computer chip. Benefitting the new Tech Museum of Innovation, Silicon Valley is already one of the most user-friendly races on the West Coast and moving up fast on the marathon super highway.

COURSE DESCRIPTION   Designed with one thing in mind—fast times—Silicon Valley's course offers a tour of the high-tech area from which the race takes its name. The essentially flat, loop course takes you past the front doors of hundreds of Silicon Valley companies that are developing the latest, fastest, and most revolutionary technologies in the world. It starts amidst the newly-planted palm trees lining the medians of Almaden and Park Streets in downtown San Jose. Within the first half mile, runners negotiate two quick turns then head down 3rd Street, a combination business and residential area which takes runners past historic St. James Park and the Unitarian Church, and then into Japantown near 2 miles. Mostly residential for the next mile, the route skirts the Santa Clara County Government Building on Hedding Street (mile 3) before a right turn onto First Street, the longest stretch of road on the marathon course. New and old hotels and law offices set up in old Victorian houses dominate mile 4 before runners head underneath highway 101 into the heart of the Silicon Valley. After passing dozens of computer companies, some complete and others still under construction, through mile 7, runners then embark on a 4-mile out-and-back section through exposed, undeveloped land paralleling highway 237. You may hardly notice this least scenic section since runners approaching from the opposite direction easily divert your attention. A right turn on Tasman (10.7 miles) leads you through "Cisco Alley'' so named because Cisco Systems occupies both sides of the street. Expect a lot of commotion through this area as the 11- and 20-mile marks and the third relay transition lie here. The next seven miles loop though the "Golden Triangle" in the city of Santa Clara. Three of the world's largest computer companies, Cisco Systems, 3 Com and Bay Networks are all within a five mile region. The roller coasters from Paramount's Great America Amusement Park as well as the 49er's former training site appear on the left as you climb a 30-foot overpass at mile 12 and another 20-footer at 12.2 miles. Though barely worth mentioning, three more bumps occur at miles 13.2, 13.5, and 16, before the course rejoins Tazman. Near 20 miles, runners turn right onto First Street for a five-mile straightaway skirting the grounds of such well known companies as Sun, Digital, Fujitsu, Hitachi, Phillips, Novellus, and Texas Instruments. Take advantage of the aid stations along this mostly shadeless stretch. Near mile 25, a couple quick turns deposit runners onto Market Street where

Silicon Valley Marathon

they pass beautiful St. Joseph's Catholic Church and the San Jose Museum of Art before turning on Park Avenue (site of the race beneficiary Tech Museum of Innovation) and the 150-meter sprint to the finish.

CROWD/RUNNER SUPPORT Due to the nature of the course, don't expect huge crowd participation. Most spectator involvement comes at the start/finish area, relay exchange points, and in Japantown. You will, however, receive excellent volunteer support—over 1,000 dot the course. Aid stations, located every mile, are enthusiastically manned by employees of twenty-five Silicon Valley companies. Light rail transportation parallels the entire route, affording spectators great viewing opportunities. Split timers sit every mile calling running time and projected finish time (a feature overlooked by most races).

RACE LOGISTICS Several downtown hotels lie literally yards from the start/finish area making race morning hassle free for most participants. If driving to the race, parking is not a problem.

ACTIVITIES Pick up your race packet, register, and attend the Sport-Tech Expo on Friday from 3:00 p.m. to 7:00 p.m. or Saturday from 9:00 a.m. to 6:00 p.m. Saturday night, don't miss the Carbo-Loading dinner featuring a spectacular laser light show set to music. A huge finish celebration featuring loads of food, beverages, live entertainment, awards ceremony, and random prizes takes place in Caesar Chavez Park.

AWARDS Every marathoner receives a T-shirt, and finishers earn the coveted computer chip medallion. Top runners and wheelchair racers compete for over $30,000 in prize money. Top age group competitors receive special product prizes and unique "high-tech" designed awards.

ELITE RUNNERS INFORMATION Men under 2:20 and women under 2:50 may qualify for travel and lodging expenses and free entry. The 1998 race featured over $30,000 in prize money, a figure expected to grow in coming years. Bonus money goes to the first sub 2:20 male and sub 2:32 female.

ACCOMMODATIONS The San Jose Hilton & Towers, 300 Almaden Blvd. (800-445-8667) serves as the official race hotel offering special rates for contestants. Other nearby hotels offering special rates include: The Fairmont Hotel, 170 South Market Street (800-527-4727); and Crowne Plaza San Jose, 282 Almaden Blvd. (800-2-Crowne).

RELATED EVENTS/RACES Race day includes a full menu of events in addition to the marathon. A half marathon and four-person relay leave with the marathon at 7:30 a.m. Short distance specialists can compete in the 5K (8:00 a.m.) where winners earn lap top computers. Kid's races begin at 10:30 a.m. for children 12 & under. Distances range from 10 yards to 1 mile.

AREA ATTRACTIONS Don't leave town without visiting the brand new Tech Museum of Innovation featuring incredible high-tech displays and an IMAX theatre. San Jose lies in the heart of the bay area, close to all of the popular locales including San Francisco, Monterey and the wine country. Treat the kids to Paramount's Great America Amusement Park in neighboring Santa Clara, or take in a San Jose Sharks hockey game.

New York City Marathon

OVERALL: 99.9

COURSE BEAUTY: 8+

COURSE DIFFICULTY: 4+ (SEE APPENDIX)

APPROPRIATENESS FOR FIRST TIMERS: 10

RACE ORGANIZATION: 10

CROWDS: 10+

RACE DATA

Overall Ranking: 2
Quickness Ranking: 52
Contact: New York City Marathon
New York Road Runners Club
9 E. 89th Street
New York, NY 10128
Tel. (212) 423-2249
Fax (212) 348-9614
E-mail: susana@nyrrc.org
http://www.nyrrc.org/mar.htm
Date: November 7, 1999; November 5, 2000
Start Time: 10:50 a.m.
Time Course Closes: NA
Number of Finishers: 30,427 in 1997
Course: Point to point
Certification: USATF
Course Records: Male: (open) 2:08:01
Female: (open) 2:24:40
Elite Athlete Programs: Yes
Cost: $35/45
Age groups/Divisions: 18-19, 20-29, 30-39, 40-49, 50-59, 60-69, 70-79,
80+
Walkers: Yes
Requirements: 18 years old
Temperature: 42° - 55°
Aid/Splits: 24 / digital clocks every mile

HIGHLIGHTS   Perhaps the most exciting marathon in the world, the New York City Marathon overwhelms the senses with its sights, smells, sounds, and energy. Over 60,000 runners vie for the 29,000 slots each year. The first Sunday each November, the lucky winners fill the upper and lower spans of the Verrazano-Narrows Bridge anxiously awaiting their trek through the five boroughs that comprise New York City and over the five bridges that connect each borough to the next. Over 2 million cheering spectators surround the course, buoying your every step.

RACE HISTORY   The New York City Marathon's humble beginnings may surprise runners new to the sport. Legendary runner Fred Lebow, who died of brain cancer in 1994, founded the marathon in 1970. Held entirely within Central Park, the race vanquished 72 of its 127 starters. One hundred hard-core spectators witnessed Gary Muhrcke's victory in 2:31:38, with the top finishers earning cheap wrist watches and recycled bowling trophies. With grueling 80° temperatures, the survivors rushed to the waiting cans of soda only to find there were no can openers!

In 1976, the race finally left Central Park for the five boroughs of the city. To keep things interesting, however, organizers threw in a flight of stairs on the course. Bill Rodgers won his first of four in a row that year, only to discover afterward that his car had been towed. In 1979, Grete Waitz of Norway entered her first marathon here, the start of her nine victories in eleven years. In 1981, both the men's and women's winners broke the then-world marathon record, with Alberto Salazar finishing in 2:08:13 and Allison Roe recording a 2:25:29. In 1994, eventual winner German Silva of Mexico nearly blew it at the end when he took his eye off the blue line and took a wrong turn in Central Park. He quickly recovered and snatched the victory in the closest finish in NYC's history. Things are never dull in New York.

COURSE DESCRIPTION Located on Staten Island, the marathon's three starting lines lie at the Verrazano-Narrows Toll Plaza. Runners use both the upper and lower spans of the bridge, the longest single suspension bridge in the world. Elite men and men under 3:30 start at the blue line on the Brooklyn-bound, right-side upper level. Local elite men and men over 3:30 start at the green line on the Staten Island-bound lower level. All women start at the red line on the Staten Island-bound upper level. After going up the bridge, about a 180-foot climb, runners hit the first mile mark at its midpoint and the second mile mark at the exit ramps. Miles 3 through 13 course through Brooklyn, passing Bay Ridge at mile 3, Fort Greene at mile 8, Bedford-Stuyvesant at mile 9, and Williamsburg at mile 11. The half-marathon point lies on the Pulaski Bridge (about a 40-foot incline) connecting Brooklyn and Queens (mile 13.1 to 15.5). The course heads through Long Island City, a manufacturing area since the industrial revolution and now home to the Silvercup Studios, often referred to as Hollywood East. At mile 15, runners climb 130 feet up the Queensboro Bridge, spanning the East River and Roosevelt Island, bringing them to Manhattan (mile 16 to 20). North on First Avenue, you pass through the Upper East Side, known as the silk stocking district; Yorkville in the East 80s, formerly a thriving German community; and then Spanish Harlem. Just before mile 20, you encounter the challenging Willis Avenue Bridge over the Harlem River. At mile 20, you make a quick trip through the ethnically diverse Bronx before hitting the final bridge, the Madison Avenue Bridge, leading back into Manhattan. The next two miles traverse Harlem, the center of black culture famous for its dance and music. The final miles tour rolling, challenging Central Park, one of the world's great urban retreats, finishing at Tavern on the Green.

HOW TO ENTER The New York City Marathon has instituted new entry procedures starting in 1998, including requiring an unfortunate (in our opinion) application fee. United States residents outside New York should request an entry form by sending a self-addressed, stamped, business-sized envelope and a $7 non-refundable handling fee (check payable to NYRRC or credit card information) to: Marathon Entries, P.O. Box 1388, G.P.O., New York, NY 10116. You can also request your form by e-mail using the electronic application request form in the NYRRC's web site (and including your credit card information). You may request your entry form at any time, but you may not return it to the New York Road Runners Club until the day after the Central Park Marathon Line-Up (noted in the race brochure). New Yorkers can attend the annual Central Park Marathon Line-Up to pick up their entry form. Standing in this line gives you slightly better odds of being accepted than receiving your entry by mail. Make sure to bring your $7 check. The first 17,000 runners are accepted on a first-come, first-served basis, with 7,500 from the Marathon Line-Up, 2,500 others drawn from New York, New Jersey, and Connecticut, and 7,000 drawn from the rest of the country. The next 3,000 runners are determined by a lottery held in July or August. The last 10,000 entries are reserved for international runners based on a quota system by country. Accepted runners are notified within about four weeks. The race maintains a wait list to fill spaces vacated by runners who are forced to cancel. For the latest entry information, check out the New York Road Runners Club's web site (see contact information).

CROWD/RUNNER SUPPORT Banners hang prominently along the race course and in midtown Manhattan, gearing up community support for the marathon. On race

New York City Marathon

day, spectators turn out in tremendous numbers, with approximately 2 million viewing the race. More than 40 bands of all flavors speckle the course, providing a lift to tired runners. Twenty-four water stations line the course every mile starting at mile 3, with electrolyte replacement drink available every two miles beginning at mile 4 and every mile beginning at mile 22. A sponge station lies just after mile 18; sponges can be replenished in the kiddie pools from miles 19 to 25. Digital clocks indicate the elapsed time every mile, and several video checkpoints ensure race integrity.

RACE LOGISTICS Since the Verrazano-Narrows Bridge closes at 9:00 a.m., we recommend taking the race buses to the start area. Although unfortunately an expensive ride at $7 a head, it will eliminate much worry and aggravation on race morning. Buses pick up runners at the New York City Public Library at Fifth Avenue and 42nd Street between 5:30 a.m. and 7:30 a.m. You must purchase a ticket ahead of time at the Runner's Expo. The race will transport your warm-ups to the finish area.

ACTIVITIES On Wednesday through Saturday before the marathon, you can attend the marathon expo at the Show Piers on the Hudson lcoated at Piers 90 and 92, 12th Avenue and 55th Street on Manhattan's West Side. Bring your registration card and a photo ID to retrieve your race packet, and check out the approximately 80 exhibitor booths. You can also buy NYC Marathon souvenirs at the marathon gift shop in the Coliseum. The race holds a number of clinics and seminars which may interest you. See your information package for this year's topics. On Saturday evening from 4:30 p.m. to 9:30 p.m., join 17,000 other runners and guests at the pasta party at Tavern on the Green under the big tent. On race morning, munch on bagels at the start area to fuel your journey. After your race, meet your family and friends at the Family Reunion Festival on Central Park West from Columbus Circle to 72nd Street. The festival features food, beverage, music, and a giant screen projecting the race. The awards ceremony and Celebration Party are held at the Roseland Ballroom and Disco, 239 West 52nd Street, at 7:30 p.m. and 8:30 p.m., respectively.

AWARDS Every NYC Marathon entrant receives an official race T-shirt and poster. Those who complete the race also receive finisher medals, and women receive a red rose. Age-group winners receive Tiffany trophies as do the top runners from each New York borough. Awards also go to the top three international teams, USATF-sanctioned teams, top five NYRRC local runners, and the oldest male and female to finish the race.

ELITE RUNNERS INFORMATION As expected, the NYC Marathon actively recruits the top runners from around the world. Elites are offered transportation, lodging, expenses, and the chance to take home a sizeable paycheck. The top six overall finishers respectively earn: $50,000 plus a new automobile, $25,000, $12,500, $7,500, $5,000, and $2,000. American citizens who finish in the top five earn double the above amounts. The race has established time bonuses for runners breaking 2:13 for men and 2:30 for women ($3,000) up to $65,000 for sub 2:07 and 2:22 times. The top three masters are awarded $3,000, $2,000, and $1,000. Prize money also goes to the top local teams and individuals, including time incentives.

ACCOMMODATIONS Two hotels serve as the NYC Marathon co-headquarters, the New York Hilton and Towers, 1335 Avenue of the Americas, between 53rd and 54th Streets (212-586-7000); and the Sheraton New York Hotel & Towers, 811 Seventh Avenue, between 52nd and 53rd Streets (212-581-1000). Runners who would like to stay at either hotel must complete an application provided with their acceptance notification. The race also provides a Hotel Guide listing scores of other possible lodgings.

RELATED EVENTS/RACES The race sponsors the International Friendship Run, a four-mile fun run held the day before the marathon at 8:00 a.m. Exclusively for international runners and their families, runners follow their country's flag from the United Nations to Tavern on the Green in Central Park. After the jaunt, runners swap T-shirts and pins with fellow marathoners from around the world.

The New York City Marathon®

*Five Bridges • Five Boroughs
and a 26.2-Mile Standing Ovation*

November 7, 1999 • November 5, 2000

www.nycmarathon.org • 212-423-2249

This is the truth.

We didn't come here to argue about shoe technology. You've probably noticed, if you've read any shoe ads, that every company bickers about their cushioning technology being the best. Good for them. We feel the same way. But we also know that a great running shoe is about more than comfort. So we also make sure it's got the technical features you need. You may not fully appreciate these features when you're standing in the shoe store. But then, you're not buying them to stand around in.

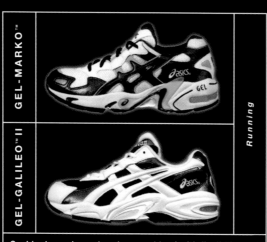

GEL-MARKO™

GEL-GALILEO™ II

Running

Cushioning only works when combined with flexibility and fit. We balanced these features for shoes that really perform. But don't take our word for it, take them out for a test ride.

OCEAN STATE MARATHON

OVERALL: 86.4

COURSE BEAUTY: 9

COURSE DIFFICULTY: 5- (SEE APPENDIX)

APPROPRIATENESS FOR FIRST TIMERS: 8

RACE ORGANIZATION: 9

CROWDS: 3-

RACE DATA

Overall Ranking:	41
Quickness Ranking:	71
Contact:	Ocean State Marathon
	5 Division Street
	East Greenwich, RI 02818
	Tel. (401) 885-4499
	Fax (401) 885-3188
	E-mail: osm26@ids.net
	http://www.osm26.com
Date:	November 6, 1999; November 4, 2000
Start Time:	9:00 a.m.
Time Course Closes:	2:30 p.m.
Number of Finishers:	Point to point
Course:	1,300 in 1997
Certification:	USATF
Course Records:	Male: (open) 2:16:12; (masters) 2:25:20
	Female: (open) 2:35:51; (masters) 2:54:01
Elite Athlete Programs:	Yes
Cost:	$30/40/50
Age groups/Divisions:	≤39, 40-49, 50-59, 60+, wheelchair
Walkers:	No
Requirements:	None
Temperature:	47° - 63°
Aid/Splits:	15 / digital clocks at miles 5, 10, halfway, 15, 20 & 25.2

HIGHLIGHTS   Believe in reincarnation? Ocean State Marathon ("OSM") organizers do. OSM, which traces Rhode Island's coast from Narragansett to Warwick, springs from the original Ocean State race held in Newport from 1976 to 1986. The current Ocean State offers a scenic, point-to-point, moderately difficult course. Weather can play a real factor in Rhode Island—you may face a Nor-Easter head on, or you may be blessed with a tailwind all the way to Warwick. Quickly on the road toward recapturing its former glory, OSM already ranks as one of the top races in New England.

RACE HISTORY   The Ocean State Marathon started in 1976 in Newport, Rhode Island. Very successful, the race peaked with more than 2,500 runners in 1979. After losing its primary sponsor, the race was canceled in 1987 when no alternative sponsor emerged. Revived in 1988 as the Rhode Island Marathon ("RIM"), the race was run on a variety of courses on Aquidneck Island until 1992 when it looped from Warwick to Providence. Around that time, several race committee members became disillusioned with the direction the RIM had taken. They began exploring the possibility of resuscitating the Ocean State Marathon. In 1993, the new Ocean State threw down the gauntlet, holding its race one week prior to RIM and within miles of each other. RIM folded the following year, and Ocean State doubled to over 1,100 entrants.

COURSE DESCRIPTION Ocean State's scenic, moderately challenging, point-to-point course starts on Kingstown Road at Sprague Park in Narragansett (adjacent to the high school). Gaining 28 feet in the first mile, runners then go downhill about 60 feet to the seawall at mile 2. As you turn onto the shoulder of Ocean Road (Scenic Route 1A), you will either be nailed by a stern headwind or graced with a pleasant tailwind. The next mile and a half along the coast remain flat and beautiful. At 3.5 miles, the course rises 40 feet and then falls 30 feet at 4 miles. Now begins the first real climb on the course, a 105-footer over 2 miles. Mostly flat, the next 3 miles (6 to 9) provide a nice respite before the second big climb from mile 9 to 10. Just after the 9-mile mark, look to your right for a great view of Narragansett Bay and the Newport Bridge. From the Casey Farm at 9 to Heffie's at 10, you climb another 85 feet. Then you face a steep downhill (120 feet) to mile 11 on a newly paved road. Try not to get too carried away here. You'll enjoy the flat stretch from mile 11 to 12.7, since you climb another 44 feet to 13, before dropping 30 feet into the charming village of Wickford. Savor these next two miles because the course's complexion soon changes. At 14.2, runners turn right on Route 1 climbing 40 feet in the process. The next five miles on Route 1 roll with about four noticeable ups and downs. This relatively tedious section may be the most difficult psychologically for many runners since it runs by fast-food joints, stores, bowling alleys, and lots of concrete. Just before mile 20, runners face the toughest hill on the course, a short, steep 80-footer. The next mile proceeds down affluent East Greenwich's Main Street. Mostly flat until mile 22.5, the route features two more down and ups from 22.5 to 23.2 and from 23.8 to 24 while becoming flat again the final 2.2 miles through residential Warwick.

CROWD/RUNNER SUPPORT Approximately 5,000 to 10,000 people come out to support the runners, with the largest clumps at 10K, miles 10, 13.1, 14, 20, 21 and the finish. Twelve aid stations offering water and electrolyte replacement dot the course at approximately miles 2.5, 4.5, 7, 9, 11.5, 14, 16, 18.5, 19.5, 21, 23, and 25. Digital clocks are located at miles 1, 5, 10, 15, 20, and 25.2, and every mile is marked. Music and other entertainment provide inspiration at several points, while four medical units provide mending.

RACE LOGISTICS You can either drive to the start or take the race bus from the finish area. Buses leave from Warwick Veterans Memorial High School from 6:30 a.m. to 7:30 a.m. If you drive to the start, park at Narragansett High School parking lot, and make sure someone will pick you up at the finish since there is no bus from the finish back to the start after the race. To get to the starting line, walk a short distance down Prospect Avenue at the back of the school to Kingstown Road. The race transports your sweats and other gear to the finish for you to retrieve.

ACTIVITIES The Health and Fitness Fair goes from 10:00 a.m. to 4:00 p.m. on Saturday. Browse informational booths, buy race apparel, pick up your race packet, or register late for the race. You can register on race morning at Narragansett High School from 7:00 a.m. to 8:30 a.m. Saturday evening, dine at the pasta dinner (about $10) at a local restaurant. After the marathon, enjoy a well-deserved massage, shower, and food, such as clam chowder, donuts, and pizza. At 2:00 p.m., the awards ceremony kicks off in the auditorium, followed by a raffle.

AWARDS Every entrant receives a long-sleeve T-shirt and a race program book. Finishers garner unique medallions, certificates, and complete results, including individual performance data. OSM offers approximately $30,000 in prize money for individuals and teams.

ELITE RUNNERS INFORMATION OSM may award elite status to men under 2:20 and women under 2:50. Elites may be offered some travel money, lodging, and free entry and compete for about $20,000 in prize money. The top five overall runners earn $2,000, $1,500, $1,000, $750, and $500; the top three masters runners (40-49) garner $500 $400, and $200; the top two seniors (50-59) earn $300 and $200; and the top veteran (60+) earns $250. Special awards also go to the top Rhode Island finishers. Additionally, over $65,000 in prize money is available for course records and time incentives.

ACCOMMODATIONS The Sheraton Tara Airport Hotel, 1850 Post Road, Warwick (800-THE TARA), serves as the host hotel. The Tara offers discount packages to Ocean State runners, about $75 a night. Other possibilities include: Comfort Inn, 1940 Post Road (401-732-0470); Radisson Hotel, 2081 Post Road (401-739-3000); Master Hosts Inn, 2138 Post Road (401-737-7400); Holiday Inn at the Crossings, 800 Greenwich Avenue (401-732-6000); Marriott Residence Inn, 500 Kilvert Street (401-737-7100); Susse Chalet Inn, 36 Jefferson Blvd. (401-941-6600); and Crossroads Inn, 20 Jefferson Blvd. (401-467-9800).

AREA ATTRACTIONS The 400 miles of coastline attract most people to Rhode Island. Perhaps most famous is Newport, site of some of the most monied homes on the East Coast and one of the world's best music spectacles, the Newport Jazz Festival held every Spring. Block Island, an excellent daytrip, lies southeast of Newport. Perhaps best toured by bicycle, Block Island offers wild natural splendor packed into 21 square miles.

SAN ANTONIO MARATHON

OVERALL: 84.1

COURSE BEAUTY: 8-

COURSE DIFFICULTY: 3+

APPROPRIATENESS FOR FIRST TIMERS: 8-

RACE ORGANIZATION: 9-

CROWDS: 4

RACE DATA

Overall Ranking: 59
Quickness Ranking: 39
Contact: San Antonio Marathon
1123 Navarro
San Antonio, TX 78205-2196
(210) 246-9652
http://www.samarathon.org

Date: November 7, 1999; November 5, 2000
Start Time: 7:00 a.m.
Time Course Closes: 12:30 p.m.
Number of Finishers: 1,500 in 1997
Course: Loop
Certification: USATF
Course Records: Male: (open) 2:22:40; (masters) 2:32:35
Female: (open) 2:47:33; (masters) 3:10:20
Elite Athlete Programs: No
Cost: $30/40
Age groups/Divisions: ≤19, 20-24, 25-29, 30-34, 35-39, 40-44, 45-49,
50-54, 55-59, 60-64, 65-69, 70+
Walkers: No
Requirements: None
Temperature: 62°
Aid/Splits: 12 / every mile including pace

HIGHLIGHTS   The cradle of Texan independence, San Antonio retains many monuments to its frontier past, and the San Antonio Marathon passes most of them. The Alamo, Mission Concepcion, Fort Sam Houston, King William District, and historic downtown all lie on the course, as well as some more modern monuments like the Alamodome and the Tower of the Americas. After the race, plenty of San Antonio remains to be explored, and we believe you will quickly understand why San Antonio is becoming one of the United States' top tourist destinations.

COURSE DESCRIPTION   The San Antonio Marathon starts north of the Alamodome, workplace of the NBA San Antonio Spurs, and heads to HemisFair Plaza, site of the 1968 World's Fair and current home to the Tower of the Americas and the renowned Institute of Texan Cultures (mile 1). After completing a semicircle of the plaza, the course returns to the Alamodome (mile 3). After crossing the freeway again, the race proceeds through historic downtown and passes the San Antonio Museum of Art (miles 4 to 5). Winding through an older commercial district (mile 5) and older residential neighborhood (mile 6), runners reach the first hill of the course, a 100-foot climb over 300 yards just before Fort Sam Houston (miles 7 to 11). Runners enter Fort Sam at the historic quadrangle and proceed slightly downhill for 100 yards. The course takes in the most scenic sections of the fort, passing stately houses of base bigwigs, the parade grounds, and the Brooke Army Medical Center (BAMC). The marathon exits Fort Sam and heads to beautiful Brackenridge Park (miles 12 to 14), passing the Witte Museum, San Antonio Zoo, and Japanese Tea Gardens. Runners then go straight down North St. Mary's Street, a fairly nice commercial road, from miles 14 to 17, with the Tower of the Americas looming ahead. By mile 16 you're back downtown and go right past HemisFair Plaza into the historic south section of town (miles 18 to 23). The turnaround point is located at Mission Concepcion, which dates from 1731. The runners then head back to the finish in the North Plaza of the Alamodome.

CROWD/RUNNER SUPPORT Several thousand race fans cheer on the runners, with the greatest concentrations near the start/finish, downtown, and the half marathon point. The aid stations, well stocked for San Antonio's weather, carry water, electrolyte replacement, fruit, and medical aid. Portable toilets are also located near each aid station.

RACE LOGISTICS The start and finish are located near many downtown hotels so transportation is not an issue unless you are staying further out. If you drive to the start, try parking on Durango Street across from the Federal Office Building or around the Alamodome.

ACTIVITIES On Friday evening and all day Saturday, you can register, pick up your race packet, and attend the Sports Expo and Health Fair at the Downtown YMCA Branch, 903 N. St. Mary's. There is no race-day registration or packet pick up. On race afternoon, enjoy music, beverages, baked potatoes, cookies, fruit, and other tidbits.

AWARDS Every marathon entrant receives a short-sleeve T-shirt, while each finisher also receives a long-sleeve T-shirt and a medal. Age-group awards range from three to five deep, with winners receiving trophies. Top runners compete for approximately $5,000 in prize money. The top four overall runners earn: $1,000, $500, $250, and $125. The top three masters runners take home $250, $125, and $75. Awards are not duplicated.

ACCOMMODATIONS The Sheraton Four Points Hotel, 110 Lexington (210-223-9461) serves as the host hotel offering special rates to San Antonio Marathon runners. Other convenient hotels include: Best Western Historic Crockett Hotel, 320 Bonham Street (800-292-1050); Days Inn at the Alamo Riverwalk, 902 E. Houston Street (210-227-6233); the historic Fairmont Hotel, 401 S. Alamo (210-224-8800); Holiday Inn Riverwalk, 217 North St. Mary's Street (210-224-2500); Howard Johnson Riverwalk Plaza-Hotel, 100 Villita Street (800-554-HOST); Hyatt Regency, 123 Losoya Street (210-222-1234); and Radisson Downtown Market Square, 502 West Durango (800-333-3333) or (210-224-7155).

RELATED EVENTS/RACES Two runners can join together to compete in the marathon relay, with each runner completing a half marathon. Road runners may consider the San Antonio Mayor's 5-mile Challenge Run, starting at 7:45 a.m., through downtown San Antonio. Walkers may be interested in the Celebration for Fitness Walk, a scenic three-mile fun walk beginning at 8:00 a.m. Finally, keep the kids happy with the Roger Soler's Sports Kids Klassic, a quarter-mile run through the Alamodome for children 10 and under (8:30 a.m.).

AREA ATTRACTIONS San Antonio boasts lots of points of interest, most of which center around its rich history. Every visitor must visit the Alamo, site of that famous stand against General Santa Anna. You will also want to explore the local missions founded by Spanish missionaries in the 18th century. Stroll down San Antonio's teeming urban canal, the famous Riverwalk, a great place to get a bite to eat, shop, or simply people watch. Worthwhile museums include Witte Museum, Pioneer Hall, Institute of Texan Cultures, and San Antonio Museum of Art. Spelunkers may want to check out the Natural Bridge Caverns about 17 miles outside of San Antonio. Basketball fans may be able to catch a San Antonio Spurs game at the Alamodome.

CITY OF SANTA CLARITA MARATHON

OVERALL: 78.2

COURSE BEAUTY: 7+

COURSE DIFFICULTY: 3+

APPROPRIATENESS FOR FIRST TIMERS: 7

RACE ORGANIZATION: 9+

CROWDS: 3-

RACE DATA

Overall Ranking: **97**
Quickness Ranking: **40**
Contact: **City of Santa Clarita Marathon, Inc.**
P.O. Box 800646
Santa Clarita, CA 91380-0646
(805) 259-7149 or (888) 823-3455
http://www.santaclarita.com/marathon

Date: **November 7, 1999; November 5, 2000**
Start Time: **6:30 a.m.**
Time Course Closes: **1:00 p.m.**
Number of Finishers: **682 in 1997**
Course: **Point to point**
Certification: **USATF**
Course Records: **Male: (open) 2:30:54; (masters) 2:47:38**
Female: (open) 3:06:28; (masters) 3:15:22
Elite Athlete Programs: **No**
Cost: **$40/50**
Age groups/Divisions: **18-24, 25-29, 30-34, 35-39, 40-44, 45-49, 50-54,**
55-59, 60-64, 65-69, 70+
Walkers: **Yes, if can finish in time limit**
Requirements: **None**
Temperature: **44° - 60°**
Aid/Splits: **26 / every mile, 10K & halfway**

HIGHLIGHTS   You had hoped to go to Orlando this winter for the Walt Disney World Marathon. Maybe you live in California and just don't have the funds for the trip. The next best thing may be Six Flags California and its Colossus roller coaster, which lies on the path of the City of Santa Clarita Marathon. This fresh, exuberant race burst on the Southern California running scene in 1995 with an impressive debut and envious budget for a first-time affair. With grand growth plans, the race may eventually become a national draw, but for now it is a nice alternative for Californians worried about spending too much money around Christmas.

COURSE DESCRIPTION   The City of Santa Clarita Marathon's point-to-point course journeys through all four Santa Clarita communities—Saugus, Newhall, Valencia, and Canyon Country—utilizing streets, trails, and paseos. Nestled among mountain ranges in view throughout the course, the rural-flavored course is completely closed to traffic. Beginning at the historic Lang Station area in Canyon Country, the route follows a gentle, downhill slope on tree-lined streets past residential communities and the flowered hillsides of Canyon Country Park. At the first intersection on the course, runners glimpse a continuous parade of restaurants, shopping centers, and homes. The course drops off the street onto the Santa Clara River trail and remains on this asphalt bike path to Golden Oak, where it jumps back onto Soledad Canyon Road. As they continue past the infamous Saugus Speedway, runners catch a peek at the bargain hunter's paradise, the Saugus Swap Meet. At mile 12, the course begins a gentle ascent until its peak at mile 16. Runners soon jump onto the South Fork Trail and eventually pass through Old Town Newhall. Again passing through tree-lined, residential streets, runners practically tiptoe through backyards as they run on the Valencia paseo system. The paseo system includes several overpass bridges and underpasses, after which runners pass the renowned California Institute of the Arts while encountering their toughest hill at 16. But, it's a downhill relief for the next mile into the main entrance of College of the Canyons, through its campus and past the baseball field to Valencia Blvd. and the Old Road. While crossing the Golden State Freeway, runners hear the roar of 30,000 Harley Davidsons as their riders motor through on their annual Love Ride. Another downhill slope leads into Six Flags California, where runners come within yards of the rollercoaster Colossus, Hurricane Harbor, and the new Superman ride. At last, the course passes through the Valencia Business Park, a flat, secluded complex of large buildings and home of several movie and sound studios. From the business park, runners emerge into a mix of empty fields and retail centers and finish at the Valencia Town Center shopping mall in the heart of Santa Clarita.

CROWD / RUNNER SUPPORT   The Santa Clarita communities genuinely support the marathon, with spectators dotting most of the course. CSCM offers outstanding runner support with 26 water stations along the course including electrolyte replacement drink from mile 5 through 25. There are five medical aid stations, toilets at every mile, and a sponge station at mile 22. Mile splits are called every mile, at 10K and the halfway point.

RACE LOGISTICS   The race designates a parking area near the finish line and offers shuttle bus service from the assembly area to the start from 5:30 a.m. to 6:15 a.m. Don't worry about your warm-ups; the race transports them from the start to the finish for you to retrieve.

ACTIVITIES   The Business, Sports, and Fitness Expo goes on Saturday, noon to 6:00 p.m. at the Hyatt/Santa Clarita Conference Center. A pasta dinner is held Saturday evening. There is no race-day registration. Family music and entertainment keep you occupied after the marathon. Expo booths also sit around the finish area for you to browse while you await the awards ceremony at noon. You can also stroll through Valencia Town Center for food, shopping, and movies.

AWARDS   All race entrants receive T-shirts, while finishers earn commemorative medals. Overall winners receive trophies, while the top finishers are awarded plaques.

ACCOMMODATIONS   The official race hotel is the Hyatt Valencia, 24500 Town Center Drive, Valencia (800-233-1234). Others convenient to the course are: Hampton Inn, 25259 The Old Road, Newhall (805-253-2400); Marriott Fairfield, 25340 The Old Road, Stevenson Ranch (805-290-2828); and Valencia Hilton at Six Flags, 27710 The Old Road, Valencia (800-445-8667); the Best Western Ranch House Inn, 27413 Tourney Road, Valencia (805-255-0555); and Country Inn, 17901 Sierra Highway, Santa Clarita (800-537-8930).

RELATED EVENTS / RACES   Santa Clarita holds two related events at the marathon finish line—a 10-Mile Run on an out-and-back route covering the final five miles of the marathon course (designated an official training run for the LA Marathon), and a Kiddie K Fun Run for children 12 and under.

AREA ATTRACTIONS   Kids and grownups alike will enjoy the Six Flags California amusement park in Valencia and Mountasia Fun Center in Canyon Country. Bargain hunters may want to check out the Saugus Swap Meet on Sundays. Several film studios mark the area, including Melody Ranch. Los Angeles lies only a short drive away.

COLUMBUS MARATHON

OVERALL: 90

COURSE BEAUTY: 9-

COURSE DIFFICULTY: 3- (SEE APPENDIX)

APPROPRIATENESS FOR FIRST TIMERS: 10-

RACE ORGANIZATION: 10-

CROWDS: 7+

R A C E   D A T A

Overall Ranking: 22
Quickness Ranking: 22
Contact: Columbus Marathon
P.O. Box 26806
Columbus, OH 43226
Tel. (614) 433-0395
Fax (614) 433-0330
http://www.columbusmarathon.com
Date: November 14, 1999; November 12, 2000
Start Time: 9:00 a.m.
Time Course Closes: 2:30 p.m.
Number of Finishers: 2,857 in 1997
Course: Loop
Certification: USATF
Course Records: Male: (open) 2:11:02; (masters) 2:20:23
Female: (open) 2:30:54; (masters) 2:38:07
Elite Athlete Programs: Yes
Cost: $35/45
Age groups/Divisions: 18-19, 20-24, 25-29, 30-34, 35-39, 40-44, 45-49,
50-54, 55-59, 60-64, 65-69, 70+, wheelchair
Clydesdales (males 200+, females 140+): 18-39, 40+
Walkers: No
Requirements: 18 years old
Temperature: 43° - 53°
Aid/Splits: 12 / digital clocks every mile & 5K, including pace &
projected finish

HIGHLIGHTS Fast, detailed, and runner-friendly, the Columbus Marathon regularly attracts 4,000 runners, many looking to improve their marathon mark. Columbus' excellent reputation led to its designation as the U.S. Men's Olympic Marathon Trials in 1992. The unique course design, called a cloverleaf by organizers, resembles the profile of a roadrunner, with the three loops depicting its tail, body/head, and leg. The layout allows runners to cover many of Columbus' most interesting neighborhoods, such as Short North, Ohio State University, Bexley, and German Village. Those not familiar with the city may be pleasantly surprised at what it offers, including museums, theaters, shopping, and diverse dining. Weather, the biggest variable, can range from cold and blustery to unseasonably warm.

COURSE DESCRIPTION Columbus' layout makes it spectator friendly, easy for tired runners to drop out, and more scenic than many loop courses. Completely closed to traffic, the race begins on High Street, the city's main drag, in front of the Nationwide Insurance Building.

After a gentle down and up start through the Short North, with its galleries, trendy shops, and restaurants, the race turns flat until about 2.5 miles. A short rise, followed by a quick downhill leads to 3.7 miles. The runners pass the Ohio State agricultural areas here as they prepare for the 85-foot ascent into Upper Arlington, a quiet suburban community with tree-lined streets and some interesting homes. Beginning at mile 4, the climb concludes at mile 6.2. After a few minor ups and downs, the course descends gradually to the Ohio State University, passing Ohio Stadium, home of perennial Big Ten power Ohio State Buckeyes football team, at 10 miles. Leaving the campus, runners traipse down Neil Avenue and Victorian Village, with its renovated, turn-of-the-century homes. Passing by shady Goodale Park, the course returns to High Street, retracing its path through the Short North. Runners return downtown at mile 13.5 and turn east for a peek into the original Wendy's restaurant, followed by the Columbus Museum of Art. At mile 16, runners make a circuit around Franklin Park, home of the beautifully restored 1895 conservatory. Affluent Bexley, site of the Ohio Governor's Mansion and other distinguished homes, awaits at mile 17. The course from downtown to Bexley is generally flat with a few minor grades. Runners exit Bexley at mile 20. From here, the race features long, gentle rolls. At mile 22, the course passes Olde Towne East, one of Columbus' oldest neighborhoods, and Topiary Garden on East Town Street, reaching German Village at mile 23. The largest privately-funded restoration project in the country, German Villages' cobbled streets (none on the runners' route), beer halls, and proud brick homes will beckon your return after the race.

CROWD / RUNNER SUPPORT   Columbus' course gives downtown onlookers a chance to catch their favorite runner four times during the race—the start, mile 13.5, mile 23, and the finish—by walking only a few blocks. Crowd support at other sections of the course is also surprisingly strong, with approximately 100,000 people cheering the runners. Runners also find entertainment, including professional and high school bands, at a number of areas, especially at Schiller Park. Many of Columbus' 2,400 volunteers man the aid stations at even miles, which stock water and electrolyte replacement drink, and the 13 portable toilet stations at odd miles. Columbus' enthusiastic helpers consistently receive high marks from runners year after year. Among the race's other notable details are the digital clocks located every mile and 5K, including overall time, pace, and projected finish.

RACE LOGISTICS   Columbus' compact downtown means most hotels lie near the race staging area, making transportation to the start unnecessary. However, a shuttle bus from the finish area will return you to the Hyatt Regency (pick-up at Broad and High Streets). For those driving into town, there is plenty of inexpensive, convenient, garage parking.

ACTIVITIES   Packet pick-up and late registration are located at the Marathon Expo in the Hyatt Regency Ballroom. Runners may retrieve their packets on Friday, 4:00 p.m. to 9:00 p.m., Saturday, 9:00 a.m. to 8:00 p.m., and Sunday, 6:00 a.m. to 8:00 a.m. There is no race-day registration. On Saturday, attend clinics on a variety of subjects, including the popular Columbus Marathon 101 which gives advice to Columbus first-timers on how to run the race. Saturday night, the race holds a pasta party (about $10) in the Nationwide Insurance Cafeteria, connected by walkway to the Hyatt Regency.

AWARDS   Every marathon entrant receives a high-quality T-shirt, results magazine, and official race program, and finishers also earn medals and certificates. Age-group awards go mostly five deep. Finally, about $70,000 in prize money is up for grabs.

ELITE RUNNERS INFORMATION   Male runners under 2:20 and female runners under 2:45 may qualify for elite status at Columbus. Elites may be offered travel, accommodations, and free entry. Promising young runners may also receive a complimentary entry. In addition, Columbus offers prize money totaling approximately $70,000, doled out to the top 5 overall finishers, top five Ohioans, and top five masters. Specifically, the top 5 finishers (male and female) earn $5,000, $2,500, $1,250, $750, and $500, respectively. Masters winners and top Ohioans receive $500, $300, $200, $150, and $100. A runner who sets a new course record

receives $10,000.

ACCOMMODATIONS Conveniently located at the start and a few blocks from the finish, the Hyatt Regency, 350 North High Street (614-463-1234), serves as the host hotel. Also convenient are the Hyatt on Capitol Square, 75 East State Street (614-228-1234); Holiday Inn City Center, 175 E. Town Street (614-221-3281); Holiday Inn Crowne Plaza, 33 E. Nationwide Blvd. (614-461-4100); Hojo Inn Downtown, 1070 Dublin Road (614-486-4554); Courtyard by Marriott, 145 N. High Street (614-228-2244); Sheraton Suites Columbus, 201 Hutchinson Avenue (614-436-0004); Holiday Inn, 175 Hutchinson Avenue (614-885-3334); and Hampton Inn, 1100 Mediterranean Avenue (614-848-9696). Alternatively, call Peoples Travel (800-336-7662) for hotel accommodations at a special marathon rate.

RELATED EVENTS/RACES Two or three runners can band together to form a marathon relay team in either corporate or non-corporate divisions. Teams may be male, female, or coed. Relay legs run 13.7, 9.5, and 3 miles. Others may choose to run in the 5K, which starts immediately after the marathon/marathon relay. Kids may want to join in the Fun Run following the marathon start. Register at the marathon expo.

AREA ATTRACTIONS A clean, wholesome city, Columbus contains lots of museums, theaters, shopping, and other places of interest. Among them are the Columbus Museum of Art, 480 E. Broad Street; Wexner Center for the Arts on the Ohio State University campus at North High Street and 15th Avenue; the hands-on Center of Science and Industry, 280 E. Broad Street; a replica of Christopher Columbus' Santa Maria at the Riverfront; German Village south of Capitol Square; Short North; and the State Capitol building.

PHILADELPHIA MARATHON

OVERALL: 87.9

COURSE BEAUTY: 8+

COURSE DIFFICULTY: 3- (SEE APPENDIX)

APPROPRIATENESS FOR FIRST TIMERS: 9-

RACE ORGANIZATION: 9

CROWDS: 5-

RACE DATA

Overall Ranking:	29
Quickness Ranking:	27
Contact:	Philadelphia Marathon
	P.O. Box 21601
	Philadelphia, PA 19131-0901
	(215) 685-0054
	http://www.philadelphiamarathon.com
Date:	November 21, 1999; November 19, 2000
Start Time:	8:30 a.m.
Time Course Closes:	2:00 p.m.
Number of Finishers:	4,000 in 1997
Course:	Loop
Certification:	USATF
Course Records:	Male: (open) 2:19:03; (masters) 2:37:10
	Female: (open) 2:39:44; (masters) 2:55:36
Elite Athlete Programs:	No
Cost:	$35/40
Age groups/Divisions:	≤19, 20-29, 30-39, 40-49, 50-59, 60+
Walkers:	Yes
Requirements:	None
Temperature:	54°
Aid/Splits:	12 / digital clocks every mile

HIGHLIGHTS   Run through history in the Philadelphia Marathon, a tour of the original U.S. capital city. The U.S. Mint, Betsy Ross House, Benjamin Franklin's Grave, Independence Hall, University of Pennsylvania, Philadelphia Zoo, and Fairmount Park all lie on the marathon trail. Fairly flat, the loop course includes a 12-mile out-and-back along the Schuylkill River. The Philadelphia Marathon is a growing regional race that could become a national draw, particularly given its setting in America's fifth-largest city.

COURSE DESCRIPTION   Starting at the Philadelphia Museum of Art, the race courses down stately, flag-lined Benjamin Franklin Parkway toward downtown, loops Logan Circle and heads back to the start line. Circling the museum oval, runners return down the parkway to Arch Street (mile 2.5), glimpsing City Hall before passing through Independence National Historical Park after mile 3. Proceeding by the U.S. Mint, Benjamin Franklin's Grave, and Betsy Ross House, the course turns right on Front Street for about two-thirds mile going by the brick fed-

254

Philadelphia Marathon

eral-style townhouses of Society Hill. Briefly on South Street, runners travel down 6th catching glimpses of Norman Rockwell Museum and Independence Hall. Near 5.5 miles, the course heads left on Chestnut crossing the Schuylkill River at 7, into University City. Rising 34 feet between 7 and 8, runners hit the edge of the University of Pennsylvania as they turn right on 34th. Traveling by the Philadelphia Zoo, the course drops about 48 feet between 8 and 9, then climbs 78 feet between 9 and 10. Winding for 2 miles through the Horticultural Center area, runners descend about 80 feet between miles 11 and 12, when the course finds West River Drive on the edge of Fairmount Park. Crossing the Schuylkill River just before 14, the race passes in front of the start before heading north on Kelly Drive tracing the river through the eastern section of Fairmount Park for a 12-mile out-and-back. Passing Boathouse Row, and Falls Bridge, runners turn around near mile 20 in Manayuk, retrace their steps and finish at the Philadelphia Museum of Art.

CROWD/RUNNER SUPPORT   The thickest crowds gather around the Philadelphia Museum of Art, which includes the first 2 miles, mile 14, and the finish line. Music entertains runners at Memorial Hall, West River Drive, and Kelly Drive. The aid stations, located every 2 miles, generally offer water, electrolyte replacement, and minor first-aid.

RACE LOGISTICS   Runners can walk from the Embassy Suites Hotel, the Wyndham Franklin Plaza, and the Holiday Inn Express Midtown to the start, about six to eight blocks away. Runners staying elsewhere have to find their own way to the start. Parking exists around the museum but arrive early.

ACTIVITIES   Go to Memorial Hall in Fairmount Park on Friday, 11:00 a.m. to 8:00 p.m., or Saturday, 10:00 a.m. to 6:00 p.m. to pick up your race packet. Memorial Hall also features a Health and Fitness Expo those same times, including massages and the usual products. On Saturday evening, see how much you can eat at the pasta party ($10) in the Wyndham Franklin Plaza on 17th and Race Streets. Unknot yourself with a free post-race massage, and then enjoy music, refreshments, and an awards ceremony.

AWARDS   Every runner who pays the entry fee receives a marathon T-shirt; those who actually finish also take home a medal and receive a certificate and individual result postcard. Up to the top five finishers in each age group receive trophies, and the front runners compete for $5,000 in prize money.

ACCOMMODATIONS   The Embassy Suites Center City, 18th Street and Benjamin Franklin Parkway (215-561-1776), serves as the headquarters hotel (about $110). Other hotels offering marathon discounts are: Wyndham Franklin Plaza (about $100), 17th and Race Streets (215-448-2000); Holiday Inn Express Midtown (about $80), 1305 Walnut Street (215-735-9300); and Sheraton University City (about $80), 36th and Chestnut Streets (215-387-8000).

RELATED EVENTS/RACES   Those not wanting to compete in the marathon should consider joining the approximately 750 other runners in the Rothman Institute 8K, which starts a half hour after the marathon.

AREA ATTRACTIONS   Much more than a capsule to America's revolutionary past, Philadelphia offers exceptional activities for almost all tastes. Sports fans can catch one of Philadelphia's many professional teams, the 76ers basketball team, Eagles football team, and Flyers hockey team. Cultural buffs should consider the Museum of Art, the Academy of Music which houses the excellent Philadelphia Orchestra, Rodin Museum, Science Center in the Franklin Institute, the Horticultural Center, and the Norman Rockwell Museum. Philadelphia also boasts outstanding restaurants, clubs, and theaters.

ATLANTA MARATHON

OVERALL: 80.2

COURSE BEAUTY: 7+

COURSE DIFFICULTY: 6+

APPROPRIATENESS FOR FIRST TIMERS: 6+

RACE ORGANIZATION: 9+

CROWDS: 2

RACE DATA

Overall Ranking: **86**
Quickness Ranking: **91**
Contact: **Atlanta Marathon**
c/o Atlanta Track Club
3097 East Shadowlawn Avenue, NE
Atlanta, GA 30305
(404) 231-9064

Date: **November 25, 1999; November 23, 2000**
Start Time: **7:30 a.m.**
Time Course Closes: **12:30 p.m.**
Number of Finishers: **1,000+ in 1997**
Course: **Loop**
Certification: **USATF**
Course Records: **Male: (open) 2:29:08; (masters) 2:40:29**
Female: (open) 2:54:14; (masters) 3:12:09
Elite Athlete Programs: **No**
Cost: **$30/50**
Age groups/Divisions: **≤19, 20-24, 25-29, 30-34, 35-39, 40-44, 45-49,**
50-54, 55-59, 60-64, 65-69, 70+
Walkers: **No**
Requirements: **None**
Temperature: **42°**
Aid/Splits: **10 / miles 1, 5, 10, halfway, 15, 20 & 25**

HIGHLIGHTS   Held on Thanksgiving morning, the Atlanta Marathon may be the best appetite enhancer for your holiday feast. Littered with hills sporting names like Cardiac Arrest and Capitol Punishment, the race challenges the most seasoned marathoner. Olympic Games buffs may recognize the course as over 90 percent of it follows the route used for the 1996 Olympic Marathons.

RACE HISTORY   The eighth oldest marathon in the United States, the Atlanta Marathon humbly began with a handful of runners completing a ten-ring merry-go-round around North Fulton Golf Course. No entry blank was needed for the March 1963 race, and no T-shirts or trophies were awarded. The race took on more formal dimensions the following year, and from 1964 to 1980, the marathon ran on a difficult two loops in North Atlanta. In the mid-1970s, the race became the Peach Bowl Marathon and moved to the week between Christmas and New Years. In a bid to attract more than 200 runners, the race moved downtown in 1981 and the race date moved to Thanksgiving. By 1982, 902 hardy souls finished the race. The race faced another course change in the early 1980s, and then in 1992, the present course debuted. The marathon now attracts about 1,000 entrants, and its accompanying half marathon draws over 7,000.

COURSE DESCRIPTION The Atlanta Marathon's loop course begins and ends at Turner Field (Centennial Olympic Stadium). The route goes north on Hank Aaron Drive, gently rising until .6 miles, then falling gently until mile 2, passing the State Capitol along the way. The ups and downs become more pronounced between miles 2 and 8, including the 100-foot Early Riser from 4.3 to 4.6, 40-foot Colina Latina before the 6-mile mark, and 125- foot Hill Too Pharr from 6.5 to 7.7. Piedmont Park, home of the Atlanta Botanical Garden, lies prior to Early Riser, and Atlanta's oldest Hispanic community surrounds Colina Latina. From miles 8 to 19, the course gently rolls giving runners a nice break for the hills ahead. Just before mile 19, the course's major downhill appears, a fairly steep drop of about 220 feet to mile 20.4. Then, runners mount short, steep Cardiac Hill, a 125-footer over half a mile. From 22 miles to 25, the course contains a series of hills, climbing approximately 175 feet. Near mile 23, the race passes Atlanta's arts district, including the High Museum, the Memorial Arts Center, and the Alliance Theatre. The final mile or so is mostly flat or downhill to the finish. Note that the course is not closed to traffic. Runners typically stick to the right-hand lane of a broad road.

CROWD/RUNNER SUPPORT Arising extra early on Thanksgiving morning does not appeal to many people, especially with the planning and preparations many must go through that day. So don't expect large crowds along the course. Aid stations are located every 2.5 miles or so and carry water, electrolyte replacement, Vaseline, and minor first aid. Portable toilets also sit at every aid station.

RACE LOGISTICS Plenty of parking exists at Turner Field for those who have cars. Alternatively, you can take MARTA to the Georgia State University station and walk ten minutes to the start. MARTA tokens are on sale at the race expo. You can check your bags at the Stadium.

ACTIVITIES The Atlanta Marathon Expo goes on Tuesday and Wednesday before the race from 11:00 a.m. to 9:00 p.m. at the Sheraton Colony Square Hotel. Pick up your race packet at the expo. If your training hasn't gone so well, or has gone better than expected, you may switch between the marathon and the half marathon prior to 2:00 p.m. on Wednesday. There is no packet pickup or registration on race day. As an appetizer to Thanksgiving dinner, fruit, drinks, and snacks await finishers.

AWARDS All participants receive long-sleeve T-shirts, and finishers receive medals in the finish chute. The top masters runner and the top three finishers in each age group are mailed awards. Overall winners receive trophies. Finishers earn medals indicating their finish time in under 3 hours, under 3:30, or under 4:00. All other finishers in under 5 hours receive a finisher's medal. Results postcards are mailed to all finishers.

ACCOMMODATIONS Race headquarters is the Sheraton Colony Square Hotel, 14th and Peachtree (800-422-7895 or 404-892-6000). The Sheraton offers Atlanta Marathon runners a special rate of $69 per night. Other possibilities include: Ramada Hotel Downtown, 175 Piedmont Avenue NE (404-659-2727); Travelodge Downtown, 311 Courtland Street NE (404-659-4545); Westin Peachtree Plaza, 210 Peachtree Street NW (404-659-1400); Best Western American Hotel, 160 Spring Street NW (404-688-8600); Comfort Inn, 101 International Blvd. NE (404-524-5555); and Days Inn, 683 Peachtree Street NE (404-874-9200).

RELATED EVENTS/RACES The Atlanta Half Marathon covers the second half of the marathon course and begins at 7:00 a.m. on Peachtree near Chamblee-Tucker Road. The half attracts over 7,000 runners, making it the largest in the South and the third largest in the United States.

AREA ATTRACTIONS While in Atlanta, you may want to witness the lighting of the Big Tree, signifying the start of the Christmas season. Or, you could visit the usual Atlanta sights: Martin Luther King, Jr. National Historical Site, Stone Mountain Park, Georgia State Capitol, Carter Presidential Center, Piedmont Park and its Atlanta Botanical Garden, the Science and Technology Museum of Atlanta (SciTrek), the High Museum of Art, the Center for Puppetry Arts, the Governor's Mansion, Atlanta History Center in Buckhead, and the New Museum of Atlanta History.

NORTHERN CENTRAL TRAIL MARATHON

OVERALL: 77.6

COURSE BEAUTY: 9+

COURSE DIFFICULTY: 2-

APPROPRIATENESS FOR FIRST TIMERS: 8+

RACE ORGANIZATION: 8+

CROWDS: 0+

RACE DATA

Overall Ranking: 101
Quickness Ranking: 9
Contact: Charles Reynolds
BRRC P.O Box 9825
Baltimore, MD 21284
(410-668-8653)
http://www.brrc.com

Date: November 27, 1999; December 2, 2000 (tentative)
Start Time: 9:30 a.m.
Time Course Closes: NA
Number of Finishers: 350 in 1997
Course: Out and back
Certification: USATF
Course Records: Male: (open) 2:25:18; (masters) 2:36:00
Female: (open) 2:54:09; (masters) 3:27:06
Elite Athlete Programs: No
Cost: $25/30
Age groups/Divisions: 16-19, 20-29, 30-39, 40-49, 50-59, 60+
Walkers: Yes
Requirements: None
Temperature: 54°
Aid/Splits: 8 / miles 1, 5, 10, 13.1, 15, 20 & 25.2

HIGHLIGHTS   Amid the spirit of Thanksgiving, the Northern Central Trail Marathon takes place in Gunpowder Falls State Park, a mere 15 miles north of Baltimore, Maryland. This fast, out-and-back marathon travels along a hard-packed former railroad bed, beautifully surrounded by the telltale signs of the season. Destroyed in 1972 by Hurricane Agnes, the tracks have been converted to a multi-use recreational trail. Local lore claims that this same route was traced by the train that carried President Lincoln's body back to his Illinois home after his assassination.

COURSE DESCRIPTION   To thin out the crowds, the first 1.5 miles of the marathon lead to the trail via country roads. The balance of the course is a wide, hard-packed dirt path decorated with trees sparsely covered with the last vestiges of fall. The soft, forgiving surface is gentle on your legs. Along a stream that runs beside the course at several points, depots of a once glorious railroad past mark the trail. To make this rustic scene complete, if you look closely, you might even spot deer along your path. Though the trail ascends gently for the first 14 miles, the second half of the course is downhill, making for a fast finish. Be forewarned that the course can become a bit sloppy under rainy conditions. Also, the race often coincides with the beginning of deer hunting season; don't be alarmed if you hear gunshots in the distance.

CROWD / RUNNER SUPPORT   Small gatherings of fans cheer at various road crossing points and at the finish line. However, because the trail is somewhat prohibitive to spectators, you have to go it alone for most of the race. Aid stations dot the course approximately every 3 to 3.5 miles. Generally, water and electrolyte replacement fluids are available at each station, which competes for the best runner support. Splits are provided at miles 1, 5, 10, 13.1, 15, 20 and 1-mile-to-go mark along the course so you can conveniently monitor your progress.

RACE LOGISTICS   Park your car at Advanced Manufacturing, 14600 York Road. From there, a shuttle van transports you to and from the start/finish.

ACTIVITIES   You may pick up your packet or register on race morning at Advanced Manufacturing. On Friday evening, there is a pasta dinner. Replenish yourself at the finish line with complimentary refreshments and massages. Afterwards, find a comfortable space to sit and enjoy the awards ceremony.

AWARDS   Every runner receives a T-shirt, and finishers receive medals. Awards for the top five overall and top three in each age group are announced on race day at the finish line tent, but the actual awards (usually plaques) will be engraved and mailed to award winners after the race.

ACCOMMODATIONS   Lodging facilities include the Marriott Hunt Valley Inn, exit 20 off I-83 (410-785-7000); Red Roof Inn, exit 16 off I-83 (410-666-0380); Holiday Inn, exit 16 of I-83 (410-252-7373); Days Inn, exit 17 off I-83 (410-560-1000); and the Hampton Inn, exit 20 off I-83 to 11200 York Road (410-527-1500). In each case, request rooms for the Northern Central Trail Marathon. All hotels are conveniently located near the marathon start/finish.

AREA ATTRACTIONS   Nearby Baltimore offers plenty to do. Browse the Inner Harbor, with its National Aquarium, the U.S.S. Constellation (the first commissioned U.S. Navy ship), and numerous shops and restaurants. Make sure to sample Maryland's famous crab cakes. A great area for fun, Fells Point offers quaint streets and historic buildings. In addition, Washington, D.C. lies about an hour and a half away.

SEATTLE MARATHON

OVERALL: 92.1

COURSE BEAUTY: 10-

COURSE DIFFICULTY: 4-

APPROPRIATENESS FOR FIRST TIMERS: 8+

RACE ORGANIZATION: 9

CROWDS: 4-

RACE DATA

Overall Ranking: 15
Quickness Ranking: 49
Contact: Seattle Marathon Association
P.O. Box 31849
Seattle, WA 98103-1849
Tel. (206) 729-3660
Fax (206) 729-3662
E-mail: sea_mara@wolfenet.com
http://www.seattlemarathon.org

Date: November 28, 1999; November 26, 2000
Start Time: 8:00 a.m.
Time Course Closes: 2:00 p.m.
Number of Finishers: 2,348 in 1997
Course: Loop
Certification: USATF
Course Records: New Course
Elite Athlete Programs: NA
Cost: $41/47/60
Age groups/Divisions: ≤19, 20-24, 25-29, 30-34, 35-39, 40-44, 45-49,
50-54, 55-59, 60-64, 65-69, 70+
Walkers: No
Requirements: None
Temperature: 44°
Aid/Splits: 14 / NA

HIGHLIGHTS In our first edition we wrote: "Like a talented runner with a questionable work ethic, the Seattle Marathon could be one of the top destination marathons in North America. The fact that it currently isn't largely results from a sup-par course and some organizational snafus." While it's probably presumptuous to think that we had something to do with it, we're excited that both deficiencies were addressed in the race's 1998 edition. With a restructured race organization and an exciting new, downtown course (changed from the former bike trail course), the 30-year-old Seattle Marathon no longer deserves its "underachiever" status.

COURSE DESCRIPTION Seattle's new, city-loop course starts in the heart of downtown at historic Seattle Center (site of the 1962 World's Fair and home to the famed Seattle Space Needle). The first two miles run mostly flat to downhill along downtown Fifth Avenue, eventually passing the Seattle Kingdom at mile 2. Miles 2.5 to 4.75 head east along highway 90 and include a steady 100-foot climb from mile 2.5 to 3.75. Losing all of this elevation gain over the next mile, runners hit the I-90 Bridge (the world's first floating bridge) near mile 4.5. The next 6.5 miles run out and back across the bridge. This section of the course runs relatively flat with the exception of two small hills (45 feet) at miles 7 and 9. Leaving the bridge, runners head north while paralleling Lake Washington for the next 3 miles. With spectacular views of the Seattle Skyline and the Olympic Mountains to the left, you face the course's greatest incline around mile 14, climbing nearly 140 feet in only one mile. Upon cresting the hill, a sharp 120-foot downhill (almost too steep for comfort) takes runners past scenic Washington Park Arboretum. After circling Lake Union between miles 17 and 21, runners head through the prestigious Capitol Hill neighborhood and into the posh Queen Anne Neighborhood. Miles 21 and 22 parallel the Ballard Locks, passing Seattle Pacific University near mile 22. A left turn onto 15th Avenue leads runners south past the Interplay Playfield and U.S. Naval Reservation between mile 23 and 24. Now it's a left turn on W. Mercer Place as runners head back downtown. A quick right turn on 3rd Avenue, and a right on Republican Street lead to a slight uphill to the finish at Memorial Stadium.

CROWD/RUNNER SUPPORT Most of the spectator support comes at the start and finish, and in the latter half of the course through the Capitol Hill and Queen Anne neighborhoods. Aid stations lie every 2 miles along the course.

RACE LOGISTICS You'll find Seattle hassle-free on race morning if you stay at the official race hotel or one of several downtown hotels within walking distance of the start/finish. If you want to conserve energy, The Westin provides bus service to the start. If driving to the start, local pay lots and street parking are available at or near the Seattle Center, the location of all event starts. Gear check facilities are located in Memorial Stadium.

ACTIVITIES Pick up your race packet, register, and browse the expo at the Westin Hotel on Friday from 12:00 p.m. to 9:00 p.m. There is no race-day entry. Saturday evening the Westin serves an all-you-can-eat pasta buffet ($15), with seatings at 5:00 p.m., 6:00 p.m., and 7:00 p.m. The Mercer Arena, within a short distance of the event finish, serves as the post-race recovery area, where finishers can receive massages ($15), get medical help, meet their families, pick up their sweatshirts, and get some hot soup and refreshments. At 1:00 p.m., the "Brag and Whine" lounge opens at the Westin with refreshments and snacks. Here, you can check the official results, and division winners can pick up their awards.

AWARDS Every participant receives a T-shirt, and finishers receive medallions and certificates. The top 10 in each age division receive an award.

ACCOMMODATIONS The Westin Hotel, 1900 Fifth Avenue (206-728-1000), serves as the host hotel, offering special rates to Seattle Marathon runners (about $90). If the Westin is full, try: Best Western Executive Inn, 200 Taylor Avenue N (206-448-9444); Travelodge By The Space Needle, 200 6th Avenue N (206-441-7878); Hilton Seattle Downtown (206-624-0500); Sheraton Seattle Hotel & Tower, 1400 6th Avenue (206-621-9000); Stouffer Renaissance Madison, 515 Madison Street (206-583-0300); Travelodge University, 4725 25th Avenue NE (206-525-4612); Inn at the Market, 86 Pine Street (206-443-3600); and Inn at Queen Anne, 505 1st Avenue N (206-282-7357).

RELATED EVENTS/RACES Attracting nearly 4,000 entrants, the Seattle Half Marathon starts at 7:30 a.m., while the recently added half marathon walk begins at 7:00 a.m. An 8K walk starts at 8:15 a.m.

AREA ATTRACTIONS Famous for its coffee houses, brewpubs, and music, Seattle offers much more to the visitor. Check out the Museum of Flight near Boeing Field, and take a tour of the huge Boeing complex. Stop by the Pike Place Market for fresh fruits, vegetables, seafood, or just plain browsing. Get a birds eye view of Seattle atop the famed Space Needle. The Pacific Science Center is great for the kids, or maybe take them to a Seattle Supersonics basketball game at KeyArena or a Seahawks game at the Kingdome. Green Lake Park offers great jogging, rollerblading, bike riding, or people watching opportunities, and be sure to wander downtown along the waterfront.

CALIFORNIA INTERNATIONAL MARATHON

OVERALL: 82.1

COURSE BEAUTY: 7+

COURSE DIFFICULTY: 2+ (SEE APPENDIX)

APPROPRIATENESS FOR FIRST TIMERS: 8

RACE ORGANIZATION: 9+

CROWDS: 5-

RACE DATA

Overall Ranking: **73**
Quickness Ranking: **15**
Contact: **California International Marathon**
P.O. Box 161149
Sacramento, CA 95816
(916) 983-4622
http://www.runcim.org

Date: **December 5, 1999; December 3, 2000**
Start Time: **7:00 a.m.**
Time Course Closes: **12:30 p.m.**
Number of Finishers: **3,000 in 1997**
Course: **Point to point**
Certification: **USATF**
Course Records: **Male: (open) 2:10:26; (masters) 2:15:35**
Female: (open) 2:29:29; (masters) 2:41:09
Elite Athlete Programs: **Yes**
Cost: **$35/45/60**
Age groups/Divisions: **≤19, 20-24, 25-29, 30-34, 35-39, 40-44, 45-49,**
50-54, 55-59, 60-64, 65-69, 70+
Walkers: **No**
Requirements: **None**
Temperature: **38° - 56°**
Aid/Splits: **12 / every mile**

HIGHLIGHTS The California International Marathon, one of the 15 fastest marathons in North America, attracts a multinational field to the Golden State's capital every December. The mostly rolling course, which starts near Folsom Dam and ends in front of the State Capitol, loses approximately 300 feet. Containing few turns, CIM runs even faster than it appears, and runners have the entire road to work with. With solid crowd support, CIM is an excellent choice to go for a PR in a winter marathon.

COURSE DESCRIPTION CIM's point-to-point course begins on a gradual downhill near Folsom Dam. Turning at a right angle up a steep incline on Oak Avenue, the course gently rolls through rural residential neighborhoods. At the 6-mile mark, the course turns left on Fair Oaks Blvd., following it for the next 15.5 miles. The next noticeable hills on the route occur from mile 6.8 to 7 and from 7.5 to 7.7. Again rolling, the race enters Fair Oaks Village on an upgrade, passing antique shops, book sellers, and other small stores. At 10.4 miles, take advantage of the terrific downhill to 11.1. Back to rolling, the course reaches the halfway point during a commercial stretch on Fair Oaks Blvd., and the hills tend to roll more gently thereafter. Continuing to go through a mixture of residential and commercial areas, the route passes a particularly nice neighborhood between 15 and 21. At this point, CIM enters the City of Sacramento. Just before mile 22, runners face a slight hill that could prove tough at this point as they cross the American River via the H Street Bridge. Past the entrance to Sacramento State University, runners soon reach one of the city's most exclusive neighborhoods, the Fabulous Forties, former home to Governor Ronald Reagan. As you turn left on Alhambra Blvd. and enter midtown, you have 2 miles to go. At 24.6, the course passes historic Sutter's Fort, nucleus of the man who started the California Gold Rush. Runners reach scenic Capitol Park, which supposedly contains at least one example of every tree species found in California, and can see the Capitol dome. After passing Capitol Park, the course makes two turns to a beautiful finish in the Capitol's shadow.

CROWD / RUNNER SUPPORT   The Sacramento community warmly supports the marathon; spectators are found most of the way along the route while nearly 2,000 volunteers take care of every runner's needs. Since the Sacramento Bee newspaper usually prints the names and numbers of entrants the day before the race, some onlookers can be seen with paper in hand, cheering for the runners by name. Various music along the course provides added inspiration, particularly the high school band playing in Old Fair Oaks just after the 10-mile mark. Marathon parties along the route are also common. Look for the John McCarthy Memorial Party at the 17-mile mark. Held in honor of the longtime Sacramento runner, cyclist, and marathon supporter, the party brings together over 50 friends and family members to cheer the runners.

RACE LOGISTICS   Runners may not park at the marathon start, which leaves two ways to get there. You can either have someone drop you off about a half mile away, or you can take the race-provided bus ($5) which leaves from the headquarters hotel. Tickets for the race bus must be purchased in advance. The race provides free transportation for all runners from the finish back to the headquarters hotel. CIM transports your sweats to the finish area.

ACTIVITIES   On Friday afternoon and all day Saturday, register, pick up your race packet, and browse the Sports and Fitness Expo at the Doubletree Hotel. After the race, plenty of food including tomato soup (a favorite in colder years), can be found in the Capitol Rotunda. Massages are also available. The awards ceremony takes place at the headquarters hotel.

AWARDS   Every runner receives a T-shirt, while finishers earn medallions. The top three age-group finishers are awarded plaques.

ELITE RUNNERS INFORMATION   Men under 2:20 and women under 2:50 could receive lodging, transportation, and free entry. The top five overall finishers take home about $50,000 in prize money. The precise breakdown varies year to year.

ACCOMMODATIONS   The headquarters hotel is the Doubletree, 2001 Point West Way (Arden Way at the Capital City Freeway) (800-733-5466) or (916-929-8855). Other hotels near the Doubletree are: Sacramento Inn, 1401 Arden Way (916-922-8041); The Beverly Garland Heritage Hotel, 1780 Tribute Road (800-972-3976); Expo Inn, 1413 Howe Avenue (800-643-4422); and the Radisson Hotel, 500 Leisure Lane (800-333-3333). Near the finish line are the Hyatt Regency, 1209 L Street (800-233-1234); and the Clarion Hotel, 700 16th Street (800-252-7466).

RELATED EVENTS / RACES   Four-person teams can enter the Corporate Relay Challenge, with three 10K legs and one 12K leg. Family and friends may want to enter the 2.62-mile Marafun Run/Walk while they wait for their marathoner. The Marafun Run starts at 8:00 a.m. and is held at the marathon finish line. Kids under 13 may enter free.

AREA ATTRACTIONS   While in Sacramento, get a taste of the Old West in Old Sacramento, just off the Sacramento River in downtown. Wood walkways, cobblestone streets, shops, restaurants, and horse-drawn carriages highlight the area. Don't miss the Railroad Museum while there. Other possibilities include State Capitol tours, and kids may enjoy exploring Sutter's Fort to learn about life in the frontier days. Centrally located, Sacramento provides easy access to Lake Tahoe for skiing or gambling, the Napa Valley and Sonoma wine country, and San Francisco.

DALLAS WHITE ROCK MARATHON

OVERALL: 92.2

COURSE BEAUTY: 9+

COURSE DIFFICULTY: 5- (SEE APPENDIX)

APPROPRIATENESS FOR FIRST TIMERS: 8+

RACE ORGANIZATION: 9+

CROWDS: 6

RACE DATA

Overall Ranking: **14**
Quickness Ranking: **66**
Contact: **Dallas White Rock Marathon**
3607 Oak Lawn
Dallas, TX 75219
(214) 528-2962
http://www.whiterock-marathon.com

Date: **December 5, 1999; December 3, 2000 (tentative)**
Start Time: **8:00 a.m.**
Time Course Closes: **2:00 p.m.**
Number of Finishers: **2,663 in 1997**
Course: **Loop**
Certification: **USATF**
Course Records: **Male: (open) 2:12:18**
Female: (open) 2:33:39
Elite Athlete Programs: **Yes**
Cost: **$40/50/60**
Age groups/Divisions: **≤19, 20-24, 25-29, 30-34, 35-39, 40-44, 45-49,**
50-54, 55-59, 60-64, 65-69, 70+
Walkers: **No**
Requirements: **None**
Temperature: **45° - 70°**
Aid/Splits: **15 / none**

HIGHLIGHTS   The Dallas White Rock Marathon ranks as one of the top six most beautiful urban marathons in the country and is our highest-rated destination race in Texas. No small feat given the competition—Houston-Methodist, Motorola Austin, Cowtown, and San Antonio, among others. In fact, Texas trails only California in the high number of quality marathons. Houston-Methodist may be bigger and faster, but The Rock (as it is affectionately known) has class, starting with its eclectic course. The Rock proves that an urban marathon does not need to pass through slums or mile upon mile of strip malls. It can encompass parkways, pleasant communities, refurbished districts, and even a lake.

RACE HISTORY   As runners, we have found that some of our best thinking is done during a run. Clearly, Talmage Morrison, founder of the Cross Country Club of Dallas, agrees. Running around White Rock Lake one bright morning in 1970, Morrison had a moment of clarity. He walked to a now famous flagpole at Winfrey Point, gazed out at the picturesque lake and the flat roads that ring it, and saw the perfect setting for a marathon. He paid $25 for a quarter-page ad in Runner's World (boy, that was a long time ago!) and had the course certified by the Amateur Athletics Union. Eighty-two runners showed up at the inaugural Dallas White Rock Marathon in 1971 to loop around White Rock Lake three times. Twenty-nine years later, The Rock has matured to nearly 3,000 runners, has added two relay events, and has changed its course. But the inspiration that launched it hasn't changed.

COURSE DESCRIPTION Completely closed to traffic, The Rock offers a loop course that starts and finishes at City Hall. Race organizers have put a lot of thought into the course and it shows. Showcasing the best of Dallas, the race passes through Highland Park Township, White Rock Lake, Swiss Avenue, and downtown. In short, the deceptively difficult course is the most scenic and entertaining in Texas. The start is slightly downhill on Young, a wide street that can handle the large number of entrants. Between miles 1 and 2, runners pass through West End, downtown's entertainment district, and face a 60-foot climb over a half mile. After a right turn on Olive, runners barrel down a 60-foot drop over 200 yards, and then go right back up. At Cedar Springs (miles 2 to 3), a quarter-mile downhill leads to beautiful, woodsy, Turtle Creek. Around the 3-mile mark, the course begins a 3.5- mile, general upward trend, gaining about 200 feet over rolling terrain through the exclusive Township of Highland Park. At mile 6, runners swing onto commercial Mockingbird Lane and begin a long (about 2 miles) downhill toward White Rock Lake. After mile 8, the course returns to a neighborhood before a short, good uphill entering White Rock Park. The next 10 miles loop the running trails around beautiful White Rock Lake. Completely flat (except for a rolling downhill between 19 and 20), this part of the course can be windy since it is relatively unprotected. At mile 20, you regret leaving the inspiration of White Rock Lake, especially as you begin two steep hills and the gradual climb through Lakewood to mile 22. Your spirits will soar again at mile 22, the head of historic Swiss Avenue with its refurbished houses, tree-laden median strip, and best of all, a long, two-mile gradual downhill. About 23.5, the course gradually becomes more commercial, and downtown and the City Hall finish are not far. Dallas' skyline comes into view about mile 25, near the renovated Farmer's Market. Although the street consists of cobblestones, they are easy to run on (though slippery when wet). After the cobblestones, weary runners have pretty much a straight shot to the finish line at City Hall.

CROWD/RUNNER SUPPORT Fifteen very enthusiastic aid stations sponsored by businesses and other groups highlight The Rock. Many of the aid stations have different themes every year. Some past themes include the Dancing Cowgirl, The Beverly Hillbillies, Christmas in Toyland, and Comedy Club. The aid stations compete against each other in three categories, with the winners chosen by the runners. Aid stations offer water, electrolyte replacement, fruit, medical personnel, and portable toilets. A variety of entertainment along the course ranges from live bands to residents blasting boom boxes. Scattered along the course, crowds are particularly thick along Turtle Creek near the entrance to Highland Park, the entrance to White Rock Lake, and from Lakewood to the finish.

RACE LOGISTICS The Rock is a loop course so little transportation is required. The headquarters hotel and other race affiliated hotels all have shuttles to the start/finish areas. Furthermore, sag wagons search the course for those unable to finish. Shuttle busses provide transportation to the relay exchange points and from the exchange points to the finish.

ACTIVITIES Race weekend begins on the Saturday before the race with a Sports Expo from 9:00 a.m. to 5:00 p.m. at the Dallas Convention Center. The expo features seminars, running clinics, exhibits, running apparel and footwear vendors. Saturday night features a pasta dinner. Doled out during the pasta dinner, the annual Award for Excellence honors an individual who has made significant contributions to distance running. Past award winners include Frank Shorter, Dave Scott, Joan Benoit Samuelson, Fred Lebow, Dr. Kenneth Cooper, and Dr. George Sheehan. An awards banquet featuring food and refreshments follows the marathon.

AWARDS   Every runner receives a terrific Rock T-shirt. Those able to finish also earn a finisher's T-shirt, medallion, certificate, and a well-conceived results booklet. Special age-group awards go up to 15 deep, depending on the number of entrants in each age group.

ELITE RUNNERS INFORMATION   The Rock recruits elite runners—men who have recently run under 2:20 and women under 2:35. Depending on your credentials, the race could offer transportation, hotel, expenses, and/or complimentary entry.

ACCOMMODATIONS   The Adam's Mark Hotel, 400 N. Olive Street (800-444-ADAM), serves as the official race headquarters hotel. Or, try the Le Meridien, 650 N. Pearl Street (800-543-4300). Both offer special rates for Rock runners and are within 4 to 6 blocks of City Hall. Other possibilities include: The Fairmont Hotel, 1717 N. Akard (800-527-4727); Holiday Inn-Aristocrat Hotel, 1933 Main Street (214-741-7700); Ramada Hotel- Convention Center, 1011 S. Akard (214-421-1083); Best Western Market Center, 2023 Market Center Blvd. (214-741-9000); and Quality Hotel Market Center, 2015 Market Center Blvd. (214-741-7481).

RELATED EVENTS/RACES   On Sunday, there are two marathon relays starting simultaneously with the marathon. Five and two- person teams in various categories compete on the marathon course.

AREA ATTRACTIONS   Dallas is a great sports town. Check out the NFL Cowboys (if they are in town), the NBA Mavericks, or NHL Stars. Dallas is also something of a shopping mecca if you need to take your mind off the big race with some mindless money-blowing.

MEMPHIS MARATHON

OVERALL: 85.5

COURSE BEAUTY: 7

COURSE DIFFICULTY: 5-

APPROPRIATENESS FOR FIRST TIMERS: 8

RACE ORGANIZATION: 10-

CROWDS: 5-

RACE DATA

Overall Ranking:	46
Quickness Ranking:	68
Contact:	First Tennessee Memphis Marathon
	P.O. Box 84
	Memphis, TN 38101
	Tel. (800) 893-7223
	Fax (901) 523-4354
	http://www.runmemphis.com
Date:	December 5, 1999; December 3, 2000
Start Time:	8:00 a.m.
Time Course Closes:	1:00 p.m.
Number of Finishers:	806 in 1997
Course:	Loop
Certification:	USATF
Course Records:	Male: (open) 2:20:31; (masters) 2:24:28
	Female: (open) 2:43:27; (masters) 2:48:40
Elite Athlete Programs:	No
Cost:	$30/35
Age groups/Divisions:	16-19, 20-24, 25-29, 30-34, 35-39, 40-44, 45-49,
	50-54, 55-59, 60-64, 65+, wheelchair
Walkers:	No
Requirements:	16 years old
Temperature:	38° - 56°
Aid/Splits:	12 / every mile

HIGHLIGHTS　　Billed as a running tour of the city, the Memphis Marathon fulfills its promise. The only problem being that the tour includes some areas you may not want to visit! The consensus on Memphis? Great city, great race, not-so-great course. David Williams of Little Rock sums up the general feeling, "*Great little marathon with only one drawback—the course! If you like hills, exhaust fumes from 10 to 20, cobblestones at 21 and 22 … and some bad parts of town …, then by all means—go for it!*" Runners do rave about the finish inside The Pyramid arena and the excellent race organization. Runners also appreciate the excitement and history of Memphis as the birthplace of blues and rock 'n' roll. Now, if we could just do something about that course.

COURSE DESCRIPTION　　Despite what you may have read elsewhere, Memphis' loop course is not particularly fast. Heading east from the start outside the majestic Pyramid arena, runners traipse the flat, tree-lined residential neighborhoods along North Parkway. Near 3.5 miles, runners may hear a baboon's howl or a lion's roar as they pass the Memphis Zoo in Overton Park. Scenic residential neighborhoods continue on East Parkway before the route heads west on South Parkway around 7.25 miles. After passing still more beautiful homes along South Parkway for two miles, the route turns left on the 4 to 6 lane-wide Elvis Presley Blvd.—full of heavy, Sunday traffic. The challenging hills and suffocating vehicle exhaust on EPB leaves one wondering whether changing the course to incorporate Graceland was a wise decision. Nonetheless, runners can have their picture taken in front of the Graceland Wall as they head for the turnaround. Police and course officials have their hands full with angry motorists at the highly congested and cruelly positioned U-turn atop a difficult hill on EPB (about 14.5 miles). Still rolling along Winchester Road between 15 miles and 16.5 miles, the race turns right starting the most unappealing section of the course along the highly commercial and lower-income areas of Third Street (another byproduct of the Graceland addition). Six miles later, the scenery improves when entering flat, cobblestone-laden Beale Street at 22.5 miles. Be careful, as the uneven edges of the cobblestones can have you singing the blues at this point in the race. Around 23 miles, the route heads southwest passing the fashionable storefronts on newly revitalized Front Street before hitting the posh South Bluffs neighborhood. Runners encounter more treacherous cobblestones (made more tricky by temporary astroturf, which, despite the good intentions of the race organizers, only hides the bumps) while passing Cybill Shepherd's home before 24 miles. After a right turn onto Riverside Drive at 24 miles, the course heads north for the final 2 miles along the breathtaking Mississippi River to the spectacular finish inside the Pyramid Arena.

CROWD/RUNNER SUPPORT Crowds along the course tend to congregate around the aid stations, with sparse support in between. The best throng can be found inside The Pyramid as runners finish at half court. Aid stations, about every two miles, offer water, electrolyte replacement, Vaseline, and band-aids. Portable toilets are located at the start/finish, miles 3.5, 13.5, and 19.5. The water stations at 13.5 and 19.5 also carry cookies and fruit.

RACE LOGISTICS Most hotels are located within walking distance of The Pyramid. If you do need to arrive by car, plenty of parking exists at The Pyramid. After the race, you can shower at The Pyramid, provided you bring your own soap, towel, and lock.

ACTIVITIES Every pre-race event on Saturday is held at the Memphis Cook Convention Center, 255 N. Main near The Pyramid. You may pick up your race packet at the expo between 10:00 a.m. and 7:30 p.m. While you can retrieve your packet on race day (at The Pyramid), you may not register for the race. Saturday night, attend the pasta dinner which features a noted guest speaker (about $8). The awards ceremony starts at 2:00 p.m. at The Pyramid, immediately followed by the rock 'n' roll victory party held one block away at High Point Finch.

AWARDS Every entrant receives a long-sleeve T-shirt. Each finisher also receives a medallion, certificate, and results. Approximately $30,000 in prize money is awarded to open, masters and age-group winners, with first place overall earning $2,000, down to $225 for fifth place. Masters winners earn $1,500, down to $225 for fifth. Age-group winners receive $125, $100 for second, and $75 for third. Masters runners are eligible for both open and masters prize money.

ACCOMMODATIONS Several convenient hotels offer discounts to Memphis Marathon runners, including: Brownstone Hotel, 300 N. Second Street (800-HOTEL-15); Comfort Inn, 100 N. Front Street (901-526-0583); Crowne Plaza, 250 N. Main Street (901-527-7300); The Peabody, 149 Union Avenue (800-PEABODY); Radisson Hotel, 185 Union Avenue (901-528-1800); and Ramada Convention Center Hotel, 160 Union Avenue (901-525-5491). You can obtain a list of other hotels in the area from the Visitor's Information Center, 340 Beale Street (800-873-6282).

AREA ATTRACTIONS Loaded with things to do, Memphis could keep you moving for some time. Make sure you check out the Beale Street Historic District, fountainhead of the blues. Visit Graceland, that beacon for Elvis lovers around the world. Tour the National Civil Rights Museum, located in the Lorraine Motel, site of Dr. Martin Luther King, Jr.'s assassination. Watch the charming duck parade in the Peabody Hotel every day at 11:00 a.m. and 5:00 p.m.

TUCSON MARATHON

OVERALL: 83.5

COURSE BEAUTY: 9-

COURSE DIFFICULTY: 1

APPROPRIATENESS FOR FIRST-TIMERS: 9

ORGANIZATION: 9

CROWDS: 2

RACE DATA

Overall Ranking:	64
Quickness Ranking:	2
Contact:	Tucson Marathon
	1643 N. Alvernon Way, Suite 108
	Tucson, AZ 85712
	Tel. (520) 320-0667
	Fax (520) 326-3627
Date:	December 5, 1999; December 3, 2000
Start Time:	7:30 a.m.
Time Course Closes:	1:30 p.m.
Number of Finishers:	980 in 1997
Course:	Point to point
Certification:	USATF
Course Records:	Male: (open) 2:19:00
	Female: (open) 2:50:01
Elite Athlete Programs:	Yes. Apply for free entry and hotel.
Cost:	$40/55
Age groups/Divisions:	20-24, 25-29, 30-34, 35-39, 40-44, 45-49, 50-54,
	55-59, 60-64, 65-69, 70+, wheelchair
Walkers:	Yes, if can finish in 6 hours
Requirements:	None
Temperature:	42°-68°
Aid/Splits:	12 / none

HIGHLIGHTS The Tucson Marathon is fast. Wait. Let us repeat that in case you didn't hear. The Tucson Marathon is fast. Avalanche fast. The course drops a just-right 1,900 feet from start to finish. The gentle slope makes the route fast without being overly jarring on your knees and body. (You should still do some downhill training, however, to accustom your quadriceps to prolonged descents.) Since the course runs along a state highway, you are relegated to the shoulder of the road, which can be a detraction for runners who are sensitive to camber. And don't expect to run through downtown Tucson, either. In fact, the course doesn't even come close to the city. But the vast majority of the race's runners don't care, because they come for speed. And this race was built for speed.

COURSE DESCRIPTION The Tucson Marathon starts in the little town of Oracle (elevation 4,514 feet), adjacent to the Circle K on Rock Cliff Road. Runners turn right on two-lane State Route 77, and, in defiance of all expectations and pre-race hype, run uphill. It's a good uphill, too. But don't worry. It's early still, and you should lose only a few precious seconds over the first 1.5 miles that are uphill. Surrounded by the high desert scenery, the course heads down, becoming fast and furious near mile 2.5 leading to the right turn on American Avenue (mile 2.8). Runners face a tough upgrade on American Avenue until about mile 3.6 where it rolls through the small town. From mile 5.5, the route becomes consistently downhill, passing the starting point near 10K and merging back onto State Route 77 (mile 6.6). The next 5.5 miles scream downhill through the shrubs, bushes, and cacti of the high desert along the Santa Catalina mountains, until a little bump at mile 12.1 briefly breaks your rhythm. You pass the road to the Biosphere-2 complex near mile 10.3. The course turns left at Oracle Junction (mile 15.7), where it flattens until mile 16.8 and then proceeds downhill on a gentle grade. Runners pass the town of Catalina at mile 19, where the road widens considerably. Directly after Mile Post 86 (about mile 20.8), the route rises slightly until 21.5 miles. By mile 22, the race resumes its downward path (with another little bump near mile 25), until the turn into the finish area at the AlliedSignal plant (elevation 2,600 feet).

CROWD/RUNNER SUPPORT   There aren't a lot of crowds pushing you down the highway, so the nice slope will have to suffice. Runners come across aid stations every 2 miles or so where they can snag sport drink and water. The aid station at mile 18 usually carries some gel, as well.

RACE LOGISTICS   Runners must take the free shuttle buses to the race start. Buses for the marathon leave every 20 minutes from Allied Signal (the finish line) from 5:45 a.m. until 6:30 a.m.

ACTIVITIES   Pick up your race packet during the pre-race expo at the Westward Look Resort's Desert Site, 245 E. Ina Road (just east of Oracle Road—SR 77— on Ina), from 9:00 a.m. to 5:00 p.m. on Saturday. You can also register for the race at the expo. After the race, have some breakfast while enjoying the music. The award ceremony kicks off at noon.

AWARDS   All entrants receive a T-shirt, while finishers also get a medal. The top 3 runners in each age group receive an award, and $100 goes to every runner who runs under 2:20 for men and 2:40 for women.

ACCOMMODATIONS   The Westward Look Resort, 245 E. Ina Road (800-722-2500) serves as the unofficial host hotel. An 80-acre retreat, the Westward has several pools, spas, a running trail, and fitness center for a little over $100 per room. Another nearby possibility is the Triangle L Ranch, with its double rooms in private cottages set in 80 acres of the oak-shaded foothills of Mount Lemmon (520-623-6732). If you want to stay cheaply in downtown Tucson, try the bohemian Hotel Congress (where the Dillinger gang was once arrested), 311 E. Congress Street (800-722-8848). You can also call the marathon's official travel agency, Travel Headquarters (800-359-6979), for accommodation information.

RELATED EVENTS/RACES   Race day also includes a super-fast half marathon that completes the final 13.1 miles of the full marathon course. Half marathoners also must take a race shuttle to the start. A band of five runners can enter the marathon relay, with legs of 6.1, 4.3, 4.6, 5, and 6.2 miles. There are categories for male, female, and coed teams (with at least 3 women).

AREA ATTRACTIONS   The historic core of Tucson along the (usually bone-dry) Santa Cruz River, bisected by Congress Street, contains many good restaurants and nightspots. You and your kids will probably enjoy the Arizona-Sonora Desert Museum in Tucson Mountain Park. The museum contains all sorts of desert animals, birds, and snakes, most of which were injured and had to be rescued from the desert. The Saguara National Monument, part of which stretches north from the Desert Museum, gives you the chance to wander through weird forests of forty-foot, multi-limbed Saguaro cacti. You can also tour the Biosphere-2 complex, where a small group of folks lived for two years sealed inside the plexiglass bubble.

WESTERN HEMISPHERE MARATHON

OVERALL: 71.4

COURSE BEAUTY: 7-

COURSE DIFFICULTY: 4+

APPROPRIATENESS FOR FIRST TIMERS: 7-

RACE ORGANIZATION: 8

CROWDS: 2

RACE DATA

Overall Ranking: 110
Quickness Ranking: 65
Contact: Western Hemisphere Marathon
4117 Overland Avenue
Culver City, CA 90230-0507
(888) 844-8474
http://www.ci.culver-city.ca.us

Date: December 5, 1999; December 3, 2000
Start Time: 8:00 a.m.
Time Course Closes: 1:00 p.m.
Number of Finishers: NA
Course: Out and Back
Certification: USATF
Course Records: Male: (open) 2:28:27
Female: (open) 2:59:09
Elite Athlete Programs: No
Cost: $32/35/40
Age groups/Divisions: ≤15, 16-20, 21-30, 31-35, 36-45, 46-50, 51-60,
61-70, 71-80, 81+
Walkers: No
Requirements: None
Temperature: 70°
Aid/Splits: 25 / None

HIGHLIGHTS   Quietly aging, the Western Hemisphere Marathon reveals few signs of its significant place in marathon annals. Reigning as the second oldest consecutively run marathon in the United States, the race celebrated its golden anniversary in 1997. Its golden years, however, date far back when the race finished in the glamorous confines of the Los Angeles Coliseum before 70,000 fans attending the Coliseum Relays track and field meet. The modern, convoluted course consists of a series of out-and-backs and a loop. Beginning in front of the Culver City Veteran Memorial Auditorium, the race runs unceremoniously through the main venues of Culver City, passing historic movie studios before heading to the coastline of the Pacific Ocean and then back.

RACE HISTORY   With 51 races under its elastic waistband, it's not surprising that WHM's scrapbook is chock full of entertaining stories. One of the best emanates from the inaugural run. For added drama, the race was timed so the winner would arrive at the Los Angeles Coliseum just before the one-mile run of the 1948 Coliseum Relays. Slowed by heavy traffic, the lead runner arrived only to find the Coliseum gates locked. After finally gaining entry, Gerald Cote of Canada found himself in the midst of the 100-yard high hurdles race. Before 70,000 cheering fans, Cote proceeded to clear a series of 39-inch hurdles finishing two races in one. The mood of the boisterous crowd soon changed to quiet dismay, however, when Cote celebrated his accomplishment by puffing on a cigar during his victory lap. Another memorable race occurred three years later when China's Lan Wen Ngau, while leading the race, suddenly veered off course. Unable to understand instructions to turn around, Ngau continued running until race officials physically altered his direction—forcing his disqualification. Sponsored by the People's Party of China, Ngau feared harsh consequences upon his return so, instead, he stayed. He's rumored to be living in the California mountains to this day.

COURSE DESCRIPTION After reading WHM's race literature, you may think you're in for an amazingly beautiful course. "A setting that is unparalleled," or "One of the most picturesque and enjoyable routes in American history." We can only surmise that these descriptions have been carried over from the days when WHM stood as one of the few marathons in the country. In reality, with the exception of a 6-mile stretch along the coastline, the course is not particularly attractive. Appropriately starting in front of Culver City's Veterans Memorial Auditorium, the veteran race loops the city passing its historic movie studios before heading west toward the ocean. Much of the course runs on Culver Blvd., a mostly flat, secondary road with two lanes in each direction, lined on both sides with retail areas, apartments, duplexes, schools, and car lots. The scenery improves as you meet a wetlands preserve before heading south up a gradual hill on Vista Del Mar. Near the halfway point, runners overlook the beach at Playa Del Rey as they make their way along the Pacific coast. Descending slightly near the Imperial Hwy., runners negotiate an out-and-back on both a service access road and Pershing Drive. Hopefully, the 6 miles along the scenic coastal bluffs inspire you for your return to the Veterans Memorial Auditorium as you encounter much of the same urban sprawl which characterized earlier miles.

CROWD/RUNNER SUPPORT Don't expect much crowd support on race day. Most of the encouragement comes from the volunteers at the aid stations which dot the course each mile. Although impressive in number, be aware that the aid stations usually don't provide electrolyte replacement drinks.

RACE LOGISTICS Race participants have to get themselves to the start. This should not pose a problem since plenty of parking exists near the Veterans Memorial Auditorium.

ACTIVITIES You may pick up your race packet or register late during the small race expo held on Friday and Saturday from at the Helms Building located at 8007 Washington Boulevard in Culver City. Race-day registration and packet pickup starts at 6:30 a.m. Food and display booths and a pancake breakfast (for a fee) begin at 7:00 a.m. After the race, enjoy a well-deserved massage before refueling on the traditional stew lunch beginning at noon at the Senior Center. The awards ceremony, also held at the Senior Center, begins at 12:30 p.m.

AWARDS Every participant receives a T-shirt and goodie bag, and finishers receive a medals. The first overall male and female finishers receive the coveted Culver City Heart of Screenland Trophy. The first three males and females in all age divisions receive trophies.

ACCOMMODATIONS You shouldn't have a problem finding accommodations in the area. Lodging options near the start/finish area include: Culver City Travelodge, 11180 Washington Place (310-839-1111); Holiday Inn, 3930 Sepulveda Blvd. (310-390-2189); and Ramada Inn, 6333 Bristol Parkway (310-839-1111).

RELATED EVENTS/RACES Race day starts with a marathon bike tour at 6:00 a.m. At 7:00 a.m., skaters navigate a separate course from the marathon runners in one of the only in-line skating marathons in California. Shortly after 8:00 a.m., the Bruce Robinson Memorial 5K runs through the heart of Culver City. A separate, elite 5K begins at 9:00 a.m. Sandwiched between the two 5Ks is a 1 Mile Fun Run for Kids.

KIAWAH ISLAND MARATHON

OVERALL: 89.5

COURSE BEAUTY: 10-

COURSE DIFFICULTY: 3-

APPROPRIATENESS FOR FIRST TIMERS: 9-

RACE ORGANIZATION: 9

CROWDS: 2

RACE DATA

Overall Ranking: 23
Quickness Ranking: 31
Contact: Dylan Jones
Kiawah Island Resort
12 Kiawah Beach Drive
Kiawah Island, SC 29455
Tel. (803) 768-2780
Fax (803) 768-6022

Date: December 11, 1999; December 9, 2000
Start Time: 8:00 a.m.
Time Course Closes: 3:00 p.m.
Number of Finishers: 845 in 1997
Course: Loop
Certification: USATF
Course Records: Male: (open) 2:21:24
Female: (open) 2:52:08
Elite Athlete Programs: No
Cost: $30
Age groups/Divisions: 13-17, 18-23, 24-29, 30-34, 35-39, 40-44, 45-49, 50-54, 55-59, 60-69, 70+
Walkers: Yes
Requirements: None
Temperature: 45° - 60°
Aid/Splits: 12 / every 2 miles

HIGHLIGHTS   Chances are you have never heard of the Kiawah Island Marathon. Until now. Offering one of the most unique marathon experiences in North America, the race runs entirely on this 10,000 acre resort barrier island off the coast of South Carolina. Using just about every inch of road on the isle, the winding course passes salt marshes, semitropical wilderness, breathtaking golf courses, and maybe even an alligator! The elegant, post-race banquet knows no equals. And after the marathon, Kiawah Island is a terrific place to relax and savor your accomplishment. So if you want to escape the December frost, the Kiawah Island Marathon may be the best destination you've never heard of.

COURSE DESCRIPTION   Covered by salt marshes, wilderness, beaches, and golf courses, environmentally sensitive Kiawah Island consists entirely of a world-class resort and exclusive residential communities. The controlled marathon course, open to limited residential traffic, consists of a series of inventive loops and out and backs up and down the island. Since the barrier isle has relatively few roads, the race covers many twice, providing ample opportunity to view the other runners. The course has many curves and turns which could annoy faster runners. However, runners should love the excellent footing and the flat route (the highest elevation on the island is 14 feet), with the largest grades consisting of golf cart paths. If you want it any flatter you'd have to send out for it!

The marathon starts and finishes in front of the East Beach Conference Center. The first six miles of the course cover the western end of the island passing 21-acre Night Heron Park, the Cougar Point Golf Course, and the tree-lined roads of Kiawah's first residential area. The following 10 miles weave through the middle and eastern sections of the island, now comprised of second and third growth maritime forest and quintessential Southern Living homes. Indigo and cotton fields covered this area over 150 years ago. The next four miles (16-20) take runners down and back on spectacular Ocean Course Drive, providing vistas of marshland, salt water creeks, gracious oaks, and the famous Ocean Course where America claimed the 1991 Ryder Cup. The final stretch guides marathoners down beautiful Flyway Drive with ponds and gators motivating runners to the East Beach Conference Center finish line.

CROWD / RUNNER SUPPORT   Kiawah Island has a small local population so most of the crowds consist of runners' families and friends. An excellent spectator course, the runners pass most points at least twice. Located every 2 miles, aid stations offer runners the choice of water, sports drink and fruit. Splits are called roughly every two miles.

RACE LOGISTICS   There is a free shuttle service to the start area for those runners staying on the island. If you are staying in Charleston, there is plenty of parking near the conference center, but as always, you should arrive early.

ACTIVITIES   On Friday evening, attend the Pasta Bash at the East Beach Conference Center. The resort catering staff does a superb job with the dinner (about $14). Kiawah Island hosts an excellent awards ceremony and party following the marathon. A generous buffet of hot and cold food and beverage highlights the festivities.

AWARDS   Each pre-registered marathon entrant receives a long-sleeve T-shirt, with finishers earning medals. Kiawah "Proud Pelican" awards go to the top five open males, top three open females, and the male and female masters winners. Age-group awards are also given to the top three finishers in each age division. Ten percent of all pre-registered runners receive awards.

ACCOMMODATIONS   The Kiawah Island Inn offers special accommodation packages for marathon runners and their families. The resort also offers numerous villa and home options, starting at about $60 per person, per night. For resort reservations call (800-654-2924). Other companies also offer home and villa accommodations, including Great Beach Vacations (800-845-3911); Pam Harrington Exclusives (800-845-6966); Benchmark Rentals (800-992-9666); Beachwalker Rentals (800-334-6308); and Charleston Resort Properties (800-845-7368). Budget lodging can be found in Charleston a short drive away.

RELATED EVENTS / RACES   Kiawah Island also sponsors a half marathon (with 1,329 finishers in 1997) and 5K, both held on the same day as the marathon.

AREA ATTRACTIONS   A true resort, Kiawah Island offers four world-class golf courses ranked among the top in the country, numerous tennis courts, ten miles of beach, and an outstanding children's program, Kamp Kiawah.

ROCKET CITY MARATHON

OVERALL: 83.6

COURSE BEAUTY: 8-

COURSE DIFFICULTY: 3- (SEE APPENDIX)

APPROPRIATENESS FOR FIRST TIMERS: 8+

RACE ORGANIZATION: 10-

CROWDS: 5-

R A C E   D A T A

Overall Ranking: **62**
Quickness Ranking: **25**
Contact: **Malcolm Gillis**
Rocket City Marathon
1001 Opp Reynolds Road
Toney, AL 35773
Tel. & Fax (205) 828-6207

Date: **December 11, 1999; December 9, 2000**
Start Time: **8:00 a.m.**
Time Course Closes: **1:30 p.m.**
Number of Finishers: **797 in 1997**
Course: **Out and back with a loop**
Certification: **USATF**
Course Records: **Male: (open) 2:12:21; (masters) 2:17:01**
Female: (open) 2:32:22; (masters) 2:44:09
Elite Athlete Programs: **Yes**
Cost: **$20/25/30**
Age groups/Divisions: **≤19, 20-24, 25-29, 30-34, 35-39, 40-44, 45-49,**
50-54, 55-59, 60+, Father-Son, Husband-Wife
Walkers: **No**
Requirements: **None**
Temperature: **45°**
Aid/Splits: **10 / every mile, 10K, halfway & 25.2**

HIGHLIGHTS   Huntsville, Alabama, a.k.a. Rocket City, USA. Home to the launch vehicles that carried man to the moon and the Space Shuttle. With such a high-flying history, you would expect the Rocket City to host a real barnburner of a marathon. And they do. It's just that most people outside the Southeast don't know it. The Rocket City Marathon is a true sleeper. Its race organization is among the most friendly and thorough in the country. And if it seems as though everybody knows your name, it's because organizers print your first name in large letters above your bib number. Only the warm and supportive community surpasses the fast course that boasts no significant hills. No other marathon provides runners with as much information about the race, course, history, and surrounding area in the form of an 84-page information book. Trained handlers greet and attend to every finisher, providing personalized care that usually can only be found at races one-tenth Rocket City's size. The race sports one of the fastest courses in the country, as attested to by the numerous age-group records that have been set here. If you are looking for an early winter marathon to bust a PR, we suggest you give Rocket City a try.

RACE HISTORY Following World War II, 100 ex-German scientists were brought to Huntsville to develop the U.S. rocket and space program. Among the results: Saturn rockets that powered man to the moon and the Space Shuttle. These achievements earned Huntsville the nickname, Rocket City. The Rocket City Marathon began in 1977 with a healthy 482 runners, becoming the first marathon held in Alabama. Participation peaked in 1981 with nearly 2,000 entrants. Lured by the fast course, many runners hoping to qualify for the 100th Boston Marathon increased participation numbers by 50% in 1995.

COURSE DESCRIPTION Run on a mixture of downtown streets (13.4%), broad avenues (21%), and residential roads (65.6%), the course consists almost entirely of asphalt. Relatively flat, with a few modest inclines and descents, the route contains no steep hills. The difference between the lowest and highest point on the course is 93 feet, with a total elevation change of 563 feet (includes ups and downs) over the 26.2 miles. The race has a large number of curves and turns, especially for a fast course, but it is well marked and patrolled.

The start/finish lies outside the Huntsville Hilton. After the start, look for the rocket launches in the park that let you know you are indeed running the Rocket City Marathon. The first 2.5 miles loop through downtown Huntsville. As you run north on Monroe Street, you pass Big Spring International Park and the Von Braun Civic Center. The course veers left, and you hit the first incline of the race, an 18-foot rise. Immediately following the 1-mile marker and a short downgrade, you turn left on Holmes Avenue and cross through the Old Town Historic District, the only predominantly Victorian neighborhood remaining in Huntsville, with most of the residences dating from 1870 to 1930. Within a few blocks, runners enter the Twickenham Historic District, one of the largest concentrations of antebellum homes in the South, through tree-canopied Randolph Avenue, accompanied by a nice downward slope. That is, until you reach Green Street and climb 20 feet. At the Madison County Courthouse, you traverse Cotton Row to the 2-mile mark in front of the 1835 Greek Revival First Alabama Bank. Runners then have a nice half-mile descent leading to a section of the course called the Downtown Connection. As you pass the Huntsville Hospital, a 24-foot climb over .3 miles precedes Governors Drive, the busiest intersection on the course. Largely flat and residential, the next 3 miles include some of Huntsville's older neighborhoods. Just before 6 miles, you encounter a short, 33-foot climb, and then you drop 41 feet over the next mile. At 6.85 miles, you begin the 58-foot climb to the highest point (668 feet) on the course at about 7.6 miles. As you cross the pedestrian tunnel under Whitesburg Drive, you are entering the 14.5-mile southern loop. The next 2 miles are through tree-lined residential streets. From the highest point to just before mile 9, the course follows a nice downward pitch. After a slight rise between 9 and 10, the course again dips to the lowest part on the route, 575 feet between miles 14 and 15. At mile 15, runners reach the biggest climb on the course, an 88-foot rise over 2 miles as you make the turn back toward downtown Huntsville. From the crest just before 17 to 19 miles, you drop 72 feet on the Chickamauga Trail. The next 3 miles roll slightly, and at 21.5, you return to the pedestrian tunnel and do the Downtown Connection in reverse. This last section of the course leading to downtown is mostly flat until the home stretch and a downhill, red carpet finish at the Hilton. Announcers call out your name as you cross the line.

CROWD/RUNNER SUPPORT Rocket City provides excellent support to the runners. Race organizers distribute 18,000 spectator flyers to homes along the course, and they promote a contest for the best spectator signs (many of which are extremely well done) boosting the runners. Crowd turnout is decent for a city of this size. The Friday paper lists all entrants so that spectators can cheer on runners by name. In addition, more than 1,000 volunteers, nearly one volunteer per runner, allows Rocket City to provide personalized service, such as the trained handlers for each and every marathon finisher.

RACE LOGISTICS Since the course is a loop, with the start and finish at the

Huntsville Hilton, transportation is not required for the vast majority of runners. If you are staying elsewhere, you need to get to the start on your own. Portable toilets are located at four locations along the course. Belongings may be left in the Runner's Check-In area and picked up after the race. Aid stations every 2.4 miles offer water, electrolyte replacement, and minor medical supplies.

ACTIVITIES Rocket City offers a number of pre-race activities. On Friday evening, members of the Huntsville Track Club lead noncompetitive group runs around historic Huntsville. The emphasis is on sightseeing and socializing. The runs begin at 4:00 p.m. and leave from the covered bridge at the Hilton. A "gabfest" greets runners at the Race Headquarters where they pick up their race packets, get information about the course, and browse the expo. The Carbo Loading Supper and clinic (about $9) at the Hilton features a noted guest speaker. After finishing the race, runners receive a snack while the official results are posted after every 50 finishers. Following the race, a panel of experts provides informal advice on any questions you may have. The awards presentation begins at 2:30 p.m. inside the Hilton. Finally, marathon weekend concludes with the Award Winners' Banquet and Party.

AWARDS One of the best marathon values around, Rocket City presents runners with an 84-page Marathon Information book that contains everything you need to know about the race, a 40-page Results Book, and a long-sleeve T-shirt. Every finisher receives a medallion, finisher's cap, and finish certificate. Rocket City offers $18,000 in prize money, plus $4,000 course record bonuses. Age-group winners (3 to 5 deep) receive special medallions. Winners must be present to receive their awards.

ELITE RUNNERS INFORMATION Rocket City maintains fairly explicit policies for elite runner recruitment. Recently, the race has moved toward offering more prize money and less in travel expenses in the hopes of encouraging faster performances. Essentially, the race offers lodging (at a hotel or possibly with a host) and entry to open males under 2:25, master males under 2:35, open females under 2:55 and master females under 3:05. Past winners also receive travel expenses. Complimentary entry and race functions are available to open males under 2:30, master males under 2:40, open females under 3:00, and master females under 3:10. The race offers prize money of approximately $18,000, with money going to the top ten open males and females, the top five master's males, and the top three master's females. There is also a $1,000 bounty for any open or masters runner who sets a new course record.

ACCOMMODATIONS Try to stay at the Huntsville Hilton if you can. All race activities begin and end there, including the marathon. A good value at $60 or so, the Hilton is located at 401 Williams Avenue (205-533-1400), and fills very early so make your reservations far in advance. Two other hotels offer special rates to marathoners: the Huntsville Marriott Hotel, 5 Tranquillity Base (205-830-2222); and the Courtyard by Marriott, 4804 University Drive (205-837-1400). The Huntsville Marriott is located next to the U.S. Space and Rocket Center Museum and offers shuttles to and from the marathon. The Marathon Information Book contains a list of other hotels in the area.

AREA ATTRACTIONS While in Huntsville, you should visit the Space Museum which is the largest in the world. The Museum contains more than 60 hands-on exhibits, space flight simulations, and a 354-foot Saturn V rocket. The Von Braun Civic Center also hosts a large craft show on race weekend.

HONOLULU MARATHON

OVERALL: 93.4

COURSE BEAUTY: 9

COURSE DIFFICULTY: 4+ (SEE APPENDIX)

APPROPRIATENESS FOR FIRST TIMERS: 8

RACE ORGANIZATION: 9+

CROWDS: 6

RACE DATA

Overall Ranking: **9**
Quickness Ranking: **62**
Contact: **Honolulu Marathon Association**
3435 Waialae Avenue, Room 208
Honolulu, HI 96816
Tel. (808) 734-7200
Fax (808) 732-7057
E-mail: info@honolulumarathon.org
http://www.honolulumarathon.org/
Date: **December 12, 1999; December 10, 2000**
Start Time: **5:00 a.m.**
Time Course Closes: **Last finisher**
Number of Finishers: **26,495 in 1997**
Course: **Near loop**
Certification: **USATF**
Course Records: **Male: (open) 2:11:43; (masters) 2:17:24**
Female: (open) 2:31:01; (masters) 2:32:13
Elite Athlete Programs: **Yes**
Cost: **$65/75/100**
Age groups/Divisions: **≤14, 15-19, 20-24, 25-29, 30-34, 35-39, 40-44,**
45-49, 50-54, 55-59, 60-64, 65-69, 70-74, 75-79,
80-84, 85-89, 90-94, 95-99, 100+, wheelchair
Walkers: **Yes**
Requirements: **None**
Temperature: **65° - 85°**
Aid/Splits: **17 / every mile, clocks every 5 miles**

HIGHLIGHTS Like the swallows' yearly pilgrimage to San Juan Capistrano, runners from East and West flock to Hawaii for the burgeoning Honolulu Marathon. In 1997, nearly 33,000 runners made the flight to the tropics, perhaps to escape the pre-winter cold or to place the ultimate bookend on their marathon year. The painfully early 5:00 a.m. start, necessary because of the impending heat and humidity, is tempered by the most entertaining staging area of any marathon. Each year, upwards of 20,000 Japanese runners add a colorful flair to the race, providing more vitality than a hummingbird on honey as they proudly sport their brightly colored running club duds, wave club banners and bellow club chants. If this spectacle doesn't get you going, the gust of fireworks will surely put some bounce in your stride as you embark on a course that includes the world-famous sights of Waikiki Beach, Diamond Head and Koko Head Crater.

COURSE DESCRIPTION Most runners congregate in the darkness of Ala Moana Beach Park or the Ala Moana Shopping Center, listening to the lively military band. Amidst

a torrent of fireworks and a Howitzer cannon blast, the 30,000+ runners stampede west toward downtown and Aloha Tower. Runners enter the Capitol District (miles 2 and 3) on South King Street, passing the Kamehameha Statue, Alliolani Hale (the Judiciary Building), Iolani Palace, the Hawaii State Library, Kawaihao Church, and Honolulu Hale (City Hall). With Christmas only weeks away, local businesses and merchants get into the marathon spirit by leaving on their Christmas lights to illuminate this predawn section of the course. Returning near the start after 5K, runners cross the Ala Wai Canal into the world-famous Waikiki strip just after 4 miles. The Hilton Hawaiian Village and Fort DeRussy lie on the way to your first glimpse of the balmy Pacific waters at Kuhio Beach (mile 5). Leaving the ocean behind, the course makes its first trip through Kapiolani Park, the eventual finish, six miles into the race. Virtually flat up to this point, the course begins ascending Diamond Head Road at 7.25 miles and peaks just past the lighthouse near mile 8 (93 feet). At 8.6 miles, the course veers left of Ft. Ruger Triangle Park, climbing to its highest point (108 feet) at 15K. A quick turn onto 18th Avenue leads runners past the Diamond Head Film Studio, home of Hawaii Five-O and Magnum P.I. The lonely next 3 miles on Kalanianaole Hwy., although barely 10 feet above sea level and absolutely flat, afford only a few places to see the ocean. Your spirits soon rise as you reach the half-marathon point just before the Aina Haina Shopping Center. After passing the Niu and Kuliouou Valleys around 14 miles, the course turns off the highway into residential Hawaii Kai, christened by a 200-yard climb over a short bridge. After retracing your steps on the lonely highway, a slight incline occurs past the Waialae Country Club (21.5 miles) before the course descends toward the ocean. At the bottom of the short decline sits the Aloha Gasoline station, site of a Hawaiian band and hula dancers in grass skirts. At mile 23, the course turns right onto Kahala Avenue, better known as the Million Dollar Mile because of the high value of its real estate. By mile 23.8, you begin the 1-mile climb up Diamond Head, gaining a modest 50 feet. From the cliffs to your left, watch the surfers and windsurfers in the water below. A 3-mile downhill from Diamond Head and you're in the homestretch—only flat Diamond Head Road (mile 25) and Kalakaua Avenue remain before the finish in Kapiolani Park.

CROWD/RUNNER SUPPORT Over 30,000 fellow runners and 50,000 spectators do their best to give you company on the course. The thousands of spouses, friends and other spectators left behind at the start get their next chance to cheer their runner at the 5K mark when the course returns near the start. Here, cheering sections from the Japanese running clubs shout, chant, blow whistles, sound horns, and jingle bells. Others cheer them from their high-rise condos and hotel lanais along Ala Moana and Kalakaua Avenue in Waikiki. Not only do they cheer you on, but their camera flashbulbs light up your predawn path. More applause and encouragement come from residents of Hawaii Kai (15-18 miles) and the Million Dollar Mile (23-24 miles). As the day grows older and the temperature rises, each of the 17 aid stations becomes more of a welcomed sight. You'll especially enjoy the enthusiastic stations in Hawaii Kai around miles 15 and 17.

RACE LOGISTICS Free bus service from Kapiolani Park to the start begins at 2:00 a.m. The last bus leaves at 4:00 a.m. Kapiolani Park is located within walking (hobbling for the return) distance of major hotels along Waikiki Beach. You can check-in any post-race clothing you need at Kapiolani Park from Friday through Saturday for pick-up after the marathon. You may not drop off your clothing on marathon morning.

ACTIVITIES Early arrivers to Honolulu have first pick at arguably the best collection of souvenirs (most display Honolulu's signature Polynesian runner) of any North American marathon. An all-in-one Sports Expo, souvenir sale and packet pick-up extends from Wednesday to Saturday 10:00 a.m. to 6:00 p.m. at the Outrigger Reef Hotel. There is no race-day registration for the marathon. Souvenir sales also take place at Kapiolani Park, Thursday through Saturday from 10:00 a.m. to 6:00 p.m. and race day from 5:00 a.m. to 4:00 p.m. On Friday evening, join runners from around the world at the carbo-loading party at the Waikiki Shell from 5:30 p.m. to 8:30 p.m. After the race, speed your recovery with post-race refreshments and a well-deserved massage as you await the awards ceremony, starting at 1:00 p.m., at the Kapiolani Park Bandstand.

AWARDS Every finisher receives a T-shirt, shell lei, and medallion. Finisher certificates are also awarded and available the day after the race at marathon headquarters. Elite runners compete for several thousand dollars in overall prize money, while the top three in each age group receive trophies. Additionally, the top 5% of each age division receive medals.

ELITE RUNNERS INFORMATION The race maintains no official criteria establishing elite status. Instead, race organizers determine elite status and appropriate expenses on an individual basis. The usually substantial prize money purse fluctuates annually depending on sponsorship commitments.

ACCOMMODATIONS The Outrigger Reef Hotel, 2169 Kalia Road (800-688-7444) generally serves as the host hotel. Additional nearby hotels include: Sheraton Waikiki, 2255 Kalakaua Avenue (800-325-3535); Hyatt Regency Waikiki, 2255 Kalakaua Avenue (800-233-1234); Royal Hawaiian Hotel, 2259 Kalakaua (800-325-3535); Hawaiian Waikiki Beach Hotel, 2570 Kalakaua Avenue (800-877-7666); and Continental Surf Hotel, 2426 Kuhio Avenue (808-922-2755).

RELATED EVENTS/RACES To insure that you're not overly peaked for the marathon, run the Diamond Head Duet couples run. This is a free, 4.2-mile run on Thursday at 8:00 a.m. in Kapiolani Park. On race day, family and friends braving the early marathon start may consider participating in the 10K Mayor's Walk, benefitting Hawaii's Special Olympics, held immediately following the start of the marathon. The walk course covers the first 10K of the marathon and finishes in Kapiolani Park in plenty of time to watch the marathon finish.

AREA ATTRACTIONS While catching some rays will surely be near the top of your "to do" list, wait until after the race for sun worshiping on famous Waikiki Beach or snorkeling at nearby Hanauma Bay. In the meantime, head to the U.S.S. Arizona National Memorial in Pearl Harbor. Although you'll pass Diamond Head Crater during the marathon, take time to hike the one mile in to the crater for a gorgeous sunrise or sunset and nice view of Waikiki.

THE MID PACK

56 LOCAL MARATHONS

OCALA MARATHON

Contact: Chuck Savage
Ocala Marathon
P.O. Box 5621
Ocala, FL 34478
(352) 732-4833

Date: February 7, 1999; February 6, 2000

So you fell behind on your winter training and aren't quite fit enough for the Walt Disney World Marathon? Don't despair. The year-old Ocala Marathon, located only 70 miles northwest of Orlando, exists as a worthy, rural substitute one month later. Featuring a rolling figure-8 loop through the beautiful horse country of north central Florida, the Ocala Marathon attracted 333 marathoners in its first year. Except for a 100-foot hill from mile 4 to 4.5, the course runs flat to rolling on asphalt country roads, passing over 50 handsome horse farms along the way. The typically dry, sunny, and cool weather conditions are perfect for marathoning. Aid stations sit every 2 miles and every mile after 20 miles. The Ocala Hilton, I-75 & SR 200 (352-854-1400), serves as the host hotel where you can pick up your race packet or register. On Saturday night, swing by O'Malley's near Courthouse Square for an outdoor carbo-load pasta dinner. The race presents long-sleeve T-shirts for each entrant, and medals to all finishers. Fast runners win unique horseshoe plaques. The race provides all finishers with post-race food and music.

TYBEE MARATHON

Contact: Anna Boyette
Savannah Striders Track Club
P.O. Box 15785
Savannah, GA 31416
(912) 921-4786

Date: February 13, 1999; February 12, 2000

Originally called the Savannah Marathon, the race moved seven years ago to the friendly and less congested surroundings of Tybee Island, Savannah's beach. The 1998 race saw 161 marathoners line up in front of City Hall for the flat, double-loop course along mostly paved roads through island marshlands and residential areas. Aid stations dot the route every 2 to 3 miles. For those not interested in going a full 26, race day includes a larger half marathon (500 runners) and 5K (385) starting with the marathon at 8:00 a.m. All entrants receive T-shirts, and marathon finishers receive either commemorative medals or mugs. The top three overall and age-group winners receive plaques.

After the race, enjoy the many tourist sites of Tybee Island, including: the Coney Island-type amusement park, water park or Marine Science Center. For more entertainment, head to River Street or the City Market in Savannah where street-side food stands and local band performances regularly attract large crowds.

THIRD OLYMPIAD MEMORIAL MARATHON

Contact: Gateway Athletics—St. Louis
c/o Marathon Sports
13453 Chesterfield Plaza
Chesterfield, MO 63017
Tel. (314) 434-9577
Fax (314) 434-9193
Date: February 21, 1999; February 20, 2000 (tentative)

The Olympiad Memorial Marathon, a tribute to those who participated in the 1904 St. Louis Olympic Marathon, runs on a USATF-certified, loop course. Commencing in Chesterfield Plaza, the race runs on rolling residential roads for the first 5 miles before proceeding onto a flat river bottom over lightly-traveled roads for the next 20 miles. At mile 25, you encounter a major hill preceding the Chesterfield Plaza finish. Starting at mile 5, aid stations are positioned along the course every 2 to 2.5 miles, and splits are called out at miles 1, 5, 10, 13.1, 15, and 20. Upon completion of the course, you receive a finisher's award and certificate. The open, masters, and age-group winners are presented awards at a post-race ceremony. The St. Louis Marriott West, about 2 miles from the race start (800-352-1175), serves as the host hotel. The hotel offers free shuttle service to and from the airport if you're flying in from out of town.

NANTUCKET MARATHON

Contact: Paul K. Daley
Nantucket Marathon
P.O. Box 401
Norton, MA 02766-401
(508) 285-4544

Date: March 5, 1999; March 3, 2000

Historic Nantucket Island, located 30 miles off the coast of Cape Cod, plays host to about 350 marathoners each spring. The beautiful course on this former whaling bastion lazily rolls along paved roads in the crisp salt air. Arrive early, and pick up your race packet and T-shirt at the Jared Coffin House, the host hotel. After check-in, mosey over to the official island greeting and Friday night Five Star CarboLoad feast, where you can ask any last minute questions about the race. Each finisher is awarded a medal, and personalized certificates are mailed to participants after the race. Special prizes go to the top five overall runners and to age-group winners. The race also hosts a half marathon. Nantucket is accessible from Hyannis, MA by express ferry (1 hr.), air (15 min.) and steamship (2.7 hrs).

B & A Trail Marathon

Contact: Thomas Bradford
Annapolis Striders
746 Mimosa Court
Millersville, MD 21108-1883
(410) 987-0674

Date: March 7, 1999; March 5, 2000

Originally created to accommodate Boston Marathon hopefuls who hadn't yet made the cut, the B & A Trail Marathon now runs on its own since Boston has moved up its qualifying date. The paved course has an unusual configuration. Technically a loop, the route contains two out-and-backs for the marathon on the B & A Trail. Starting on the residential streets of Severna Park, you embark on the B & A Trail, an asphalt bike and running path along the Rails-to-Trails Park, at mile 3. Runners complete an out-and-back from miles 3 to 13.1; half marathoners finish on the trail, while full marathoners continue on for another out-and-back to finish near the race start. Though mostly level, the race contains a couple of slight grades at miles 2 and 7. Take care on the course as you share it with cyclists, rollerbladers and walkers. Volunteers greet you at miles 3, 7, 11, 13.1, 15, 20 and 24 with refreshments, first aid and other necessities. Though crowd participation is small, the race allows doting friends and relatives to cheer you on at numerous spectator access points.

All registered runners receive T-shirts, and each finisher earns a medal. Additional awards are presented to the first three finishers in each age group, and bonus prizes go to the overall and masters winners. All winners are recognized at the post-race awards ceremony held at noon.

Athens Marathon

Contact: Athens Marathon Committee
P. O. Box 5780
Athens, OH 45701
(800) 878-9767

Date: TBA (typically last weekend in March or early April)

Greece is beyond your budget? Will Athens, Ohio do? Each year this community hosts a marathon and half marathon starting at high noon in front of the Athens County Courthouse. The USATF-certified marathon heads straight for the country and finishes in Ohio University's Peden Stadium. Aid stations and medical assistance are provided every three miles. To save you from splashing yourself uncontrollably, the water cups come equipped with lids and straws.

Cash prizes are presented to the top three overall finishers, top two masters runners, and age-division winners. Wreaths (from Greece, of course) are also presented to the marathon winners. All preregistered marathoners receive long-sleeve T-shirts. Located 75 miles southeast of Columbus, Athens contains several hotels near the course. Most convenient is the Ohio University Inn (614-593-6661).

CAMP LEJEUNE MARATHON

Contact: Mike Marion
Morale, Welfare & Recreation
Attn: MSAD/Race
1401 West Road
Camp Lejeune, NC 28547
Tel. (910) 451-1799; Fax (910) 451-2093
Date: April 10, 1999; April 8, 2000

A lesser known U.S. Marine-sponsored marathon lies a few hundred miles south of Washington, D.C. in Camp Lejeune, North Carolina. And while you won't find historic monuments, Al Gore, or Oprah Winfrey at the Camp Lejeune Marathon, you will find a great value. For a paltry $15 ($10 for active duty military) marathoners receive a T-shirt, commemorative finisher's award, post-race meal, and an excellent opportunity for a PR. Held entirely on Camp Lejeune, one of the largest U.S. Marine bases, the race features a flat, loop course with very few turns. Nearly 300 runners finished the 1998 race, 40 percent of whom were military personnel. One runner commented that it was the only marathon he had run where some of the runners had arms as big as most marathoner's legs. A small expo and pre-race pasta party take place on Friday at Marston Pavilion. Those not interested in running the marathon can participate in the 5K run or walk. Following the race, relax at one of the beautiful Carolina coast beaches lying only minutes away.

CBK COUNTRY TRAIL MARATHON

Contact: Bill & Cheri Kissell
301 N. Jenifer Avenue
Covina, CA 91724
(818) 339-5251

Date: April 25, 1999; April 23, 2000

A trail marathon conveniently located in the midst of a city, the CBK Country Walnut Creek Trail Marathon begins with a flag ceremony by local boy scouts and the singing of our National Anthem. The challenging out-and-back passage starts with a 3-mile trek through downtown Covina, then travels through country terrain, across bubbling streams, and over the rolling hills of Bonelli Regional Park. As you make your way through the second half of the course, the sight of the cool waters of Puddingstone Lake and Raging Waters Park rejuvenate and push you toward the live entertainment at the Covina Park finish line. All runners are treated to race T-shirts, a post-race pancake breakfast and live entertainment, and all finishers receive medallions.

GLASS CITY MARATHON

Contact: Pat Wagner
Glass City Marathon
130 Yale Drive
Toledo, OH 43614
(419) 385-7025

Date: April 25, 1999; April 23, 2000

Known as the glass capital of the world, Toledo, OH hosts the Glass City Marathon every spring. Organized by the Toledo Roadrunners, this small marathon features a loop course run entirely along the scenic Maumee River. The flat route travels through Toledo and three adjoining suburbs. The Toledo Zoo, several parks, and some of the area's most exclusive residential neighborhoods pop up along the route. You also pass hundreds of fishermen, between miles 12 and 16, during the spring walleye run. All race entrants receive a unique polo shirt, and finishers (usually about 300) earn a commemorative glass. A two- or four-person marathon relay runs concurrently with the marathon.

JERSEY SHORE McMARATHON

Contact: Jersey Shore McMarathon
P.O. Box 198
Oceanport, NJ 07757
(732) 542-6090

Date: April 25, 1999; April 23, 2000

One of only two New Jersey marathons, the Jersey Shore McMarathon benefits the Ronald McDonald House of Long Branch. The race features a diverse, scenic point-to-point course along the northern New Jersey coast. The first 8 miles of the route loop through Gateway National Recreation Area (Sandy Hook), passing historic Fort Hancock, which years ago played a role in defending New York Harbor. While skirting the shore of Sandy Hook Bay near 5 miles, runners enjoy a spectacular, across-the-bay view of Navesink Twin Lights Lighthouse. While leaving Sandy Hook near mile 9.5, you encounter the only hill on the course, a 40-foot overpass leading into Sea Bright. The remainder of the course heads along a straight, two-lane road through residential and commercial areas of Sea Bright and the three other coastal boroughs of Monmouth Beach, Long Branch, and Deal. Along the way, you run along the Ocean Promenade in Long Branch, past historic St. Michael's Church, and along Lake Takanassee, site of the George Sheehan Memorial Monument. Fittingly, the race passes the Long Branch Ronald McDonald House before finishing on the all-weather track at Long Branch High School's Bresett Stadium. Ocean lovers may be disappointed that the course, with the exception of the Ocean Promenade, offers few ocean views. In addition to the marathon, Jersey Shore features a Friday night Mile Race, kids' races, and a 15K fitness walk. All marathon entrants receive T-shirts, and finishers receive medals and certificates.

IDAHO GREAT POTATO MARATHON

Contact: Tim Severa
YMCA
1050 State St.
Boise, ID 83702
(208) 344-5501

Date: May 1, 1999; May 6, 2000

Beginning in 1978 as a Boise YMCA fitness challenge, the Idaho Great Potato Marathon features a relatively fast, point-to-point course (shuttle buses are provided to the start) with a net drop of 500 feet. Starting outside of Boise, the City of Trees, the race provides beautiful views of the city and the Boise foothills. Runners enjoy more of the area's springtime beauty while running along the Boise River Greenbelt System, which comprises 40% of the race course. Approximately 150 runners typically compete in the marathon with hundreds more participating in the accompanying half marathon, 10K run and walk, and 2.2-mile run and walk. Every entrant receives a T-shirt, unless choosing the reduced entry fee, while division winners receive plaques and bags of potatoes. If you're not fast enough to win your division, you're still eligible to go home a winner. Sport your best Mr. Potato Head garb and enter the costume contest to win dinner at one of Boise's finest restaurants. Speaking of food, post-race activities include a carbo reload party with, you guessed it, a large potato feed. So, if you're a potato lover and a marathoner, consider placing the Idaho Great Potato Marathon on your race menu.

LONG ISLAND MARATHON

Contact: Patti Kemler
NC Recreation & Parks
Sports Unit, Eisenhower Park
East Meadow, NY 11554
(516) 572-0248

Date: May 2, 1999; May 7, 2000

The Long Island Marathon (originally called the Earth Day Marathon) attracts more than 7,500 participants to one of New York's most popular sandy summer refuges. The loop course starts in Eisenhower Park, winding through suburban streets on its way to Wantagh Parkway. Here, with water on both sides, you make an out-and-back to Jones Beach with the Jones Beach tower in the background. Aid stations await you at least every 2 miles. Runners can also choose to do the half marathon in mid race. Starting together, the full and half races split near mile 7.7; you may go in either direction depending on how you feel that day. After the race, runners receive refreshments prior to the awards ceremony.

With the race behind you, set out to see the sights of Long Island. Start at Nassau's Jones Beach State Park with its 1.5 miles of boardwalk offering activities such as miniature golf, deck games and rollerblading. If you haven't quite recovered from your run, head to Fire Island to enjoy the national seashore and protected wilderness of this 32-mile barrier island. If you want to toast your accomplishment, then work your way to wine country where the vineyards of the North Fork produce wines from Riesling to Chardonnay.

BAYSHORE MARATHON

Contact: Dave Taylor
1211 E. Front Street, #116
Traverse City, MI 49684
(616) 941-8118
E-mail: tctc@northlink.net
http://www.users.northlink.net/tctc
Date: May 23, 1999; May 28, 2000

Celebrating its 17th anniversary in 1999, Traverse City Track Club's Bayshore Marathon features a scenic, flat USATF-certified course. Starting on the grounds of Northwestern Michigan College, the out-and-back course winds through one mile of residential neighborhoods before joining the shores of East Grand Traverse Bay on the beautiful Old Mission Peninsula. Aid stations are located every 2 miles along the mostly shaded course. Marathoners face a five-hour time limit, although the 1999 race features a one hour early start for walkers. For those not wanting to run the full 26 miles, the race includes an accompanying 10K event. After the race, snacks are provided, and an awards ceremony is held to recognize the top five male and female finishers. All participants receive T-shirts, and finishers receive medals. Top open and masters runners vie for $2,400 in prize money. Race results are available on the Traverse City Track Club web site or by mailing a self-addressed stamped envelope. Host hotels include the Days Inn (616-941-0208) and Hampton Inn (616-946-8900). Traverse City, one of the top resort destinations in the Midwest, features many water activities, great restaurants, the Interlochen Center for the Arts, and the Sleeping Bear Dunes National Lakeshore.

ANDY PAYNE MEMORIAL MARATHON

Contact: J.R. Cook
United National Indian Tribal Youth, Inc. (UNITY)
P.O. Box 25042
Oklahoma City, OK 73125
Tel. (405) 236-2800; Fax (405) 971-1071
E-mail: unity@unityinc.org
Date: May 29, 1999; May 27, 2000

When Andy Payne, a Cherokee from Claremore, Oklahoma, stepped across the finish line first at the 1928 Los Angeles to New York City "Great Cross-Country Marathon Race," he could not have anticipated that nearly 70 years later runners would come out to Lake Overholser in Oklahoma City to pay tribute to his life. In an effort to uphold Andy Payne as a role model, the United National Indian Tribal Youth, Inc. has sponsored the Andy Payne Memorial Marathon and related 10K and 5K runs since 1978.

Starting along the shore of Lake Overholser, this paved, USATF-certified course, dubbed the "Bunion Run," makes a short, out-and-back before looping the lake three times. Four aid stations are positioned throughout each loop.

An awards ceremony is held after the race where prizes are presented to the overall male and female winners and the top three in each age division. Every participant who preregisters receives a commemorative T-shirt, while finishers receive medals.

LONE STAR PAPER CHASE MARATHON

Contact: Jo Tyler Bagwell
Amarillo Globe-News
P.O. Box 2091
Amarillo, TX 79166
(806) 345-3451

Date: May 29, 1999; May 27, 2000

Founded by a veteran long-distance runner who worked for the Amarillo Globe-News, the Lone Star Paper Chase Marathon benefits the Newspapers in Education (NIE) program which supplies subscriptions to area schools. The mostly flat point-to-point course begins in front of Northwest Texas Hospital in the Harrington Regional Medical Center. The course follows Soncy Road along Amarillo's newest neighborhoods, before joining Route 66 to Hope Road. Returning on Route 66, runners head through the city and the newly repaved historic antique district before finishing at Wonderland Amusement Park in shady Thompson Park. Aid stations are positioned at least every 2 miles. Though this USATF-certified marathon normally attracts a small field of around 60 runners, more competitors take part in the accompanying half marathon, 10K , 10K relay, and 1-mile runs.

The Ambassador Hotel traditionally serves as the race headquarters. Transportation is available from the airport to the hotel and back. Transportation is also available to and from the start/finish for all runners staying at the Ambassador Hotel. A finish line celebration and awards ceremony follow the race. If you plan on extending your stay, consider visiting the Wonderland Amusement Park, Funfest '99, a three-day outdoor festival, or the Palo Duro Canyon State Park.

WYOMING MARATHON

Contact: Brent Weigner
Wyoming Marathon
402 West 31st Street
Cheyenne, WY 82001
Tel. (307) 635-3316; Fax (307) 635-5297
E-mail: RunWyo26point2@compuserve.com

Date: May 30, 1999; May 28, 2000

Wyoming's new, out-and-back course still runs over the hilly dirt and gravel roads of beautiful Medicine Bow National Forest. Thankfully, however, the new route excludes the 10 miles on I-80. Those prone to altitude sickness may choose to Chey away from this one as the route hovers between 7,500 and 8,640 feet. And don't expect to be babied by race management; as noted on the race entry blank, the race motto is, "Where the race director promises you nothing, and he delivers." He's actually relented a bit recently by adding an aid station every 6 miles and a pasta dinner the night before. A growing field of 46 marathoners finished the 1998 race and an additional 18 completed the accompanying double marathon. Each finisher receives a medal in the finish chute, and T-shirts are available for sale after the race. Bring warm clothes; the weather is typically chilly (40 ° to 55°), especially with the 6:00 a.m. race start.

Palos Verdes Marathon

Contact: Walt Walston
W2 Promotions
1666 Ashland Avenue
Santa Monica, CA 90405
(310) 828-4123
E-mail: W2Promo@aol.com
Date: June 5, 1999; June 3, 2000

As one of the oldest marathons on the west coast, the Palos Verdes Marathon celebrates its 33rd annual race in 1999. Featuring a rolling out-and-back course, the race starts and finishes at San Pedro's Point Fermin Park and runs along tree-lined streets of the Palos Verdes Peninsula with breathtaking ocean vistas—if not obscured by the early morning fog. Race day also includes a half marathon, 3-person marathon relay and 5K run/walk. Each marathon finisher receives a T-shirt and medal, and the top three finishers in each five-year age group receive special medals. Local bands provide on-going entertainment at the runner's expo in the finish area. The Palos Verdes Marathon is a community-supported fundraising event of the Kiwanis Club of Palos Verdes Peninsula.

Ridge Runner Marathon

Contact: Angel Adams
North Bend State Park
Rt. 1 Box 221
Cairo, WV 26337
(304) 643-2931 or (800) CALL WVA

Date: June 5, 1999; June 3, 2000

The Ridge Runner Marathon's figure-8 course, starting and finishing in North Bend State Park in northwestern West Virginia, journeys through the neighboring towns of Cairo and Harrisville. Containing some difficult hills, the mostly paved course ranges from 500 to 1,300 feet in elevation. Typically 150 runners tackle the marathon. Aid stations are present approximately every 2 miles along the route. For those not interested in running the marathon, race day also includes a 10-mile event. All runners receive T-shirts in their race packets, and marathon finishers receive participation awards and certificates. Trophies are awarded to the overall male and female winners. The Ridge Runner Marathon coincides with the North Bend Rail Trail Festival which includes mountain bike rides, sounds of the trail contest, and a luminary walk. Dinner and music are provided at the post-race celebration.

SUNBURST MARATHON

Contact: Kim Smoyer
615 N. Michigan St.
South Bend, IN 46601
(219) 674-0900 Ext. 6262

Date: June 5, 1999; June 3, 2000

If you love college football and you're a big fan of the Fighting Irish, then the Sunburst Marathon is for you. The race currently draws 500 marathoners and over 4,500 other participants in the accompanying 10K run, 5K run, and 5K fun walk. The point-to-point course begins in downtown South Bend at the College Football Hall of Fame, winds along the beautiful St. Joseph River on the East Bank Trails, and runs past the man-made white water rapids of the East Raceway (South Bend's kayak and rafting recreational waterway). After heading toward historic downtown Mishawaka, the route makes its way back to South Bend through the tree-lined campus of the University of Notre Dame to finish at the 50-yard line of the Notre Dame football stadium. Course support comes from approximately 3,000 spectators and 12 aid stations along the way. The finish line festivities include: food, music, and an awards ceremony where a $3,500 prize purse is distributed among the top three masters finishers in the marathon. Each marathoner receives a T-shirt.

NIPMUCK TRAIL MARATHON

Contact: David Raczkowski
P.O. Box 285
Chaplin, CT 06235
(860) 455-1096

Date: June 6, 1999; June 4, 2000

Beginning in 1984 when race director David Raczkowski decided he wanted a trail marathon near his home, the NipMuck Trail Marathon ("Capital M is for Muck") has grown from a sparse inaugural field of 15 to its current average of 150 runners. One of the few marathons with qualification standards (you must have already run a road marathon or a trail half marathon), NipMuck offers directions to the nearest hospital on the course map and a race entry blank commencing with a warning: "It is possible to get a serious injury in this race." To invoke more fear and trepidation, Raczkowski has first-timers read a letter from a past participant explaining his distaste for the race and his desire never again to receive an entry blank. Despite Raczkowski's many tongue-in-cheek race caveats, NipMuck is a very enjoyable race. Featuring a double out-and-back course on a well-maintained, wooded, and narrow trail, NipMuck runners must endure an overall elevation gain of 2,300 feet and an occasional fence scaling. Though the spectacular mountain laurel may take your mind off your time, bank on adding an hour or two to your road marathon time to get an idea of your NipMuck journey. Like most trail events, NipMuck is an informal event. In fact, the winners are awarded apple pies baked by Raczkowski (using his mom's recipe).

HOOSIER MARATHON

Contact: Bob Hockensmith
Fort Wayne Track Club
P.O. Box 11730
Fort Wayne, IN 46860
(219) 436-2234

Date: June 12, 1999; June 10, 2000

Essentially a series of loops, northeastern Indiana's Hoosier Marathon never strays more than four miles from the start. Spectator friendly, the course starts behind a city park golf course, makes a 2-mile loop around it, and then heads to an adjacent city park for three 8-mile loops before finishing 385 yards from the start. Since most of the race runs on a narrow, shaded, asphalt path along a river, the field is limited to 400 runners. Two separate hills occur along the route: the first takes place in the opening two miles and the other on each of the remaining loops. Local youth groups provide aid at four separate stations along each loop, and splits are called each mile. Both the music of local bands and the announcement of your name by a celebrity radio personality welcome you to the finish.

The evening before the race, a pasta dinner is accompanied by authentic German music. Post-race refreshments are provided, and awards are presented in the park, but don't leave at the completion of the ceremony—it's the first day of Fort Wayne's Germanfest.

MARATHON-TO-MARATHON

Contact: Marathon-to-Marathon
Box 262
Marathon, IA 50565
Tel. (712) 289-2246
Fax (712) 289-2146

Date: June 12, 1999; June 10, 2000

Created in 1996 to celebrate Iowa's Sesquicentennial, Marathon-to-Marathon features a flat, certified, point-to-point course beginning at the local high school in northwestern Iowa's Storm Lake community and finishing at the Marathon Community Center. Along the mostly paved rural route, runners see farmers tilling corn, cattle grazing in green pastures, quaint country churches, and aid stations every 2.5 miles.

Pick up your race packet on Friday night during the Pasta Party held at Storm Lake High School from 5:30 p.m. to 9:00 p.m. If you anticipate having an appetite after you finish, tickets for a post-race breakfast are also available for purchase. Other activities related to the marathon include kids' games and on-stage entertainment. For those not wanting to run the whole distance, Marathon-to-Marathon features a five-person relay consisting of four 5-mile legs and one 6.2-mile leg. All participants receive T-shirts, and all finishers receive medallions and official race results.

NANISIVIK MIDNIGHT SUN MARATHON

Contact: Midnight Sun Marathon
P.O. Box 225
Nanisivik NT X0A 0X0
Canada
(819) 436-8000

Date: July 4, 1999 (tentative); July 2, 2000 (tentative)

Meant for runners seeking a far-flung adventure marathon, the Nanisivik Midnight Sun Marathon runs almost on top of the world on the northern shore of Canada's Baffin Island, about 500 miles north of the Arctic Circle. Starting at sea level in the Inuit village of Arctic Bay, the course winds through the Terry Fox Pass up to an elevation of 1,749 feet at 15.5 miles, then drops 656 feet over the next 3 miles to the mining town of Nanisivik. At this point, the most strenuous part of the marathon begins. Affectionately termed "The Crunch" by the earnest few who have conquered it, the road drops 984 feet over the next 3.1 miles, down to the dock of Nanisivik, and then loops back over the same steep and winding road to the townsite. The entirely gravel course is in various states of repair so watch your footing! Come outfitted for extremes, since the temperatures on race day may vary anywhere from 23° to 50°, and parts of the barren course are quite gusty. The desolation of the region partly makes the course a laborious one; you encounter bare, gray hills and endless expanses of rock. Silence surrounds you all along the course, except for the sounds of the howling wind and your own breathing. Combine all this with the season's endless sun that burns 24 hours a day. Participants are lodged with local families or placed in single-status accommodations in Nanisivik. Consequently, the number of entrants is limited to 110, and only runners are allowed. Inuit carvings are awarded to race winners, and every finisher receives a commemorative medal, T-shirt, and certificate at the post-race awards dinner.

NOVA SCOTIA MARATHON

Contact: Raymond Green
Barrington Municipal Recreation
P.O. Box 100
Barrington, NS B0W 1G0
CANADA
(902) 637-2760
Date: July 25, 1999; July 23, 2000

The Nova Scotia Marathon charms runners with its fresh breezes, hearty post-race chowder, and friendly organization. Since its inaugural running in 1970, the event consistently draws nearly 70 participants between its full and half marathons. Starting at Barrington Municipal High School, the race loops about three miles around Barrington before crossing the causeway to Cape Sable Island. Here the route makes a figure-8 loop of the island on secondary highways running near the coast most of the way. The race finishes on the Barrington side of the causeway. While open to vehicle traffic, race officials request local dog owners to leash their pets, so you should have a pooch-free course. Rural and moderately rolling, the Nova Scotia Marathon contains three hills of note: a 500-yard moderate climb at mile 19, a 500-yard tough grade at mile 21, and a .75-mile rise at the 23-mile mark. Water stations are available every 3 miles. All entrants receive T-shirts, while finishers are awarded completion certificates. Enjoy the homemade chowder, bread and desserts.

FRANK MAIER MARATHON

Contact: Ben Van Allen
Southeast Road Runners
6731 Gray Street
Juneau, AK 99801
(907) 586-8322
E-mail: runjuneau@aol.com
Date: August 7, 1999; August 5, 2000

Named for a passionate supporter of local running, the Frank Maier Marathon takes advantage of Juneau's incredible setting pinched between the Gastineau Channel and Mt. Juneau. Starting at Savikko Park in Douglas (a community on Douglas Island just across the Gastineau Channel from downtown Juneau), this moderately hilly out-and-back course follows a coastal, two-lane asphalt road north along the Douglas and North Douglas highways where you catch some panoramic views of mountain peaks, glaciers, the Gastineau Channel, Stephens Passage, and southeast Alaska's forested habitat. Just before the turnaround, you attack a formidable hill. Aid stations are at your disposal every 2 to 3 miles, and vehicular traffic is generally negligible. Few spectators come out to observe this small race (about 35 marathoners and 70 half marathoners), so you need to bring your own fan club. A medal is presented to every finisher. Following the race, either enjoy the finish line feast or pig out at the pizza social at downtown Bullwinkle's Pizza Parlor. And, if you're inclined to extend your stay in Juneau, and we suggest you do, look forward to experiencing an endless list of outdoor activities.

EDMONTON FESTIVAL MARATHON

Contact: John Stanton
Running Room
8537 109 Street
Edmonton, AB T6G 1E4
CANADA
(403) 433-6062
Date: August 22, 1999; August 20, 2000

Held to coincide with the Fringe Festival, the Edmonton Festival Marathon drew over 400 marathoners in 1998. Arrive on Friday to attend the Runners' Fair held in conjunction with the Carbo Load Dinner at the impressive Kinsmen Sports Centre. The relatively fast out-and-back race starts at 7:00 a.m., runs through the university, along a river valley, and through picturesque parks. You also parade past many spectators attending the Fringe Festival. Runners encounter a good upgrade at mile 3.75, but it becomes a decent downhill on the way back so it all balances out. Aid is available every 5K, and if you have joined the "back-of-the-pack gang," then an ice-cream stop along the way is essential! All finishers receive a long-sleeve T-shirt, medal, and certificate. Runners not ready for the marathon may choose between the accompanying half marathon or 5K. After the race, join other festival-goers or wander the humongous West Edmonton Mall with its full-scale replica of Columbus' Santa Maria.

KONA MARATHON

Contact: Jim Lovell
JTL Timing System
P.O. Box 5316
Kailua-Kona, HI 96745
(808) 325-0287

Date: August 22, 1999; August 27, 2000 (tentative)

Why run the Kona Marathon? If you need a reason other than to enjoy the scenery of the beautiful Kona Coast, then you can enter to say you've run on the famous Ironman Triathlon marathon course. Started in 1994 by race director Jim Lovell, the Kona Marathon draws just over 50 participants. The relatively flat, out-and-back race starts at the host Keauhou Beach Hotel heading south for 2 miles before proceeding north through shady residential streets until reaching mile 9. This is the beginning of a 10-mile stretch through lava fields before returning along Alii Drive to the finish. Race entry includes a T-shirt and a pre-race Carboload party catered by Bianelli's Pizza. If pasta and salad aren't to your liking, choose from Bianelli's world-famous regular menu. After the race, not only do you receive a pound of Kona coffee, but you are eligible for random drawings for round trip inter-island flights.

TURTLE MARATHON

Contact: Bob Edwards
715 E. Linda Vista
Roswell, NM 88201
(505) 627-5507

Date: September 6, 1999; September 4, 2000

Perhaps better known for hosting the UFO Encounter Festival to celebrate the alleged crash of a flying saucer in 1947, Roswell also hosts a marathon. Beginning in 1987 as a training venue for 15 runners training for the Duke City Marathon, the Turtle Marathon remains an intimate affair. Present day entries number around 30 to 35 runners with all finishers receiving plaques. Competitors run two miles along a residential bike path before joining rural Highway 70 for the next 11 miles before returning along the same route. Trying to keep runners from crashing in the late summer heat, race organizers start the marathon at 5:30 a.m. The early start allows you ample time after the race to explore the surrounding area including Carlsbad Caverns—America's best-known subterranean national park—one hundred miles south of Roswell, and the 12,000-foot Sierra Blanca Mountain in Ruidoso.

AMERICAN ODYSSEY MARATHON

Contact: Joel Braatz
American Odyssey Marathon
8720 28th Avenue
Merrill, WI 54452

Date: September 11, 1999 (tentative); September 9, 2000 (tentative)

No need traveling to Greece to run from Marathon to Athens, simply head to rural, central Wisconsin's American Odyssey Marathon. Though you won't retrace the steps of the famous messenger who brought news of the Greek victory over the Persians, you do run by some pretty cool barns, not to mention (for you geography buffs) mile 19 where you pass the village of Poniatowski—the exact center of the northern part of the Western Hemisphere. It is one of four places on this planet where the 90th meridian of longitude bisects the 45th parallel of latitude. Starting at the Marathon High School parking lot, your Odyssey heads northwest over mostly paved and challenging, rolling terrain to the finish at the bandstand in downtown Athens. If you have family or friends who would like to participate in a less-grueling event, direct them toward the marathon relay also held on race day. Relay teams consist of two to five runners with hand-offs allowed only at the 5, 10, 15, and/or 20-mile marks. Transportation is provided between the start and finish line both before and after the race, and nine aid stations dot the course. All marathon finishers receive official running shorts, and overall and division winners receive commemorative posters. An all-you-can-eat spaghetti dinner is held the night before the race at the Marathon High School cafeteria. The race celebrated its 21st anniversary in 1998. At our press time, however, race organizers were unsure whether the race will continue.

BISMARK MARATHON

Contact: Bill Bauman
YMCA
P.O. Box 549
Bismarck, ND 58502
Tel. (701) 255-1525
Fax (701) 255-0365
Date: September 11, 1999; September 9, 2000

North Dakota's only marathon, the Bismarck Marathon provides an opportunity to set a personal record on its flat, out-and-back course along the Missouri River bottomlands. The USATF-certified race is well ensconced on the trail of those runners seeking to complete a marathon in each of the 50 U.S. states. A bargain at $25, race entry includes an official race T-shirt and post-race pizza picnic. Marathon finishers receive special medallions and certificates. Race day also includes a half marathon. An international Pow Wow is held the same weekend, giving children and adults the chance to see the native culture firsthand. The Kelly Inn, Exit 159 off I-94 (800-635-3559), is the race motel, offering a special marathon rate.

SASKATCHEWAN MARATHON

Contact: Ray Risling
Saskatoon Road Runners Assoc.
128 Ottawa Avenue S.
Saskatoon, Sask. S7M 3L5, CANADA
(306) 382-2962

Date: September 12, 1999 (tentative); September 10, 2000 (tentative)

The handsome valley of the South Saskatchewan River is where the Saskatchewan Marathon, originally the venue of the Western Canada Games trials, takes place. Participation has steadily increased since 1979 on this figure-8 course beginning on the Victoria Bridge in downtown Saskatchewan. Every 2.5 miles you find refreshment at aid stations, and you can track your splits at the 1K, 10K and halfway points. After making your way through a residential area, you proceed along Saskatchewan Crescent, through the shady respite of Diefenbaker Park. Runners continue through flat residential areas before turning around (near 10K) and retracing their steps to Victoria Bridge at the halfway point. The second half continues along Spadina Crescent with a moderate incline between 16.5 and 17.5 miles. After turning around at mile 18.5, runners retrace their path and finish on the red carpet near Broadway Bridge. All finishers receive medals, and overall winners receive modest cash prizes and get their name inscribed on perpetual trophies. Saskatoon's Radisson Hotel (306-665-3322) serves as the race hotel and site of the post-race meal and awards ceremony.

YONKERS MARATHON

Contact: A.J. Cambria
Yonkers Marathon
Yonkers Parks & Recreation
285 Neperhan Avenue
Yonkers, NY 10701
(914) 377-6430
Date: September 19, 1999; September 17, 2000

For a good part of running history, the Yonkers Marathon rivaled Boston as the country's most prestigious marathon. Held merely one month apart, both races started at noon over challenging courses. To earn a space in the Olympics, American hopefuls had to compete in both races with the team decided by competitors' average pace. A new course and date change have given today's Yonkers Marathon a much different look. Gone are most of the pitiless hills and the hot, muggy weather. The race starts at historic City Recreation Pier on the Hudson River. The double-out-and-back course travels over city streets, and though flatter, still contains some of the hills of its predecessor. Every entrant receives a T-shirt, and finishers earn medals and certificates. Top runners compete for at least $10,000 in prize money—divided according to percentage of division registrants compared to overall registration. All runners can enjoy the post-race meal in the finish area. If you arrive in town early, catch Saturday's "Riverfest," an annual Yonkers event full of top-name entertainment.

KOKOPELLI TRAIL MARATHON

Contact: Mike Heaston
Event Marketing Group
747 Centauri Drive
Grand Junction, CO 81506
Tel./Fax (970) 242-7802

Date: September 25, 1999; September 23, 2000

Formerly part of the Old Kokopelli Super Marathon (six races over five days), the Kokopelli Trail Marathon now runs in conjunction with a half marathon and 50K ultra. As the race name suggests, all races take place on the famed Kokopelli Trail—named for the magical hunchbacked flute player of the Flute Clan of the Hopi Indians. Legend has it that he was able to drive back winter with his flute playing and as a symbol of fertility, was welcome during spring planting. With average elevation between 4,600 and 4,900 feet, the point-to-point course rolls along dirt trails and jeep roads featuring the spectacular scenery of the high desert, canyonlands, slickrock, and the Colorado River Basin. The well-organized event is managed by the Pikes Peak Marathon organizers. Bus transportation is provided from the finish to the start. Aid stations sit every 5K to 7K; if you require more frequent aid, plan on bringing your own. All entrants receive T-shirts; finishers receive mugs, finish-line refreshments, and a chance to win random draw prizes. On race afternoon, head to Old Chicago, 120 North Avenue, Grand Junction, for the "Runner Appreciation Party."

ARKANSAS MARATHON

Contact: Dale Burns
Arkansas Marathon
1200 Clardy Street
Malvern, AR 72104
(501) 337-0007

Date: September 26, 1999; September 24, 2000

Aging gracefully, the 31-year-old Arkansas Marathon unveiled a new course in 1997. The race now starts at the National Guard Armory in Malvern (45 minutes southwest of Little Rock) and finishes at Tyndall Park in Benton. The hilly, point-to-point course tours scenic back roads along Hot Springs National Park. The race provides bus transportation from the finish line to the start. Aid stations with water and electrolyte replacement drink are placed at 1-mile intervals beginning at mile 2. Every participant receives a T-shirt, and finishers receive a certificate of completion. The first five finishers in each, five-year age group earn trophies.

DUKE CITY MARATHON

Contact: Duke City Marathon
P.O. Box 3088
Albuquerque, NM 87190
(505) 890-1018

Date: September 26, 1999; September 24, 2000

Recently becoming a training mecca for many of the world's top long distance runners, high altitude Albuquerque hosts one of the Southwest's most popular running events, the Duke City Marathon. With seven races to choose from, Duke City allows everyone to participate. Although the marathon course rises and falls only 300 feet throughout, the 5,000-foot average elevation provides little hope for low-land PR chasers. The route takes you past a nature center and waterpark, along the Rio Grande bike path, past the University of New Mexico and trendy Nob Hill, and through downtown Albuquerque on legendary Route 66. Duke City features the Family Fitness Expo on Saturday at the Albuquerque Convention Center. Each entrant receives a long-sleeve T-shirt, and finishers earn pins. The top three overall and first masters runners receive modest prize money; age-division awards extend three deep. Other race-day events include a half marathon, marathon relay, 5K, and kids' 1K.

ISLAND MARATHON

Contact: Dave Campbell / Wayne Long
City of Charlottetown Parks & Recreation Department
PO Box 98
Charlottetown, PE
Canada C1A 7K2
(902) 566-3966
Date: September 26, 1999; September 24, 2000

In 1979, the Prince Edward Island (PEI) Roadrunners Association designed a course that revealed the windswept scenery of the island from Cavendish to Charlottetown, the largest city and provincial capital. Now city-run, the race remains a double loop in and around the city of Charlottetown with two steep grades (1-1.5 and 14-14.5) on the otherwise rolling course. Aid stations are positioned at five points along the course, so runners obtain relief every 2.5 miles. Spotty crowds in this quiet and quaint city encourage you to the finish line at the City of Charlottetown Recreation Department. In general, Canadian races tend to be great value and the Island Marathon is no exception. Each participant in the marathon and accompanying half marathon and 10K receives a T-shirt and tickets to a number of social events including a wine and cheese party (Friday night), Spaghetti Dinner and award social.

If you can muster up your remaining energy, make certain to visit some of Canada's finest beaches, wind-sculpted sand dunes and salt marshes at PEI National Park—if you're lucky, you might catch a glimpse of the endangered piping plover.

SACRAMENTO MARATHON

Contact: Sacramento Marathon
Sport Scene Promotions
P.O. Box 995
Dixon, CA 95620
(707) 678-5005

Date: October 3, 1999; October 1, 2000

The Sacramento Marathon has an admittedly sentimental appeal for us. It was at this race in 1977 where a short, scrawny thirteen-year-old boy named Rich Hanna ran his first marathon in 3:01:14 on his mom's bacon and eggs breakfast. With the arrival of the California International Marathon (Sacramento's larger and more prestigious marathon) in 1982, the Sacramento Marathon's numbers have steadily declined. These days the race attracts about 150 runners—down from nearly 1,500 in its heyday—to its pleasant, flat course. Essentially a double-out-and-back route, the race starts in shady William Land Park running through its grassy landscapes for the first 1.75 miles. The course then winds through nice area neighborhoods to mile 4.5, turning slightly industrial for a short period. The next 2 miles run along the Sacramento River to the turn-around in Old Sacramento, a restored riverfront from the Old West. Runners then retrace their way back to the park before repeating. All race entrants receive a long-sleeve T-shirt, and finishers earn medals. The overall winner and top three in each division win special prizes (usually coffee mugs). All runners can enjoy free massages, refreshments, live music, and a picnic in the park after the race. A larger half marathon runs concurrently with the marathon, usually attracting 800 runners.

LAKE TAHOE MARATHON

Contact: Les Wright
2261 Cold Creek Trail
So. Lake Tahoe, CA 96150
Tel.(530) 544-7095; Fax (530) 544-6061
E-mail: Leswright@oakweb.com
http://www.laketahoemarathon.com
Date: October 10, 1999; October 8, 2000

The three-year-old Lake Tahoe Marathon circles one-third of North America's largest, and arguably most beautiful, mountain lake. Starting at Fanny Bridge in Tahoe City, the pine-lined, point-to-point course journeys alongside the west shore of Lake Tahoe, past the pristine waters of Emerald Bay and Cascade Lake, over the spawning salmon in Taylor Creek, and by historic Valhalla and Camp Richardson in route to the finish at South Lake Tahoe's city limits. Disguised by the beauty of the course is the awesome challenge it presents. Flat to rolling near lake level (6,225 feet) through 14 miles, the route then poses a few long, steep uphills and downhills to 20 miles. The final 10K gradually descend to the finish. All entrants receive long-sleeve T-shirts, and finishers receive medals. The race uses the ChampionChip timing system, guaranteeing accurate results. Speaking of results, the race institutes a unique option for women runners: they can choose to start 14:42 (the difference between the men's and women's world records) early, and compete for the overall win. Shuttle bus service is provided to the start. A host of events accompany the marathon including a kids fun run, half marathon, 10K, and 5K; the latter three feature point-to-point courses ending at South Lake Tahoe's city limits. If you arrive on the eve of the marathon, partake in the pasta party aboard a sunset cruise boat (for a fee). Unfortunately, frequent organizational miscues keep the Lake Tahoe Marathon from reaching its potential as a great destination marathon. With a little more seasoning (perhaps more emphasis on race preparation), Lake Tahoe may someday leave the mid pack and join the list of elite marathons. **303**

Pueblo River Trail Marathon

Contact: Ben Valdez
Pueblo Family YMCA
700 N. Albany Ave.
Pueblo, CO 81003
Tel. (719) 543-5151
Fax (719) 543-7960
Date: October 10, 1999; October 8, 2000

The Pueblo River Trail Marathon began in 1984 with 135 runners, but currently averages about 360. The rolling point-to-point course contains aid stations every 2 to 3 miles. Throughout the course, the Sangre De Cristo Mountains lie in the distance. Starting at 5,173 feet, the course rolls or slightly descends for the first 10.6 miles through the barren subdivision of Pueblo West. At mile 10.6, the route moves onto a bike path which passes the Pueblo Reservoir and follows the cottonwood-lined Arkansas River. The most noticeable uphills take place just after the half-marathon point. From there, the route is mostly flat except for the largely ascending final mile. In Pueblo, the wall near 20 miles takes on a new meaning as you reach the longest (4.5 miles) urban art mural in the world painted on the levee wall on the opposite side of the river. Included in the entry fee is an all-you-can-eat pasta dinner at the Gold Dust Saloon (where you can pick up your race packet), a long-sleeve T-shirt, complete race results, and a shuttle from the finish to the start. Awards are presented to the top three overall and age-division winners.

Valley Harvest Marathon

Contact: Steve Moores
RR 1
Wolfville, NS B0P 1X0
CANADA
(902) 542-1867

Date: October 10, 1999; October 8, 2000

The Valley Harvest Marathon, named as a tribute to the fall harvest in this primarily agricultural valley, is appropriately held on Canada's Thanksgiving weekend. The gently rolling, out-and-back course ambles through the Annapolis Valley on a lightly-traveled rural road through the golden seasonal brilliance of the region. The marathoners convene on Main Street, just west of the Kentville Fire Hall, loop once around downtown Kentville, cross the Cornwallis River, and proceed to the turnaround in Somerset. At miles 10 and 18, the trees along the course form a tunnel to give you shady respite. What's more, a probable tailwind on the second half of the course pushes you toward the finish line at Centre Square in downtown Kentville. Aid stations are positioned every 2 miles. You find few fans along the course, but you might come upon a grazing cow or two. After the race, a reception and awards ceremony are held to honor all finishers. All preregistered runners receive T-shirts, and finishers receive certificates in the mail.

GREEN MOUNTAIN MARATHON

Contact: Howie Atherton
6010 Main Road
Huntington, VT 05462
(802) 434-3228
E-mail: hatherton@pipeline.com

Date: October 16, 1999; October 21, 2000

For over a decade, the state of Vermont has served as the setting for the Green Mountain Marathon. More than 125 runners typically compete in the marathon, while approximately twice that participate in the accompanying half marathon. The rolling, out-and-back course starts at Folsom School, close to where Clarence DeMar (7-time winner of the Boston Marathon) once lived. It then winds along the west shore of South Hero and Grand Isle, ambling through apple orchards and running past farmland. Tracing the beautiful shore of Lake Champlain, the route passes quaint summer cottages before returning to the finish lined with the crimson fall leaves of 100-year-old maple trees. Although the course rolls throughout, at mile 24 be aware of a 100-foot hill. Primarily paved, the race does consist of some well-maintained hard-packed dirt roads on this sparsely-populated isle. Cool weather can make the air very dry so be sure to stop at all of the aid stations every 3 miles. Upon completion of the race, certificates are awarded to all finishers, with awards and trophies presented at the post-race ceremony.

INDIANAPOLIS MARATHON

Contact: Joel Sauer
Indianapolis Marathon
P.O. Box 36214
Indianapolis, IN 46236
(317) 826-1670
http://www.rocketboy.com/Indy26
Date: October 16, 1999; October 21, 2000 (tentative)

Better known for hosting the country's largest half marathon, not to mention a 500-mile auto race, Indianapolis also holds a relatively new marathon. The three-year-old race features a flat to rolling route with two separate out and backs. After an initial 2-mile loop through historic Fort Benjamin Harrison in neighboring Lawrence, IN, runners head through the suburb of Oaklandon. On the return, runners cut through the tree-lined Fort Harrison Parade Grounds—former housing area of the fort's officers. The second out and back traipses through the new Fort Harrison State Park before running along Fall Creek Corridor Park. The race benefits Youth Development, Inc., a not-for-profit organization designed to meet the physical, emotional, and spiritual needs of area youth. The marathon and accompanying half marathon and 5K start in front of the Benjamin Harrison YMCA (site of the race expo). All entrants receive long-sleeve T-shirts, and finishers take home medals. Top runners split over $2,000 in prize money. All runners receive a free, post-race meal.

WICHITA MARATHON

Contact: **Clark Ensz**
P.O. Box 782050
Wichita, KS 67278
Tel. (316) 636-1266
Fax (316) 636-1288

Date: **October 16, 1999; October 21, 2000**

Changes are in store for the Wichita Marathon as it celebrates its 20th year in 1999. Race organizers intend to introduce a new point-to-point course starting in neighboring Derby, KS and finishing in Wichita's Sedgwick Park. The south to north course promises a prevailing tailwind 80% of the time over a route encompassing a mix of country, city, and Arkansas River bike path running. Aid stations are positioned every 2 miles along the way. Refreshments and massages are provided after the race. All entrants receive long-sleeve T-shirts, and finishers receive medals. The top two males and females earn small cash prizes. Age-group winners are also recognized.

ATLANTIC CITY MARATHON

Contact: **Barbara Altman**
Boardwalk Runners Club
P.O. Box 2181
Ventor, NJ 08406-0181
(609) 601-1RUN

Date: **October 17, 1999; October 15, 2000**

Past its heyday, frayed Atlantic City accommodates East Coast runners who want to combine some high-stakes action amongst the geriatrics with some fast-paced running with the fit. Or, if you're not up to the 26.2 miles, perhaps the half marathon, 10K, 5K or the American Cancer Society 2-mile Healthwalk on the boardwalk will better suit your abilities. Whichever race you choose, arrive early at the Sports Fitness Clinic at the Sea Skate Pavilion on the Boardwalk at Mississippi Avenue to pick up race packets and enjoy the many exhibits. The pre-race pasta party, also at the Sea Skate Pavilion, is hosted by the All Star Cafe. Soak in the sights of the city, a Las Vegas for senior citizens, including beaches, the Atlantic City Boardwalk, Brighton Park, or one of the many casinos. But, conserve some of your energy for the marathon which starts at 8:30 a.m. This USATF-certified marathon starts and finishes on the boardwalk in front of the Atlantic City Convention Center. It follows a flat route running the length of the Atlantic City and Ventnor Boardwalk and along the ocean where you can enjoy scenic seashore vistas and clean, fresh sea breezes. Aid stations are abundant; there's one at 16 points along the course. All marathon finishers are awarded medals, and every participant receives a T-shirt. Plenty of post-race activities also take place with refreshments, music, runner expo and an awards presentation on the boardwalk. Overall and masters winners receive cash prizes, and age-group awards are also presented. Also at the awards ceremony, there is a drawing for a trip for two to the Walt Disney World Marathon.

BAYSTATE MARATHON

Contact: Bill Smith
BayState Marathon
6 Proctor Road
Townsend, MA 01469
(508) 597-5204; E-mail: baystate@empire.net
http://www.baystate.org
Date: October 17 1999; October 15, 2000

Featuring New England's flattest marathon course, BayState's *raison d'etre* is to help area runners qualify for Boston. The parasitic, two-loop race starts in Tyngsboro at Greater Lowell Regional Vocational High School and runs along the Merrimack River. An annual field of 2,500 runners participates in the marathon and accompanying half marathon, with the vast majority of marathoners hoping to crack the Boston barrier. Kicking off with the Health Fair and Expo on Saturday, race weekend also includes a 5K Walk and pasta dinner. Though spectators are sparse along the route, members of the Greater Lowell Road Runners Club provide good support at the aid stations. All preregistered entrants receive long-sleeve T-shirts. Shower and changing facilities are available at the start/finish.

MOHAWK-HUDSON RIVER MARATHON

Contact: Mohawk-Hudson River Marathon
P.O. Box 4146
Albany, NY 12204
(518) 435-4500
E-mail:nylp@.albany.net
http://www.crisny.org/users/hmrrl/index.html
Date: October 17, 1999; October 15, 2000

Named for the two rivers it parallels, the Mohawk-Hudson River Marathon features a point-to-point course through upstate New York's beautiful fall foliage. Typically run under cool, clear skies, the race starts in Schenectady's Central Park and runs along roads and bike paths to the finish at City Square in downtown Albany. Though containing a net elevation loss of 370 feet, the route contains one noteworthy hill between miles 12 and 13. You may pick up your race packet during the mini-sports expo at the downtown Albany Ramada Inn on Saturday from 12:00 p.m. to 6:00 p.m. After the event, enjoy refreshments and an awards ceremony. All preregistered runners receive T-shirts, and finishers earn commemorative medals and certificates. A $500 bonus goes to the male runner who breaks the course record (2:20:59), while $250 goes to the female who dips under the women's record (2:50:12).

ST. LOUIS MARATHON

Contact: **Tom Eckleman**
St. Louis Track Club
2385 Hampton Avenue
St. Louis, MO 63139
(314) 781-3926

Date: **October 17, 1999; October 15, 2000**

Featuring a loop course, the 28-year-old St. Louis Marathon starts on Market at Union Station and travels along gently rolling city streets through downtown St. Louis, Laclede's Landing, and across the spectacular Mississippi Riverfront and Arch Grounds. From there, you venture through pleasant Forest Park, past the neighborhoods of West and South St. Louis, and finish in front of the Soldier's Memorial. Aid stations replenish runners at 12 points along the course, and splits are provided at each mile. Each entrant receives a long-sleeve T-shirt, and finishers receive custom finisher's medallions, personalized certificates, and results booklets. The marathon winners are awarded John Furla Memorial medals and have their names inscribed with past winners on the John Furla Memorial Cup, dedicated to the only St. Louis resident to run the 1904 Olympic Marathon. Prize money, totaling about $10,000, is divided amongst the open, masters, seniors and age-division winners. The post-race festivities, including refreshments and musical entertainment, begin at 1:30 p.m. in the finish area.

BATON ROUGE MARATHON

Contact: **Jeff Ravlin**
13380 Greenview Avenue
Baton Rouge, LA 70816
(504) 275-1576

Date: **October 23, 1999; October 28, 2000**

Named after a beach along the Louisiana State University Lake, the Baton Rouge Beach Marathon started in 1993 with just seven marathoners. More recently, the race attracts over 50 runners to its double-loop course through the LSU campus and along the Mississippi River. The course takes you by Alex Box Stadium (home of the LSU baseball team), Tiger Stadium (football), Bernie Moore Track (Women's National Champions), Peter Maravich Assembly Center, LSU Tower, Sorority and Fraternity Mansions, lakes of LSU, City Park Golf Course, and Centenial Oaks. Primarily flat, the course contains short hills at approximately miles 8, 10, 11, 21, 23, and 24. Those not ready for the marathon can enter the half marathon running over one loop of the marathon course. Every participant receives a T-shirt, and finishers receive medals and certificates. The post-race food may be the most unique of any North American marathon. The race director claims to have enough gator meat to have "the only post-race dish worth having—ALLIGATOR SAUCE PIQUANT." If you can't make the marathon, at least write for a race entry blank; it's one of the most humorous we've seen!

THE RIB RUN

Contact: Karen Raymer
The Rib Run
P.O. Box 1216
Raymore, MO 64083
(816) 331-4286

Date: October 31, 1999; October 29, 2000

Formerly called the Greater Kansas City Marathon (the self-proclaimed nation's first green marathon), the event now has adopted The Rib Run as its moniker. Despite its apparent identity crisis, the race features a new, two-loop course through the dynamic new Power and Light District, the River Market, and the revitalized 18th and Vine Jazz District. The route passes several Kansas City points of interest including: Union Station, Gem Theatre, Negro Baseball Museum, City Market, and Midland Theatre. Non-marathoners can participate in the accompanying half marathon, marathon relay, or 5K. Each entrant receives a T-shirt, while finishers earn commemorative awards. All runners are invited to the Afterglow Barbecue celebration.

ANDREW JACKSON MARATHON

Contact: Bob Saffel
Les' Photos
P.O. Box 3832
Jackson, TN 38303
(901) 668-1708
E-mail: JSweeney@fhu.edu
Date: November 6, 1999; November 4, 2000

The 27-year-old Andrew Jackson Marathon starts at Union University (the location of the pre-race spaghetti supper), heads three miles through urban Jackson, and then continues through surrounding farm country for 3.5 miles. Here, you meet expansive fields of cotton and soybean while making a 13-mile loop through seemingly endless agricultural land before you return on the first leg of the course for the last 6.2 miles to the finish. Rolling and completely paved, the course features aid stations every 2 to 3 miles. On the flat portions of the unprotected route, wind direction determines the difficulty of the section.

After receiving your medal, take advantage of the post-race activities which include a catered buffet and free massages. At the post-race awards ceremony, prizes are presented to the overall and age-division winners in the marathon as well as in the accompanying 5K. All entrants are eligible for drawings for prizes donated by local businesses. Though the attendance is modest at this event, many enjoy the small-town charm of local attractions, such as the Casey Jones Museum and the many country stores that fill the area. The race headquarters, Garden Plaza Hotel (800-3-Garden), offers special group rates to marathon entrants.

CHICKAMAUGA BATTLEFIELD MARATHON

Contact: Chris Levan
Chattanooga Track Club
2428 Fox Run Drive
Signal Mountain, TN 37377
(423) 886-4099

Date: November 6, 1999; November 4, 2000

You've completed the training, are dressed in the appropriate attire, prepared to battle the 26.2 miles of the Chickamauga Battlefield Marathon. Held mostly in Chickamauga Battlefield Park, the rigorous, out-and-back route starts at Gordon Lee High School running over paved roads as it heads for Battlefield Park, site of one of the Civil War's fiercest battles. There, you loop through the park two times before charging toward the finish line. En route you encounter three series of enemy hills at miles 9, 17, and 25 on the otherwise rolling course. Located every 2 to 2.5 miles, aid stations supply water, electrolyte replacement drink, fruit, and petroleum jelly. At the end of your personal skirmish, celebrate your victory with post-race food and refreshments. An awards presentation follows, honoring the overall, masters and age-group winners. There are also special awards for first-timers. Perhaps the most convenient lodging for runners is found at the Best Western Battlefield Inn, Highway 27 just north of Battlefield Parkway in Fort Oglethorpe, GA, 5 miles from the start (706-866-0222). Chattanooga lies about 40 minutes from the race staging area.

HARRISBURG MARATHON

Contact: HARRC
c/o Walt Greene
431 Springhouse Road
Camp Hill, PA 17111
(717) 761-5178

Date: November 7, 1999; November 5, 2000

Celebrating its 27th Anniversary in 1999, the Harrisburg Marathon features a flat, out-and-back course starting in front of the Pennsylvania State Capitol Building and ending at City Island on the Susquehanna River. An annual field of about 350 marathoners and several relay teams navigate a course that blends urban, suburban and rural areas. All race-related activities occur at race headquarters, the Crown Plaza Inn, 23 South and 2nd Street. Packet pick-up and late registration take place Saturday from 1:00 p.m. to 5:00 p.m. Race-day registration occurs from 6:30 a.m. to 7:30 a.m. A pre-race pasta dinner takes place from 5:00 p.m. to 7:30 p.m. on Saturday night. Every runner receives a T-shirt, medal, certificate of completion, and complete results. The awards ceremony begins at 2:00 p.m., with open, masters and age-group winners receiving awards and others having a chance to win random prizes.

SPACE COAST MARATHON

Contact: Bill Dillard
1480 Meadowbrook Road, NE
Palm Bay, FL 32905
(407) 724-2510

Date: November 28, 1999; November 26, 2000

Boasted as the oldest marathon in Florida, the Space Coast Marathon had its inaugural running in December of 1971. The course has been modified a number of times since the early 1970s to accommodate both increased traffic and construction. The current course offers an exceptionally flat loop that starts/finishes in front of the Brevard Community College gymnasium and winds along shady streets through residential areas studded with spectacular new homes. Many of the 100 marathoners are from out of the area, combining the race with a Thanksgiving weekend family visit. Aid stations are placed strategically along the route, as you can expect warm weather later in the day. Refreshments are available at the finish line, and an awards presentation takes place after the race. The overall male and female winners and top three in each 5-year age group receive trophies. T-shirts are guaranteed to all preregistered runners. A companion half marathon covers the first 10 miles of the marathon course (plus three more). Afterwards, relax at nearby Cocoa Beach. The Kennedy Space Center, site of the space shuttle launches, is definitely worth a look.

DELAWARE MARATHON

Contact: Wayne Kursh
Marathon Sports
P.O. Box 398
Wilmington, DE 19899
(302) 654-6400

Date: December 5, 1999; December 3, 2000

Prospective members of the 50 states club can rejoice! After a one-year hiatus due to sponsorship problems, the Delaware Marathon (the state's only marathon) revived in 1997. The USATF-certified five-loop (ouch!) course runs on mostly flat country roads, starting and finishing at Middletown High School (45 minutes from Wilmington). This modest race provides each entrant a dri-release long-sleeve T-shirt. Finishers earn medals, while top overall runners win merchandise prizes. The top three age groupers receive plaques. Those not ready for a marathon can recruit a friend or three and enter the two-person or four-person relay.

MISSISSIPPI MARATHON

Contact: **Mississippi Track Club**
P.O. Box 1414
Ridgeland, MS 39157
(601) 856-9884

Date: **December 11, 1999; December 9, 2000**

Starting and finishing at the Mississippi College Coliseum in the small town of Clinton, the small (120 marathoners in 1997) Mississippi Marathon follows an essentially flat, out-and-back course along the Natchez Trace. A 10K run and 5K walk also cover part of the course. Aid stations are available approximately every 3 miles, and splits are called at miles 1, 5, 10, 15, 20, and 25. All marathoners completing the course within 5 hours are awarded commemorative medals, while all preregistered participants receive long-sleeve T-shirts and gloves. After the race, refreshments are provided, and the top male and female overall, masters, grandmasters and age-group winners receive special awards.

Hotel accommodations are conveniently located near the race start/finish, including: the Holiday Inn, 103 Johnston Place (601-924-0064); the Clinton Inn, 400 Highway 80E (601-924-5313); Comfort Inn, 103 Clinton Center Drive (601-924-9364); and the Days Inn, 482 Springridge Road (601-925-5065).

JACKSONVILLE MARATHON

Contact: **Doug Alred**
1st Place Sports
3853 Baymeadows Rd.
Jacksonville, FL 32217
(904) 739-1917

Date: **December 18, 1999; December 16, 2000**

The Jacksonville Marathon attracts about 1,700 competitors to its shady and flat course. Although the main attractions of the race are its Florida location and level route, it does pass through some beautiful mandarin trees. Most support is found in the neighborhoods and at the aid stations available every two miles. Splits are provided every other mile, many by digital clocks. Age-group prizes go three deep. The top three overall finishers receive a small amount of prize money ($300 for first, $200 for second, and $100 for third). Rejuvenate those aching muscles with a free massage, and if you've depleted all your stores from Friday night's carboload, then refuel at the post-race meal. If you can muster the strength, join your fellow competitors for the Saturday night victory party. In recent races, the Holiday Inn, Baymeadows Road and Interstate 95 (904-737-1700), served as the host hotel.

APPENDIX

MARATHON RANKINGS
AND COURSE PROFILES

TOP 110 DESTINATION MARATHONS

Name of Marathon	Crowd	Course Scenery	Race Organization	Overall Rating
1. Big Sur (p. 61)	5	10+	10	100.0
2. New York City (p. 237)	10+	8+	10	99.9
2. Twin Cities (p. 197)	9-	10	10	99.9
4. Chicago (p. 226)	9+	8+	10	99.3
5. Boston (p. 58)	10+	8	10	99.0
6. Marine Corps (p. 230)	5+	10-	10-	96.6
7. St. George (p. 184)	4-	9+	10-	94.0
8. San Francisco (p. 136)	5-	10-	9	93.6
9. Honolulu (p. 280)	6	9	9+	93.4
9. Maui (p. 48)	3+	10-	9+	93.4
11. Vermont City (p. 110)	6+	9	10-	93.0
12. Los Angeles (p. 40)	10	7	9+	92.8
13. Grandma's (p. 124)	5	9-	10	92.4
14. Dallas White Rock (p. 265)	6	9+	9+	92.2
15. Seattle (p. 261)	4-	10-	9	92.1
16. Clarence DeMar (p. 172)	4	9+	9	91.3
16. Portland (p. 191)	6	8+	10	91.3
18. Vancouver (p. 85)	6	8+	9+	90.8
19. Houston (p. 14)	9-	7-	10	90.6
20. Royal Victoria (p. 211)	4	9	9	90.4
21. Catalina Island (p. 43)	1+	10	9+	90.3
22. Columbus (p. 251)	7+	9-	10-	90.0
23. Kiawah Island (p. 274)	2	9	10-	89.5
23. Walt Disney World (p. 11)	4	9-	9	89.5
25. Cape Cod (p. 224)	3-	9+	9	89.4
26. Wineglass (p. 202)	4	9	9	88.9
27. Pittsburgh (p. 82)	8	8-	10-	88.6
28. Napa Valley (p. 36)	2	9+	9	88.3
29. Philadelphia (p. 254)	5-	8+	9	87.9
29. Silicon Valley (p. 234)	4-	8+	10-	87.9
31. Deseret News (p. 143)	7-	9	8	87.7
32. Ave. of the Giants (p. 74)	1-	10	9-	87.6
32. Humboldt Redwoods (p. 220)	1-	10	9-	87.6
34. Adirondack (p. 179)	2	10-	9-	87.1
35. Crater Lake (p. 147)	0+	10	9-	87.0
35. Kilauea Volcano (p. 145)	0+	10	9-	87.0
37. Steamtown (p. 213)	5	8+	9	86.8
38. Fox Cities (p. 176)	7-	8-	10-	86.7
38. National Capital (p. 96)	4	9	9	86.7
40. Madison (p. 106)	4	9	9	86.5
41. Ocean State (p. 244)	3-	9	9	86.4
41. Steamboat (p. 121)	1-	9+	9	86.4
43. Canadian Internat'l (p. 216)	5-	8-	9+	86.1
43. Marathon By The Sea (p. 151)	4+	8-	10-	86.1
45. Myrtle Beach (p. 32)	3	9	9	85.9
46. Austin (p. 26)	5-	8	10	85.5
46. Mayor's Midnight Sun (p. 127)	1+	9	9-	85.5
46. Memphis (p. 268)	5-	7	10-	85.5
49. Grandfather Mountain (p. 134)	2	9+	8	85.3
49. Silver State (p. 158)	1	9	9	85.3
51. Mount Rushmore (p. 209)	1+	9	9	84.9
51. Quad Cities (p. 195)	4+	9	9	84.9
53. Mule Mountain (p. 54)	1	9+	9	84.7
53. Wild Wild West (p. 90)	1	10-	9	84.7
55. Shamrock (p. 46)	2	9-	9+	84.4
56. Capital City (p. 99)	3+	8+	9	84.3
56. Gold Country (p. 117)	1+	9+	9-	84.3

TOP 110 DESTINATION MARATHONS

Name of Marathon	Crowd	Course Scenery	Race Organization	Overall Rating
56. Lakefront (p. 207)	3+	8+	9	84.3
59. San Antonio (p. 247)	4	8-	9-	84.1
60. Pikes Peak (p. 153)	1-	9	9+	83.9
60. Cleveland (p. 76)	5+	8-	9+	83.9
62. Mardi Gras (p. 19)	3-	9-	9-	83.6
62. Rocket City (p. 277)	5-	8-	10-	83.6
64. Harford (p. 204)	4	8	10-	83.5
64. Tucson (p. 270)	2	9-	9	83.5
66. San Diego (p. 17)	2	8+	9+	83.2
67. Smoky Mountain (p. 34)	1	9	9	82.9
68. Calgary (p. 132)	3-	8	9	82.4
68. Charlotte (p. 56)	3-	8	9	82.4
68. Detroit (p. 218)	3-	8+	10-	82.4
68. Coeur d'Alene (p. 101)	1+	9	9-	82.4
72. Rock 'n' Roll (p. 103)	4	8	7+	82.3
73. California Internat'l (p. 263)	5-	7+	9+	82.1
73. New Hampshire (p. 181)	0+	9+	8+	82.1
75. Cowtown (p. 30)	5-	8	9-	81.5
75. Johnstown (p. 187)	2+	9+	8+	81.5
77. U.S. Air Force (p. 162)	4-	8-	9+	81.2
77. Lake County (p. 66)	3-	7+	9	81.2
77. Whiskey Row (p. 72)	1-	9+	8+	81.2
77. Ghost Town (p. 113)	1+	9	8+	81.2
81. Eriesistible (p. 160)	3-	9-	8+-	80.9
81. Towpath (p. 222)	1-	9+	9-	80.9
83. Lake Geneva (p. 92)	1	9	8+	80.8
84. God's Country (p. 115)	2	9	9-	80.5
85. Lincoln (p. 79)	3+	7+	10-	80.3
86. Atlanta (p. 257)	2	7+	9+	80.2
87. Equinox (p. 164)	0+	9-	9-	80.0
88. Maine (p. 189)	2	9-	8+	79.9
89. Blue Angel (p. 28)	2	8	9+	79.3
89. Las Vegas (p. 23)	2	7+	8	79.3
91. Burney (p. 168)	1-	9	8+	78.8
91. Monster Trail (p. 156)	0+	9	8	78.8
93. Shiprock (p. 70)	2+	8+	8+	78.5
93. Walker North (p. 166)	1-	9	9-	78.5
95. Forest City (p. 94)	2	8+	9-	78.4
95. Leadville Mosquito (p. 139)	0	9	8-	78.4
97. Santa Clarita (p. 249)	3-	7+	9+	78.2
97. Taos (p. 119)	1-	8+	8+	78.2
99. Dutchess County (p. 170)	2-	8	9	77.9
99. East Lyme (p. 174)	1-	9-	8+	77.9
101. No. Central Trail (p. 259)	0+	9+	8+	77.6
101. Univ. of Okoboji (p. 141)	0+	9+	7+	77.6
103. Paavo Nurmi (p. 149)	2	8	9-	77.5
104. Carolina (p. 21)	1+	8	9	77.3
105. Michigan Trail (p. 68)	1-	9-	8+	76.4
106. Med-City (p. 108)	2	8+	9	76.3
107. Manitoba (p. 130)	3-	8-	9-	74.6
108. Race of Champions (p. 82)	1-	8	8+	74.3
109. Trail Breaker (p. 52)	1-	8	8	73.4
110. W. Hemisphere (p. 272)	2	7-	8	71.4

THE PR CHASE
TOP 30 FASTEST MARATHONS

Name of Marathon	Crowd	Race Organization	Difficulty	Overall Rating
1. Chicago (p. 226)	9+	10	1+	100.0
2. Tucson (p. 270)	2	9	1	98.5
3. Las Vegas (p. 23)	2	8	1+	94.6
4. Steamtown (p. 213)	5	9	2-	93.1
5. Houston (p. 14)	9-	10	2	93.0
6. Shamrock (p. 46)	2	9+	2-	91.9
7. Mount Rushmore (p. 209)	1+	9	2-	91.3
8. Silicon Valley (p. 234)	4-	10-	2	90.2
9. No. Central Trail (p. 259)	0+	8+	2-	90.1
10. Myrtle Beach (p. 32)	3	9	2	89.2

Name of Marathon	Crowd	Race Organization	Difficulty	Overall Rating
11. Grandma's (p. 124)	5	10	2+	88.2
12. Ave. of the Giants (p. 74)	1-	9-	2	87.7
12. Humboldt Redwoods (p. 220)	1-	9-	2	87.7
14. Cleveland (p. 76)	5+	9+	2+	87.6
15. Cal. Internat'l (p. 263)	5-	9+	2+	87.3
16. Detroit (p. 218)	3-	10-	2+	86.7
16. Clarence DeMar (p. 172)	4	9	2+	86.7
16. Wineglass (p. 202)	4	9	2+	86.7
19. Twin Cities (p. 197)	9-	10	3-	86.1
20. Mardi Gras (p. 19)	3-	9-	2+	85.8

Name of Marathon	Crowd	Race Organization	Difficulty	Overall Rating
21. Napa Valley (p. 36)	2	9	2+	85.7
22. Columbus (p. 251)	7+	10-	3-	85.1
23. Towpath (p. 222)	1-	9-	2+	84.8
24. Austin (p. 26)	5-	10	3-	84.1
25. Rocket City (p. 277)	5-	10-	3-	83.8
26. Canadian Internat'l (p. 216)	5-	9+	3-	83.4
27. Philadelphia (p. 254)	5-	9	3-	83.1
28. Walt Disney World (p. 11)	4	9	3-	82.8
29. Pittsburgh (p. 82)	8	10-	3	82.5
30. Lakefront (p. 207)	3+	9	3-	82.4

MARATHON RANKINGS

The Raving Beauties

Most Scenic Marathons

1. Big Sur
2. Catalina Island
3. Crater Lake
4. Avenue of the Giants
5. Humboldt Redwoods
6. Kilauea Volcano
7. Twin Cities
8. Maui
9. Kiawah Island
10. Adirondack
11. Lake Tahoe
12. Wild Wild West
13. Marine Corps
14. San Francisco
15. Seattle
16. Cape Cod
17. Mule Mountain
18. New Hampshire
19. Steamboat
20. Clarence DeMar
21. Napa Valley
22. St. George
23. Gold Country
24. University of Okoboji
25. Grandfather Mountain

Get Outta Town

Top Seasonal Destination Marathons

Winter
1. Honolulu (9)
2. Dallas White Rock (14)
3. Houston (19)
4. Kiawah Island (23)
4. Walt Disney World (23)
6. Myrtle Beach (45)
7. Austin (46)
7. Memphis (46)
9. Mardi Gras (62)
9. Rocket City (62)

Spring
1. Big Sur (1)
2. Boston (5)
3. Maui (9)
4. Vermont City (11)
5. Los Angeles (12)
6. Vancouver (18)
7. Catalina Island (21)
8. Pittsburgh (27)
9. Napa Valley (28)
10. Avenue of the Giants (32)

Summer
1. San Francisco (8)
2. Grandma's (13)
3. Deseret News (31)
4. Crater Lake (35)
4. Kilauea Volcano (35)
6. Steamboat (41)
7. Marathon By The Sea (43)
8. Mayor's Midnight Sun (46)
9. Grandfather Mountain (49)
9. Silver State (49)

Fall
1. New York City (2)
1. Twin Cities (2)
3. Chicago (4)
4. Marine Corps (6)
5. St. George (7)
6. Seattle (15)
7. Clarence DeMar (16)
7. Portland (16)
9. Royal Victoria (20)
10. Columbus (22)

In My Own Backyard

Top Destination Marathons by Region

Pacific Region
1. Big Sur (1)
2. San Francisco (8)
3. Honolulu (9)
3. Maui (9)
5. Los Angeles (12)
6. Seattle (15)
7. Portland (16)
8. Catalina Island (21)
9. Napa Valley (28)
10. Silicon Valley (29)

Southwest/Mountain Region
1. St. George (7)
2. Dallas White Rock (14)
3. Houston (19)
4. Deseret News (31)
5. Steamboat (41)
6. Austin (46)
7. Silver State (49)
8. Mount Rushmore (51)
9. Mule Mountain (53)
10. San Antonio (59)

Midwest Region
1. Twin Cities (2)
2. Chicago (4)
3. Grandma's (13)
4. Columbus (22)
5. Fox Cities (38)
6. Madison (40)
7. Quad Cities (51)

South Region
1. Kiawah Island (23)
1. Walt Disney World (23)
3. Myrtle Beach (45)
4. Memphis (46)
5. Grandfather Mountain (49)
6. Shamrock Sportsfest (55)
7. Mardi Gras (62)
7. Rocket City (62)
9. Smoky Mountain (67)
10. Charlotte (68)

Northeast Region
1. New York City (2)
2. Boston (5)
3. Marine Corps (6)
4. Vermont City (11)
5. Clarence DeMar (16)
6. Cape Cod (25)
7. Wineglass (26)
8. Pittsburgh (27)
9. Philadelphia (29)
10. Adirondack (34)

8. Lakefront (56)
9. Cleveland (60)
10. Lake County (78)
10. U.S. Air Force (78)

Canada

1. Vancouver (18)
2. Royal Victoria (20)
3. National Capital (38)
4. Canadian International (43)
4. Marathon By The Sea (43)
6. Calgary (68)
7. Forest City (95)
8. Manitoba (107)

Looking for a Fast Time?

Fastest Seasonal Marathons

Winter
1. Tucson (2)
2. Las Vegas (3)
3. Houston (5)
4. Myrtle Beach (10)
5. California International (15)
6. Mardi Gras (20)
7. Austin (24)
8. Rocket City (25)
9. Walt Disney World (28)
10. Kiawah Island (31)

Spring
1. Shamrock Sportsfest (6)
2. Avenue of the Giants (12)
3. Cleveland (14)
4. Napa Valley (21)
5. Pittsburgh (29)
6. Rock 'n' Roll (32)
7. Lake County (34)
8. Boston (37)
9. National Capital (38)
10. Forest City (43)

Summer
1. Grandma's (11)
2. Calgary (34)

Fall
1. Chicago (1)
2. Steamtown (4)
3. Mount Rushmore (7)
4. Silicon Valley (8)
5. Northern Central Trail (9)
6. Humboldt Redwoods (12)
7. Detroit International (16)
7. Clarence DeMar (16)
7. Wineglass (16)
10. Twin Cities (19)
11. Columbus (22)
12. Towpath (23)
13. Canadian International (26)
14. Philadelphia (27)
15. Lakefront (30)

Looking for a Fast Time in Your Own Backyard?

Fastest Marathons by Region

Pacific Region
1. Silicon Valley (8)
2. Avenue of the Giants (12)
2. Humboldt Redwoods (12)
4. California International (15)
5. Napa Valley (21)
6. Rock 'n' Roll (32)
7. Santa Clarita (40)
8. Portland (44)
9. Maui (48)
10. Seattle (49)

Southwest/Mountain Region
1. Tucson (2)
2. Las Vegas (3)
3. Houston (5)
4. Mount Rushmore (7)
5. Austin (24)
6. St. George (33)

Midwest Region
1. Chicago (1)
2. Grandma's (11)
3. Cleveland (14)
4. Detroit (16)
5. Twin Cities (19)
6. Columbus (22)
7. Towpath (23)
8. Lakefront (30)
9. Lake County (34)
10. Fox Cities (44)

South Region
1. Shamrock Sportsfest (6)
2. Myrtle Beach (10)
3. Mardi Gras (20)
4. Rocket City (25)
5. Walt Disney World (28)

Northeast Region
1. Steamtown (4)
2. Northern Central Trail (9)
3. Clarence DeMar (16)
3. Wineglass (16)
5. Philadelphia (27)
6. Pittsburgh (29)
7. Marine Corps (36)
8. Boston (37)
9. Dutchess County (42)
10. Hartford (46)

Canada
1. Canadian International (26)
2. Calgary (34)
3. National Capital (38)
4. Forest City (43)
5. Royal Victoria (55)
6. Manitoba (59)
7. Vancouver (66)
8. Marathon By The Sea (69)

Easy Riders

Easiest Courses

1. Tucson
2. Las Vegas
3. Chicago
4. Shamrock Sportsfest
5. Northern Central Trail
6. Steamtown
7. Mount Rushmore
8. Myrtle Beach
9. Houston
10. Silicon Valley
11. Humboldt Redwoods
11. Avenue of the Giants
14. Cleveland
15. Mardi Gras
16. Detroit
17. California International
18. Wineglass
19. Clarence DeMar
20. Napa Valley

MARATHON RANKINGS

21. Towpath
22. Grandma's
23. Canadian International
24. Columbus
25. Twin Cities

What Was I Thinking?
Most Difficult Marathons

1. Leadville Mosquito
2. Pikes Peak
3. Monster Trail
4. Equinox
5. Nanisivik Midnight Sun
6. Whiskey Row
7. Kilauea Volcano
8. Crater Lake
9. Wild Wild West
10. NipMuck Trail
11. Michigan Trail
12. Gold Country
13. Catalina Island
14. Lake Tahoe
15. Wyoming

Shower and Shampoo Specials
Top Trail Marathons

1. Catalina Island
2. Kilauea Volcano
3. Wild Wild West
4. Gold Country
5. Pikes Peak
6. Equinox
7. Monster Trail
8. Walker North Country
9. Leadville Mosquito
10. Michigan Trail

The Well-Oiled Machines
Best Organized Marathons

1. Portland
2. Chicago
3. New York City
4. Boston
5. Houston
6. Grandma's
7. Twin Cities
8. Big Sur
9. Austin
10. Columbus
11. Pittsburgh
12. Marine Corps
13. St. George
14. Memphis
15. Vermont City
16. Fox Cities
17. Hartford
18. Lincoln
19. Rocket City
20. Silicon Valley
21. Detroit
22. Marathon By The Sea
23. Los Angeles
24. Honolulu
25. Dallas

Screamin' Meemies
Marathons With Best Crowd Support

1. New York City
2. Boston
3. Los Angeles
4. Chicago
5. Houston
6. Twin Cities
7. Pittsburgh
8. Columbus
9. Fox Cities
10. Deseret News

Virgin Voyages
Top Marathons For First Timers

1. Chicago
2. New York City
3. Marine Corps
4. Twin Cities
5. Portland
6. Walt Disney World
7. Columbus
8. Vermont City
9. Houston
10. Pittsburgh
11. Los Angeles
12. Grandma's
13. National Capital
14. Cleveland
15. Fox Cities
16. Dallas
17. Honolulu
18. Austin
19. Cleveland
20. San Francisco

The Road Less Traveled With Plenty of Leg Room
Best Small Marathons (under 500 runners)

1. Clarence DeMar
2. Avenue of the Giants
2. Humboldt Redwoods
4. Adirondack
5. Crater Lake
6. Kilauea Volcano
7. Steamboat
8. Marathon By The Sea
9. Grandfather Mountain
10. Silver State
11. Mule Mountain
12. Wild Wild West
13. Gold Country
14. Mardi Gras
15. Smoky Mountain
16. Coeur d'Alene
17. New Hampshire
18. Johnstown
19. Whiskey Row
20. Ghost Town

COURSE PROFILES

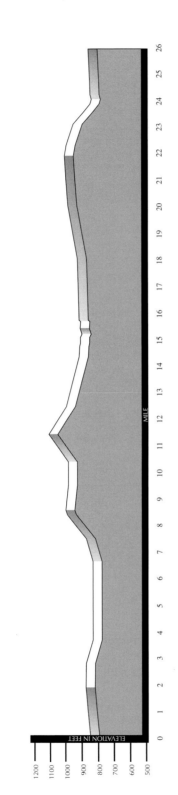

ADIRONDACK MARATHON

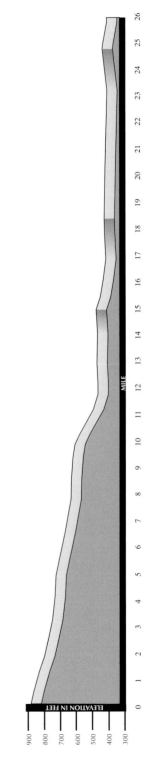

AUSTIN MARATHON

COURSE PROFILES

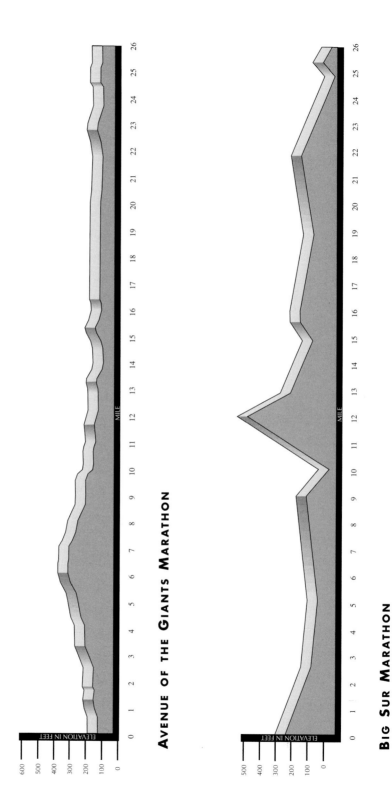

AVENUE OF THE GIANTS MARATHON

BIG SUR MARATHON

Course Profiles

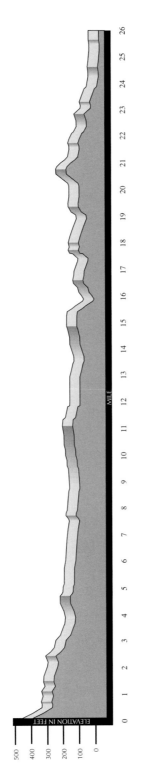

Boston Marathon

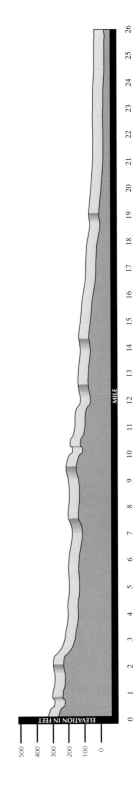

California International Marathon

Course Profiles

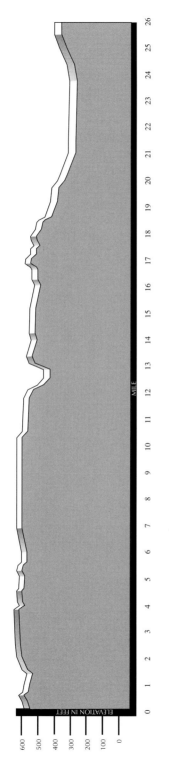

Canadian International Marathon

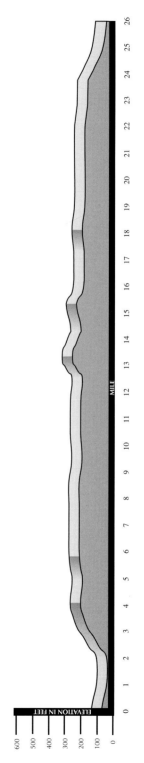

Capital City Marathon

Course Profiles

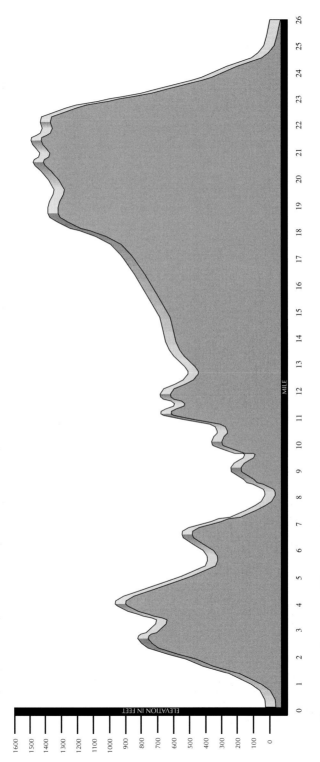

Catalina Island Marathon

ELEVATION IN FEET

MILE

COURSE PROFILES

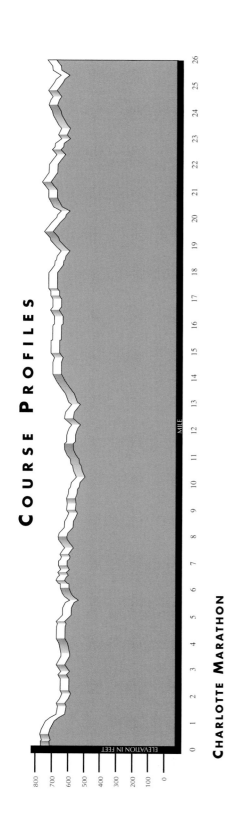

CHARLOTTE MARATHON

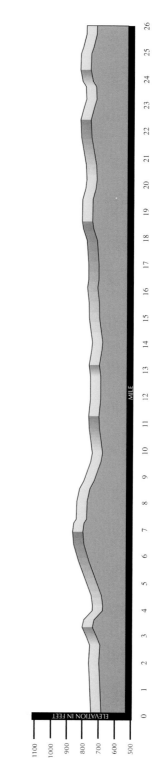

COLUMBUS MARATHON

COURSE PROFILES

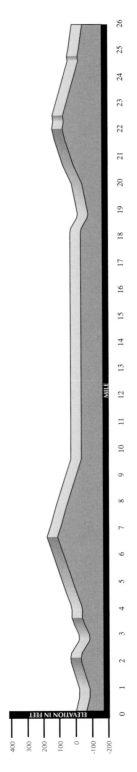

DALLAS WHITE ROCK MARATHON

COURSE PROFILES

EQUINOX MARATHON

ELEVATION IN FEET

COURSE PROFILES

ERIESISTIBLE MARATHON

ELEVATION IN FEET: 800 700 600 500 400 300 200 100 0

MILE: 0 1 2 3 4 5 6 7 8 9 10 11 12 13 14 15 16 17 18 19 20 21 22 23 24 25 26

GOD'S COUNTRY MARATHON
(NOTE VERTICAL SCALE IS 500 FEET)

ELEVATION IN FEET: 3000 2500 2000 1500 1000 500 0

MILE: 0 1 2 3 4 5 6 7 8 9 10 11 12 13 14 15 16 17 18 19 20 21 22 23 24 25 26

COURSE PROFILES

GOLD COUNTRY MARATHON
(NOTE VERTICAL SCALE IS 200 FEET)

GRANDMA'S MARATHON

COURSE PROFILES

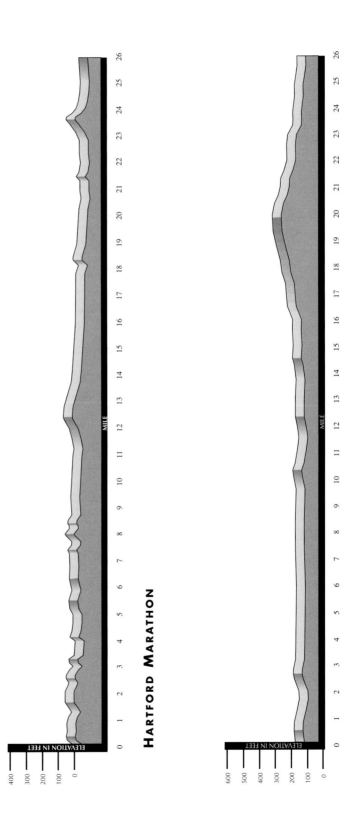

HARTFORD MARATHON

HUMBOLDT REDWOODS MARATHON

Course Profiles

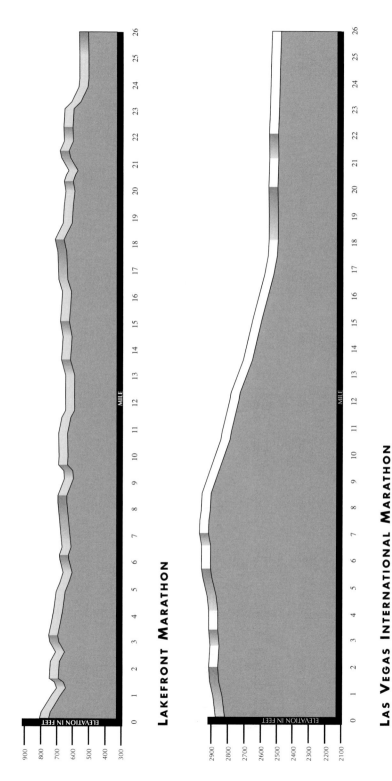

Lakefront Marathon

Las Vegas International Marathon

COURSE PROFILES

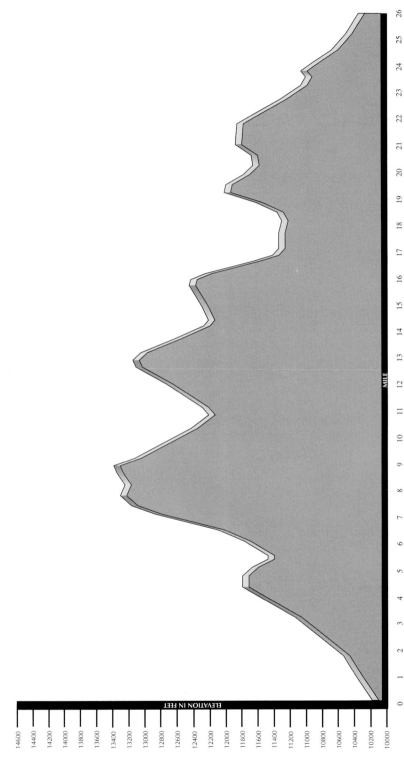

LEADVILLE MOSQUITO MARATHON
(NOTE: VERTICAL SCALE IS 200 FEET)

Course Profiles

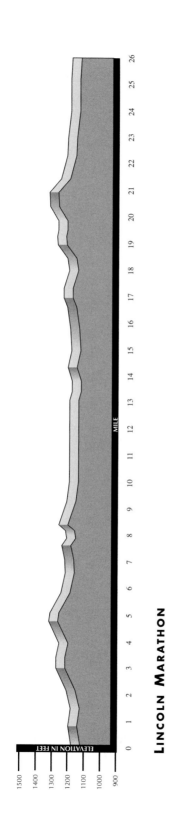

Lincoln Marathon

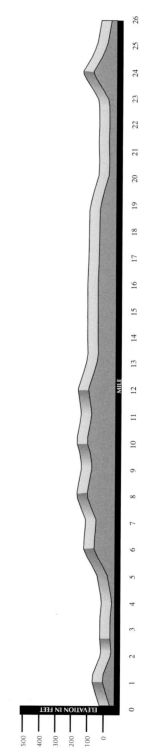

Marathon by the Sea

Course Profiles

Mayor's Midnight Sun Marathon

Monster Trail Marathon

COURSE PROFILES

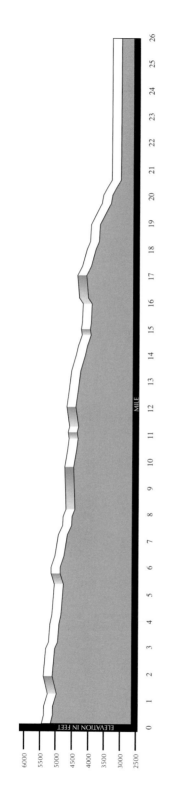

MOUNT RUSHMORE INTERNATIONAL MARATHON
(NOTE: VERTICAL SCALE IS 500 FEET)

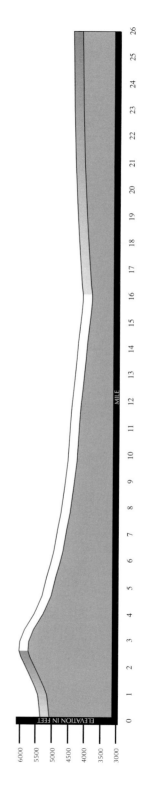

MULE MOUNTAIN MARATHON
(NOTE: VERTICAL SCALE IS 500 FEET)

Course Profiles

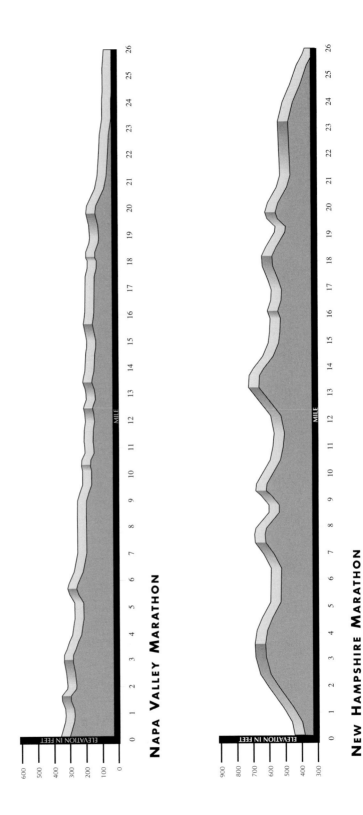

Napa Valley Marathon

ELEVATION IN FEET

600 500 400 300 200 100 0

MILE

0 1 2 3 4 5 6 7 8 9 10 11 12 13 14 15 16 17 18 19 20 21 22 23 24 25 26

New Hampshire Marathon

ELEVATION IN FEET

900 800 700 600 500 400 300

MILE

0 1 2 3 4 5 6 7 8 9 10 11 12 13 14 15 16 17 18 19 20 21 22 23 24 25 26

COURSE PROFILES

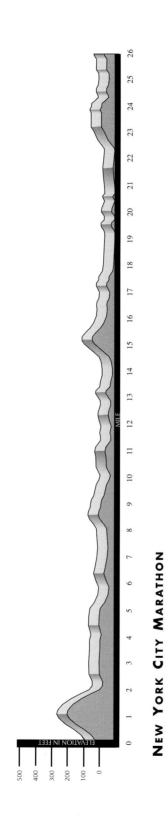

NEW YORK CITY MARATHON

OCEAN STATE MARATHON

Course Profiles

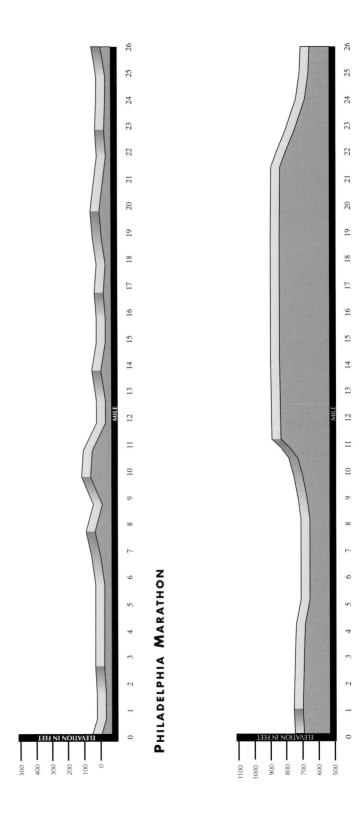

Philadelphia Marathon

Pittsburgh Marathon

COURSE PROFILES

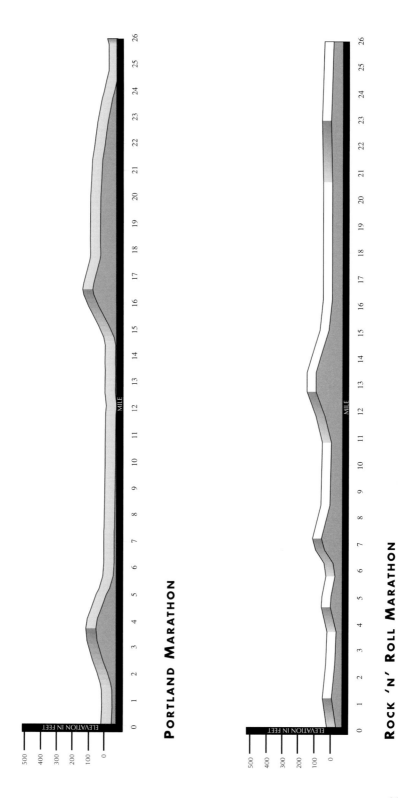

PORTLAND MARATHON

ROCK 'N' ROLL MARATHON

Course Profiles

Rocket City Marathon

Royal Victoria Marathon

340

Course Profiles

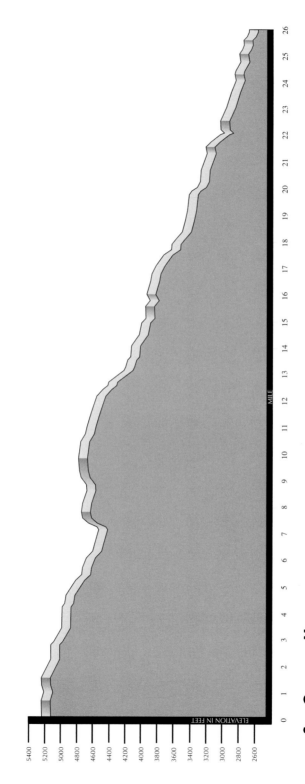

St. George Marathon
(Note: vertical scale is 200 feet)

ELEVATION IN FEET

MILE

5400 5200 5000 4800 4600 4400 4200 4000 3800 3600 3400 3200 3000 2800 2600

0 1 2 3 4 5 6 7 8 9 10 11 12 13 14 15 16 17 18 19 20 21 22 23 24 25 26

COURSE PROFILES

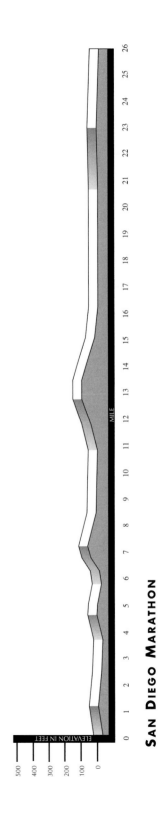

SAN ANTONIO MARATHON

SAN DIEGO MARATHON

Course Profiles

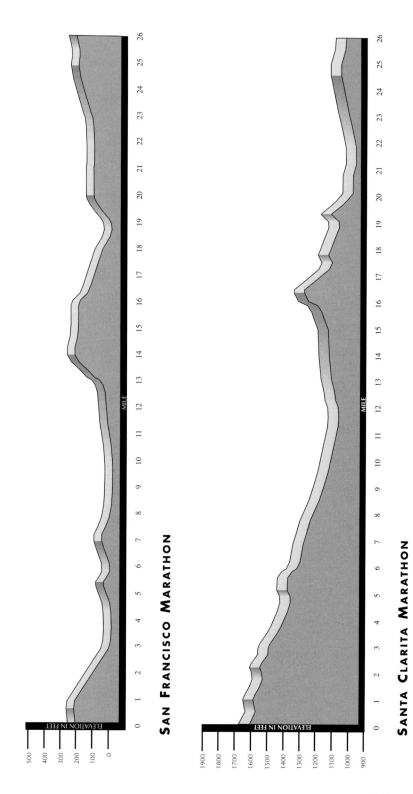

San Francisco Marathon

Santa Clarita Marathon

Course Profiles

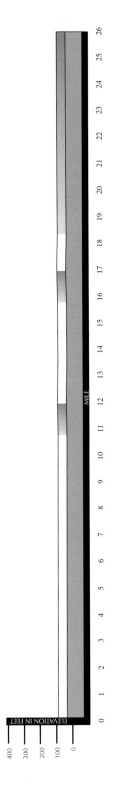

Seattle Marathon

Silicon Valley Marathon

Course Profiles

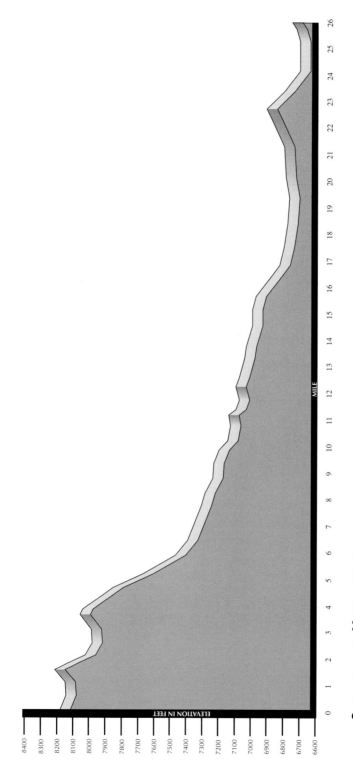

Steamboat Marathon

ELEVATION IN FEET

8400
8300
8200
8100
8000
7900
7800
7700
7600
7500
7400
7300
7200
7100
7000
6900
6800
6700
6600

MILE

0 1 2 3 4 5 6 7 8 9 10 11 12 13 14 15 16 17 18 19 20 21 22 23 24 25 26

Course Profiles

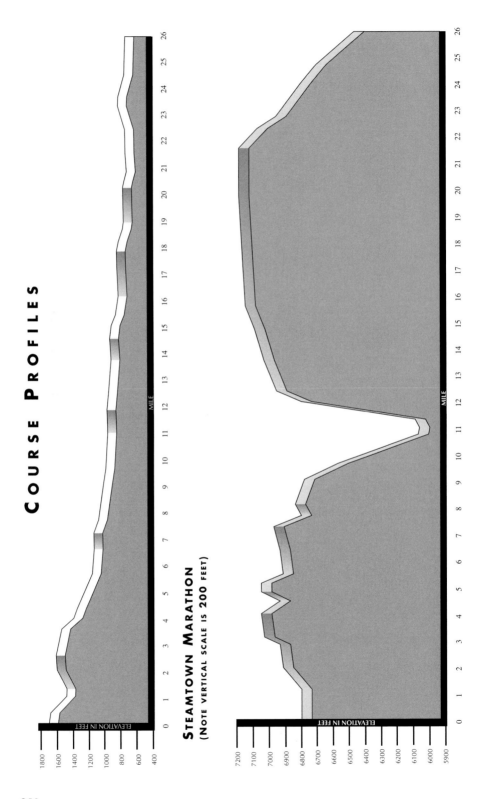

Steamtown Marathon
(Note vertical scale is 200 feet)

COURSE PROFILES

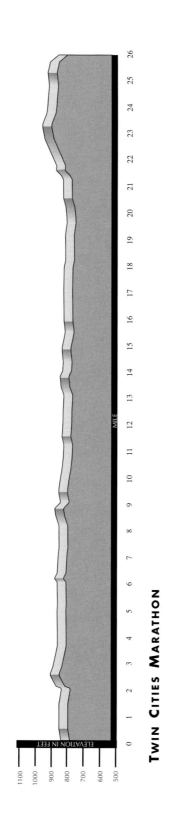

TWIN CITIES MARATHON

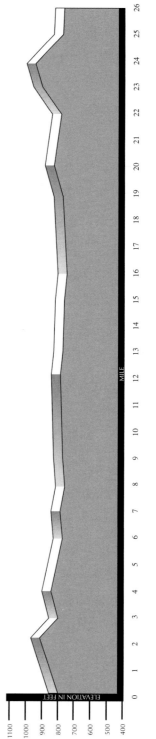

U.S. AIR FORCE MARATHON

COURSE PROFILES

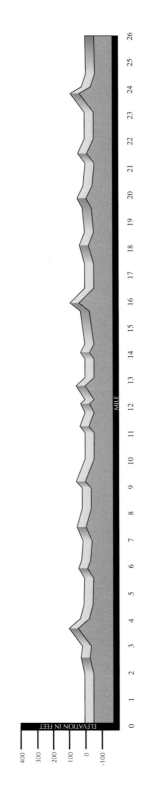

VANCOUVER INTERNATIONAL MARATHON

ELEVATION IN FEET

400 300 200 100 0 -100

MILE

0 1 2 3 4 5 6 7 8 9 10 11 12 13 14 15 16 17 18 19 20 21 22 23 24 25 26

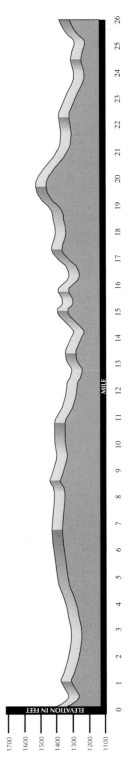

WALKER NORTH COUNTRY MARATHON

ELEVATION IN FEET

1700 1600 1500 1400 1300 1200 1100

MILE

0 1 2 3 4 5 6 7 8 9 10 11 12 13 14 15 16 17 18 19 20 21 22 23 24 25 26

Course Profiles

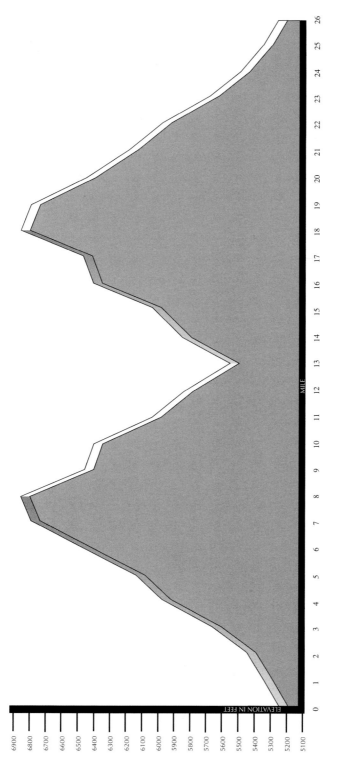

Whiskey Row Marathon

ELEVATION IN FEET

6900 6800 6700 6600 6500 6400 6300 6200 6100 6000 5900 5800 5700 5600 5500 5400 5300 5200 5100

MILE

0 1 2 3 4 5 6 7 8 9 10 11 12 13 14 15 16 17 18 19 20 21 22 23 24 25 26

COURSE PROFILES

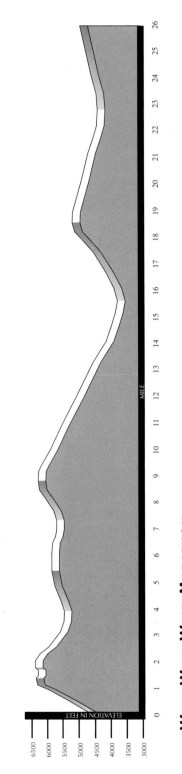

WILD WILD WEST MARATHON
(NOTE: VERTICAL SCALE IS 500 FEET)

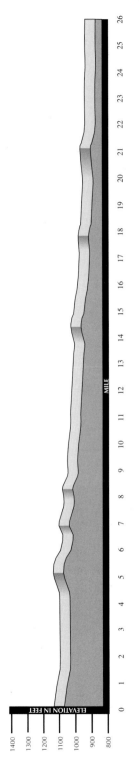

WINEGLASS MARATHON

INDEX

BY LOCATION

UNITED STATES